Intelligence and Crime Analysis

# Critical Thinking Through Writing

**Second Edition**

# David Cariens

HighTide
Publications, Inc.

High Tide Publications, Inc.
1000 Bland Point Road
Deltaville, Virginia 23043
www.HighTidePublications.com

Ordering Information: Quantity sales. Special discounts are available on quantity purchases by corporations, associations, and others. For details, contact the "Special Sales Department" at the address above.

Intelligence and Crime Analysis
CRITICAL THINKING THROUGH WRITING

David Cariens /2nd ed.
Printed in the United States of America

ISBN   978-0692577004

# Contents

# Note to Readers

All statements of fact, opinion, or analysis expressed in this book are those of the author and do not reflect the official positions or views of the Central Intelligence Agency (CIA) or any other U.S. Government agency. Nothing in the contents should be construed as asserting or implying U.S. Government authentication or information or CIA endorsement of the author's views. This book and its contents have been reviewed by the CIA to prevent the disclosure of classified information.

# Introduction

I have spent over forty years working in intelligence analysis, and in the last ten of those years have expanded into teaching crime analysis. There are a few textbooks that touch on one or the other of these analytical styles, but I do not know of any text that draws close parallels between the two, teaches how to do the analysis for both through writing, and dispels some of the myths about intelligence, the Intelligence Community, and intelligence writing. Therefore, I decided to write this book.

Intelligence and crime analysis writing is difficult. But much can be done to better explain how to do these kinds of analyses, and I hope to do just that in the pages of this book. Furthermore, the texts I am familiar with all have one glaring shortcoming—how does one deal with the real world that all intelligence and crime analysts exist in? This book touches on attempts to manipulate intelligence by consumers and producers of intelligence, and gives examples of those attempts.

This textbook is not just a book about analysis and writing. Intelligence analysts face a wide number of problems not confronting other professions. For example, all consumers of intelligence have an agenda; they are looking to get some sort of support for their policies, prejudices, or biases from intelligence. Few other professions are subjected to such close scrutiny by the public and the media. The media too have a political bias. Furthermore, far too few members of the media go to the primary sources, the intelligence reports, as a basis for their reporting. As a result some of their reporting is based on unsubstantiated information instead of primary sources. Often these primary sources are available, but are not checked out. I have also folded in the difficulties all intelligence officers face—real world problems.

Intelligence and crime analysts are privileged and honored to have access to highly sensitive information related to the security of the country—security issues from both abroad and from within. Critical decisions are made on the reports that intelligence and crime analysts produce. The responsibility is great, and the rewards are great. The intelligence and crime analysts will never get wealthy in monetary terms, but the job satisfaction is incredible. If and when your analysis plays a role in making this country safer, or bringing a criminal to justice, you will walk on cloud nine.

Your name may never be known, and you will probably not get credit for much of your work. When you are wrong you will be called on the carpet. When you are right, little or nothing will be said to you. When your intelligence is right and policy-makers ignore and adopt policies that result in the loss of lives—you have no recourse. It will be called "an intelligence failure," and when you call to the attention of the policy-maker that the intelligence was right, you will be told it is still your fault because your argument was not strong and convincing enough.

In both intelligence and crime analyses, the degree of clarity and precision in the written text must be second to none. For the purposes of this book, I define all aspects and all levels of intelligence (CIA, DIA, state police fusion centers, FBI, and police) investigation as intelligence. Indeed, any analysis of a crime is an intelligence report. Two prominent and significant examples are the official reports of the shootings at Columbine and Virginia Tech. Each falls into the category of an intelligence analysis of a major crime.

The underlying principles used in intelligence writing—such as precision of language, clarity of thought, and correct English sentence structure—apply whether you are a CIA analyst, a military intelligence officer, or a police officer. Many police do not see themselves as intelligence officers, but they are. Whether the written product is the initial crime scene report or a product of a fusion center, they are intelligence. These reports require keen observation, accurate rendering of details, analytical skills, good judgments, and a solid understanding of the English language and the idiosyncrasies of the language. These reports are the first critical step to the production of a piece of finished intelligence. The main differences between a CIA or DIA writing on the one hand, and a police product on the other, center on the audiences. I will go into the differences in the chapter dealing with criminal investigations and analysis.

# Chapter I

# Why Intelligence Analysis and Writing Are Demanding

Intelligence and crime analyses are both demanding and difficult. Indeed, the intelligence analyst's profession is not just demanding but extremely difficult. Not everyone is cut out to be an intelligence officer. The profession demands that judgments be made on fragmentary evidence—risk is not part of the business, risk is the business. Furthermore, those doing intelligence and crime analysis must take complicated problems or situations, put their analysis in English that is clear and concise—and, not lose any of the complexity. That is a formidable task. It is not uncommon for an analyst to have to write a short analysis on a one line press release or one line clandestine report, and do it immediately. It has happened to me. It has happened to nearly every intelligence officer I know. That is the worst-case scenario—in that one instant you are asked to bring all your analytical and writing skills to bear on one fragmentary bit of information.

I have combined the words analysis and writing in the title of this chapter because, in our profession, the two cannot be separated. Analysis is taught through writing, not through methodologies. Methodologies are invaluable tools for intelligence officers because they help the analyst bring order and structure to vast amounts of information she or he faces every day. Without methodologies it is next to impossible to process the vast amounts of information an intelligence officer handles every day. Methodologies are critical to the analytical process that eventually results in an intelligence product useful to the consumer. I have to emphasize, and will repeat several times in this book, that without expertise on a given subject or field, all the methodologies and all the structuring in the world will not produce good intelligence analysis.

Bringing some sort of organization and structure to the sources is a first step in the analytical process. Many individuals mistake the use of methodologies as analysis; they have the idea that all you need are a few methodologies and presto—you are an intelligence analyst. That is not true. Methodologies are indispensible tools for intelligence officers. Methodologies help intelligence officers sift through mountains of raw intelligence and bring some sort of order or structure to the information in front of them. But, the intelligence analysis begins when you have to tell someone what the information means. I define intelligence analysis in the following way:

*Intelligence analysis is the ability to process intelligence sources, capture the intelligence significance of the subject being dealt with, and then present the intelligence findings in clear, concise, and well written English so that your analysis is clear to both the novice and the expert.*

The analyst must take complicated situations and problems and put her or his conclusions in simple, direct English so it can be understood by someone who knows nothing about the subject and still be of interest to the expert in the field. Intelligence analysts rarely have all the pieces to the puzzle—if they do, then the analysts are, more often than not, writing history and not intelligence.

Intelligence analysts are paid for their substantive expertise. It is this expertise that allows the analyst to make judgments and to present his or her analysis in a clear and concise format so that an intelligent person, who is not an expert in the field, can understand what is in front of him or her.

Intelligence analysts must tell the consumer what, in their judgment, the evidence and information means. Intelligence analysts should answer questions, not raise them.

To put it another way, intelligence writing demands the analyst take complicated and complex problems and situations and put them in a simple form of English, without losing any of the complexity of what is being addressed. The consumer must be able to read the intelligence through one time and not have to ponder over this or that. The analyst must make the subject intelligible to all readers while not appearing to simplify or talk down to the specialist. The task is formidable.

In the words of retired senior CIA officer, Martin Petersen, "There are several certainties that are common to all intelligence: first, you will probably never have all the evidence you need to feel one-hundred-percent certain about your judgments; second, the chances of being wrong are present every day; and third, sooner or later you will be wrong. These certainties underscore the imperative of not only careful thought and analysis, but the need for precision in observation, analysis, and writing at all times—at every step from the initial investigation to the final report."

Our profession, then, is exacting and demanding in unique ways. Furthermore, there is confusion about what intelligence analysis is, and what it is not. First, what it is not: Intelligence analysis is not just collecting and writing down facts, and it is not just timelines and matrices; these things are important, but they are only part of the whole. Intelligence analysis is the ability to make sense out of situations and problems that are not readily clear and apparent, which requires a clear understanding of the difference between opinion and analysis. The intelligence officer is not being asked to give an opinion. Therefore it is imperative to understand the difference between *an opinion* and *analytical judgment*. The following are definitions of the two:

—    *An opinion is a statement of preference whose grounds are wholly personal.*
—    *An analytical judgment is one whose grounds of support do not depend on the individual who holds them.*

Intelligence analysis must be free of personal biases and preferences, objective, thorough, clear and concise. Furthermore, intelligence analysis and intelligence organizations must guard their objectivity and resist all attempts to corrupt the intelligence product.

Maintaining objectivity and integrity are critical factors in the production of intelligence and are part of why the intelligence profession is so demanding and difficult. The most common term for the attempts to undercut the integrity of intelligence is "politicization." Politicization of intelligence is an omnipresent problem and it comes from both within intelligence organizations and from without. One of the largest impediments to the production of intelligence is that all consumers of intelligence have an agenda; they will be looking for the intelligence product to justify their policies, their theories of the crimes, their biases, and their prejudices. It is a rare consumer who does not want to manipulate intelligence.

The secret to countering politicization is to produce well-written, well-documented, clear and precise papers that make it difficult for managers of intelligence officers or consumers to distort. In the final analysis, if you have done your job well and the manager does not want to put the product out, he or she can block its publication. If you have done your job well and the product is published and your work is so well written that the consumer who wants to cannot distort your words, he or she will simply ignore what you have produced.

If the consumer does not like your analytical conclusions, because those conclusions point to flawed policies or do not fit their bias or prejudice, he or she can turn to interest peddlers or "think tanks." Who pays for "think tanks?" The answer is people and interest groups with agendas. These "think tanks" can and do produce well-written, well-researched papers. The problem is the papers and authors have a bias from the outset. Think tanks often cherry-pick evidence to strengthen their point of view and ignore opposing, compelling evidence. Does anyone reading this believe that a conservative "think tank" will produce analysis not in line with conservative doctrine, or that a liberal "think tank" will produce analysis that undermines the liberal agenda? Furthermore, the "think tanks" are out to make money to sell their services—and even if they are non-profit, they certainly will not do anything to annoy their financial backers.

An example of selectivity in the use of facts and evidence was an analysis of the shooting at Virginia Tech done by a private company in the business of selling its services to members of the law enforcement community. The company's analysis of police action on the morning of April 16, 2007, is clearly intended to exonerate those actions, or lack of action that terrible day. The company's analysis is an excellent account of the police action once the shooting started at Norris Hall. But that is not the real issue; the real issue is what the police were doing at the time of the double homicide at West Ambler Johnston Hall, two hours before the slaughter at Norris hall.

The following are examples of manipulation of facts:

1. There were bloody footprints leading away from the murder scene at West Ambler Johnston Hall. Introductory Crime Analysis tells you the killer is still loose and quite possibly still on the campus. Yet, the police chose to concentrate on a single suspect—the female victim's boyfriend—in part because he owned a gun. It is hard to find males in Southwest Virginia who do not own a gun. Common sense dictates caution and preventive measures, such as warning the campus and locking the school down. No such actions were taken. The company's analysis glosses over this fact.

2. The report does not tell the reader that Virginia State Police and the ATF declined to turn over to the governor's review panel the reports and documents dealing with the killer's application to buy weapons. In other words, these two organizations refused to cooperate in the investigation of the worst mass shooting in this nation's history, but this is not touched upon in the analysis.

3. The report failed to examine or even mention the legal concepts of premise liability, foreseeable threats of violence, or negligence. All these concepts should have been examined in a thorough analysis of the events of April 16, 2007.

4. There is an overwhelming body of legal evidence and opinion that underscores the duty of campus police to protect faculty, staff and students. Students in particular are vulnerable to attacks by other students. They are congregated in open spaces, such as classrooms and libraries. They are encouraged to depend upon institutional safety measures—to rely, for example, on the campus police, or judicial affairs–when they feel endangered by other students. The report never touches on the duties and responsibilities of campus police forces, and whether these duties and responsibilities were met on April 16, 2007.

5. In order to vindicate the Virginia Tech Police for not locking down the campus, the company asserts, "If locked down inside any building, it would have made it all the easier for Cho to trap his quarry." In fact the opposite is true, if a lockdown had been instituted after the first two shootings, the killer would not have been able to get into Norris Hall and slaughter thirty people. Furthermore, if there had been a lockdown, two students would not have been allowed to leave West Ambler Johnston Hall and go to their deaths in Norris Hall.

6. Finally, the report does not mention that the Virginia Tech Police Department and school administration did not follow their own well-established security procedures. For example, on April 21, 2006, Virginia Tech did close and all students were sent home because of a manhunt for William Morva, accused of killing two people in Blacksburg. There was no indication that Morva was on the campus, yet the school and police acted. Why they did not chose to act some eight months later, when two students were found shot dead in West Ambler Johnston Hall is not even speculated on in the report.

Let me give you an example of manipulation of intelligence on the federal level. The manipulation centers on two words related to the crisis in Bosnia in the 1990s. Those words were "ethnic cleansing." The American policymaking community, the U.S. Intelligence Community, and the news media all used the words "ethnic cleansing." They should have used the word "genocide."

Ethnic cleansing is defined as "the systematic elimination of an ethnic group or groups from a region or society, as by deportation, forced emigration, or genocide." What went on in Bosnia was genocide, not deportation or forced emigration.

Having spent a great deal of my professional life working on the Balkans, having traveled and lived there, I was very interested in what happened in Bosnia. I was also puzzled why the words "ethnic cleansing" were being used and not "genocide." I began asking in my intelligence analysis classes, "Why isn't the Intelligence Community using "genocide" to describe the massacres taking place in Bosnia?"

The answer invariably was the same, "Every time we try to use 'genocide' we are told we are not allowed." Everywhere I taught I asked the same question, "Why aren't you calling the slaughter of people in Bosnia 'genocide'?" Always the same answer, "We are not allowed."

On one occasion when I asked, a hand went up in the back of the class. A young woman said, "I can tell you why. I am a lawyer specializing in international law. The U.S. is a signatory to a UN treaty stating that any signatory using the word "genocide" will activate the treaty." (She never explained what "activate the treaty" meant.)

My response was, "Fine, it works for me. Isn't that why we signed the treaty in the first place?" But she persisted and said that the word "genocide" could not be used in intelligence writing when referring to Bosnia.

I thought for a moment and then said, "Do you mean to tell me, that if the Department of Agriculture uses the word 'genocide' the treaty will be activated?"

"Yes," she responded.

"Well if that is the case; if the U.S. hired lawyers who allowed our government to sign such a treaty, then all of them should be fired. No member of the Intelligence Community speaks for the U.S. government. The Intelligence Community, in fact, advises policy-makers, it does not make policy. Those lawyers—if what you are saying is true—clearly do not understand the role intelligence plays in supporting the government. Nor do they understand the need for any member of the Intelligence Community to use any word necessary in the English vocabulary to analyze a problem or situation."

Needless to say I did not gain a friend.

In April of 2008, I spoke at the annual conference of the International Association of Law Enforcement Intelligence Agencies (IALEIA) and the Association of Law Enforcement Intelligence Units (LEIU). I made the same point about the danger of word games in the production of intelligence, citing the "ethnic cleansing" example. At the end of the presentation a man came up and said he was very interested in what I had to say about word games. He then said that he taught law at an Ivy League university and used that treaty in his class.

The gentleman then said, "You are right, and the lawyer is wrong. There is nothing in the treaty to prevent anyone, anywhere in the Intelligence Community from using the word 'genocide,' if it is appropriate." He then added, "You know why intelligence officers have been told they cannot use it, don't you?"

"Yes," I said, "but I want my students to tell me the reason CIA analysts are being told they cannot use genocide." We cannot use the word "genocide" in official publications because it would force the politicians to make a decision!

I told this story in a class not too long ago and a young man raised his hand. He said he was a former military intelligence officer who had encountered the same problem. He had been stationed in Italy when the fighting was taking place in Bosnia and tried to use the word "genocide" in his intelligence reports.

I asked why he hadn't been allowed to use the term, and he responded that his commanding officer would not allow use of the word "genocide" because it would be an insult to Israel and the Jewish people.

I could only respond by saying, "Incredible, absolutely incredible!"

It is amazing to me how people who know nothing about a subject will make up any justification to enforce their point of view. That was the case of the commanding officer.

I lived in Yugoslavia in the early 1980s and spent time in Sarajevo. My wife and I went to the synagogue in the Bosnian capital and talked with a survivor of the holocaust. Apparently the commanding officer didn't know that Israel recognized the killings in Bosnia for what they were—genocide. In fact, the Israelis evacuated the remaining members of the Jewish faith still living in Bosnia because they recognized it would only be a matter of time before the genocide turned on the Jewish community.

I would argue that contrary to the officer's assertion, to *avoid* calling the killings in Bosnia genocide is an insult to the Jewish people!

What can any of us do to prevent politicization of intelligence and crime scene analyses? A number of things:

1.   To paraphrase the title of Virginia Tech Professor Lucinda Roy's book, "No Right to Remain Silent," we cannot remain silent. All of us have a right and responsibility to speak out when confronted with evil or danger. Many of the people in positions of authority who refuse to act are little more than playground bullies. When you confront them or threaten action, they almost always back down.

2.   File a complaint with the Inspector General. Most large institutions have one.

3.   Many large institutions also have an Ombudsman whose job it is to investigate charges of abuses or capricious acts by public officials. Charges of corruption of intelligence or abuse of power, such as failing to respond when people feel their lives are endangered, will be investigated.

The most disgusting of all pressure to manipulate intelligence is when it comes from the intelligence professionals. I have heard such things as, "The President doesn't want to hear this or that." When those words are uttered at a time when this country is at war, it is tantamount to treason. Of all people, trained intelligence professionals should know that the minute we deviate from our analytical conclusions either for the customer or for our own careers, we have damaged the intelligence beyond repair and betrayed the taxpayer.

Nearly every intelligence officer I know has, at one time or another, been told by other intelligence officers to distort the truth or out-and-out lie. It happened to me.

In the early 1980s, following the death of Yugoslav President Tito, I was told to write a major paper on the prospects for stability in Yugoslavia. I concluded that the prospects for stability were high—around 80 to 90 percent. Furthermore, I believed that as long as the Soviet Union existed, the constituent republics and provinces would see their best chance to survive as national entities as being within the Yugoslav federation. The real danger for the federation would be if the Soviet Union and Warsaw Pact disbanded. That is exactly what happened.

But when senior management reviewed the paper, I was told to change my conclusions. I was told to say the federation was in danger of breaking apart and there was a real danger of civil war and bloodshed. I was told if I made the change it would be good for my career and good for my supervisor's career. If I said the federation would hold together and it did not, then that would be bad for our careers. If I said there would probably be civil war and bloodshed and it never happened, no one would remember, and that would be good for our careers.

I held my ground. The paper was eventually published exactly the way I wrote it. But remember, no good deed goes unpunished. I had stood up to a senior official and won. I was not promoted for four years.

Finally, we need to take a quick look at the problem facing the Intelligence Community in general, and intelligence analysts specifically—the false impressions put out by the media. If you look at the media coverage and analysis of the post-Iraq invasion you hear or read over and over again that the Intelligence Community was unanimous in the view that Saddam Hussein had weapons of mass destruction. The media, and most politicians, want the public to believe the Intelligence Community spoke with one voice. That is simply not true. I doubt if those members of the media or those politicians read the primary sources on the Iraq's program for weapons of mass destruction.

Please read the following unclassified version of the National Intelligence Estimate (NIE) on "Iraq's Continuing Programs for Weapons of Mass Destruction." Please note the dissenting positions by the Department of State's Intelligence and Research Bureau (INR) and Air Force intelligence.

# Key Judgments (from October 2002 NIE)

## Iraq's Continuing Programs for Weapons of Mass Destruction

We judge that Iraq has continued its weapons of mass destruction (WMD) programs in defiance of UN resolutions and restrictions. Baghdad has chemical and biological weapons as well as missiles with ranges in excess of UN restrictions; if left unchecked, it probably will have a nuclear weapon during this decade. (See INR alternative view at the end of these Key Judgments.)

We judge that we are seeing only a portion of Iraq's WMD efforts, owing to Baghdad's vigorous denial and deception efforts. Revelations after the Gulf war starkly demonstrate the extensive efforts undertaken by Iraq to deny information. We lack specific information on many key aspects of Iraq's WMD programs.

Since inspections ended in 1998, Iraq has maintained its chemical weapons effort, energized its missile program, and invested more heavily in biological weapons; in the view of most agencies, Baghdad is reconstituting its nuclear weapons program.

- Iraq's growing ability to sell oil illicitly increases Baghdad's capabilities to finance WMD programs; annual earnings in cash and goods have more than quadrupled, from $580 million in 1998 to about $3 billion this year.

- Iraq has largely rebuilt missile and biological weapons facilities damaged during Operation Desert Fox and has expanded its chemical and biological infrastructure under the cover of civilian production.

- Baghdad has exceeded UN range limits of 150 km with its ballistic missiles and is working with unmanned aerial vehicles (UAVs), which allow for a more lethal means to deliver biological and, less likely, chemical warfare agents.

- Although we assess that Saddam does not yet have nuclear weapons or sufficient material to make any, he remains intent on acquiring them. Most agencies assess that Baghdad started reconstituting its nuclear program about the same time UNSCOM inspectors departed–December 1998.

How quickly Iraq will obtain its first nuclear weapon depends on when it requires sufficient weapons-grade missile material.

- If Baghdad acquires sufficient fissile material from abroad it could make a nuclear weapon within several months to a year.

- Without such material from abroad, Iraq probably would not be able to make a weapon until 2007 to 2009, owing to inexperience in building and operating centrifuge facilities to produce highly enriched uranium and challenges in procuring the necessary equipment and expertise.

- o Most agencies believe that Saddam's personal interest in and Iraq's aggressive attempts to obtain high-strength aluminum tubes for centrifuge rotors—as well as Iraq's attempts to acquire magnets, high-speed balancing machines, and machine tools—provide compelling evidence that Saddam is reconstituting a uranium enrichment effort for Baghdad's nuclear weapons program. (DOE agrees that reconstitution of the nuclear program is underway but assesses that the tubes probably are not part of the program.)

- o Iraq's efforts to re-establish and enhance its cadre of weapons personnel as well as activities at several suspect nuclear sites further indicate that reconstitution is underway.

- o All agencies agree that about 25,000 centrifuges based on tubes of the size Iraq is trying to acquire would be capable of producing approximately two weapons' worth of highly enriched uranium per year.

- In a much less likely scenario, Baghdad could make enough fissile material for a nuclear weapon by 2005 to 2007 if it obtains suitable centrifuge tubes this year and has all the other materials and technological expertise necessary to build production-scale uranium enrichment facilities.

We assess that Baghdad has begun renewed production of mustard, Sarin, GF (cyclosarin), and VX; its capability probably is more limited now than it was at the time of the Gulf war, although VX production and agent storage life probably have been improved.

- An array of clandestine reporting reveals that Baghdad has procured covertly the types and quantities of chemicals and equipment sufficient to allow limited CW agent production hidden within Iraq's legitimate chemical industry.

- Although we have little specific information on Iraq's CW stockpile, Saddam probably has stocked at least 100 metric tons (MT) and possibly as much as 500 MT of CW Agents—much of it added in the last year.

- The Iraqis have experience in manufacturing CW bombs, artillery rockets, and projectiles. We assess that they possess CW bulk fills for SRBM warheads, including for a limited number of covertly stored Scuds, possibly a few with extended ranges.

We judge that all key aspects – R&D, production, and weaponization – of Iraq's offensive BW program are active and that most elements are larger and more advanced than they were before the Gulf War.

- We judge Iraq has some lethal and incapacitating BW agents and is capable of quickly producing and weaponizing a variety of such agents, including anthrax, for delivery by bombs, missiles, aerial sprayers, and covert operatives.
  - o Chances are even that smallpox is part of Iraq's offensive BW program.
  - o Baghdad probably has developed genetically engineered BW agents.
- Baghdad has established a large-scale, redundant, and concealed BW agent production capability.
  - o Baghdad has mobile facilities for producing bacterial and toxin BW agents; these facilities can evade detection and are highly survivable. Within three to six months* these units probably could produce an amount of agent equal to the total that Iraq produced in the years prior to the Gulf war.

Iraq maintains a small missile force and several development programs, including for a UAV probably intended to deliver biological warfare agent.

- Gaps in Iraqi accounting to UNSCOM suggest that Saddam retains a covert force of up to a few dozen Scud-variant SRBMS with ranges of 650 to 900 km.

- Iraq is deploying its new al-Samoud and Ababil-100 SRBMs, which are capable of flying beyond the UN-authorized 150-km range limit; Iraq has tested an al-Samoud variant beyond 150 km–perhaps as far as 300 km.

\* (Corrected per Errata sheet issued in October 2002).

- Baghdad's UAVs could threaten Iraq's neighbors, US forces in the Persian Gulf, and if brought close to, or into, the United States, the US Homeland.
  - An Iraqi UAV procurement network attempted to procure commercially available route planning software and an associated topographic database that would be able to support targeting of the United States, according to analysis of special intelligence.
  - The Director, Intelligence, Surveillance, and Reconnaissance, US Air Force, does not agree that Iraq is developing UAVs primarily intended to be delivery platforms for chemical and biological warfare (CBW) agents. The small size of Iraq's new UAV strongly suggests a primary role of reconnaissance, although CBW delivery is an inherent capability.

- Iraq is developing medium-range ballistic missile capabilities, largely through foreign assistance in building specialized facilities, including a test stand for engines more powerful than those in its current missile force.

We have low confidence in our ability to assess when Saddam would use WMD.

- Saddam could decide to use chemical and biological warfare (CBW) preemptively against US forces, friends, and allies in the region in an attempt to disrupt US war preparations and undermine the political will of the Coalition.

- Saddam might use CBW after an initial advance into Iraqi territory, but early use of WMD could foreclose diplomatic options for stalling the US advance.

- He probably would use CBW when he perceived he irretrievably had lost control of the military and security situation, but we are unlikely to know when Saddam reaches that point.

- We judge that Saddam would be more likely to use chemical weapons than biological weapons on the battlefield.

- Saddam historically has maintained tight control over the use of WMD; however, he probably has provided contingency instructions to his commanders to use CBW in specific circumstances.

Baghdad for now appears to be drawing a line short of conducting terrorist attacks with conventional or CBW against the United States, fearing that exposure of Iraqi involvement would provide Washington a stronger cause for making war.

Iraq probably would attempt clandestine attacks against the US Homeland if Baghdad feared an attack that threatened the survival of the regime were imminent or unavoidable, or possible for revenge. Such attacks – more likely with geological than chemical agents – probably would be carried out by Special Forces or intelligence operatives.

- The Iraqi Intelligence (IIS) probably has been directed to conduct clandestine attacks against US and allied interests in the Middle East in the event the United States takes action against Iraq. The IIS probably would be the primary means by which Iraq should attempt to conduct any CBW attacks on the US Homeland, although we have no specific intelligence information that Saddam's regime has directed attacks against US territory.

Saddam, if sufficiently desperate, might decide that only an organization such as al-Qaida – with worldwide reach and extensive terrorist infrastructure, and already engaged in a life-or-death struggle against the United States – could perpetrate the type of terrorist attack that he would hope to conduct.

- In such circumstances, he might decide that the extreme step of assisting the Islamist terrorists in conducting a CBW attack against the United States would be his last chance to exact vengeance by taking a large number of victims with him.

State/INR Alternative View of Iraq's Nuclear Program

The Assistant Secretary of State for Intelligence and Research (NR) believes that Saddam continues to want nuclear weapons and that available evidence indicates that Baghdad is pursuing at least a limited effort to maintain and acquire nuclear-related capabilities. The activities we have detected do not, however, add up to a compelling case that Iraq is currently pursuing what INR would consider to be an integrated and comprehensive approach to acquire nuclear weapons.

Iraq may be doing so, but INR considers the available evidence inadequate to support such a judgment. Lacking persuasive evidence that Baghdad has launched a coherent effort to reconstitute its nuclear weapons program, INR is unwilling to speculate that such an effort began soon after the departure of UN inspectors or to project a timeline for the completion of activities it does not now see happening. As a result, INR is unable to predict when Iraq could acquire a nuclear device or weapons.

In INR's view Iraq's efforts to acquire aluminum tubes is central to the argument that Baghdad is reconstituting its nuclear weapons program; but INR is not persuaded that the tubes in question are intended for use as centrifuge rotors. INR accepts the judgment of technical experts at the U.S. Department of Energy (DOE) who have concluded that the tubes Iraq seeks to acquire are poorly suited for use in gas centrifuges to be used for uranium enrichment and finds unpersuasive the arguments advanced by others to make the case that they are intended for that purpose. INR considers it far more likely that the tubes are intended for another purpose, most likely the production of artillery rockets. The very large quantities being sought, the way the tubes were tested by the Iraqis, and the atypical lack of attention to operational security in the procurement efforts are among the factors, in addition to the DOE assessment, that lead INR to conclude that the tubes are not intended for use in Iraq's nuclear weapon program.

## Confidence Levels for Selected Key Judgments in this Estimate

**High Confidence:**

- Iraq is continuing and in some areas expanding, its chemical, biological, nuclear and missile programs contrary to UN resolutions.
- We are not detecting portions of those weapons programs.
- Iraq possesses proscribed chemical and biological weapons and missiles.
- Iraq could make a nuclear weapon in months to a year once it acquires sufficient weapons-grade fissile material.

**Moderate Confidence:**

- Iraq does not yet have a nuclear weapon or sufficient material to make one, but is likely to have a weapon by 2007 to 2009. (See INR alternative view, page 84).

**Low Confidence:**

- When Saddam would use weapons of mass destruction.
- Whether Saddam would engage in clandestine attacks against the US Homeland.
- Whether in desperation Saddam would share chemical or biological weapons with Al-Qaida.

\*    \*    \*

Given the problems and pressures discussed on the preceding pages in this chapter, the importance of clear, precise, well-argued intelligence becomes abundantly clear. Our integrity is our life-blood, if we lose that we lose everything. For intelligence analysts to approach their job in a slip-shod fashion or to look the other way when faced with attempts to manipulate, would be toxic to our democratic system. Intelligence analysts must be islands of integrity and objectivity in seas of deceit and duplicity.

# Chapter II

## This Beast The English Language

I often tell my classes that all intelligence officers need to be recertified every five years to use the English language correctly. I am half joking, half serious. A survival level skill in English is relatively easy to learn; a superficial look at the language leaves the impression that English is simple and logical. Nothing could be further from the truth. English is riddled with contradictions and inconsistencies. The net result is that English requires more education to use correctly than any other Western language.

There are three major U.S. government language schools, the Defense Language

Institute in Monterey, California, the State Department's Foreign Service Institute, and the CIA Language School. All three rate languages in order of difficulty—from "5" the most difficult, to "1" the easiest. The scale is based on the ability to use the languages correctly, not to gain simply a survival skill. All three rank English as a "5."

Native English speakers find it hard to believe that English is a "5." After all, we do not attach genders to our nouns (no masculine, no feminine, no neuter), and we don't change vocabulary or word endings depending on whether a man or woman is speaking. How could English possibly be a "5?"

There are many reasons why English is difficult to use correctly:

1.  A rule is not a rule in English; a rule is a suggestion and a place to start. Many of our rules have nearly as many exceptions as they have adherents. I recently read a book by an English scholar who described English grammar and punctuation as three-quarter rules and one-quarter common sense. That is a heck of way to run a language. By the way, if anyone reading this has a child in school struggling with English, the best thing you can do is enroll him or her in one of three foreign languages: German, Latin, or Spanish. All three have rules and abide by them. That is how I learned correct English. I took three years of German in high school and reverse engineered. By drilling on German rules, I came to understand English rules and their exceptions.

2.  English is not phonetic; you cannot spell in English based on the sounds of our words. English spelling is probably the most inconsistent and confusing of all the major European languages. Moreover, in writing we rarely use an accent mark, which further complicates the problem. At least in French, which is also non-phonetic, accent marks are used in writing to help the reader.

3.  There are eight basic parts of English according to grammarians, and one of those, prepositions, is one-hundred-percent idiomatic—there are no rules! We make it more complicated by using prepositions to change the meaning of our sentences. The following three sentences are identical except for the prepositions. Notice how the preposition nudges the reader's expectations about what is to follow:

    –   I work <u>in</u> an office.

    –   I work <u>at</u> an office.

    –   I work <u>for</u> an office

4.    English is the fastest changing major language in the world. Unlike other languages that resist change, English is open to it. For example, the Academie Francaise has the job of preventing foreign words from being used in French. In fact, it is an offense (legally) if products are sold under their English names. Indeed, there are many languages which do not allow borrowing from other languages. This resistance to foreign words most often has to do with the politics of languages.

5.    English does not have genders on our nouns, English only has three articles—"the" (the definite article), and "a" and "an" (the indefinite articles). Yet even the use of them is a bit confusing and at times idiomatic. For example, you say, "I am going to <u>the</u> movies," putting the article in front of the noun, but you also say, "I am going to bed," leaving the article out.

How do you know when to use "a" or "an?" Simple, right? Not really. The rule or suggestion in English is that if the noun starts with a consonant, use "a." If the noun starts with a vowel, use "an." So, the following must be a correct English sentence: Ralph has a herb garden. In British English, it is correct, but in American English it is not. The British pronounce the consonant "h" so they use "a." In American English we swallow the "h" and pronounce the vowel "e." So you use "an."

The reason for this is based on sounds—on how you pronounce the first letter of the noun. So, in American English, you use "an" with all vowel sounds except those words starting with a long "u" or silent "h." Are you seated for this one? In speech, according to the *Gregg Reference Manual*, both "a historic occasion" and "an historic occasion" are correct, depending on how you pronounce the word "historic." In written American English, "a historic occasion" is the most common and accepted form. You don't get much more screwed up in the world of languages than having a non-phonetic language with a rule that trumps its other rules, based on sounds!

We need to take a moment and look at the history of English in order to put it into context and to better understand why the language is so difficult to use correctly. English belongs to the broad category of Indo-European languages and traces its origins to around 500 B.C. English language has dramatically changed and altered as invasion after invasion swept over the British Isles.

I know historians and linguists disagree with me, but I consider the foundation of modern English to date from 1066 and the Battle of Hastings, when the French-speaking Normans conquered the Anglo-Saxons. French is arguably the most difficult of the Romance languages; it has difficult grammar, difficult punctuation, *and* is non-phonetic. The Anglo-Saxon tongue had simpler grammar, simpler punctuation and simple one and two syllable words. From 1066 on, the mixing begins. What does that mean for modern English in general, and intelligence writing specifically? Essentially, that English is a mix of rules and exceptions to those rules, and that in English, a rule is a suggestion.

Thus, in the mixing of the new language, the upper class words became French as the new rulers imported their language and left the Anglo-Saxon to the swineherders. Most words dealing with sophisticated ideas and thoughts, abstractions, nuances, and innuendos owe their roots to French. The grammar and vocabulary of the common worker remained Anglo-Saxon—simple and to the point.

This means that at the heart of our language, we have two core groups of words, the multi-syllable, French-based words, and the one and two-syllable words of Anglo-Saxon origin. For those of us in intelligence, it means we fall back on the simpler words wherever possible. We do not deal in abstractions; we do not deal in innuendos or nuances. We are not academic—we do not reach for words, and we minimize adjectives. Our work must be objective. Where adjectives add color or emotion to the text, we do neither. Our writing is a straightforward, unvarnished presentation. It is logical expository writing.

The study of the English language is very useful for historians, who can trace the rise in power of the Anglo-Saxon nobles by looking at legal English. As the nobles became more powerful they insisted their vocabulary be inserted into the law. Thus you have the phenomenon of the double noun in legal

English. When you go to your attorney to have your will drawn up, the first sentence may begin as follows:

*My last <u>will</u> (Anglo-Saxon) and <u>testament</u> (French for will)...*

The periodic appearance of the Anglo-Saxon nouns alongside French nouns marked a step forward for the Anglo-Saxon nobility and another step forward in the mixing of the two vocabularies.

The willingness to grow and change, then, is an inherent part of modern English. English is receptive to change—particularly American English. Because English is so willing to borrow from other languages and coin new words, English vocabulary is always in flux. This willingness to change gives English a vitality and panache lacking in other languages. It also makes English difficult. Every year a new list of correct American English words appears. As new waves of immigrants come to the United States they bring different foods, different concepts, and different words to describe things. Many of these words become standard American English. The impact of Spanish on American English is already apparent and will continue.

You may say the above is interesting and will give you some answers when you play Trivial Pursuit, but what does it have to do with the production of intelligence? Well, it underscores the difficulty of the problem we face. We are not writing for the beauty of the sentence or the paragraph and we are not trying to win a Pulitzer Prize; we are writing sentences and paragraphs upon which critical decisions will be made. We are rarely, if ever, in the room when the consumers of intelligence read our products. We are not there to say, "No, that is not what I meant, I meant this ...." Critical decisions are made concerning the safety of this country based on our analyses, and at that point it is too late to revise.

Whether the threat is from al-Qa'ida, organized crime, street gangs, foreign intelligence services, or drug cartels, the stakes are too high to give short shrift to writing.

Following the tragedy of September 11, 2001, the need for all members of the intelligence and law enforcement communities to communicate using the same writing principles reached paramount importance. Different templates were and are used by different members of the intelligence/law enforcement communities (at the federal and state levels), but these templates are, for the most part, based on the same writing principles. Where differences do exist, once they are understood, the intelligence or police officer can easily adjust his or her writing.

Failure to understand the basic writing principles, as well as the variations on those principles, can and does lead to misunderstandings and confusion. One of the basic differences centers on the use of active voice versus passive voice. Most of the non-law enforcement members of the community insist on the active voice. Some writing templates at the FBI and in the state and local police forces, however, emphasize passive voice sentences.

The passive voice allows for greater interpretation and from the law enforcement perspective these sentences make a great deal of sense. Who are the primary consumers of FBI and police reports? Lawyers. Lawyers prefer the passive voice because such sentences allow greater flexibility in courtroom argumentation. Other members of the Intelligence Community (IC) prefer the active voice, a clearer and more direct form of written communication. The active voice in its purist form leaves little in doubt.

Analysts throughout the IC must be well versed in both active and passive voice sentences; they must know when and how to use them.

I know that the readers of this chapter understand the difference between the two types of sentences, but let's take a moment to review both.

Here is a passive-voice sentence: *Prime Minister Schmidt was wounded today during a military parade, but a coup does not appear to be in progress.* The sentence is passive and raises the question of who wounded the prime minister. You could rewrite the sentence to say: *Prime Minister Schmidt was wounded today by members of a radical right-wing group, but a coup does not appear to be in progress.* The problem is you still have a passive construction because you identify the actor after the verb. To turn this sentence into active voice construction, put the actor ahead of the verb: *A member of a radical right-wing group wounded Prime Minister Schmidt today, but a coup does not appear to be in progress.*

The decision to use active or passive voice may well depend on your audience—even within the same organization. The director of the FBI wants his or her intelligence in concise, active voice sentences. But, FBI lawyers who want to use the intelligence reports as part of the prosecution of a criminal probably want passive sentences. The director wants things pinpointed; lawyers like a little leeway.

In some cases, FBI and law enforcement officers may have to write two separate reports on the same subject, the main difference being active or passive voice. An officer may craft an active voice paragraph or two to go to senior management, such as a synopsis of a longer report (crime investigation), pulling out the main conclusions and facts in active voice, while the report itself is written in passive voice.

In the case of the active-voice report, the key thing to remember is to begin with a strong topic sentence telling the reader the main point, or the "so-what." Think of it this way: if the primary recipients only read the topic sentence, tell them the most important thing you want them to know.

This principle of conceptualizing what you want to say in one sentence should be basic to all intelligence officers' writing, no matter what the format. You should be able to tell someone verbally or in writing, in one sentence, the main point you want the listener or reader to take away. The ability to conceptualize your main point in one sentence applies whether you are writing one paragraph or one hundred pages. This conceptualization is difficult, but it will make your writing easier and clearer.

This need for conceptualization applies everywhere—at all levels of intelligence and crime analysis. It is not enough just to throw ideas and facts down. Taking the time to conceptualize before putting fingers to keyboard or pen to paper will help the drafter construct a logical case.

Active voice sentences are the overwhelming choice of most senior intelligence officers and managers. Much of the detail and the bits of evidence that were critical for you in making your judgments will lie on the editorial floor. By the way, this direct, active voice, concise way of writing is the preferred style of the Office of the Director for National Intelligence (ODNI).

Some of you may be horrified to think, "I have spent my whole career just putting the facts down on paper in passive voice sentences. Are you telling me this is wrong?" No, I am not. You will continue to do that. I *am* telling you that if you are required to write a series of facts or observations, take the time to conceptualize, in your mind, what all these things mean—even if you do not put that in your report. There should be some order and thought in your writing. Furthermore, for those of you with an attachment to the passive voice, let's take a look at reasons to use it, and be clear when, where, and why it is appropriate. Use a passive-voice sentence:

1.  When you don't know who the actor is—that is just common sense.
2.  When you want to emphasize something other than the actor. For example: *A bumper crop of wheat was grown by the Russians.*
3.  When your main audience consists of lawyers. The passive voice allows them greater argumentation and interpretation.
4.  When you intentionally want to obscure the actor. This type of passive construction is the lifeblood of politicians, who during elections want to give the impression they are coming clean with the electorate. For example: *"Mistakes were made!"* Yes! By whom? Tell us so we can vote the culprits out of office.

The intelligence profession—across the board—puts a high premium on correct English usage. Most of the errors I have found in intelligence officers' writing center on four parts of English:

1.  Verbs—all aspects ranging from tenses, through verb selection, and subject-verb agreement.

2.  Prepositions—English, unlike other languages, uses prepositions to change the meaning of sentences. And, English complicates the problem because prepositions are one hundred percent idiomatic—***there are no rules***.

3.  Pronouns—Minimize the use of pronouns in intelligence writing. Other forms of writing encourage the use of pronouns as a way of adding variety, but with that variety comes the danger of ambiguity. What or who does the pronoun refer to? If you use a pronoun make sure that the antecedent of the pronoun is clear. The pronouns "this, that, these, and those" are frowned upon in intelligence writing. They are the demonstrative pronouns and are considered crutches. For example, if you begin a topic sentence with "This means...," what or who does the "this" refer to? If you use the demonstrative pronouns make sure that you identify the reference to "this decision…" or "that rule change…."

4.  Sentence structure and grammar—Remember that intelligence writing puts a high premium on short declarative sentences with little or no internal punctuation. If you have trouble with English, you have found the right profession. Be careful of commas. An English sentence can be correct with or without a comma. For example:

    A.  *I hereby leave all my earthly belongings to the first of my children who lives a good life.* Message: The first of my eleven offspring to shape up and live a good life gets the loot.

    B.  *I hereby leave all my earthly belongings to the first of my children, who lives a good life.* Message: I am leaving the family fortune to my first born because I am rewarding the child for living a good life.

There is also a rule in commas that runs counter to other forms of writing. In intelligence writing, you must have a comma in a series of three or more just before the "and." For example:

*I hereby leave all my earthly belongings to Sally, Paul and Grace.* What is Sally's reaction? "I knew Dad loved me the best, I get 50 percent of the estate." The Intelligence Community at both the state and federal level has adopted the legal standard—the failure to have the comma after Paul's name means that he and Grace are equal to Sally. To be correct, if you want all three to share equally, the sentence must be written: *I hereby leave all my earthly belongings to Sally, Paul, and Grace.*

Before I leave commas, I have to mention a student I had not too long ago in class. He had just graduated from a major university and one of his professors had told him not to worry about commas because they were becoming passé and soon would disappear from English. "No!" I wanted to say, "What university did you go to? I want to advise every young person I know to stay away from that school." Commas are of paramount importance to understanding written English. Look at the difference a comma makes in the following sentences:

1.  *Ralph quit, saying he was fed up with office politics.*
2.  *Ralph quit saying he was fed up with office politics.*

English sentences can be correct with or without a comma, and the difference can be significant.

By now some of you may be thinking, "This is an English grammar and punctuation book—not a book in intelligence and crime analysis." The problem is that many intelligence officers pay too little attention to the basics of English, and errors creep into the final product… errors that can have catastrophic consequences.

There are a couple of other issues involving English and intelligence writing. First, almost all members of the Intelligence Community have their own style guides—there is overlap, but there are differences. Wherever you work in the IC, you need to be familiar with the accepted style of the intelligence organization employing you. If the use of commas or semi-colons does not conform to standard academic American English—so be it. You may disagree with the style guide, but I would remind you, "Who pays your salary?" Don't argue. You are not going to change anything; you are just going to get a bad reputation.

Second is the problem of the supervisor who "knows everything about English." When I worked at the CIA I witnessed a strange phenomenon—a metamorphosis, of people becoming "gods." I am not sure what causes this transformation, but I know it is not unique to any one government agency or private business; it happens everywhere.

Where do these "gods" decide to exercise their godly powers? Invariably it is in the use of English. What is sad is that they got to this new position for reasons that have nothing to do with their understanding of, much less use of, the English language. Nevertheless, they are there and their word is law. Again, and for reasons I cannot explain, to question their use of English attacks their masculinity or femininity in ways that defy description. Indeed, if you question them (even though you are right and may prevent embarrassment to this "god") you do so at your own risk. You may have to swallow hard and say, "Sorry, my mistake." It comes with the territory.

I once read a book on crime analysis in which the author told the readers not to worry about grammar and punctuation in reports, just get the facts down. No! If you have gotten anything from this chapter, it should be how important grammar and punctuation are to our profession.

English is the major tool of our trade. The message you send when your work is riddled with errors or is confusing is that you are sloppy, uneducated, and careless, and pay no attention to detail. Why should anyone believe you if your products are confusing and error-ridden? There is, therefore, a personal career aspect to all of what I have just written.

Enough, I think I have made the point sufficiently about using correct English. Now, let's turn our attention to the specifics of intelligence analysis and writing. On to Chapter III.

# Chapter III

## The Nitty-Gritty of Intelligence Writing

Before we get into the actual mechanics of intelligence analysis and writing, there are still a few things we have to touch on. One is the difference between a personal opinion and an analytical judgment. Critics of intelligence sometimes scoff at intelligence products saying they are simply someone's opinion; young people coming into the profession often are concerned that our products are opinion and not analytical judgment.

Intelligence analysis is not opinion. To understand the difference between an opinion and an analytical judgment you need to know the following definitions:

<u>Opinion</u>

*An opinion is a statement of preference
whose grounds are wholly personal.*

<u>Analytical Judgment</u>

*An analytical judgment is one whose grounds of support
do not depend on an individual.*

### *RULES FOR INTELLIGENCE WRITING*

Writing is thinking on paper. When you write you give the reader a glimpse of your thinking abilities—you are saying something about yourself. Like it or not, people form images about you based on how you write. If there are a number of spelling or grammar mistakes what are you saying about yourself—that you are careless, not well educated, lack pride? Writing can be easy if you will remember a few simple rules:

**<u>Rule One</u>:**    Think before you write. Know what you want to say before you put pen to paper or fingers to keyboard.

**<u>Rule Two</u>:**    Organize your thoughts. If you are writing a longer paper or memorandum, take time to organize your thoughts so you can present a logical argument.

**<u>Rule Three</u>:**  Use simple sentences wherever possible--in the active voice.

**<u>Rule Four</u>:**   Pick your words carefully. Use shorter English words based on the Anglo-Saxon roots of the language. Usually these words are clear and void of nuance and innuendo.

**<u>Rule Five</u>:**   Pursue economy of language. Make each word count and use familiar terms.

**<u>Rule Six</u>:**    Make the majority of your sentences short and to the point.

**<u>Rule Seven</u>:**   Self-edit and proofread. (If you have time, have someone proofread your final product.)

The Intelligence Style is expository writing. It is plain talk, straightforward and matter-of-fact communication. Expository writing efficiently conveys ideas, requires precision, and stresses clarity. A major goal of expository writing is to *never* make the reader wonder what the main point is in the paper or paragraph. Expository writing emphasizes the use of the active voice, although the passive voice is not wrong and should be used at times in your writing.

If you are an intelligence officer reading this, you have been selected for your profession because of your intelligence and hopefully, your writing and analytical ability. Analysis and writing are the two main tools of intelligence officers—our analysis is most often presented through writing (briefing is also an important tool, but not part of this textbook). As an intelligence officer, if your writing is riddled with errors, your prose will be hard to understand. If you cannot correctly use the tools of your trade, people will not listen.

Having said the above, if you have problems with English grammar and punctuation, you have found the right career. Intelligence analysis and writing falls back on the simplest and clearest forms of English. Intelligence writing is not academic writing—you are not trying to demonstrate your intellect through multi-syllable words and abstract concepts. Intelligence writing is not creative writing—you are not trying to create a mood, and you do not deal in nuance and innuendo. In intelligence writing use words and sentences an intelligent person with no understanding of the subject can understand without talking down to the specialist. You never want to send the reader of intelligence to the dictionary.

Our analysis and writing should do all or part of the following:

1.  Define intelligence problems and issues concisely and clearly.
2.  Anticipate or identify trends and developments.
3.  Provide the consumers with analytical judgments and insights that are clear and precise.
4.  Be responsive to decisionmakers' needs.
5.  Give the customer your best judgment about what has or is happening.
6.  Make clear why you are writing and why it is important.
7.  Evaluate raw information critically to determine its relevance and reliability, as well as weigh the evidence.

8. Make meaningful characterizations about data by synthesizing them into judgments that are greater than the data they are based on. By this, I mean conceptualization which I will return to later.

Intelligence reports, whether at the crime scene or in the finished product, are based on fragmentary evidence, incomplete information, and sources of varying degrees of reliability. If you have all the evidence and all the information, you are writing history, not intelligence. It is the intelligence officer's task to bring some sort of meaning and order to problems and situations that, on the surface, defy logic and understanding. Intelligence writing should provide the best possible answer to a problem or situation at any given time with what information is available. We should not provide data dumps, and we are certainly not historians.

## Conceptualization

I was once asked to conduct a one-day intelligence-writing workshop for a major law-enforcement agency. I asked for a good example of their work, but when I read it I had difficulty figuring out what crime had been committed. Structurally the report was fine—no problems in grammar, punctuation, or sentence structure. But, conceptualization was missing. What was the crime? What was the point of the report? Reading the report was something akin to reading a book with no thesis. I was adrift in a sea of words.

Active-voice sentences are the overwhelming choice of most senior intelligence officers and managers. Here, the topic sentence with the "what" and "so-what" is mandatory. As an intelligence officer, you will comb through mountains of evidence in order to make your judgments. But, much of the detail and the bits of evidence that were critical for you in making your judgments will lie on the editorial floor. (Remember we are not academic writers who put every shred of evidence into our finished intelligence. The exception to this is a crime-scene report where *all* the observations and details are vital.)

Hardly any readers are interested in every piece of evidence. They want just the most important, and by implication, persuasive evidence. Every now and then a consumer does want the details. When the request comes in, it is like manna from heaven. At last someone cares.

---

**ODNI**

IC ANALYTIC STANDARDS

A. OBJECTIVITY
B. INDEPENDENT OF POLITICAL CONSIDERATIONS
C. TIMELINESS
D. BASED ON ALL AVAILABLE SOURCES OF INTELLIGENCE
E. EXHIBITS PROPER STANDARDS OF ANALYTIC TRADECRAFT

*SPECIFICALLY:*

1. *PROPERLY DESCRIBES QUALITY, RELIABILITY OF SOURCES*
2. *PROPERLY CAVEATS AND EXPRESSES UNCERTAINITIES OF CONFIDENCE IN ANALYTIC JUDGMENT*
3. *PROPERLY DISTINGUISHES BETWEEN UNDERLYING INTELLIGENCE AND ANALYSTS' ASSUMPTIONS, JUDGMENTS*
4. *INCORPORATES ALTERNATIVE ANALYSIS WHERE APPROPRIATE*
5. *RELEVANCE TO US NATIONAL SECURITY*
6. *LOGICAL ARGUMENTATION*

7.    *CONSISTENCY, OR HIGHLIGHTS CHANGE*

8.    *ACCURATE JUDGMENTS, ASSESSMENTS*

For more information, please visit the ODNI Web site, Intelligence Community Directive

Let's take just a moment to look more closely at these four problem areas, starting with verbs.

1.    <u>You May Change Tenses in an English sentence</u>—<u>if you have a reason!</u>
The problem is that we Americans have the shortest attention span of any people on the face of the earth. We only go as far as "you may now change verb tenses in an English sentence" and ignore the most important part of the rule—you must have a reason. The net result is that people incorrectly overuse the present tense.

In intelligence writing, much of what you analyze and write about will have taken place in the past. Use the past tense. The analysis, however, may be in the present or future tenses.

2.    <u>The Concept of the Universal Present Tense</u>: Even when the rule was you could not change tenses in an English sentence in formal writing, you could because of the universal present tense. The principle of the universal present tense rests on the idea that there are certain universal truths; there are things that do not change. Therefore, when you write about those truths you do so in the present tense. For example: "The earth's gravity *holds* us on the planet's surface." To put this in the past tense would set us adrift in space. This principle holds true in writing: "Huck is always floating down the Mississippi."

An example of the universal present tense in intelligence writing deals with overhead photography. "Satellite images show more work on the Iranian nuclear plant." Every time you look at the image that is what it shows. Until new images indicate something different, keep the sentence in the present tense.

3.    <u>Subject-Verb Agreement</u>: The principle is very simple. If you have a plural subject, you need a plural verb. If you have a singular subject, you need a singular verb. The problem is that many people fail to identify the simple subject in a sentence. The result is a mistake in one of the basic rules of the language. (This mistake is a hot-button issue for many supervisors of intelligence analysts. I know of one intelligence organization that threatened to fire *all the analysts* if one more paper went to senior management with lack of subject-verb agreement.)

4.    <u>Active or Passive Voice</u>: The preferred style of writing for most intelligence is the active voice, aside from the exceptions we have discussed above. Here again the principle is simple—put your subject ahead of the verb: "*John bounced the ball down the road*" (active voice) rather than "*The ball was bounced down the road by John*" or "*The ball was bounced down the road*" (passive voice).

If you name the actor after the verb, or do not name the actor at all, you have a passive voice sentence.

5.    <u>Verb Selection</u>: Take time to select the correct verb. Verbs carry the power of your argument. You do not want to overstate the point you are making; neither do you want to understate it. It can also save you verbiage, because an accurate verb can stand without an adverb, while a more general verb may need to be embellished in order to be clear. An example would be *"She wrote her name quickly and sloppily,"* (general) as opposed to *"She scrawled her name."* (accurate).

6.    <u>The Six Tenses You Will Use Most Often in Intelligence Writing</u>:

    a.    *Simple Present Tense:* Indicates what a person does every day, every year, or each month.

b. *Present Continuous Tense:* Indicates action taking place while the speaker is speaking.

c. *Simple Past Tense:* Indicates an action that is finished or completed.

d. *Past Continuous Tense:* Indicates an action of prolonged duration that is taking place in the past.

e. *Simple Future Tense:* Indicates a planned action to take place in the future.

f. *Future Continuous Tense:* Indicates an action of some duration that will be taking place in the future.

**Note:** When nouns and other words in English are used as verbs, they are verb forms in transition. They are not fully accepted in formal documents. Among these words are: author, critique, debut, distance, emit, host, impact, pressure, and reference.

There is one more problem that undercuts good writing, the correct use of commas, which are governed by more than 300 rules. You need only be concerned with eight of them:

## Eight Basic Rules For Commas

1. A sentence can be correct with or without commas, but the meaning can change significantly:
   A. Ralph claimed Bob was not telling the truth.
   B. Ralph, claimed Bob, was not telling the truth.

   A. Sally quit saying she was looking for a job.
   B. Sally quit, saying she was looking for a job.

2. Use commas in compound sentences to separate clauses with "and" between them.
   The storm hit the coast at 9:00 AM, and Orlando was suffering the full brunt of it by noon.

3. Use commas to separate a series of things or actions.*
   The American flag is red, white, and blue.

4. Use commas before and after the names of people you are talking to:
   Good-bye, Dad.

5. Use commas before and after a quotation.
   Prunella asked, "Are we there yet?"

6. Use a comma after an introductory phrase—if a pause is intended.
   As usual, he turned off the light.

7. Use a comma around an aside.
   Her good friend, the one with the tattoos, is entering college.

8. Use commas around "which" (or nonessential) clauses.
   The sandwich, which I bought at the deli, was terrible.

*Mandatory in intelligence writing

*     *     *

## Words

We need to take just a moment to discuss the use of words in intelligence writing. Here again, we fall back on the basics. Intelligence writing does not reach for multi-syllable words. Let's take another look at our language.

As I said in the previous chapter, I always point to the Battle of Hastings (1066) as one of the defining moments in the development of the English vocabulary.

From 1066 on, the mixing of the languages begins. There are several things to keep in mind about the development of English. First, English has built into it a willingness to change. All languages change, but English is the fastest changing major language. Second, English has one of the largest working vocabularies of all major languages. Scholars estimate English's active vocabulary is around 100,000 words. Third, English has more words than any other language that sound the same, may or may not be spelled the same way, and yet have different meanings. Fourth, because English is a fast changing bastard language, its rules are not rules—a rule in English is a suggestion. Fifth, rules change; stay up-to-date with what is current. For example it is now correct standard American English to use one space after a period—I was taught to use two.

What does this mean for those of us in intelligence? It means several things. First, wherever possible fall back on the one- and two-syllable Anglo-Saxon words. These words cut down the chances of misunderstanding and manipulation. I am not saying to never use the multi-syllable sophisticated words. Use them if they are appropriate, and if they are the best words to convey your meaning. Just do not reach for complicated words. Second, because the English vocabulary is willing to adopt foreign words, make sure you know the correct meanings. Third, make sure you select words that an intelligent individual with no knowledge of the subject will understand, and that do not appear to be talking down to a specialist reading the report.

One other point before we leave the subject of words. Cut down or nearly eliminate adjectives and adverbs. We over-use both, to the point that their impact has been watered down. In particular, use adjectives sparingly. Adjectives add color and emotion, and we do not engage in colorful or emotional writing. Indeed, it is through the inadvertent use of an emotion-charged adjective that the intelligence analyst's reaction or feelings can creep into the written product. The minute the reader can see the emotions of the analyst, objectivity and credibility suffer.

*         *         *

## Sentence Structure

Now that we have reviewed some of the more troublesome aspects of English grammar and punctuation, as well as word selection, we need to look at the English sentence. The Intelligence Community prefers sentences with little or no internal punctuation. So, here again intelligence writing is different from academic and creative writing.

Every English sentence has three essential elements: subject, verb and complete thought. Exceptions to this rule are exclamations such as "Oh!" One or two words expressing emotions are sentences. They are also called "interjections" and are often rude—you probably will never use them in intelligence writing unless you are doing a source report quoting a very colorful source. These sentences do not have subject, verb, and complete thought—they do have complete emotion.

There are sentences where the subject "you" is understood, such as: "Hand me the book." Another exception to this rule is the ellipsis sentence where dots substitute for words. Creative writing thrives on these sentences. For example, a romance novelist I once had in class made her bread-and-butter with these sentences. She would write the following about her lovers: "Gwendolyn looked longingly into Raul's eyes and said, 'Oh darling …!'" The author is doing two things: mimicking the way we speak—

we all let sentences trail off without finishing them—and, more importantly, trying to draw out the reader's imagination. What is on Gwendolyn's mind? The author wants your imagination to run wild. We never want the imagination of intelligence consumers to be drawn into what we write (some are singularly lacking in imagination in the first place.)

Getting back to intelligence writing, if there is a subject and a verb, but the words do not express a complete thought—you do not have an English sentence. Without the complete thought, you have a sentence fragment. Without the complete thought, you are inviting the consumer to fill in what is missing. You are inviting them to fill in with their bias or prejudice.

The function of language is to communicate meaning and grammar. Complete, correct sentences are a vital part of that communication. Meaning can be clear and grammar faulty, just as meaning can be clear in a sentence with misspelled words.

There are four basic types of English sentences: the simple sentence, the complex sentence, the compound sentence and the compound-complex sentence. This text emphasizes the use of simple, compound, and complex sentences. Let's take a closer look at the four sentences.

Simple sentences: Simple sentences are straightforward and leave little in doubt. They are easily understood and visually digestible. The point to remember about these sentences is active versus passive voice. (Yes, I know I have raised this point before, but it is important and worth repeating.) Wherever possible use active voice construction. Briefly:

1. Mary bounced the ball down the road. (active voice)
2. The ball was bounced down the road by Mary. (passive voice because the actor comes after the verb)
3. The ball was bounced down the road. (passive voice because no actor is named.

Some critics of intelligence writing turn up their noses at the extensive use of simple sentences. They miss the point. We are vying for busy decisionmakers' time, and they need complex problems and judgments put in a concise form—without losing any of the complexity of what is being presented. A good simple sentence can do this.

Complex sentences: I am going to bend the definition of the complex sentence and say that it is a simple sentence with a dependent clause or phrase. I added the word "phrase" to the definition because it captures one of the most common sentences in intelligence writing;

> *There will be a coup in Uganda tomorrow, according to a reliable source.*
>     *(simple sentence)*                                    *(phrase)*

The question that frequently comes up with the complex sentence is where to put the source citation. When it comes to the topic sentence, it is suggested that the source citation come at the end of the sentence. The reasoning is that you do not want anything to stand in the way of the point—there will be a coup in Uganda tomorrow—and the reader. Furthermore, if you lead with the main point or judgment, the next question in the reader's mind will be, "How do you know?"

In all writing a rule is a suggestion, and intelligence writing is no different. Why might you discard this suggestion and begin with a source citation? Well, suppose you have a source that has reported over the last five years on some of the most sensitive problems you deal with, and that source has been 100 percent accurate. It will never happen, but work with me and pretend this time it has. One day a report comes in from this incredible source that appears to be outrageous and flies in the face of everything you know and believe to be true. You cannot ignore the report. You probably will be forced to go into print. If you want the reader to at least consider what you write, you lead with the source citation to give your following words some credibility.

The reverse is also true. I remember the management of one Intelligence Community agency dictated that every time a report mentioned Osama Bin Laden, it would be cited in that organization's publication. (This sort of requirement cheapens intelligence and sends the message that the reporting agency has either no standards of analytical judgment or is running scared.) To put this requirement in some perspective, the intelligence officers began their articles with the source citation: "According to an untested source who claims to have met with the third cousin of the defense minister every fourth Thursday of the month, the defense ministry thinks Osama Bin Laden is in Afghanistan." By the time the reader wades through the source citation, he or she knows that what follows is not worth much.

Compound sentences: Compound sentences consist of two simple sentences joined by a conjunction—AND, that conjunction must be preceded by a comma. The absence of a comma in a compound sentence is one of the twenty-five most frequent mistakes made in written English, according to Dartmouth University. The thing to remember is that if what precedes the conjunction and what follows it can each *stand alone* as a simple sentence, put the comma ahead of the conjunction. Look at the following:

*I like apples, and I like pears.*

Both "I like apples," and "I like pears" are simple sentences; therefore you must have the comma before the conjunction. Having said that, if your writing passes under the pencil of a trained intelligence editor, most of these sentences will be broken into two simple sentences.

Compound-complex sentences: A compound-complex sentence usually consists of at least two independent clauses joined by conjunctions such as *and, but, or,* or *nor*, and one or more dependent clauses. They are often, but not always, very long. These sentences may be correct English, but the author has put so much in them that the reader rarely takes time to slow down and digest all the content. Just the length of these sentences is intimidating—what is your reaction when you come to a sentence that is eight or ten lines long? Skip over it, doze off? Few, if any, busy decisionmakers read them.

Bullets: If you find you have written a compound-complex sentence, there are several ways to correct the problem. The obvious is to rewrite and turn it into several smaller sentences. Another is to use bullets. The Intelligence Community loves bullets. The following are a few pointers about their use.

---

## BULLETS

1  Bullets need a topic sentence to put them into perspective and frame their meaning. Do not just throw bullets down willy-nilly.

2.  Bullets do not have to be sentences; they can be sentence fragments.

3.  You have a choice of putting or not putting punctuation at the end of bullets. If the bullets are sentences, I recommend putting a period at the end of each one. If the bullets are sentence fragments, I recommend a semi-colon at the end of each until the last bullet and then a period.

4.  The first word of a bullet is always capitalized.

5.  Use parallelism with the first word of a bullet. For example, if you use a verb form to begin the bullet, make sure that each subsequent bullet begins with the same verb form.

6.  Bullets, in intelligence writing, do not have to be preceded by a complete sentence. You can use the following sentence fragments: "for example," "the following."

Now, take a look at the following example of bullet construction:

TITLE:    The Contract With the Reader
          Topic Sentence—the "What" and "So What"—Deliver on the Contract.
          For example:
          –    Using simple sentences;
          –    Placing commas correctly; and,
          –    Limiting use of the passive voice.

*NOTE: The use of the semi-colon along with "and" followed by a comma is correct intelligence style. It is not correct standard American English.*

So, in intelligence writing, keep your sentences short and to the point. Before we move on to the most important sentence in intelligence writing—the topic sentence of the first paragraph—the following are a few pointers to improve your sentences:

1.    Omit redundant or otherwise unnecessary words or phrases.

2.    Omit words or phrases that are ambiguous.

3.    If there are elements in a sentence that are parallel in meaning and in grammatical function, make them parallel in grammatical form. (For example: He liked sailing, swimming, and to fish. This sentence should read: He liked sailing, swimming, and fishing."

4.    Do not reach for multi-syllable words if a one or two syllable word will capture what you are saying.

Be concise, clear and to the point. Word choice is extremely important. In selecting the one word that captures the meaning you are trying to convey, you will probably eliminate a number of unnecessary words. Improving word choice means improving your vocabulary—you can begin to do this by reading more and looking up the meaning of words you do not know.

## Topic Sentences

The most important part of a paragraph is the topic sentence, which contains the main point of the paragraph. If the reader does not read any further, he or she will know your main point or idea. In intelligence writing this sentence has several different names: core assertion, main point, topic sentence, the "what" and "so-what," the statement of synthesis, and big picture-bottom line.

Whether your intelligence product consists of one paragraph or one hundred paragraphs, conceptualize the main point in one sentence. Make it clear in the topic sentence why the reader should take time out of his or her busy day to read what you have written. I call it the "what" and "so what." What is the reason or hook for your writing and what is the significance, meaning, or analytical judgment you want the reader to take away?

Conceptualization right up front becomes the contract with the reader and the rest of what you write should support, buttress, or illustrate the main argument you are making. Let me give you a worst-case scenario. Suppose your primary consumer is interrupted after reading just the topic sentence of your intelligence report and goes to a meeting where decisions will be made on the subject you have analyzed. At least she or he will know the main analytical judgment you have made on the problem.

Topic sentences in intelligence writing do not normally begin with a dependent word, phrase, or clause. The reason is that a dependent word, phrase, or clause stands between the reader and the main point you want to make. However, there is a major exception: if the clause gives the reader an idea of how or why you know what follows— put the clause first. For example: According to a reliable source, the military will lead a coup in France on 31 October. The phrase tells the reader why he or she should believe an assertion that runs against common or excepted wisdom.

The busy policy-maker or manager may only read the topic sentences of your work. If you move your main point to other sentences (valid in other forms of writing), the reader of intelligence may become confused and stop reading because their reason for continuing to read is not readily apparent.

Let's take a moment and do an exercise in crafting a topic sentence that contains the main intelligence point of what you want the reader to know. Please read the following article and then craft a topic sentence that captures the "what" and "so what." You are crafting the sentence for a U.S. policy-maker.

## Hezbollah Cracked Israeli Code

BY MOHAMAD MOHAMAD
Middle East Correspondent

September 20, 2006

AITA SHAAB, LEBANON – Hezbollah guerrillas apparently hacked into Israeli radio communications during last month's battles in southern Lebanon, an intelligence breakthrough that helped them thwart Israeli tank assaults, according to Hezbollah and Lebanese officials.

The technology was most likely supplied by Iran, allowing Hezbollah to monitor the constantly changing radio frequencies of Israeli troops on the ground. That gave Hezbollah a picture of Israeli movements, casualty reports and supply routes. It also allowed Hezbollah anti-tank units to be more effective.

"We were able to monitor Israeli communications, and we used this information to adjust our planning," said a Hezbollah commander involved in the battles, speaking on the condition of anonymity.

The Israeli military refused to comment on whether its radio communications were compromised, citing security concerns. But a former Israeli general, who spoke on the condition of anonymity, said Hezbollah's ability to secretly hack into military transmissions had "disastrous" consequences for the Israeli offensive.

"Israel clearly underestimated Hezbollah's capabilities," he said.

Like most modern militaries, Israeli forces use a practice known as "frequency-hopping" —rapidly switching among dozens of frequencies—to prevent radio messages from being jammed or intercepted.

It also uses encryption devices to make it difficult for enemy forces to decipher transmissions even if they are intercepted. The Israelis mostly rely on a U.S.-designed communication system called the Single Channel Ground and Airborne Radio System (SINGARS).

Western intelligence sources speculate that Hezbollah's capability came from its two main backers, Iran and Syria.

During thirty-four days of fighting, which ended Aug. 14 under a cease-fire brokered by the United Nations, Hezbollah repeatedly surprised Israel by deploying new types of missiles and battlefield tactics.

"The Israelis did not realize that they were facing a guerrilla force with the capabilities of a regular army," said a senior Lebanese security official who asked not to be identified. "Hezbollah invested a lot of resources into eavesdropping and signals interception."

Besides radio transmissions, the official said Hezbollah also monitored cell phone calls among Israeli troops. But cell phones are usually easier to intercept than military radio, and officials said Israeli forces were under strict orders not to divulge sensitive information over the phone.

Hezbollah eavesdropping teams had trained Hebrew speakers who could quickly translate intercepted Israeli transmissions. That information was then relayed to local commanders, the Hezbollah sources said.

With frequency-hopping and encryption, most radio communications are difficult to hack. But troops in the battlefield sometimes make mistakes in following secure radio procedures and can give an enemy a way to break into the frequency-hopping patterns. That might have happened during some battles between Israel and Hezbollah, according to the Lebanese official. Hezbollah may also have had sophisticated reconnaissance devices that intercept radio signals even while they were frequency-hopping.

An Israeli raid into southern Lebanon found a Hezbollah office equipped with jamming and eavesdropping devices. The base also had detailed maps of northern Israel, lists of Israeli patrols along the border, and cell phone numbers for Israeli commanders, according to Israeli intelligence sources.

Hezbollah's ability to hack into Israeli communications made its arsenal of anti-tank missiles deadly. Throughout the ground war, Hezbollah deployed well-trained anti-tank teams to transport these missiles.

Four kinds of missiles were used to disable Israel's most powerful armor: Merkava tanks. The Merkava is reinforced with several tons of armor, a virtual fortress on tracks.

All the missiles used by Hezbollah are relatively easy to transport and can be fired by a single guerrilla or a two-person team. They all rely on armor-piercing warheads. The most prevalent of Hezbollah's anti-tank weapons is the Russian made RPG-29, a powerful variation on a standard rocket-propelled grenade. The RPG-29 has a range of 500 yards.

Hezbollah also used three other potent anti-tank missiles: the Russian-made Metis, which has a range of 1 mile and can carry high-explosive warheads; the Russian-built Kornet, which has a range of 3 miles and thermal sights for tracking the heat signatures of tanks, and the European-built MILAN (a French acronym for Anti-Tank Light Infantry Missile), which has a range of 1.2 miles, a guidance system and the ability to be fired at night.

The Kornet and RPG-29 were most likely provided to Hezbollah by Syria, which bought them from Russia in the late 1990s.

Western intelligence officials, who declined to be identified by name, say Hezbollah used all its capabilities—eavesdropping, anti-tank missiles and guerrilla fighting skills—to maximum effect. These officials also asserted that the information collected by signals intercepts was used to help direct fighters on the battlefield, demonstrating the tactics and skills of a modern army.

Now, in one sentence, what is the main point you want the reader to take away from this open intelligence source?

---

<u>ONE SENTENCE ANSWER</u>

U.S. radio communication security is at risk, if Hezbollah's ability to breach Israeli tactical communications is transferred to other radical groups.

---

## PARAGRAPHS

Strong topic sentences are the key to organizing your written work and will help you keep the rest of the paragraph focused on the main point you are making. The remaining sentences in the paragraph support the topic sentence, and should be arranged in descending order of importance. This is called the Inverted Pyramid paragraph structure.

Look at the Hezbollah topic sentence exercise you just did. The following is an example of how you might capture the main point in a short paragraph based on that topic sentence:

---

Hezbollah: Potential Ability to Intercept US Tactical Communications

US radio communication security is at risk, if Hezbollah's ability to breach Israeli tactical communications is transferred to other radical groups. Hezbollah's recent tactical success against Israeli units gives credence to this ability. The technology used by Hezbollah was most likely supplied by Iran or Syria. Israeli units rely on the same Single Channel Ground and Airborne Radio System (SINGARS) used by US military units. SINGARS uses sophisticated frequency hopping and encryptions technology to keep communication from being compromised.

---

There are many ways the above paragraph could have been written, but note that it answers the critical question of where Hezbollah probably got the intercept capability and expands the U.S. angle.

The sentences that follow your topic sentence should do one of the following:

- Give the evidence and source or sources used to support your analytic judgments.
- Elaborate on the main point in the topic sentence;
- Explain or clarify the point(s) in the topic sentence;
- Provide details about your topic sentence;
- Give factual information or proof about your topic sentence; and,
- Define your topic sentence.

There are several reasons for using the Inverted Pyramid paragraph structure. First, it keeps you tightly focused on the main point; second, it provides the organization for multi-paragraph reports (the reader can skim read using the topic sentence and get a clear understanding of your analytic judgments and the logic of your argument); and third, it is the hook that captures the reader's interest.

There is another important reason for using the Inverted Pyramid paragraph, and it has to do with keeping the reader's attention. Almost all consumers will read and understand the topic sentence. But as they go through the paragraph, their comprehension begins to wane. Your topic sentence has 99 percent of their attention; the second sentence may drop to 80 percent; the third sentence comprehension may be around 65 or 70 percent; by the fourth sentence (and last sentence), their comprehension may have dropped to 50 percent. In traditional writing, the main point is put in the last sentence—but 50 percent reading and comprehension is not good enough for intelligence writing.

# The Inverted Pyramid Paragraph

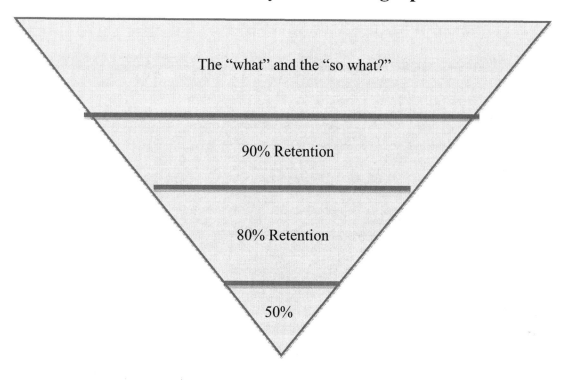

The "what" and the "so what?"

90% Retention

80% Retention

50%

# TWO-PARAGRAPH INTELLIGENCE SEPARATING ANALYSIS FROM FACTS

## TITLE: CONTRACT WITH THE READER

### TOPIC SENTENCE CONTAINS THE MAIN ANALYTIC JUDGMENT—IT DELIVERS ON THE CONTRACT

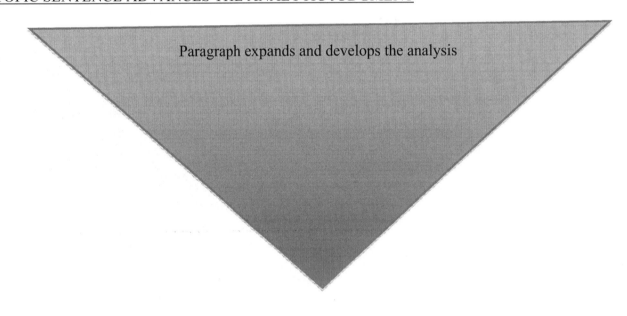

Paragraph contains evidence and facts. Analysis is developed further in the second paragraph

### TOPIC SENTENCE ADVANCES THE ANALYTIC JUDGMENT

Paragraph expands and develops the analysis

# MULTI-PARAGRAPH INTELLIGENCE

## TITLE: YOUR CONTRACT WITH READER

Deliver on the contract in the topic sentence of the Executive Summary

### TOPIC SENTENCE: MAIN ANALYTIC JUDGMENT

Captures all the main analytic judgments
Might include substantiation of key analytical judgment, outlook implications for the U.S.
Usually no more than six sentences

### TOPIC SENTENCE

Paragraph advances, substantiates, or advances the analysis

*EXECUTIVE SUMMARY*

(Approximately six sentences)

### TOPIC SENTENCE

Paragraph advances, substantiates, or advances the analysis

### TOPIC SENTENCES ADVANCES ANALYSIS

This paragraph may contain some historical references for perspective

### TOPIC SENTENCE

Paragraph advances, substantiates, or advances the analysis

### TOPIC SENTENCE

Paragraph advances, substantiates, or advances the analysis

### TOPIC SENTENCE

The last paragraph often goes into outlook and prospects for the U.S

There are many templates in the production of finished intelligence. The above are just a couple of examples. No matter what your template, the key to using the Inverted Pyramid Paragraph structure is to put your main analytic point (the "what" and "so-what") in the first topic sentence. Then, put the main analytic point (the "what" and "so-what") for each subsequent paragraph in the topic sentence of that paragraph.

By the way, I have used four sentences to illustrate because four or five sentences make up the ideal intelligence paragraph. If you need more sentences by all means use them, and if you need fewer, use fewer. You will note that in many intelligence products, there are one-sentence paragraphs. That is correct intelligence writing and it is now correct standard American English paragraph structure. Not too long ago, we were taught in school that all paragraphs had to have at least three sentences, a beginning, a middle, and an end or conclusion. That is still the preferred academic style, but the one sentence paragraph is now correct, even in the academic world.

Are you up for another exercise to practice the paragraph structure? If you are, read the following article on Japan and then write an intelligence paragraph of no more than 125 words. Once you are done, compare your paragraph with the answer.

# JAPAN: FINANCIAL SCANDAL

Arrests At Finance Ministry

<u>The Daily Press</u>
By Ralph Finkelmeyer

Tokyo – They wore dark coats, said little, and carried briefcases. About one hundred of them marched into the Finance Ministry last week. The Tokyo District prosecutor had sent them. Within hours, they were carting away boxes of documents. Japanese officials later announced the arrest of two senior officials of the Finance Ministry, the most powerful institution in Japan.

The arrested men, who were bank inspectors for the Finance Ministry, are accused of accepting tens of thousands of dollars in bribes and gifts—including golf outings and champagne suppers—from big Japanese banks. In return, the officials are said to have tipped off bank executives to surprise inspections. These tips gave the banks time to conceal bad loans. Two other bureaucrats under investigation hanged themselves.

The scandal spotlights what has gone wrong with Japan's and, indeed much of Asia's economy: badly supervised banks. The Finance Ministry admitted earlier this year that bad and doubtful debt in banks amounted to $610 billion, nearly three times what was previously disclosed. Confidence in Japan's financial system has been sapped because each time a financial institution has failed, it has gone down with a huge previously undisclosed portfolio of bad loans.

The bribery charges led to the sudden resignation of Finance Minister Hari Hashimoto and his deputy, who took responsibility even though they were not directly implicated in the scandal. Their departure may be a blow to Prime Minister Nobiki Nippon's government or it could also clear the way for stronger leadership. Hashimoto, in particular, was widely seen by the public as bumbling. The Asahi Shimbun newspaper ran a cartoon showing Hasimoto erasing a single stroke from his name, changing the pronunciation to "futsuzuka," "meaning the "incompetent."

The Finance Ministry dominates and directs Japan's economy. Now many Japanese are wondering who will lead them out of their severe economic crisis. Hasimoto presided over a disastrous hike in taxes last year and kept a tight lid on government spending. But Japanese politicians have been dropping hints everywhere that they may spend more money, or cut taxes, to boost the economy. That is one reason Japan's financial markets stayed surprisingly calm last week in the face of the turmoil at the core of Japan's government.

ANSWER:

*JAPAN: Finance Minister Resigns*

*The resignation of Finance Minister Hari Hasimoto and his deputy in the middle of an economic crisis may open the door to badly needed reforms. Hashimoto's departure is a blow to Prime Minister Ryutaro Nippon's government, but clears the way for new—and possibly stronger—financial leadership. The crisis centers on badly supervised banks. The Finance Ministry acknowledges that bad loans total $610 billion—three times the amount previously thought. Two senior ministry officials were arrested and charged with taking bribes in return for alerting banks to surprise inspections. The Japanese financial markets have remained calm in part because Japanese politicians have hinted they may spend more money or cut taxes to stimulate the economy.*

Let's take a few moments and explain the textbook solution. The real intelligence in the newspaper article does not come until the latter half of the article. Remember, the journalist is an excellent source of intelligence, but she or he has a different reason for writing and will emphasize the colorful and sensational, not the intelligence. That is exactly what has happened in the Japan story.

Ask yourself, why I am writing now? Why should I take the reader's time? Clearly the scandal has been going on for some time, and the arrests took place a week ago—that is not new. What is new is the sudden resignation of one of the most powerful men in Japan in the midst of the crisis. Therefore, the resignation of Hasimoto is your hook or reason for writing. After that, tell the reader what the resignation means. Then you need to tell the reader what the scandal is about—badly supervised bank loans. The third sentence gives the evidence of just how serious the scandal is—$610 billion dollars in bad loans, three times the amount previously thought. The fourth sentence further explains the scandal. The fifth sentence supports the topic sentence's assertion that new policies may be on the way because of the hints Japanese politicians are dropping.

In sum, the five-sentence paragraph gives the busy reader a quick understanding of what has happened and its significance. Yes, some interesting information has been left out. For example, the paragraph does not mention that neither Hasimoto nor his deputy was involved in the scandal. The public's sagging confidence is not mentioned (that would almost be a given—think of the banking crisis in the U.S.), and there is no mention of the fact the same banking problems may exist throughout the rest of Asia (that is the subject for a broader look at banking practices in Asia and the potential for more crises). This latter point about Asia is a prime candidate for a sixth sentence because it alerts the reader that more problems may be coming. I chose not to put it in, to keep the paragraph at five sentences.

If you have ever been handed back a paper with the comment, "It may just be me, but I don't understand your logic or what you are trying to say," the problem probably rests with poor topic sentences. Rather than start all over, read just the topic sentences of your paper. Those sentences should include your main analytical point (topic sentence) and subsequent points or judgments. The topic sentences should also carry the logic of your argument. If they do not, then begin your rewrite with the topic sentences. Once you have done that, then look at each paragraph to make sure it focuses on the point or points made in the paragraph's topic sentence.

We should look at one more use of the Inverted Pyramid paragraph. No matter what type of intelligence analysis you are involved in, at some point or another, you will be asked to write a typescript memorandum. Those memoranda almost always begin with a summary of the main points. When I wrote this type of memorandum at the CIA, they were called the "Executive Summary." The "Executive Summary" is all many high level officials or executives read—they leave it to their assistants to read the complete memorandum. Therefore the "Executive Summary" must do two things: stand alone as a complete document in and of itself and capture all the analytical judgments of the longer document.

Let's take a moment and do one more exercise—an "Executive Summary." This is the scenario; you are an intelligence analyst in a major intelligence organization. The director of your organization is making a fact-finding trip to India and Sri Lanka. You are the Sri Lanka analyst and have been asked to write an intelligence memorandum briefing him on the current situation in Sri Lanka. You may mention, India, but remember that the India analyst will write a similar memorandum on India. Your "Executive Summary" may be no longer than 130 words and six sentences. If you can do it in fewer words and fewer sentences, great.

Here is the memorandum. Read it and then write your Executive Summary.

## SRI LANKA: SITUATION REPORT

EXECUTIVE SUMMARY

Despite President Jayewardene's recent efforts to reconcile militant Tamils and Sinhalese, tensions have remained high and terrorism has continued in the country. According to Embassy reporting, this latest round of attacks is strongly reminiscent of the violence that led to the July 1983 riots, and, in our judgment, may presage another outbreak on the same scale.

Internal control in Sri Lanka is deteriorating as the various Tamil separatist groups—although disunited—continue terrorist attacks and the Sinhala-dominated government responds with measures, which probably will incite further violence rather than calm the situation. The National Security Minister has been given paramount authority in the predominately northern and eastern regions, and is embarking on a program to survey Tamil households, branding all absent persons as "terrorists," according to press reports. The newly-appointed Minister is known for his tough stand on the Tamil issue, and according to journalists, has even assured Sinhalese community leaders in private that extra-legal methods might be applied to the Tamil terrorists.

A prolonged period of violence will probably divide the government and may threaten President Jayewardene's regime. New hard-line factions have arisen as the various attempts to end the communal tensions have failed. According to an untested source, the National Security Minister sees Jayewardene as too accommodating to Tamil demands, and potentially out-of-touch with mainstream Sinhalese sentiments.

Colombo's relations with India are also faltering as New Delhi juggles its domestic and foreign policy priorities, often at perceived Sri Lankan expense. The recent reports of Sri Lankan Tamil separatist training camps in the Tamil Nadu state are exacerbating the situation and adding weight to Sri Lankan charges of Indian interference in its domestic affairs.

Although New Delhi recognizes that such activities on its soil limits its ability to play honest broker between Colombo and the Tamils, conflicting goals and sentiments between Madras and New Delhi make it unlikely that the Indian government will shut down the camps in the near future. New Delhi has moved carefully to avoid inciting domestic Tamil separatist feelings and, according to Embassy reporting, believes that permitting the camps open operation allows for better control in the area without crossing the genuine support for the Sri Lankan Tamils in Madras.

New Delhi's ambition to be a regional superpower and peacekeeper will also ensure keen interest in Sri Lanka's ethnic problems. According to a Tamil separatist leader, the camps in India serve as a not-so-subtle reminder to Colombo that New Delhi itself has various options to control the situation and is unlikely to tolerate a "bleeding sore" on its southern flank.

Faced with such domestic and international pressure, we believe that Colombo will request additional aid from the US—probably funds and small weapons to bolster its weak army—but will not offer US military access to Trincomalee port as payment. Indian and Sri Lankan sensitivities to the US presence in the region are high and considerable attention is focused on this contentious issue. Jayewardene probably hopes that US strategic interests alone will dictate a policy of quiet support for a pro-West government in a region where Russian influence traditionally has been strong.

New Delhi will be wary of extensive US aid to Colombo, which, it believes, the Jayewardene government can only repay by granting the US military access to Trincomalee. India will fear that such access will translate into US interference in other regional conflicts—Indian-Pakistani tensions and flare-ups in the Persian Gulf—and the eclipse of its own regional predominance.

## ANSWER

### EXECUTIVE SUMMARY

*Sri Lanka may be on the brink of ethnic violence that could undermine the stability of President Jayewardene's government and pose problems for US interests in the region. The Sinhala-dominated government is divided over how to handle the demands of the minority Tamils. The hard-line National Security Minister views Jayewardene as too accommodating, and has responded with actions that are inciting, rather than calming, tensions. Sri Lanka's relations with India are deteriorating as Colombo chafes at New Delhi's ambitions to be the region's superpower and perceived interference in Sri Lankan domestic affairs. Colombo will probably request US aid in the form of money and weapons, but will not offer the US military access to the port of Trincomalee, because of Indian sensitivities to any US military presence in the region.*

Again, let's look at the textbook solution. The topic sentence gives the "what"—a new round of ethnic violence and then gives the "so what"—an undermining of government stability and possible problems for the US. The director is then told the government is divided over how to meet the challenge. Your director will probably meet with most high-level officials so he needs to know the National Security Minister opposes Jayewardene's policies and has adopted measures that may be making the situation worse. The paragraph then alerts the director to the fact there are tensions between Sri Lanka and India, and that President Jayewardene will probably ask for aid, but will not repay that aid by offering the US military access to the port of Trincomalee. While not in a position to make a judgment about US aid to Sri Lanka, your director is high enough that President Jayewardene will almost certainly float the request.

A good way to begin constructing the Executive Summary is to write a simple sentence summarizing each paragraph. Then rank the sentences in order of importance, going from most important to least important. Once that is done, craft a broad topic sentence capturing the over-riding significance of the whole memorandum. Don't forget to have a U.S. angle—make sure your topic sentence is clear on why the memorandum is important for a busy U.S. decisionmaker to read.

## TITLES

Before we go any further, we need to talk about titles. I don't know about you, but titles have always been a bigger problem for me, than topic sentences. Titles are extremely important. How many of you decide whether or not to read an article based on the title? We all do, therefore your title may be the determining factor in whether your intelligence is read.

All too frequently I have writer's block when it comes to constructing a title. So there is a formula I use to get over that block. Even if you do not use this formula it is a great way for you to begin and then adapt the title to whatever form your intelligence organization uses. It goes like this: use the geographic area or subject matter as the first word. Then give the reader an idea of the subject matter in four or five words.

UGANDA: xxxxxx xxxxxxx xxxxxx xxxxxx

NARCOTICS TRAFFICKING: xxxxxx xxxxxx xxxxxx xxxxxx

Once you have selected the title (which is the contract), deliver on the contract in the topic sentence with the "what" and "so-what." Here is an example of what I mean. Please read the phony State Department cable from Tashbur and then look at the proposed title and topic sentence.

Background:     The country is Klapistan

The capital is Tashbur

The president's name is Chazir

The vice president is Mohamad

The minister of defense is Bin Abu

FM EMBASSY TASHBUR
TO SECSTATE WASHDC    IMMEDIATE

(CLASSIFICATION) TASHBUR 1234

E.O. XXXXXXXXXXXXXXXXXXXX (FLOVINA, CLYDE S.)

1.    (CLASSIFICATION)

2.    ABOUT 1300 TODAY (DATE), WHEN ARTILLERY UNITS WERE PASSING A REVIEWING STAND DURING ARMED FORCES DAY PARADE, TRUCK TOWING AN ARTILLERY PIECE STOPPED DIRECTLY IN FRONT OF PRESIDENT CHAZIR WHO WAS SEATED AT STREET-LEVEL ON THE FIRST ROW OF THE REVIEWING STAND WITH NO BARRIER BETWEEN HIM AND THE STREET. SEATED ON BOTH SIDES AND BEHIND CHAZIR WERE ALMOST ALL SENIOR EXECUTIVE BRANCH, LEGISLATIVE, MILITARY AND RELIGIOUS LEADERS OF REPUBLIC OF KLAPISTAN. AN OFFICER JUMPED OUT OF THE TRUCK AND THREW A GRENADE HIT GENERAL TABULI, SEATED AT CHAZIR'S LEFT, BUT DID NOT EXPLODE. A SECOND GRENADE WAS THROWN WHICH DID NOT EXPLODE. AN OFFICER AND FIVE OTHER SOLDIERS ALSO JUMPED OUT OF THE TRUCK AND BEGAN TO FIRE INTO THE CROWD.

   –    CHAZIR APPEARS TO HAVE BEEN HIT BY AT LEAST TWO BULLETS. INITIAL REPORTS OVER RADIO TASHBUR SAY HE IS IN SATISFACTORY CONDITION, BUT WE CAUTION THERE HAS BEEN NO OFFICIAL MEDICAL BULLETIN. VICE PRESIDENT MOHAMAD AND MOD BIN ABU WERE HIT BUT OUR INITIAL INFORMATION IS THAT THEIR WOUNDS ARE NOT SERIOUS.

3.    OUR BEST INFORMATION AT THIS TIME IS THAT THE ATTACK WAS AN ISOLATED ASSASSINATION ATTEMPT AND NOT REPEAT NOT AN ATTEMPTED COUP. THERE IS NO INDICATION OF RELATED MOVES ON GOVERNMENT FACILITIES OR PERSONALITIES IN KLAPISTAN. TASHBUR APPEARS CALM. THERE ARE HEAVY CONCENTRATIONS OF TROOPS AROUND THE RADIO/TV BUILDING, THE MILITARY HOSPITAL AND THE OTHER KEY LOCATIONS.

4.    THREE VISITING U.S. MILITARY PERSONNEL AND A LOCALLY-ASSIGNED CIVILIAN WERE INJURED DURING THE ATTACK. DETAILED INFORMATION ON THEIR CONDITION WILL BE PROVIDED THROUGH MILITARY CHANNELS. THE BRITISH AMBASSADOR AND THE CHINESE FIRST SECRETARY WERE ALSO HIT.

5.    THE CABINET IS NOW MEETING WITH, WE ARE TOLD, VICE PRESIDENT MOHAMAD. WE HAVE HEARD THAT MARTIAL LAW MAY BE DECLARED.

SHERMAN

END OF MESSAGE

ANSWER:

---

KLAPISTAN: ASSASSINATION ATTEMPT ON CHAZIR        (CONTRACT    WITH    THE READER)

PRESIDENT CHAZIR WAS WOUNDED TODAY DURING A MILITARY PARADE IN AN APPARENT ASSASSINATION ATTEMPT BUT A COUP DOES NOT APPPEAR TO BE IN PROGRESS. (DELIVER ON THE CONTRACT)

---

HERE IS WHAT A WHOLE PARAGRAPH MIGHT LOOK LIKE:

---

KLAPISTAN: ASSASSINATION ATTEMPT ON CHADZIR

PRESIDENT CHAZIR WAS WOUNDED TODAY DURING A MILITARY PARADE IN AN APPARENT ASSASSINATION ATTEMPT BUT A COUP DOES NOT APPPEAR TO BE IN PROGRESS. ACCORDING TO THE U.S. EMBASSY IN TASHBUR, NO OFFICIAL MEDICAL BULLETIN HAS BEEN RELEASED. VICE PRESIDENT MOHAMAD, ALSO WOUNDED IN THE ATTACK, IS MEETING WITH THE CABINET. TASHBUR, ACCORDING TO THE EMBASSY, IS CALM AND TROOPS ARE CONCENTRATED AROUND GOVERNMENT INSTALLATIONS. THREE U.S. MILITARY PERSONNEL WERE INJURED IN THE ATTACK.

---

Before the chapter closes, here are five intelligence writing principles to keep in mind.

## THE FIVE PRINCIPLES BEHIND INTELLIGENCE WRITING

**LISTEN:**    Listen to what you are being asked to do. If the reader asks a question, you must answer the question.

**READ:**    Read your source or sources (this is a continual process).

**THINK**:    Many analysts struggle to think as intelligence analysts and not academics. We are *not* academics. We are not writing as an intellectual exercise. We deal with very real problems; problems centering on national security. Decisions may be made that affect our national security—lives may be at stake. Intelligence analysts should approach each problem as if a major decision is going to be made based on what they have written.

**CONCEPTUALIZE**:    Every intelligence analyst should conceptualize why she or he is writing before her or his fingers touch the keyboard. Intelligence analysts write when they have something to say. Every analyst should know what he or she brings to the understanding of a problem or situation. In other words, he or she should conceptualize—at the outset—how the current written product helps the reader understand the problem or issue the intelligence is addressing.

**WRITE:**    Every intelligence analyst should be able to write in one sentence what is happening or has happened, and what it means. You will hear that concept referred to as the "what" and "so-what," "the big picture, bottom line," "the statement of synthesis," or "the strong topic sentence." Even if your format does not require the intelligence style of writing using such a topic sentence, if you can write such a sentence before you begin drafting, the writing of your intelligence product will be much easier.

We have now taken an extensive look at why intelligence analysis and writing is so demanding, the pitfalls of the English language, and the basic building blocks of intelligence analysis and writing. Now, let's turn our attention to mistakes, problems, and pressures that plague intelligence analysis.

# CHAPTER IV

## Mistakes, Problems, and Pressure

### *Mistakes*

Six mistakes are common to all new intelligence analysts, mistakes that must be corrected to have a career in intelligence analysis:

1. Breaking away from the more verbose academic writing style. The simple truth is, if you cannot write in the tighter intelligence style, you do not have a career.

2. Being content with throwing down numbers and facts and not making judgments. These analysts do not identify gaps in knowledge, nor do they identify opportunities. In the case of new law enforcement analysts, they do not make recommendations.

3. When new analysts do make judgments, they do not give their strongest evidence to support their analysis.

4. When they write, they often write something that is very interesting, but their draft is not intelligence—it does not address an intelligence problem or question.

5. They do not conceptualize their main point at the outset, and their drafts do not have a U.S. angle. If the intelligence is not clear, if there is no indication as to why a U.S. policy-maker should take his or her time to read their product, they have lost the reader.

6. They overuse adjectives and colorful language; their goal seems to be to elicit an emotional response. The net result is sensationalism. This emotionalism undercuts the objectivity and credibility of the intelligence.

Let's examine the six mistakes just listed in greater detail. Correcting them is vital to getting an intelligence career off on the right footing.

First: Breaking the academic writing habit is difficult. Most new intelligence officers learned to write in undergraduate and graduate schools, and in the academic world, more is better. In intelligence, space and time are at a premium, We are vying for just a few minutes of the consumer's time. The President's day, for example, is planned in ten-minute intervals. You cannot give him, or any busy consumer, a graduate school paper that drones on for pages. Your intelligence will be lost. No one will read it. Your intelligence must be in the intelligence style: clear, concise, and addressing an intelligence problem, issue, or question. If you cannot write in the intelligence style, you do not have a career in this profession.

Second: Many new intelligence analysts are content with just throwing down facts or numbers. They think that a matrix or a timeline is the end-all in intelligence. No. We are paid to make a judgment based on fragmentary information. We must tell the reader what the facts mean. What does the timeline tell you that you can tell the reader? We are paid to come to some sort of conclusion about a problem or situation. Matrices, timelines, tables, graphs, and charts are all important: they are invaluable in helping analysts bring structure to the vast amounts of information that crosses their desks on a daily basis.

These tools are vital to helping intelligence analysts organize their thoughts, but what do all the tables and matrices mean? You are not presenting a piece of intelligence unless you tell the reader the "so what," or what this or that means? Your judgment will be based on preliminary or fragmentary evidence, but that is what you are paid to do. We write for a reason: to answer an intelligence question and to bring meaning to situations and problems that defy explanations.

Intelligence analysts do not stop at telling the consumer the "so what." They also must identify gaps in knowledge—this helps both the reader and the collector—and they are frequently called on to identify opportunities for both the policy-maker and the collectors of intelligence, particularly case officers dealing with human sources. In the case of crime analysts, they frequently are required to make recommendations and give guidance to a criminal investigation. This latter point is one of the areas where intelligence analysis, as it is done at CIA, differs from crime and even military analysis. The CIA is strictly prohibited from giving recommendations or policy guidance. Policy formulation is the job of the Department of State and the White House, as well as others in the executive branch of government.

Third: New analysts often fail to give the evidence for their assertions or judgments; instead they just throw conclusions and pontificate. If you are dealing with fragmentary information, you must give the reader some idea of how you reached your conclusions. Here, source citations become extremely important if you are to convince the reader of the merits of the argument. New analysts frequently are not precise in their source citations. Is it better to say, "There are press reports" or "The Chinese Communist Party daily reported…"? Clearly the latter source citation gives greater strength to the point you are making.

Readers of intelligence expect (and have a right) to know what you based your analysis on and how you reached your conclusions.

Fourth: We do not write just because the subject is interesting. We are not academics. We do not value information for its own sake, no matter how interesting or fascinating the information is, and we do not rush into print with interesting reports that have no intelligence value. We should be and are interested in that information, because it adds to the depth of our knowledge and helps us gain understanding. Policy-makers only want intelligence that helps them formulate policy, and safeguard and promote the interests of the nation.

Throughout the career of every intelligence analyst, then, he or she will read vast amounts of information that has no intelligence significance. Because we become specialists in a given field or area, all of us have to resist the temptation to write for the sake of writing, or because *we* find it interesting. This information helps us gain greater depth and understanding of the problems we deal with, but is of little or no interest to the intelligence consumer.

Our products must be grounded in intelligence problems and questions. As one senior intelligence officer said, "It is the difference between saying, 'We need a piece on the riots in Greece,' and 'We need a piece on what the outcome of the riots will be and what options are open to Athens in dealing with them.'"

Fifth: A mistake that nearly every intelligence analyst makes when starting his or her career is the failure to conceptualize the main point of the written product. Without conceptualization, there is little logic or organization to the product, and again, no one will read it. When intelligence analysts fail to conceptualize the main point or conclusion, there is no identification of key drivers or variables in the paper. Once again the reader loses interest.

By the time the intelligence officer has a conclusion, it is at the end of the paragraph or paper—the academic style. The problem is that 90 percent of the readers have stopped reading, and the point of the intelligence message is lost. Putting the conclusion or main point in the last sentence is the style followed by most academic pursuits. I tell my students that if you put the following in front of the last sentence— "And most importantly, dear reader, don't forget…," —then you have flunked standard intelligence writing. "Most importantly" goes in the lead sentence, and is not needlessly repeated.

Sixth: Young analysts coming into the intelligence profession frequently fall prey to the siren's song of emotionalism through use of adjectives. As I mentioned earlier in the chapter on the use of English in intelligence, adjectives add emotion and color. We want neither in intelligence. The minute the consumer sees the analyst in the report, credibility goes downhill.

Other problems include an over abundance of qualifiers. Because analytic conclusions are based on fragmentary evidence, analysts often are timid in their analytic judgments. Sometimes this timidity stems from a fear of being wrong; sometimes it comes from a fear of telling the consumer what he or she does not want to hear; and sometimes the timidity reflects a desire to avoid a nasty coordination struggle. No matter what the reason, the net result is poor intelligence that more often than not states the obvious, is shallow and superficial, and is unsophisticated by any measure.

*   *   *

Every time I begin working for a new intelligence component, I try to get from them a list of the ten most frequent problems they see in their employees' drafts. My classes cannot correct those mistakes, but I can at least raise the problems and sensitize the students to them. The lists are remarkably similar. The following summarizes them, beginning with the most frequently cited.

*1. Paragraphs do not begin with a strong topic sentence that contains the main point or the "what and so-what". The reader must search to understand why she/he is reading the paragraph.* We covered this in point five of my previous list and have dealt with topic sentences extensively in the previous chapter, so there is no reason to repeat. However, the fact that it keeps coming up should tell you just how important that "what" and "so-what" sentence is, as well as how frequently it gets buried by inexperienced writers.

By the way, if you have taken intelligence from other instructors in the IC, you may have heard them refer to the "what" and "so what" as: "the statement of synthesis," "the big picture-bottom line," or "the strong topic sentence." We all mean exactly the same thing. Think of the topic sentence as the only sentence the consumer will read. When viewed in that light, you see its importance. The topic sentence must contain the main point you want readers to take away. They may not read anything else.

*2. Spelling errors. Remember, all spell-check does is tell you if you are using an English word, not whether it is the correct English word.* I can identify with this problem. I am a horrible speller. I simply do not hear the letters, e.g. the difference between *"ible"* and *"able,"* between *"ance," "ence,"* and *"ience,"* between *"per"* and *"pur."* Those are just a few of the problems I have. The thing to remember is to check, check again, and then double-check your spelling. Spelling is complicated by the fact English has more words than any other language that are pronounced the same way, may or may not be spelled the same way, and have different meaning. Furthermore, unlike French (which is also non-phonetic), we rarely use accent marks to help the reader. Adding to this spelling problem is the failure to standardize the (transliteration) spelling of names and places that are not written in a Latin-based alphabet. Yes, I know Congress dictated that the same transliteration would be used, but as of this writing (late 2011) not everyone is abiding by the same transliterations.

*3. Poor use of acronyms. The failure to follow the rules of standard American English when using acronyms can lead to confusion.* For example, if you can pronounce the abbreviation, do not use periods. Therefore it is "NASA," not "N.A.S.A." But it is correct to write "FBI," and we cannot pronounce those initials. Here the rule says that if an organization is so well known, you do not need periods. That is subjective. There are well-educated and traveled Americans who think that CIA stands for the Culinary Institute of America. Acronyms can be a cause of major misunderstanding. Intelligence analysts live in a world of government acronyms. The best rule to follow is, if in doubt, spell it out, and then define or explain.

*4. Classification errors. Failure to classify paragraphs properly; failure to use the proper overall classification.* Every intelligence agency has slightly different rules on where and how to put classifications on written documents. Some put them at the beginning of each paragraph, some put them at the end. At one time when I worked for the CIA, if the memorandum was based on sources whose classifications were no higher than "confidential," then all you did was put the "confidential" at the top and bottom of the page. The important thing to remember is to know the rules of your organization, and stick to them.

*5. Poor and inconsistent source citations. Failure to clearly identify the source of the information— press sources, HUMINT, clandestine source, embassy, or liaison. For example, "diplomats report..." is not as clear a saying, "the US Embassy Seoul reports..."* Intelligence consumers expect to know where your information comes from; therefore, it is important that you source your sentences and paragraphs appropriately. If the source is a human source, remember that you, the analyst, rarely have knowledge of the source's true identity. It is important you abide by the source description provided by the originating agency.

*6. Poor and over use of background information.* Intelligence is not history. Use background information sparingly. Background and history are vital to the intelligence analyst's understanding of the problem. They give her or him depth and insight into what is being analyzed, but the consumer is not interested in these details. Furthermore the consumer does not have time to read history. If consumers want background, they will ask you.

*7. Selecting the strongest evidence to make your case.* You do not have room to put all the evidence in your paragraph; you must make an analytical judgment and select the one or two strongest pieces of evidence. Keep the other sources ready to pull out, if the consumer or supervisor is not convinced and wants more evidence in order to accept your argument.

*8. Starting the topic sentence with dependent words, phrases, or clauses.* The rule in intelligence writing is to go right to the point you are making and put the source citation at the end—unless you have a reason to do otherwise. This rule applies specifically to topic sentences. You do not want anything to stand between the reader and the main point you are making. Therefore, unless told otherwise, the topic sentence should read, "There will be a coup in Uganda tomorrow, according to a reliable source," not "According to a reliable source, there will be a coup in Uganda tomorrow."

In the body of your paragraphs you may want to periodically begin with a source citation in order to add variation to your style. But, even here most editors will put the source citation at the end of the sentence.

I have just given you the rule for placing sources in a sentence, but when might you start your topic sentence with a source citation? Suppose you have an incredibly reliable source who is always right even on some of the most sensitive and important intelligence problems. One day this source reports something that either defies logic and reason, or runs counter to accepted wisdom and reason. You will be forced to write. So, if you want the reader to take your intelligence seriously, lead with the source citation.

*9. Passive voice.* We have already gone into the active versus passive voice issue in Chapter II. Unless you are in law enforcement intelligence, avoid using the passive voice, use active voice sentences whenever possible. The two main reasons to use the passive voice in intelligence are: one, if you do not know who the actor is (that is obvious), and two, if you want to emphasize something else in the sentence. The passive voice can be used to manipulate the readers. Analysts need to be aware of this manipulative effect from a professional and ethical standpoint. The Virginia Tech Case Study at the end of this book, asks you to look at the use of the passive voice in the Governor's Review Panel Report, and to determine if it was used to manipulate, conceal, or downplay aspects of the report.

*10. Poor word choice and grammar errors.* The first part of this problem, word choice, is difficult. The words you select when you write may technically not be wrong; the problem is that your words may not make your point as clearly and concisely as needed. Poor word choice may open the door to confusion and misunderstanding. Look at the following wordy and confusing sentence:

*"Reports from consulates in the region of North Korean defecting and seeking asylum, compounded by thousands of North Koreans fleeing over Chinese and South Korean borders,*

*have put both these countries on high alert, moving troops to border cities and transportation hubs, fearing an onslaught of refugees there-by creating further tensions in the area."*

The student needed to break the sentence into at least two sentences and improve word choice. Here is what the student meant to say:

*Troop movements on both sides of the Chinese-North Korean border appear to be efforts to stem the flood of Korean refugees seeking refuge in China. The U.S. consulate in Wuhan reports North Korean officials seeking asylum in China, adding to the tensions between the two countries."*

Key points are sometimes lost because of unnecessary or poor words. Take a look at the following topic sentence I was given in class:

*Seemingly dismissive of its ongoing and worrisome economic and social crisis, growing and violent civil unrest, food and energy shortages, repression, and defections of political asylum-seekers, the North Korean government appears bent on nuclear proliferation.*

First, the syntax of the sentence is badly flawed. Second, the student was writing based on several reports dealing with several subjects including: North Korea's decision to restart work on its nuclear reactor, widespread civil unrest stemming from food and energy shortages, and a growing number of defections. The mistake was to try putting all that in one sentence. What is the most important intelligence in the student's sentence? It is Pyongyang's decision to restart its nuclear reactor—and that point comes at the end. The student should have written:

*North Korea's decision to restart it nuclear reactor in defiance of threatened international sanctions underscores Pyongyang's determination to become a nuclear power. (Not, proliferation as the student wrote. Proliferation is the end result of North Korea's becoming a nuclear power.)*

Once you have a short, crisp topic sentence with a "so-what," in the following sentences you can say that Pyongyang is pursuing its nuclear goal while ignoring the country's economic crisis.

As for grammar errors, keep in mind the Intelligence Community puts a high premium on sentences with little or no internal punctuation. Your intelligence writing, therefore, will have a high number of active voice, simple, declarative sentences. Break yourself of the habit of using semi-colons. The semi-colon is the most frequently incorrectly used punctuation in English. It is too bad, as I like the semi-colon; it can make for a powerful sentence when used to replace the comma and conjunction in a compound sentence. The basic grammar points of intelligence writing were reviewed in Chapter II, "This Beast, The English Language."

*       *       *

Another mistake intelligence officers make is to take the coordination process personally, and to resent their colleagues for disagreeing with them. Intelligence analysts have to be willing to go at it tooth-and-nail without being obstinate, and then when the issue is settled, to put the argument behind them and not take it personally. Leave the argument on the table.

As a young analyst, I vividly remember a dispute between my CIA mentor and his counterpart at State Department's Bureau of Intelligence and Research (INR). It was quite heated and my mentor's words could be heard throughout the office as he tried to coordinate over the secure phone. After a long period of time, the INR officer acquiesced and my mentor's analysis went to print with the State Department's concurrence.

A week or so later, a cable came in from the field showing the CIA analysis was correct. The morning the cable came in, the INR officer was the first to call with congratulations and to say he had been wrong. I have never forgotten that. From that time on I knew I wanted to be an intelligence officer who was big enough, and secure enough to admit being wrong. I wanted to be of the quality of the INR officer.

Intelligence analysts must have the courage of their analytic convictions, but not be stubborn. Disagreements and arguments over substance are a necessary part of the profession. But these differences over substance should never turn personal. And, don't hold a grudge. I am always suspicious of intelligence analysts who coordinate too quickly without some discussion or tense moments. But once the issue is settled, that is it. Remember, you will not be right all the time. No one has a lock on knowledge and insight.

# *Problems*

Many of the problems intelligence analysts face are not "mistakes" per se so much as a failure to assume that in every product, a critical decision will be made on that product. We cannot afford to slack off in our determination to produce the very best each time we put pen to paper or fingers to the keypad. In other words, intelligence analysts are often content to report things and not analyze them. As a result there is no clear conclusion or story line, and the intelligence will not be read. It is difficult in the daily grind of work for intelligence analysts to remember the product that day may provide the missing piece to a critical puzzle— that the intelligence may tip the scales and a decision will be made that could save or cost lives.

One problem that plagues all analysts is becoming too wedded to our analysis and failing to challenge our assumptions. We often resist information that changes our analytical line. To paraphrase a Canadian intelligence analyst at the Police College in Ottawa: "One of the greatest paradoxes of our physical senses is that our eyes show us what we want to believe, not what we see."

The young Canadian captured the problem beautifully. We see what we want to see. Too often we don't challenge our assumptions and conclusions; often we go out of the way to find support for our analysis and make excuses as to why the new evidence is flawed. There are also times when we do not realize the significance of the conflicting information or evidence, and do not take it as seriously as we should. For example, an Iran analyst said in 1978, "Don't worry, this is nothing new, the students always riot this time of the year." That attitude has the makings of an intelligence failure.

Another problem that plagues all intelligence analysts throughout their career is the unwillingness to change their analysis when new information comes in. Somehow they see the change as a personal affront. It is not? Analysts are paid to make judgments on fragmentary information; they cannot be right all the time; they cannot afford to hide their heads in the sand when confronted with evidence that their analysis has not been accurate.

Robert Jervis in his excellent book, *Why Intelligence Fails*, puts it this way, "It is conventional wisdom that good analysis questions its own assumptions, looks for alternative explanations, examines low-probability interpretations as well as ones that seem more likely to be correct, scrutinizes sources with great care, and avoids excessive conformity," (page 173). We have to put our egos aside. There is too much at stake not to recognize the value of new evidence even if it shows we have been wrong.

Often, the longer intelligence analysts have toiled in academia, the more difficult it is for them to learn the key trick of presenting intelligence—particularly current intelligence. They have to stop looking backward and documenting, and start looking forward and predicting. As another Canadian intelligence officer put it to me, "The intelligence consumer does not want the History Channel. He or she wants the Discovery Channel."

Intelligence analysts ply their trade using language parsimoniously. It does no good for intelligence analysts to know everything in the world about tribal customs in Afghanistan, if they cannot present that knowledge succinctly and relate that knowledge to the policy-makers' immediate concerns. The most expert writing in the world will not be read if it does not answer an intelligence question or address a policy-maker's concerns.

Another problem is that intelligence analysts must be realistic enough to realize that power does not have to listen. The only way analysts can deliver a truly unpopular message is to stand firmly upon the facts and to repeat them over and over. Our experience during the Vietnam War made it clear that analysts can speak the truth, but they cannot make unwilling policy-makers listen. However, if the analysts keep hammering away, facts will eventually vindicate them. Clearly, this can be a Pyrrhic victory and small comfort to the analysts, but there is some comfort in knowing, "I told it like it was." Intelligence analysts often lose sight of the fact that men and women in the field put their personal safety and their lives on the line to get the raw intelligence analysts collate, summarize, synthesize, analyze, and present. I used to tell the new analysts I taught, if people are putting themselves in harm's way to get the information to do your job, then you cannot shy away from doing your best to get your analysis disseminated.

Now, let's take a closer look at the pressures intelligence analysts face.

## *Pressure*

Analysts must be willing to be brave enough to challenge managers—especially at the highest levels—if their analysis is solidly based on demonstrable facts. Such a confrontation is truly one of the greatest challenges analysts may face. It helps if analysts have immediate supervisors who are willing to back them up, but this is not always the case. In general, other analysts will present a united front if they believe one of their own is being bulldozed by managers who are trying to be "politically correct."

Crime analysts experience similar kinds of pressure. They too face pressure to be politically correct and to not challenge a manager's preconceived notions or bias that the evidence points to something else. One state police officer told me he came under strong pressure from a prosecuting attorney to lie about the evidence, because the evidence did not fit the attorney's theory of the case. The officer did not lie and the judge threw the case out.

History suggests all intelligence analysts will face some kind of pressure. All intelligence analysts need to be prepared for the price they may pay for showing the courage to speak up. Remember even if you are 100 percent right and save your agency or the U.S. government from making a mistake, you have embarrassed a senior supervisor or official, and— "no good deed goes unpunished."

Pressure comes in all shapes and sizes. Indeed every line of work has pressure—pressure to make a profit, to meet a deadline, to develop a product, or to satisfy the customer. I could go on and on. So why go into the pressures that intelligence analysts face? Because so much is at stake for the safety of the nation's citizens and or the nation's security. And, in a perverse way, this pressure is a good thing because it keeps us on our toes.

The most blatant pressure occurs when intelligence agencies or analysts are explicitly told what their conclusions should be. Failure to bend to this pressure can result in the removal of people who produce the "wrong" answers, and their replacement with individuals whose views are consistent with senior managers or policy-makers. A particularly effective form of pressure is to reduce the resources going to analytical units whose analyses are troubling to key consumers. Finally, there is the subconscious pressure that all intelligence analysts feel: the fear their careers will be damaged by producing undesired reports that run counter to policy or the bias of key individuals. [Jervis, page 172.]

The American public in general is suspicious of the Intelligence Community because it functions in a world that runs counter to the nation's values—the world of secrecy and covert action. The public intuitively sees the need for intelligence, but they are uncomfortable with it.

The following is an excellent quote to which I would add the words "intelligence officers" as part of the government officials.

*"The natural bureaucratic response is to be defensive. Officials hide behind the veil of secrecy or national security, or executive privilege. They fear embarrassment, personal or institutional.*

*Elected officials fear retribution from the electorate. Yet demanding accountability from elected and appointed officials of the government, and insisting on revealing and correcting their shortcomings, are the most basic rights and duties of citizens in a democracy."*

Craig R. Whitney, New York Times,
Introduction to The 9/11 Investigations,
PublicAffairs, New York, 2004

Intelligence analysts are under pressure to get it right at every turn. They deal with fragmentary and often contradictory evidence—they never have all the sources they need to feel comfortable. Yet they do their work and they have been remarkably successful.

While intelligence organizations in general and analysts specifically need to be right, there has to be room for error. You will be wrong periodically. I tell my classes the worst thing you can do is say nothing. If you write an intelligence report on Friday based on the information you have, and the critical information you were lacking comes in on Monday showing your analysis was wrong, you must correct the record. The important thing to remember is that if you can defend why you wrote one way on Friday, but now are changing the analysis, you will be ok. I should quickly add that you don't want to do this too often. It is not career enhancing.

Bottom-line: there has to be room for all intelligence analysts to be wrong. If intelligence analysts feel pressured to be right at every turn, they will hold back on making judgments, or produce intelligence that is so filled with qualifiers, it will come close to stating the obvious and will be of little or no value.

The most insidious pressure an analyst faces is when it comes from within his or her own organization. I have already relayed my story of the pressure I came under to say, in 1984, that Yugoslavia was on the verge of bloodshed and civil war. Well, it did not stop there. Even after the paper came out saying that was not the case, my superiors pressured me to change my analysis. The net result is that they undercut me at the highest levels. I was now working for a new office chief. She was equally insistent I should say civil war was coming in Yugoslavia, but I would not—not without the evidence.

During this period Solidarity was becoming a serious challenge to the communist government in Poland. The National Security Council (NSC) requested a briefing on Solidarity and one of my friends, the Polish analyst, was tapped to accompany our office chief to the Executive Office Building to deliver the briefing.

When the Polish analyst was through and about to leave, an NSC staffer asked if the two would briefly comment on Yugoslavia. The office chief jumped in. She said there was danger of civil war and bloodshed. When she could not get me to go into print saying that, she took the first opportunity to protect her career. In one or two sentences she undercut months of carefully thought out and written intelligence analysis. She could now say that she personally warned the NSC—despite what her analyst said. She must have heaved a sigh of relief, because now, in her mind, her job was safe.

Again, no lives were at stake; what was at stake was the integrity of intelligence. I have always considered myself a professional intelligence analyst—I have made mistakes, but they have been honest mistakes. I never intentionally misled intelligence consumers. Shortly after that incident, I transferred out of East European affairs.

Why have I told this story? Because intelligence analysts work hard to get at the truth and they are all too often undercut in ways the public knows nothing about. The most important service intelligence analysts perform is to deliver their objective analysis to the policy-maker free of considerations about their careers. Another invaluable service intelligence performs is to deliver analysis to the policy-maker even when the policy-maker does not want to hear it.

Despite all the lip service about the need for good intelligence, almost all policy-makers are skeptical of intelligence they receive because it frequently challenges their beliefs, ideology, and predisposition, making decisions more difficult. Or as John Maynard Keynes put it, "There is nothing a government hates more than to be well-informed; for it makes the process of arriving at decisions much more complicated and difficult."

Robert Jervis gives an excellent example of this pressure when he writes, "... pessimistic CIA assessments about the planned American invasion of Cambodia in 1971 were not forwarded to the president when DCI Helms realized that Nixon and Kissinger had made up their minds and would only be infuriated by the reports, which turned out to be accurate." (pages 168-169.) Jervis also makes the point on page 170, that "... policy-makers are entitled to their own policies but not their own facts." Unfortunately, Mr. Helms caved in and the intelligence process was corrupted.

Why am I spending so much time on the subject of pressure? I do this because all intelligence analysts need to go into their profession with their eyes wide open. You need to know what lies ahead and consider how you will react to the pressure. You will lose some battles and intelligence will be corrupted, but one of the worst things an analyst can do is throw in the towel—if you do, then the snake-oil salesmen win.

Let me give you one more story. Even allowing for my faulty memory, the story is essentially correct. The Reagan administration made a high priority of stopping the flow of illegal drugs into the U.S. The policy was for a while considered the crown jewel of Reagan's foreign initiatives—and it appeared to be highly successful. The policy was so successful the CIA decided to send an analyst to Latin America to do first-hand analysis and write the definitive intelligence paper on the interdiction of narcotics coming to the U.S.

What he found was that the ambassador had been blocking reports which noted the once highly successful program to halt the flow of drugs into the U.S. was now failing because of corruption in the host country. The Drug Enforcement Agency (DEA) officers in the country, whose reports had been blocked, showed the analyst their evidence. The net result would be a marked increase in the flow of drugs into the U.S. in the next twelve to eighteen months.

When the ambassador questioned the CIA analyst and learned what the analyst proposed to write, the analyst was ordered out of the country within the next twenty-four hours and sharply reprimanded for undercutting the policies of our president. The ambassador did not stop there, he called the State Department to complain about the analyst and the department in turn called the CIA to pass along the complaint.

When the analyst returned to headquarters, he was told to write his report just as he saw the situation. He was an excellent intelligence analyst and wrote an outstanding, well-documented report. Just as the report reached senior Agency management, something happened that broke the story wide open. DEA undercover agent Enrique Camarena was kidnapped on February 7, 1985, tortured and murdered. The news hit Washington like a bombshell and the National Security Council (NSC) called the CIA asking what the Agency knew about the problem.

The Agency responded by sending the analyst to brief members of the NSC. The briefing was thorough and well received. The result was U.S. policy was immediately changed in response to the intelligence findings and the Reagan administration was saved embarrassment.

You may say that is ancient history, and that it doesn't happen today. You are wrong. I have worked with trained linguists who are going to Iraq and Afghanistan to work with our troops, our operations officers, and our analysts. More than one has come to me highly upset saying they have been instructed to change the translation because it does not fit what the person in charge wants to hear.

Decisions about the allocation of resources—men, women, and materiel—are made on these translations. Wrong translations will result in wrong decisions, which will result in people being killed or wounded. Pressure to corrupt intelligence does exist and it never goes away. It is present today.

The electorate has the right to demand better. For a professional intelligence officer to intentionally distort or lie, is not only unethical, it is unconscionable.

Intelligence is a *profession*, not a *business*. Many inside and outside government chafe at the vast amounts of money the Intelligence Community gobbles up every year. Sometimes rightly and sometimes wrongly they see intelligence costing huge sums, and they see little in return. Perhaps they are not looking very hard for the returns on their dollars. The fact that there has been no major terrorist attack on the continental U.S. since 9/11 is not just luck. It is in part the result of intelligence tracking down terrorists around the world. Here both operations officers and analysts deserve our undying gratitude. Much of this effort has been the result of analysts working hand-in-glove with operations officers—levying requirements, using their expertise to check the bona fides of sources, and getting solid intelligence to policy-makers so they can adopt correct policies to aid in the struggle against terrorism.

# CHAPTER V

## Editing and Analytic Reviewing

All intelligence analysts must keep in mind their product is a corporate product and not the property of any one individual. The organization the intelligence analyst works for must be willing to stand behind the product. Therefore, editing takes on an additional significance, and all analytic products are subject to an intensive review. Review guarantees a quality of style, and that the message and the standards of finished intelligence are met. The intelligence analyst also must learn to welcome this editing process and to recognize an editor will almost always improve the text.

The editing process, then, is critical to the production of finished intelligence, and it involves several steps. The process begins with the analyst. From the very outset, analysts edit and re-edit their drafts just to get their ideas down in an intelligible form. In fact, editing is present the first time the intelligence officer begins to put her or his thoughts on paper. It is difficult for anyone to edit her or his own drafts adequately; however, primarily because the author knows exactly what he or she means to write. Furthermore, the author will often read right through simple errors, such as dropping the "r" from the end of "your" so that it unintentionally reads "you."

There are, generally, four stages to writing, and they are all part of the self-editing process. The first is simply putting your thoughts down on paper and then finding the appropriate words to express them. This stage includes brainstorming. At this point don't worry about spelling, sentence structure, grammar, or punctuation—just get the ideas out.

The second stage is where you begin both the critical thinking and actual editing. Look at your ideas and begin to group them together. Then, to start the process you must edit to make sure you have English sentences—specifically, intelligence sentences telling what your analysis means. You are both analyzing and editing at this stage—the two cannot be separated.

The third stage is a multi-step analyzing and editing process. Make sure you have answered all the questions related to your analysis. Review and edit for the organization and for the logic of your argument. Edit for sentence structure, spelling, grammar, and punctuation, and finally for style and professionalism. All this assures is that have you presented the best intelligence possible. At the same time, however, you must recognize you are tied so closely to the intelligence that you cannot put it in the final form.

The fourth and final stage is giving up the draft. Have someone else read and edit it. This is the stage most of us think about when we think of editing. You, the intelligence analyst, have invested a lot of yourself in the draft. You intuitively know your draft is telling a great deal about you—how well you can construct a logical argument, your command of the intelligence style, and your attention to detail as well as accuracy. Therefore, when your draft comes back covered in editorial changes, your first reaction is to be defensive. You feel you have failed. In fact, you have not. Having been an editor, I can tell you some excellent drafts are edited extensively because the editor can see how to turn an excellent draft into something that is outstanding.

At the same time, having been edited, I can tell you that, even when I did not decided to accept a change from an editor, well thought out comments have helped to make my writing stronger. By forcing the writer to examine and defend the wording and facts included in a piece of analysis, a good editor makes the writer more confident that what was written is getting the right message across to the reader.

A good editor is worth her or his weight in gold.

## Being the Editor

Some of the friction that exists between intelligence analysts and editors is the failure of the editor to explain the reasoning behind the changes made to the text. The editor or reviewer must give the intelligence officer clear editorial feedback if the analyst is to understand what is required and avoid making the same mistakes in the future. This is the only way one can develop into a good intelligence officer. It is not acceptable to tell a drafter, "This is not what I want. I don't know what I want; do it over again. I'll know it when I see it."

There will absolutely be times when you are on the other side of the blue pencil. You will have to be conscientious, clear, and organized. You will need to double check certain basic facts, such as the time line of events and intelligence being used, as well as being aware of the correct use of English in all its problematic glory. You will need to remember the person behind the text you are editing or reviewing is a colleague and deserves your respect, whether you agree with him or her, or not.

## Balancing on Both Sides of the Blue Pencil

Not too long ago, when I was teaching for a major component of the Intelligence Community, I was asked to include a segment on the responsibility of the analyst to accept editing. All intelligence analysts should welcome editing. Apparently, the request grew out of a near fist-fight between an intelligence analyst and an editor. I really don't think changing "glad" to "happy" or "happy" to "glad" is worth trying to knock someone's lights out. However, accepting editing does not mean becoming a doormat. My rule is if I can defend the editorial change, I accept it. If the editor changes the substance, I dig in my heels.

Intelligence analysts, and all writers, need to remember that an editor can improve nearly every written draft. I believe there is something that stands in the way of the creator of a draft and getting that draft in the best possible finished form. All good writers need and should highly value editors. The problem is that every time we write we intuitively know we are exposing something of ourselves. Rightly or wrongly, as I have said before, we are telling the reader how well educated we are and how well we understand and use correct English. Therefore editing hurts and unfortunately we all take it personally—at least early in our careers. Once we get over the fact that editing is not a personal assault or insult, we have the battle nearly won.

## FOR EDITORS AND REVIEWERS:

---

### FIVE EDITING AND REVIEWING PRINICIPLES OF INTELLIGENCE WRITING

Principle One: Apply standard intelligence writing principles to your feedback. For example:

1. Write strong topic sentences that capture the "what" and "so what."
2. Use the inverted pyramid paragraph structure, if the template calls for it. If not, explain the logic and organization of the paragraph required.
3. Know when to use accepted "Intelligence English" in lieu of standard American English.
4. Double check basic facts, such as the timeline of events.

Principle Two: Do not rewrite the paper. Do give the author examples of how the argument should be made and the correct sentences and words she or he should use.

Principle Three: Tell the author where he or she can find the justification for the editorial changes. For example: The CIA's Style Manual & Writer's Guide for Intelligence Publications or The Gregg Reference Manual.

Principle Four: Be specific and if possible differentiate between the mandatory style and the editor's personal preference.

Principle Five: DO NOT SAY, "This is not what I want. Do it over again. I will know it when I see it."

---

## FOR WRITERS:

To cut down on the editor's blue pencil, look at the following ten points for writing and self-editing. They are also handy for editing others:

### Editing for Clear Sentences

1. Edit for simple, readable sentences. A simple easy-to-read sentence avoids rambling ideas and multiple clauses. Simple sentences are easy for the eye to digest.
2. Keep the average sentence length to fifteen to seventeen words.
3. Keep one main idea to a sentence.
4. If the sentence is too long (twenty-five words or more), try to break it into two or more sentences.
5. Periodically throw in a sentence of five or six words—or less.
6. Use a conjunction or connective (and, but) to start a sentence. (This is tricky to use correctly. I would advise not using "and" or "but" to start a sentence.)
7. Occasionally, long sentences are fine. Just double check to make sure they are clear, punctuated correctly, and can be read once and understood.
8. Use proper word order. For example, make sure modifiers are in the correct place—close to the words they modify.
9. Make sure the message conveyed is the one that is intended.
10. Keep related parts of the sentence together.

### SUPERVISORS AND EDITORS TAKE NOTE

At one point in my career at the CIA when I was teaching the new analyst classes, we received a request from the Directorate of Intelligence to develop a course to help struggling analysts who, in the first eighteen months of their careers, were in danger of being fired. The problem was this: they could not write in the intelligence style.

I would like to take credit for the course we developed, but I cannot. The course was the brain-child of a former analyst and my teaching partner. I will not go into the content of the course itself, but I will say that the vast majority of the problem was not the analysts, but the supervisors, who did not know how to give editorial feedback. So, for supervisors and editors here are some guides for you:

1.   Do not begin editing until you have read the draft through once.

2.   Begin your editing process by reading and placing a check in the margin by words, phrases, and sentences that do not flow smoothly (but don't correct them during the first reading).

3.   Questions to keep in mind as you begin editing:

   A.   Will my editorial changes be understood by the writer?

   B.   Have I used clear and precise words to make my point?

   C.   Are any parts of my editing superfluous—contributing little or nothing?

   D.   Is the order logical and easy to follow, or do I have to make organizational suggestions? Is the timeline accurate?

   E.   Are some sections too wordy? (Has the writer selected the best words?)

   F.   Is the grammar correct?

   G.   Does the writing conform to intelligence style?

   H.   Have I checked and double-checked for spelling errors?

4.   Communicate clearly to the writer the reasons for the editorial changes.

5.   Be precise in suggesting outline or organizational changes.

6.   Identify changes that are unique to standard intelligence style.

7.   Resist changing the writer's style to match your own style.

8.   Give feedback on "borderline" writing that went out this time, but only because of time constraints.

9.   If the writer's use of English is poor, suggest classes he or she should take to improve.

10.  Return unacceptable drafts with specific suggestions and comments on what needs to be changed and why.

11.  Give positive feedback to the writer regularly and when appropriate.

12.  Make sure the writer has considered appropriate graphics such as text boxes, photographs, maps, and charts.

Now that you have looked at the above twelve guides for editing, here are the eight most common feedback mistakes. Try to avoid cases where the editorial feedback:

1.   Judges the individual not the written work.

2.   Is too vague.

3.   Is exaggerated with generalities.

4.   "Psychoanalyzes" the motives for writing a piece a certain way.

5.   Rambles and goes on too long.

6.   Contains implied threats.

7.   Uses humor inappropriately.

8.   Takes on a questioning tone, rather than giving guidance.

## CHECK-LIST FOR BOTH THE WRITER AND THE REVIEWER

1.  Check your title and topic sentence. Is the title your contract with the reader and is it delivered in the topic sentence?

2.  Is your topic sentence a statement of synthesis with a "what" and "so what" that makes it clear why the reader should spend the time reading your intelligence?

3.  Have you used an internal formula to lay out your piece? By that I mean, does each paragraph begin with a strong topic sentence that advances or clarifies your contract?

4.  If your piece begins with an Executive Summary, can you read that summary and understand your entire piece?

5.  Can you follow the logic of your intelligence by reading the topic sentences of each paragraph?

6.  Have you used the active voice wherever possible?

7.  Is the grammar correct?

8.  Are the antecedents to all pronouns clear?

9.  Have you chosen clear and concise words?

10. Is your spelling correct?

## ANALYTIC REVIEWS

One of the best articles I have ever read explaining "the editing and analytic review" process is by Martin Petersen, retired senior member of the CIA. Rather than paraphrase or quote individual sections, I have his permission to print the article below in its entirety.

# *Making the Analytic Review Process Work*

# *By Martin Petersen*

Former senior CIA officer in the Directorate of Intelligence

Studies In Intelligence
Vol. 49, No. 1
2005

If there is a first principle in producing written intelligence, it is that finished intelligence is a corporate product, not a personal one. Intelligence officers all have a stake in everything that leaves the building. A rigorous, focused review process is the best guarantee that the style, message, and tradecraft of every piece of finished intelligence meet the standards that the mission requires.

Like the tides, criticism of the analytic review process is predictable, relentless, eternal, and potentially destructive. Those who argue for more power to the drafter present a bill of particulars that alleges the process does little to improve the product, reduces judgments to the lowest common denominator, stifles creativity, and takes analysis out of the hands of the experts. Those who defend the review process counter argue that it sharpens focus, guarantees that the piece addresses policy-maker concerns, taps all relevant expertise, and ensures a corporate product. Both sides agree on one thing— that there ought to be fewer layers of review—and both miss the key point.

The problem with the review process is not the layers of review but rather the quality of the review. In an imperfect business, this is the one thing that intelligence officers need to get right. My thirty-plus years of experience leads me to conclude that there should be *three levels of review* and *three broad areas of review* for each piece of finished intelligence.

Editing is NOT review. Editing is a mechanical task that should be accomplished by the first-level reviewer or by a staff. Review is about thinking, about questioning evidence and judgments. It focuses on the soundness of the analytic points that are being made and the quality of the supporting evidence. *Levels* of review is NOT synonymous with *layers* of review. Layers of review speaks to how many cooks are involved with the broth; levels of review is about ascertaining the quality of the soup.

Each level of review has a different focus. The strength of the review process is directly related to the different perspective that each level brings, with succeeding levels focusing on ever broader issues that are hard for the author and firstline reviewer to see because they are so close to the substance.

Analytic Review Process at a Glance

| Level of Review | Checking for Style | Clarifying the Message | Monitoring Tradecraft |
|---|---|---|---|
| **First:**<br><br>Reviewer: Firstline supervisor, who is close to the subject matter.<br>Focus: What is in the piece. | • **Are grammar, spelling, and other technical aspects correct?**<br>• **Is language crisp?**<br>• **Is the flow logical?** | • Are key points clear and argued with evidence?<br>• Can assertions be supported?<br>• Is the what/so-what for the US evident? | • **Are facts correct?**<br>• **Are sources described accurately?**<br>• **Is the evidence correctly characterized?**<br>• **Has all relevant evidence been considered?**<br>• Are alternate interpretations acknowledged? |

| | | | |
|---|---|---|---|
| | | | • Is the piece consistent with previous analysis?<br>• Is it clear what is known and not known, and what the level of confidence is?<br>• What assumptions underpin the analysis?<br>• What are the key drivers and variables? |
| **Second**<br><br>Reviewer: Middle manager, who is somewhat expert but has a broader perspective with respect to substance and audience.<br>Focus: What underpins the piece. | • Any confusing technical language or jargon? | • **Are key points clear and argued with evidence?**<br>• **Can assertions be supported?**<br>• Is the what/so-what for the US evident? | • Are alternate interpretations acknowledged?<br>• Is it clear what is known and not known, and what the level of confidence is?<br>• What assumptions underpin the analysis?<br>• What are the key drivers and variables?<br>• **Is the piece consistent with previous analysis?**<br>• **Have the right questions been asked? Any information gaps?**<br>• Are policy-makers' concerns addressed? |
| **Third**<br><br>Reviewer: Office-level manger or senior officer of organization, who is not expert but has a very broad context.<br>Focus: The audience. | • Any confusing technical language or jargon? | • Are key points clear and argued with evidence?<br>• Can assertions be supported?<br>• **Is the what/so-what for the US evident?** | • Is it clear what is known and not known, and what the level of confidence is?<br>• Is the piece consistent with previous analysis?<br>• What assumptions underpin the analysis?<br>• What are the key variables and drivers?<br>• Have the right questions been asked?<br>• **Is the piece clear to the non-expert?**<br>• **Are policy-makers' concerns addressed?** |

## First-Level Review

The drafter's supervisor is almost always the first-level reviewer. Of all the reviewers, this individual is usually the most expert and closest to the substance, and therefore bears the greatest responsibility—

after the author—for the substantive accuracy of the piece. The focus of first-level review should be the content of the piece.

**Style.** Of the three broad areas of review—style, message, and tradecraft—style is the exclusive domain of the first-level reviewer. He or she does the "blue pencil" edit, assuring the language is clear and crisp and the piece flows logically. The second- and third-level reviewers should resist mightily the all too human temptation to "tweak the prose" or "polish the draft."

**Message.** The first-level reviewer shares with the next two levels the responsibility for the clarity of the message. Review at this point is about thinking, not editing, and the first thing the reviewer should be thinking about is why anyone should take a minute out of his or her busy schedule to read something that took days to produce. Because it is interesting is not sufficient.

The "what" and "so-what" of the paper have to be crystal clear in the title or the first sentence. Without the ability to attract the reader, there is no point in producing the piece. The first level is the expert's eye view. The second level is the perspective of someone steeped in the subject matter but not genuinely expert, and the third level is from the point of view of the intelligent generalist. When they agree, the "what" and "so-what" is as clear as it is going to be. If the expert has a vulnerability, it is assuming too much knowledge on the part of the audience and its ability to see the connections.

Assertions are among the vehicles for conveying the message. Assertions are not facts. That Beijing is the capital of China is a fact. That Chinese military leaders take a harder line than civilian leaders on Taiwan issues is an assertion—a judgment based on earlier analytic work and evidence not cited. Assertions are necessary; intelligence is not geometry, and analysts have neither the time nor the space to prove every point. But, assertions are dangerous, too. They need to be questioned periodically, especially if long held and based on earlier analysis, for they have a tendency to become unconscious assumptions over time. Questioning assertions needs to begin at the first level, but the second and third-level reviewers play an even more critical role here.

**Tradecraft.** The analyst and the first-level reviewer bear the primary responsibility for the quality of tradecraft. They have near total accountability for those things that higher levels of review are unlikely to catch, specifically:

*Accuracy of information presented as facts.* Silly things do slip through. I remember seeing a piece early in my career that made reference to the China-Thai border area. Thailand does not share a border with China.

*Descriptions of the sources and what the reporting says precisely.* It matters a great deal whether the source states that a country is attempting to acquire some technology or whether the country has actually acquired the technology, and the analysis must reflect this distinction, even if, on balance, the analyst believes the country succeeded in acquiring the technology. Why? Because if intelligence officers are called on to explain the analysis and to present the evidence, the evidence will only reflect the attempt; success in this instance is an analytic judgment. It also matters—at least to the audience— whether the source has direct knowledge or indirect knowledge. The rule is simple: the more politically sensitive the subject matter, the greater the requirement for absolute precision, because on a politically charged issue a small slip in one piece will be used to discredit all analytic work.

*Characterizations of the body of evidence.* A "majority of the reporting" means a majority, and "almost every" is not 60 percent.

These are right or wrong issues—either the piece correctly reports what the source says or it does not. The other six tradecraft issues the first-level reviewer must consider are even more difficult, and therefore more important to pay attention to. In ascending order of difficulty:

*Has all the relevant evidence been taken into consideration?* Considered means just that: thought about.

*Is there an alternate explanation or interpretation of the evidence and is it acknowledged?* The drafter is not obligated to walk the reader through all of the various interpretations or permutations of the evidence. There ought to be a presumption that the analyst considered alternate interpretations before arriving at the interpretation presented. That said, an author owes it to the reader, especially on complex or controversial subjects, to inform him or her another view exists, especially if that view has a measure of acceptance by other experts. "Suggests" and "indicates" may be the two most favored verbs of analysts. My experience is that what follows "suggests" or "indicates" is the analyst's pet theory, for which there is some but not compelling evidence. My first question as a reader—and it ought to be the first question of the reviewer—is what else might this development suggest or indicate and why is the theory put forth as the best possibility?

*Is this piece consistent with previous analysis?* If it is a departure, then that must be acknowledged explicitly and explained. Also, if it has been some time since the subject was treated, caution dictates a quick review of previous work, so the preparers know precisely what has been said, and probably some language in the piece by way of background for the reader.

*Is it clear what is known and what is not known? And has the analyst conveyed the level of confidence in the judgments and conclusions put forth in the piece?* There is a difference between "sharpening judgments" and "firming up judgments." To sharpen a judgment is to be very clear about what the judgment is and how confident the analyst is in that judgment. To firm up a judgment begs the confidence level at best and in all likelihood conveys a greater degree of confidence than actually exists.

*What assumptions underpin the analysis?* There is no tougher issue to get at, nor one with graver consequences if left unexamined. Assumptions are different than assertions—assertions are explicit statements whereas assumptions tend to be implicit to the analysis. The CIA Directorate of Intelligence's work on the fall of the Shah of Iran in the 1970s and Iraq's weapons of mass destruction in the early 2000s share a common characteristic: each was premised on a strong, widely held assumption. In the case of Iran, it was assumed the Shah was strong and the opposition weak and divided; in the case of Iraq, it was assumed Saddam would not allow his stockpiles of chemical and biological weapons to erode. In both instances, the assumptions led analysts to interpret "could be" behavior as "is" behavior. …If the analyst and the reviewer cannot articulate the assumptions on which the analysis rests, then they are flying blind. They have no idea how they can be wrong and no means to test if they are.

*What are the key variables, a change which would alter the assessment?* The variables are the drivers and the causal links in the analysis, the "if A, then B" part of the analysis. They are closely tied to the assumptions but generally are more evident. Most of the key variables will not be mentioned in the piece, especially if US actions are one, as they almost always are. The easiest way to get at the variables is to ask "what if." A change in one of these variables should alter the analysis, and indeed, should help the analyst think through how it might change. Spelling out, discussing, and periodically revisiting what the analyst believes to be the key drivers and shapers of the issue are also the best ways to identify and illuminate the underlying assumptions.

## Second-Level Review

The second-level reviewer is usually the issue manager, who is well steeped in the subject matter but not as expert as the analyst or the first-line supervisor. As a rule, this individual is closer to the policy-maker. The comparative advantage in the review process is a broader perspective, with regard to both the substance and the audience. The second reviewer is better positioned to see how the piece at hand fits in with other work being done and how it relates to the audience's needs. The focus of review at the second level should be those things that underpin the piece.

**Style.** The second-level reviewer should not be editing the piece—the blue pencil function. Flow and presentation are checked at the first level, and the odds are good there is a staff that will do the final technical edit. The one thing the second-level reviewer should keep an eye out for is technical language or jargon that would not be immediately clear to the audience.

**Message.** The real work of the second-level reviewer starts here. Whereas the firstline supervisor bears the principal responsibility for the substantive *accuracy* of the piece, subsequent reviewers, by virtue of their greater perspective, bear responsibility for the *clarity* of the message for the audience, ensuring the points the piece is attempting to make are apparent and the supporting evidence is compelling (at best) or supportive (at a minimum). If the analyst and the first-level reviewer have done their job, this should not be that demanding. The key question for the second-level reviewer is whether the "what" and "so-what" will engage the target audience and whether the key points will seem convincing. By virtue of expertise and perspective, the second-level reviewer is in the best position to judge whether the analyst has made the case for whatever is being argued.

With regard to assertions, the second-level reviewer needs to ask: Does the assertion make sense? Can it stand on its own merit without further explanation or evidence needed to convince the audience? It is the audience that matters in making this judgment, not the analyst. On issues where there are sharp policy divisions or great uncertainty, it is especially important to pay attention to the assertions, because they are an easy way to question or discredit the overall message. An overdrawn or unexamined assertion is one of the easiest ways to go wrong quickly.

**Tradecraft.** This is where the second-level reviewer does his heavy lifting. As the chart shows, four of seven tradecraft issues for consideration are exactly the same as they are for the first-level reviewer and should be looked at in the same way: Is there an alternate explanation or interpretation of the evidence, and is it acknowledged? Is it clear what is known and what is not known, and has the analyst conveyed the level of confidence in the judgments and conclusions put forth in the piece? And what assumptions underpin the analysis and what are the key variables, a change in which would alter our assessment?

Three other tradecraft issues are similar to ones at the first level of review, but have a different focus here largely because of the broader perspective of the second-level reviewer:

*Is this piece consistent not only with previous work on this topic but also with other analysis being done in the issue group?* Policy-makers generally have a broader set of responsibilities than analysts, and any differences, real and perceived, across issues will be readily apparent to them. It is not unusual for different observers (and thus different analysts) to have different perceptions of multiparty talks, for example, and this can create the impression that analytic products are all over the map on the issue under discussion. It is also important for reviewers at this level to be alert to linkages between issues—increased tension in the Taiwan Strait has implications for Japan as well.

*Does the piece ask the right questions and are there gaps in our knowledge that could have a major impact on our analysis?* This is where the second-level reviewer has the greatest potential impact. More than at the first stage, the second-level reviewer ought to be the "what if" person—the one with enough expertise and perspective to get above the piece in hand. Specifically, it falls to the second-level reviewer more than anyone else to assure that the right questions are being asked, that blind spots in information are identified and factored in, and that alternate possibilities for key variables are considered. In the case of Iran in the 1970s, the points of views of the Shah and the opposition were well understood, but the views of wider Iranian society—the "swing vote"—were a key information gap. Some basic questions were not asked, including about the Shah's ability to follow a coherent course and the opposition's ability to work together. The willingness and ability of religious moderates to act as a third force was a key variable. Once a crisis becomes full blown, it is easy for analysts to get eaten up by the daily demand. This is precisely the moment when it is most necessary to step back and reconsider assumptions and variables, and ask the big "what if" questions.

*Does the paper address known policy-maker concerns and likely questions?* Because the second-level reviewer is closer to the audience than the firstline supervisor, he or she is better positioned to ascertain whether the piece is likely to scratch the policy-maker's itch. This reviewer is also better positioned to know whether the piece in hand is likely to generate additional questions, perhaps on related matters.

## Third-Level Review

The third-level review should be done by the office director or the staff of a senior officer in the organization. On a particularly sensitive piece, both may weigh in. Their comparative advantage is that of the intelligent generalist who operates in a broad policy context. The third-level reviewer focuses on the piece almost exclusively from the perspective of the audience.

**Style and Message.** As at the previous stage, attention to style should be minimal, with an eye only for inappropriate or confusing jargon or technical language. One question should dominate the third-level review: will the intended audience find the piece convincing?

**Tradecraft.** The questions and concerns of the third-level reviewer are not significantly different than those of the second-level reviewer. The value added is in the broader perspective at this level, both in terms of the reviewer's contact with a wider range of policy-makers and an improved ability to see the forest for the trees. Like earlier reviews, the third level needs to ponder core tradecraft questions: Is it clear what is known and not known and what the level of confidence is? What assumptions underpin the analysis? And does the piece address policy-maker concerns?

The third-level reviewer should primarily be concerned with two pairs of tradecraft issues. The first set relates to clarity: Will the non-expert understand the piece, and is it consistent with other work being done in the office or directorate? The second set is the more challenging, and it goes to the "what if" questions. As an intelligent general reader, the third-level reviewer is best positioned to ask the "dumb questions" that never would occur to the expert. The third-level reviewer should focus most on whether the right questions have been asked and what the key variables are.

## Shared Responsibilities

In making sure the all-important review process works, reviewers and analysts share two obligations: to do all they can to create an environment that facilitates an exchange of views and to keep the discussion professional and not personalize the issues or get emotional. Beyond these common responsibilities, they each have their own set of responsibilities:

*Reviewers* must respect the views of analysts. A reviewer's experience and perspective are strengths, but so are an analyst's expertise and command of detail. Reviewers must be open to discussing substantive differences raised by analysts. Although the final say goes to the reviewers, the process should be a dialogue not a decree. Reviewers, moreover, have an obligation to put analysts at ease and to draw out their views. They should be specific about their concerns or issues. If a reviewer cannot explain what the problem is, the problem may be the reviewer. Reviewers should complete their work quickly. If the piece is a priority for the analyst, it has to be a priority for the reviewer. Finally, reviewers must be prepared to stand behind the analysts and their analysis at the conclusion of the review process.

*Analysts*, for their part, should submit the best draft they are capable of. They should respect the experience, perspective, and expertise of the reviewers, and accept that the final say belongs to them. An analyst can and should seek clarification if he or she does not understand what a reviewer is saying or wanting, raising any concerns about what the reviewer is suggesting by using data, history, alternate theories, or intelligence reporting. If analysts are unhappy with what reviewers have done, they should be ready to offer other language or suggest another approach to the issue at hand.

To be effective, the review process must remain collegial. There is no monopoly on either expertise or broad insight, and now more than ever the nation's security is linked to a fusion of both.

\*　　\*　　\*

Now that we have read the Petersen article, let's take a moment and look at problems with words. English has more words than any other language that are pronounced the same way or similarly, may or may not be spelled the same way, and have different meanings. Below is a list of problem words. Many times spelling errors or the inadvertent use of the wrong word can undercut the intelligence and seriously damage the analyst's credibility.

## FINE-TUNING YOUR INTELLIGENCE PRODUCT

Because the English language is the main tool of our trade, we need to know its idiosyncrasies:

1.    The use of "if" is always a problem. There are times when you write or say, "If I were…" and there are times when you write or say, "If I was…"

    Use "if I were…" when what you are talking about is contrary to fact. For example: "If I were king, I would give everyone a palace."

    Use "if I was…" when the statement may be true. For example: "If I was rude, I am sorry." The fact is you were rude, so "was" is the correct form.

2.    The difference between "might" and "may" can be confusing. One way to think about it is that "might" is a weaker form of "may." Something that "might" happen is a longer shot than "may" happen.

    The dictionary tells you that "might: is the past tense of "may." In the present tense it is correct to use both: "She may break a leg," or "She might break a leg." You select the one you mean by the likelihood of her breaking her leg. If you think it is a strong possibility, use "may."

3.    There are times when you use the "be" form of the verb "to be" rather than "was" or "were." Use "be" when someone *suggests, demands, asks, requests, requires,* or *insists*. For example:

    –    The judge ordered that he *be* executed.
    –    I demanded that I *be* allowed to attend.
    –    I was asked if I would *be* there.
    –    The law requires that you *be* in court.

4.    Here is an idiosyncrasy: some verb forms ending in *t* or *d* have dropped *ed* endings in the past tense.

    Once we said: "Mr. Jones *betted* on the wrong horse and lost all his money." "His suit *fitted* well." "She *wedded* her high school sweetheart." Now we say, "Mr. Jones *bet* on the wrong horse and lost all his money." "His suit *fit* him well." "She *wed* her high school sweetheart."

5.    The Intelligence Community loves the dash and dashes; they are frowned upon by many professional writers. The Gregg Reference Manual (William Sabin) offers this definition of dashes and guidelines for their use:

    "Although the dash has a few specific functions of its own, it most often serves in the place of a comma, the semicolon, the colon, or parentheses. When used as an alternative to these other marks, it creates a much more emphatic separation of words within a sentence. Because of its versatility, some writers are tempted to use a dash to punctuate any break within a sentence."

1.    **Use dashes to mark the beginning of a sharp or heavy interruption in thought.**

    EXAMPLE: The office manager was here with—what was the name of the man to whom we sold the desk?

2.    **Use paired dashes to replace the commas around an interrupting element that is heavily punctuated internally.**

    EXAMPLE: Several members of the president's staff—the administrative assistant, the budget analyst, and the secretary—attended the personnel committee meeting.

3. **Use the dash to mark the break into an idea that ends a statement with particular force.**

    EXAMPLE: The vice president was the only one authorized to write checks—and she was not available.

4. **Use the dash before such words as these, they, and all when these words stand as subjects summarizing a preceding list of details.**

    EXAMPLE: Tension, quarrels, low morale, and laid-off employees—these are the facts of the company.

# EDITING TIPS

1. Words that end in "o" can be confusing. Here are the plurals of a few: *tomato, tomatoes*; *potato, potatoes*; *patio, patios*; *torpedo, torpedoes*; *hero, heroes*; *cameo, cameos*; *domino, dominoes*; *piano, pianos*; *echo, echoes*; *radio, radios*; and *video, videos*.

2. Who and whom: These two words always confuse writers. Remember it this way, *who* is in the nominative case, where a nominative pronoun can be used. If you can substitute the words *I, we, he, she, you*, or *they*, then <u>who</u> is correct. *Whom* is in the objective case. If you can substitute *me, us, him, her*, or *them* use <u>whom</u>.

3. Email or e-mail? The bottom line is that both are correct. Which one you use will depend on your personal preference or your employer's style. Email is generally preferred, and from that preference the words *ebusiness, ebooks*, and *ecommerce* have evolved. Be wary of using these three words—all three are shorthand, they stand for: *electronic business, electronic books*, and *electronic commerce*. Go with whatever your employer dictates.

4. The words *bachelor, master*, and *doctor* are capitalized when following a person's name (Sally Smithenheimer, Doctor of Divinity). They should be lowercased with an apostrophe in the following: I have a *master's* degree. I am enrolled in a *master's* program in education.

5. The words *blatant* and *flagrant* are often mixed up. *Blatant* means offensively loud, conspicuous, or obtrusive. *Flagrant* means glaringly offensive or deplorable; scandalous.

6. *Per* and *as per*: Do not use these. Instead, in professional writing use *as, according to*, (in some instances) *as usual*, or *in response to*.

## PROBLEMS WORDS

| | |
|---|---|
| accede | to adhere to an agreement |
| exceed | to surpass |
| adverse | opposed |
| averse | disinclined |
| adapt | to adjust |
| adept | proficient |
| affect | to influence, move, bring about a change |
| effect | the result of; something produced by a cause |
| assure | to make confident |
| insure | insurance |
| ensure | to make sure something will happen |
| boy | male child |
| buoy | a float |

| | |
|---|---|
| broach | to open, to introduce |
| brooch | ornament |
| canvas | a heavy, coarse fabric of cotton, used for sails, tents, and for a artist to paint on |
| canvass | to solicit opinions or votes |
| ceded | to surrender possession of officially or formally |
| seated | to be sitting on something |
| seeded | the past tense of the verb to seed (to plant or to sow), or to indicate a ranking (the team is seeded third) |
| climatic | referring to climate |
| climactic | referring to a climax |
| compliment | an expression of praise |
| complement | something that completes or makes up the whole |
| comprise | to consist of |
| compose | to make up or constitute |
| cyber | computer network |
| cipher | the mathematical symbol (0) denoting the absence of quantity; zero |
| defuse | to make less harmful |
| diffuse | to spread, wordy or badly organized |
| depraved | morally debased |
| deprived | taken away from |
| discrete | individually distinct; separate |
| discreet | having or showing caution or self-restraint |
| disinterested | impartial |
| uninterested | not interested |
| dying | near death |
| dyeing | changing the color of |
| elusive | baffling; hard to catch |
| illusive | misleading or unreal |
| allusive | alluding to or hinting at |
| emigrate | you emigrate from a country |
| immigrate | you immigrate to a country |
| everyday | common or ordinary |
| every day | each day |
| exalt | to hold someone in high regard; to raise someone to a high standard |
| exult | to celebrate, to show jubilation |
| ex-patriot | one who no longer supports his/her country |
| expatriate | one who no longer lives in his/her native country |
| extant | still in existence; not extinct |
| extent | range or size, breath, or scope of something |
| faint | weak or pass out |
| feint | to trick |

| | |
|---|---|
| farther | use farther for physical measurement |
| further | use further for everything else |
| fatal | resulting in death |
| fateful | determined by fate |
| flare | (verb) to blaze brightly; to burst out in anger |
| flair | natural ability or aptitude; style; flamboyance |
| flesh out | to realize, to fill out or to give substance to |
| flush out | to force an animal or person into the open |
| fowl | domestic birds used for food |
| foul | offensive to the senses |
| forego | to go before in place, time, or degree |
| forgo | to do without or abstain |
| fortunate | luckily |
| fortuitously | by chance |
| gaffe | a social blunder or an embarrassing mistake |
| gaff | a large hook on a large pole to land large fish; a pole attached to a ship's mast used to extend a sail |
| gamble | to play games of chance; to bet; to take a risk or put at risk |
| gambol | to skip or leap about playfully; to frolic |
| gourmand | a lover of food who eats to excess |
| gourmet | a connoisseur of fine food and drink |
| guerrilla | a terrorist; a member of a band of volunteer soldiers bent on defeating a more established army |
| gorilla | a large powerful ape; a thug |
| grizzly | grayish; a North American bear |
| grisly | causing horror |
| guarantee | something assuring a particular outcome or condition |
| guaranty | financial security |
| hangar | a building that houses airplanes |
| hanger | a device used to hang cloths and other items |
| heroine | the principal female character in a story |
| heroin | a highly addictive drug derived from morphine |
| historical | relating to history |
| historic | having importance in history |
| hoard | a hidden stock of something, a cache |
| horde | a large group of people, a crowd |
| home | as a noun it means a place where one lives; as an adverb it means on target |
| hone | a fine grain whetstone for sharpening a tool |
| illicit | forbidden by law or custom; unlawful |
| elicit | to call forth; to draw out; to provoke |
| immerge | to submerge in liquid |

| | |
|---|---|
| emerge | to come forth or to become evident |
| impermeable* | not allowing fluids to pass through |
| impervious* | not affected by |
| | *both words mean impenetrable |
| incredible | unbelievable |
| incredulous | not believing |
| ingenious | clever |
| ingenuous | frank, naïve |
| imply | to hint or suggest |
| infer | to believe as a result of a hint or suggestion |
| impossible | not possible |
| impracticable | not possible under present conditions |
| incinerate | to burn |
| insinuate | to imply |
| inquire | to ask or ask about |
| enquire | variation of inquire |
| its | the possessive form of it |
| it's | the contraction of "it is" |
| leave | to depart from |
| let | to allow, to permit |
| lay | to set down |
| lie | to recline |
| libel | a damaging public statement made in print |
| slander | a damaging public statement made orally |
| missal | a book of prayer |
| missile | a rocket, a projectile |
| militate | to fight or argue |
| mitigate | to soften or moderate |
| majority | more than 50 percent |
| plurality | the largest group |
| ordinance | law, prescribed practice or usage |
| ordnance | military supplies |
| persuade | to move by argument |
| convince | the extreme form of persuade, to persuade beyond doubt |
| physical | relates to the body or material world |
| fiscal | relates to finances or revenue |
| plaintiff | a party to a lawsuit |
| plaintive | mournful |
| precede | to go before |
| proceed | to begin, to continue |

| | |
|---|---|
| principal | main or main person |
| principle | fundamental idea |
| rain | falling water |
| rein | part of a bridle, to give free rein to your imagination; rein (verb) to stop as in to rein in health care costs. |
| reign | to rule |
| reluctant | disinclined, unwilling, or hesitant |
| reticent | inclined to be silent |
| respectfully | courteously |
| respectively | each in the order given |
| rout | a disorderly retreat or flight |
| rout | to dig for food with the snout |
| route | road or course |
| sew | stitch |
| sow | to scatter seeds |
| so | therefore |
| spacious | having ample room |
| specious | outwardly correct but inwardly false |
| specially | exceptional, distinct, particular |
| especially | to an extend or degree deserving of special emphasis |
| therefor | for or in exchange for this; for it |
| therefore | consequently |
| venal | corrupt; bribable |
| venial | forgivable (as in venial sin) |
| veracious | truthful |
| voracious | greedy |
| vial | small flask for liquids |
| vile | disgusting; despicable |
| you | second person pronoun |
| yew | an evergreen tree |
| ewe | a female sheep |
| wain | a large open farm wagon |
| Wayne | a man or boy's name |
| wane | to decrease gradually in size, amount, intensity, or degree |

# CHAPTER VI

## Crime Analysis*

## Report Writing Principles

This chapter goes into greater detail on individual types of intelligence crime analysis reporting. If you are looking for a one specific type of report, below is an outline of what can be found in this chapter:

Raw Reports
Gist and Comment Reports
Working Intelligence Reports
File Summaries
    Case Analysis Reports
    Violator File Summaries
Activity Reports
    Security Alert Bulletins
    Security Intelligence Reports
    Warnings
Analytic Reports
    Investigative Chronologies
    Premonitories
    Case Summaries
Analytic Assessments
    Criminal Intelligence Assessments
    Threat Assessments
    Estimates
    Vulnerability Assessments
    Encyclopedic Reports
    Forecasts
Intelligence Publications
    Spot Items
    Weekly Reports
    Oral Reports

*This chapter is adapted from the chapter that I wrote for the LEIU/IALEIA publication *Criminal Intelligence for the 21$^{st}$ Century*.

Intelligence analysis, whether it is dealing with international issues or crime scenes, relies on summary paragraphs and larger reports. Summary paragraphs produced by state police or federal organizations, are almost always identical in their goals and objectives—to present all the main analytical points in a concise four-to-six sentence paragraph. These paragraphs are almost always written in the active voice. The longer crime analysis (or report) however, frequently differs from reports produced by CIA, DIA, or State Department because of their heavy use of passive voice sentences. Let's take a closer look at crime analysis and the various formats used in police crime intelligence.

When an officer writes her or his observations of a crime scene, she or he is making intelligence judgments—the first step in solving a crime is taking place. Every step of the way, careful attention needs to be paid to accuracy in writing. All police officers should remember they will not be in the room to explain what a sentence, word, or phrase means. There is a Murphy's Law that if there is ambiguity in a written product, whatever the writer meant to say is not the interpretation the reader will take away from the document.   While at times ambiguity is unavoidable, such as early in the investigation when not all the facts are known, it should never be used to cover up or obfuscate what actually happened.

# CONCEPTUALIZATION

I would like to return to the subject of conceptualization (I addressed it in earlier chapters) because it is so important. No matter what form of writing is involved, conceptualization is the necessary first step. The intelligence officer needs to know the format, objectives, and goals of what she or he is writing. What is the report intended to do—give crime scene observations and analysis? Analyze a possible threat? Indicate where and what terrorists may target next?

Taking the time to conceptualize at every step of an investigation will also pay added dividends. The conceptualization process will help you identify gaps in your knowledge. It is not a bad idea to make a list of the gaps at each stage of the investigation as you turn out your written products. This list of gaps can be invaluable in helping to direct and guide investigations.

All the best ideas, crime scene analyses, and intelligence judgments are not worth the paper they are written on, if they are not clear and readily understandable.

I know I have said it before, but it is worth repeating—clarity and accuracy trump everything in intelligence writing. The intelligence officer's reports must be logical, accurate, and complete. Police and law enforcement writing must be logical and the intelligence officer needs to ask, how does my written product help the reader understand the situation? It is the job of the intelligence officer to present his or her conclusions clearly so they can be understood on the first reading. The reader should not have to ponder this or that. Ask yourself the following:

First, what do I know?
Second, when did I know it?
Third, what does it mean?
Fourth, what am I going to do about it?

Remember, writing is thinking on paper and if an individual's words are muddled, confused, or riddled with poor English, his or her credibility suffers. If written English is a main tool of communication and an officer cannot use that tool, what impression is given? What are you saying about yourself as a law enforcement/intelligence officer? Furthermore, the nation's police forces, the Department of Homeland Security, the DIA, the CIA, the FBI, and all members of the Intelligence Communities must be able to communicate with each other through written products.

## Raw Reports

The collection of raw data or raw intelligence is the vital first step in the intelligence process. Raw data is collected in a variety of ways—the most common are observations at a crime scene, recording the words of an eyewitness, and through sources or agents.

The reporting officer at a crime scene has the duty and obligation to write down all the details and observations he or she sees. Use descriptors or precise measurements—be specific wherever possible. It is best to err on the side of too much detail, rather than too little. Subsequent reviews of the crime scene report in comparison with other evidence will help the investigating team put all the pieces together.

Accuracy and thoroughness in taking down the words of an eyewitness can make or break a case. The importance of recording an eyewitness account while it is still fresh in his or her mind cannot be overestimated. Here, the reporting officer has the duty to question the witness for greater detail without leading the witness. If the eyewitness is not a native speaker of the officer's language, the questioning may be much more extensive in order to make sure the officer accurately captures (in the standard dialect that the report will be written in) what the eyewitness saw.

As time goes by, witnesses' memories may fail, they may become reluctant to talk, or they may want to put the incident behind them. Therefore, the clarity of the officer's initial raw report is vital and will help reduce the chances of ambiguity and misunderstanding.

It is a good idea for the officer to draft a few lines of his or her impressions. Was the eyewitness reluctant to talk? Did the eyewitness look the officer in the face? Did the witness's body language indicate the individual was telling the truth.

Raw reports are the first input into the official record of the crime. The raw intelligence report is designed to do three things:

- Convey the essentials in a readable way.
- Identify each source of data being used.
- Improve the quality of the information by putting it in a written format, rather than by keeping it in the officer's head.

It is important to keep the raw intelligence report tightly focused. As new information becomes available, it is best to do new reports, rather than try to update the existing one. Do not put too many things in one report, draft separate reports—this aids in analysis, dissemination, and the review and purging of files.

The raw intelligence report (also referred to as a "field report" or an "intelligence report") may be divided into one or all of the following sections each time information is received:

- **File Number or Project Number**: This is assigned in accordance with each agency's policies and procedures.
- **Identification of Sources**: In many instances corroborating information about the same subject, activity, or event is often collected from different sources at the same time or within a very short period of time. Space should be available in each report for providing information from more than one source. Give as much information about the source as possible. For law enforcement sources, use rank/title, name, agency, city/state, and telephone number. You may use yourself as a source.

  Be sure to specify what was collected from each source. That way the same report will allow comparison of differing accounts. This comparison also has the benefit of identifying gaps in the overall information, which in turn will help direct resources to fill those gaps.

  If it is necessary to protect someone's identity, generally the word *anonymous* is used. If someone offers to provide information on a continuing basis and wants anonymity, you can also put in *true name withheld*. Or, if it is unknown whether he or she will be used again, and you want to maintain anonymity, you can also assign an *informant number*.
- **Security Classification**: Attention to security classification is extremely important. In my training throughout the Intelligence Community, I repeatedly ask senior managers what are the most

frequent mistakes they encounter. The response invariably includes a reference to incorrect security classifications.

In many instances it is necessary to protect not only the information contained in the report but the identity of the source. At the state level, classification guidelines vary from one agency to another. At the federal level there are well defined classification rules and guidelines. For example, the author of a report must justify the use of a particular classification. Management or security members in the Intelligence Community can tell you where to find the federal guidelines.

In general there are four levels of classification:

1. Public record or "open source" information is usually unclassified. But under certain circumstances "open source" or public record information may carry some sort of restrictor such as "For Internal Use Only," the theory being, that because the information is being used in an intelligence report, some control or restriction is needed.

2. Information that can generally be disseminated within the law enforcement community should carry the lowest classification possible. Too high a classification can prevent dissemination to people who need to know, or who may have information related to an investigation.

3. Active or ongoing investigations should have a mid-level classification in order to prevent the accidental disclosure of sensitive intelligence, investigative techniques, and strategy. This level of classification will probably have a designated time frame, which should be indicated. Because of the increasing cooperation between state and federal agencies, if you are working for or in a state police intelligence unit, you may want these mid-level classifications to conform to the classification guidelines of the Department of Homeland Security or the FBI—or both.

4. The highest level of classification may be used for a variety of reasons. The most common are to prevent compromising the identity of undercover personnel; when misconduct of public officials is being investigated; and when the intelligence is part of a broader national security issue such as terrorist activity, drug trafficking, and trafficking of humans.

— **Source Evaluation**: More than one source can be used in an intelligence report. It is important to identify each source and the information that each source provided. By identifying the information with the source you are taking the first vital step in the analytical process. Specifying what was collected from each source allows comparison of differing accounts; can provide corroboration of facts, details, and times; and may make gaps in information readily apparent.

For law enforcement sources, use rank/title, name, agency, city/state, and telephone number. You may use yourself as a source. Be specific about various inquiries and records checks so that if questions arise there will be no doubt where to go to recheck the information. If information from several sources is contained in the same report, be explicit in identifying which sources corroborate which information.

Remember to leave enough room to provide as much detail as possible; specifying what information was collected from each source. This detail is a vital part of the initial analysis and can be an invaluable aid if the same or similar information is received from other sources in other reports. The bona fides of sources can be determined early-on by paying careful attention to the "Source Evaluation" of your report.

— **Crime**: The computerized file formats that are used today allow for a text search of the narrative. This search can provide a quick summary of an individual's criminal activities. Therefore, in order to aid in future database searches, make sure that you put keywords in your report related to individuals and to crimes. Be consistent in your use of words—for example, switching between the terms "assault" and "beating" would confuse a text search. Many intelligence reports do not have a link to specific criminal activity, therefore the use of keywords related to crimes will aid in the future retrieval of the report.

- **Summary**: The summary or "synopsis" of the intelligence report is extremely important. This part of your report is closely tied to the uniform intelligence style of writing. This is where the conceptualization I talked about earlier comes into play. The topic sentence of the summary needs to capture the reader's attention by telling him or her the "what" and the "so-what." This sentence—and indeed the whole summary paragraph—frames your whole report. In theory, the reader can read this portion of the report and understand the significance of what happened and get an overview of the events. The details in the report will then fall into place within this framework.

  The summary should not be a reproduction of the detailed narrative contained in the body of the report, it should contain the salient points—what the reader needs to know. You may have heard the summary paragraph referred to as the "big picture," "bottom-line," or "the synthesis of the report." No matter what you call it, the important thing to remember is the summary should tell the reader quickly and concisely the main points contained in the report as well as any and all conclusions the reporting officer has about the information and the sources. The summary should not be long. The law enforcement summary is almost identical to summaries used in intelligence reports throughout the Intelligence Community. The ideal summary is usually no more than 250 words.

  Some members of the Intelligence Community use these summary paragraphs as the basis of morning briefings. Therefore, it is vital that your paragraph or paragraphs be clear and concise. You may want to make reference to what you do not know, as well as what you know.

- **Date of Information, Date of Acquisition, and Date of Report**: The date of information is the time or period of time when the criminal activity occurred or may have occurred. The date and time span when the information was obtained (date of acquisition) is included, because this information helps the reader determine the timeliness of what is being reported. You should also include the date you prepared and submitted the report.

- **Officer's Notes/Details—Reporting Office and Agency/Unit**: This section of the report is where you put the details and observations of the information you collected. This section requires good judgment on the part of the officer, because it should not contain non-pertinent details. What is pertinent and non-pertinent is difficult to determine in a raw report, so it is better to follow the rule—*if in doubt, put it in.* Comments about the difficulty in obtaining the information should not be in this section, *unless* those comments reflect on the source's reliability.

  The following are examples of topics in an officer's notes or details:

  - Indicate the identity of someone requesting to remain anonymous, or who may or may not be assigned a code name or number until their willingness and capability to be used as a cooperating individual is determined.

  - Report a source's motivation and willingness to provide information. This can be critical and plays a role in determining whether or not the source should be assigned a code name or number. (An individual who provides information one time is rarely given a code name or number.)

  - Report any information you have on a source's reputation and background. This information is very important for establishing reliability. Information such as past or current substance abuse, emotional stability, prejudices, reasons for revenge, or deceptiveness should be included if known.

- Note any conflicts in different accounts by different sources. Here, your judgment as to which version is the most reliable and why, is very important.
- Give any information or facts about the situation or area that is not readily apparent or reported elsewhere.
- Refer to significant information in other reports. But, be careful not to provide too much linkage to material in a criminal intelligence file or report that should be protected from inadvertent disclosure.
- Give detailed information from the source, but opinions of the drafting officer—underscoring discrepancies—should be in an addendum. Placing this information on a separate page helps prevent confusion.

# Gist and Comment Reports

Gist and Comment Reports are very common and have a specific format. Raw reports lack any kind of analysis; they simply put down facts and observations. The Gist and Comment Reports usually summarize events or issues and add an analytical component to tell us why that event or issue is important and meaningful. Here again the format of these law enforcement reports is identical to formats used by others in the Intelligence Community.

These reports may be part of a daily routine for intelligence officers or analysts. They rest on sound intelligence writing principles that are used throughout the Intelligence Community at the federal and state levels—the separation of facts from analysis. These reports play a vital role in keeping police executives informed and able to make solid decisions.

The format for Gist and Comment Reports consists of two parts:

1.  A gist or summary of an article, report, or activity that has occurred.
2.  A comment section that analyzes the report's significance.

Steps to consider in preparing a Gist and Comment Report include the following:

1.  Use a recent case, incident, or article as the basis.
2.  Capture and summarize salient facts in the case, incident, or article.
3.  Do background research (as much as time allows—often only files close at hand can be culled for information).
4.  Keep the gist and comment portions separate from one another.
5.  Note any omissions in the source case, incident, or article.
6.  Foreshadow events in the near future.

An example of a Gist and Comment Report is on the next page.

# GIST AND COMMENT

The FBI issued an Information Bulletin on December 29, xxxx, warning of possible al-Qa'ida attacks in the United States prior to the upcoming New Year's holiday. Recent intelligence indicates that al-Qa'ida may be planning an attack, possibly targeting highly populated areas in large U.S. cities. The FBI is also investigating an increase in the smuggling of Iraqi and other Middle East nationals across the Rio Grande from Mexico.

Until recently, the United States has kept its door all but shut to the estimated two million refugees fleeing Iraq. So far, the United States has taken fewer than 800 Iraqi refugees, according to State Department officials. The administration, however, has recently agreed to take 7,000 refugees by the end of next year.

United Press International (UPI) reports unnamed FBI sources as expressing concern that al-Qa'ida may use this increase in refugees to sneak in operatives for future attacks. The FBI Information Bulletin, however does not mention this possibility, nor does it indicate how many terrorists may have already been smuggled into the United States.

The UPI indicates that the modus operandi is to have the Iraqis and Middle East nationals meet at a safe house in Mexico, and then move across the border where contacts are waiting to drive them to train or bus stations in El Paso, Texas or Belen, New Mexico. Federal prosecutors in New Mexico told UPI they have no current cases involving illegal smuggling of Iraqis or anyone else.

Comment:

Although the FBI and the Department of Homeland Security (DHS) possess no further, specific information on the smuggling or the terrorists' targets, tactics, or locations for operations, law enforcement officials should be on heightened alert to potential indicators of terrorist activity or planning.

Surveillance and probing of potential targets is consistent with known practices of al-Qa'ida and other terrorist organizations that seek to maximize the likelihood of operational success through careful planning.

Law enforcement personnel should be on the lookout for any suspicious activity, and specifically for the following indicators of terrorist activity:

1.  Unusual or prolonged interest in security measures or personnel, entry points and access control or perimeter barriers such as fences and walls.

2.  Unusual behavior such as staring or quick movements away from personnel or vehicles entering or leaving designated facilities or parking areas.

3.  Observation of security reaction drills or procedures.

4   An increase in anonymous telephone or email threats to facilities in conjunction with suspected surveillance incidents.

5.  Foot surveillance involving two or three individuals working together.

6.  Mobile surveillance using vehicles such as bicycles, scooters, motorcycles, cars or trucks.

7.  Prolonged static surveillance using operatives disguised as panhandlers, shoeshiners, food or flower vendors, news agents, or street cleaners.

8.  Discreet use of still cameras, video recorders or note taking at non-tourist locations.

## Working Intelligence Reports

For intelligence reports to be useful, they must be up-to-date and timely. Therefore, an officer should keep a "Working Intelligence Report" or a "working file" between the time the information was gathered or received, and the time a report is submitted for approval into the official file. An up-to-date "working report" will contain much more than is put in the final—official report.

Management of these files is extremely important. Non-criminal information contained in the "working file" should not be included in the official report. As the file is built, the officer should consider marking the non-criminal and other peripheral information. That way when the final report is prepared, the officer will more easily be able to determine what should be placed in a separate, sub-set of files or documents outside the legal purview. Good management of these "working files" will also allow the officer or analyst to have on hand a quick resource.

## File Summaries

### *Case-Analysis Report*

At the outset of a case, an analyst compiles all available information on the topic, extracting and reassembling material from different individuals. It is also a good idea to conduct additional research at the outset of a case using the Internet, commercial databases, other agencies' files, and any other sources available. Thorough research at the beginning of a case provides a solid starting point for the intelligence process.

This case-analysis report should be as complete as possible because it may provide invaluable insights into where additional information gathering is necessary. The case-analysis report should also include any recommendations on what investigative steps might prove fruitful, given the information known.

### *Violator File Summaries (Target Identification Reports)*

A summary of all data available on an individual violator—or suspected violator—should accompany other types of analytic reports, such as the case analysis report. The violator file summaries should include as many of the following as possible:

1. Name of the violator or suspected violator
2. Physical description of the violator or suspected violator
3. Date of birth of the violator or suspected violator
4. Place of birth of the violator or suspected violator
5. Any known aliases or other names of the violator or suspected violator
6. The social security number of the violator or suspected violator
7. The FBI number assigned to the violator or suspected violator
8. Any vehicles registered to the violator or suspected violator
9. The violator or suspected violator's telephone number(s)
10. Any real estate owned by the violator or suspected violator
11. The names of any known associates of the violator or suspected violator
12. Any history you have about the violator or suspected violator
13. Any patterns or methods of operation associated with the violator or suspected violator
14. Any geographic area where the violator or suspected violator is known to have worked, lived, or operated
15. Reference to any other agencies that have an interest in the violator or suspected violator
16. Supporting documents
17. The driver's license number of the violator or suspected violator
18. The Bureau Criminal Identification (BCI) number
19. Miscellaneous Criminal Number
20. Last known address of the violator or suspected violator
21. The violator's or suspected violator's employer or business
22. Utilities paid by the violator or suspected violator
23. Photographs of the violator or suspected violator

24.   Any past criminal activity which involves the violator or suspected violator

25.   Violence potential or patterns associated with the violator or suspected violator.

## Activity Reports (Security Alert Bulletins, Security Intelligence Reports, Warnings)

### *Security Alert Bulletin*

A Security-Alert Bulletin conveys information of a security nature to agencies or organizations that have a need to know, or may be in a position to respond to the alert.

### *Security-Intelligence Reports*

The Security-Intelligence Report should be provided to the tactical force and to senior commanders on situations with potential for violent confrontation.

### *Warnings*

There are Tactical Warnings and Strategic Warnings. A Tactical Warning reflects imminent danger; a Strategic Warning reflects long-range problems that decisionmakers or policy-makers need to be addressing. In both warning cases, the analyst or officer may use the "gist and comment" format to describe the threat and suggest ways of dealing with the threat. Warnings and threat or vulnerability assessments go hand-in-hand. The warnings are actually the results of vulnerability or threat assessments.

## Analytic Reports (Investigative Chronologies, Premonitories, Case Summaries)

### *Investigative Chronologies*

An Investigative Chronology is a report that places each event in date-and- time order to better understand how the activity unfolded. Think of the Investigative Chronology as an elaborate timeline where each event is summarized, and the source document from which it was obtained is referenced. Other pertinent information, such as an individual's potential as a witness, should also be included in the Investigative Chronology.

### *Premonitories*

A Premonitory is a short-term assessment that focuses on a particular crime group or criminal activity. The Premonitory looks at the most effective way of investigating and prosecuting a criminal group. Data in a Premonitory should include surveillance information, background record checks of targets, information on similar groups or activities, and informant data. The four key areas that should be covered are:

−   What illegal activities the targets are involved in;
−   What the strengths and weaknesses of the group are;
−   What the recommendations for investigative activities are; and,
−   What the probability of success is for those investigative activities.

The following is a suggested Premonitory format:

I.   Introduction

    A.   Definition, description, and background
    B.   Purpose of the report and intended audience
    C.   Sources of information

     D.   Working definitions
     E    Limitations of the study
     F.   Scope of the inquiry

II.   Collected Data

     A.   First topic of investigation
        1.   Definition
        2.   Findings
        3.   Interpretation of findings

     B.   Second topic of investigation
        1.   Definition
        2.   Findings
        3.   Interpretation of findings

III.  Conclusions

     A.   Summary of findings
     B.   Overall interpretation of findings
     C.   Recommendations (adapted from a federal reporting format)

## *Case Summaries*

In the final stages of a case, the analyst often assists the prosecuting attorney by providing compiled data and charts derived from intelligence analysis as aids in presenting the case. These case summaries can be, and often are, vital bridges between the investigation and the prosecution of a group of violators. In addition, the analyst can take these summaries—often in the form of charts or tables—into the grand jury or court as a summary witness. This can be followed by analytic testimony as an expert witness in a particular type of criminal activity.

## Analytic Assessments (Criminal Intelligence Assessments, Threat Assessments, Estimates, Vulnerability Assessments, Encyclopedic Reports, and Forecasts)

### *Criminal Intelligence Assessments*

A good model to follow in producing Criminal Intelligence Assessments is the one used by the California Department of Justice. According to California authorities the following eight areas should be included in all Criminal Intelligence Assessments:

    <u>Executive Summary</u>—The summary should tell the busy reader exactly what he or she should know about the report. If the reader goes no further he or she will know your main conclusions about the criminal group. The summary should be concise.

    <u>Capabilities</u>—This section of the assessment should cover the criminal groups' abilities, capabilities, and skills—and how these might grow and develop in the future. Any previous reports on the group or the group's activity should be included here.

    <u>Intentions</u>—Here, the criminal purpose of the group, network, and criminal activities engaged in by the subjects or group should be covered.

    <u>Organization</u>—The organizational structure should be examined in as much detail as possible. This section should include the leadership chain of command, the names of key individuals and what positions they hold, any noted changes in organization size or leadership, and detectable "weak links," informants, members with ties outside the group, and the group's relationship to other groups. This is the section to comment, if you can, on the stability or instability of the group.

Trends—An historical overview of the development and trends of the group or organization can be very helpful. This overview can relate to changes or development in the group's size, criminal activity, propensity for violence, and past leadership changes.

Forecasting—Based on what has happened in the past, where do you see the group going? What is happening now and what may happen in the future?

Charts—Tables, graphs, charts, maps and other graphics are highly effective in underscoring critical points. They also have the added advantage of not only removing tedious detail from the text but being visually digestible and readily understandable for the busy consumer of your product.

Conclusions—The conclusion is usually a lengthier summary than the Executive Summary. The conclusion helps the reader understand the main points you want him or her to take away from the information he or she has just read. The conclusion also reinforces and *slightly* expands the Executive Summary and often refers back to the forecasts you have made. Be careful—never make over-generalizations or draw conclusions that are unsupported.

Another format for a Criminal Intelligence Assessment is:

Executive Summary—The Executive Summary states the purpose of the assessment, gives the key findings, and provides policy implications.

Statement of Issues—This section is intended to give the significance and fundamental issue to be explored.

Review of Previous Assessments—If there are any, capture the findings of previous assessments and studies.

Limitations of Assessments—Identifying the limitations of the assessment or gaps in knowledge is a critical part of the assessment. This section helps the reader put the assessment into the proper perspective. By identifying limitations, you also help managers allocate resources.

Methodologies—This section should discuss the methods you used in collecting data. An explanation of any methodologies you used in analyzing the evidence should be put in this part of the assessment. The use of methodologies can buttress your credibility by underscoring the meticulous and thorough approach you took in analyzing and drafting the assessment.

Findings—Empirical (experience and observation) data can be folded into this section. This data may be presented in charts, tables, graphs, and summaries.

Analysis and Policy Implications—In addition to the Executive Summary, this section is one of the most important in the Assessment because it contains the analysis and the implications for policy. Some of this is captured in the Executive Summary, but here you give much more detailed evidence to substantiate your conclusions.

Bibliography—List all the sources you consulted in drafting the assessment.

## *Threat Assessments*

A Threat Assessment is a formal estimate in which an intelligence unit analyzes pertinent information about a new or continuing threat. If a Threat Assessment is produced it is almost always serious. In other words, the raw intelligence has met the threshold required to draw the threat to consumers' attention. There are, however, Threat Assessments that are done on an annual basis to review and update the status of an ongoing threat. This is the case with al-Qa'ida.

A Threat Assessment should contain the degree of probability of a criminal or terrorist act. By definition, that probability is most likely high, or you would not have decided to write it. The Assessment should address the time frame of the threat and identify the possible target(s). The Assessment must contain conclusions about the probability that the threat will materialize, along with recommendations for countermeasures.

## Estimates

Across the board in the Intelligence Community "Estimates" are considered to be one of the premier intelligence products. At the federal level, the National Intelligence Estimate (NIE) or the Special National Intelligence Estimate (SNIE) bring together the best minds of the Intelligence Community to examine problems of national security and to make projections—to give policy-makers the Community's best analysis of a situation or problem and an indication of what to expect or where the problem is going.

The estimating process at the federal level bears marked similarities to the process at the state level. Indeed, the strategic estimate by state police intelligence units is an intelligence product that requires considered judgments on an array of key intelligence problems or issues in order to provide a backdrop against which to make projections for the near future. That is parallel to what is done at the federal level.

Estimates may be produced on an annual basis, such as the Narcotics Intelligence Estimates of the National Narcotics Intelligence Consumers Committee and the National Drug Intelligence Estimate of the Royal Canadian Mounted Police.

## Vulnerability Assessments

Vulnerability Assessments are studies to determine the potential for harm to a person, event, or location as a result of criminal activity. The traditional use for Vulnerability Assessments is for executive protection and special events planning. However, they might also be used to determine the possible market for a new criminal product or service, or the likelihood that the jurisdiction will be impacted by a crime group or activity. The Vulnerability Assessment includes many aspects of the estimative process—the motto for most Vulnerability Assessments is "forewarned is forearmed."

## Encyclopedic Reports

Encyclopedic Reports give an overview of a topic such as a geographic area. These are done by such organizations as the Drug Enforcement Administration and deal with the areas of drug production and the transit routes for drug trafficking. An Encyclopedic Report would include such information as a country's population, political situation, economics, terrain, major exports and imports, and relations with other countries. The Encyclopedic Report provides a standard reference and basis for dealing with a given country.

## Forecasts

A Forecast, as its name indicates, is a prediction about what will happen in the future. Forecasts are more limited in scope than a full-blown Estimate. The two share much in common, however. They both make judgments based on limited evidence; they both take risks because they are produced on fragmentary facts and information; and they often are built on speculation that the near future will be similar to the recent past. Some intelligence analysts are uncomfortable writing Estimates or Forecasts, but keep in mind the axiom that "the worst sin for an intelligence analyst or officer is to say nothing when the available evidence indicates a warning, estimate, or forecast should be issued."

The following are some guidelines to consider in the drafting of a Forecast:

1.  Is the expected future trend new or a continuing development?
2.  If there is some sort of change in modus operandi, leadership, strategy, or any aspect of the group, indicate what it is and the significance of the change.
3.  Differentiate between mid-term and long-term change.

4.  Discuss the cause of the change.
5.  Point out limiting factors that may have an impact on the change.
6.  Identify important contingencies or raise doubts, where appropriate.
7.  Acknowledge areas of uncertainty.
8.  Acknowledge assumptions that were critical to making the prediction.

## Intelligence Publications (Spot Items, Weekly Reports)

### *Spot Items*

Spot Items are often prepared for intelligence periodicals—that is, regularly published intelligence bulletins disseminated by law enforcement or security agencies. The Spot Item resembles the "Gist" part of the "Gist and Comment" publication. Your goal is to take a source or sources and pull out the key points *without* providing additional explanation or analysis. The following is a 118-word Spot Item on possible Mara expansion in the US:

---

**Spot Item**

# (Date) Maras: Potential Expansion

Highly violent, rival Hispanic gangs called MS-13 and 18th Street (collectively *Maras*) will pose a threat to the US by establishing one or more cliques here within thirty-six months. *Mara* members who are already in the US will likely form the leadership by recruiting and organizing locals. *Maras* gangs are highly mobile and have relocated previously in response to opportunities or threats. They may be seeking new territory due to pressure from law enforcement in Mexico (where they are an enforcement priority) as well as Honduras and El Salvador (where they are a national security threat). Links to transnational organized crime groups give the *Maras* strategic depth and increases the threat potential of these groups once they become established.

### *Weekly Reports*

In some agencies, the intelligence units are responsible for producing weekly reports on trends, developments, and emerging patterns in crime and emergent groups to alert management and officers on the street to problems that may arise. These publications are usually a mix of "Gist and Comment" and "Spot Items."

## Review and Approval of Intelligence Reports

It is the responsibility of a Quality Control Officer to give the final approval of material to be put into a criminal intelligence file. It is not possible to file all the information received, so this officer has the unpopular task in many organizations of ensuring that rules are enforced.

The major responsibilities of this officer include ensuring a raw intelligence report is crime-related and those criminal activities are within the current mission statement. The officer also checks to make sure that cross-referencing to all appropriate sources is critical to the subsequent retrieving of information. Giving short shrift to grammar and punctuation errors can create serious problems. Remember, an English sentence may be correct with or without a comma, but the meanings are dramatically different. Therefore, the Quality Control Officer should look at sentence structure, punctuation, and spelling. Then, after double-checking the sourcing, the source evaluation, and the initial classification, a sequential file number is assigned by intelligence unit personnel.

One of the last steps in the approval process is to determine how long the material will be retained rather than where it should be filed. The answer to this question often hinges on the ability to verify information. Initially, the answer to this question may be unknown, in which case it is a good idea to mark the file for review in one year. Rather than keep it in a separate file, special markings can be made on the cover page and/or on index cards to indicate retention of up to one year—some organizations lump these one-year files into a "temporary file" category. File retention of five years or more is usually referred to as a permanent file. If verification of the information in the temporary file is made during the first year, the Quality Control Officer should then move the file into the permanent, five-year category.

## *The Oral Report*

Oral briefings are very important. Some consumers as well as managers of intelligence and consumers prefer an oral briefing to a written report. Usually, an oral briefing is short and to the point—it is a presentation of a situation or analysis. The oral briefing often provides the audience with information needed to guide operations or make decisions about resource allocation. Traditionally the most common audiences include investigators, task force personnel, investigative managers, and prosecutors. But, as the Intelligence Community has drawn closer in the wake of September 11, 2001, police intelligence officers and analysts are being called upon to brief state level officials and members of the federal Intelligence Community.

Careful consideration should be given to preparing an oral briefing. Some things to consider include:

1.  Find out how much time is allotted for the briefing.

2.  Identify who will be in the audience; their backgrounds and their "need to know." If your briefing is classified, you must make sure everyone in the room has the proper clearances.

3.  Organize your briefing carefully. Begin by determining in your mind the main point or points you want the listeners to take away. A good rule to follow for organization is the following:

    a.  Introduction—allow 10 percent of your time to this part of your presentation. You should put your main conclusions in this section. If you have not been introduced you should lead with a short introduction of yourself and your credentials.

    b.  Body—allocate approximately 70 percent of your time to your supporting evidence and sub-points. You may want to consider organizing along one of three lines—strictly analytical, straight reporting and update, or informative and background.

    c.  Conclusion—save approximately 20 percent of your time for your conclusion. Here, you reiterate the main points made in the introduction and tie them to some of the key evidence. You also may want to end by telling the audience (if you can and if appropriate) where you see the problem going.

4.  Develop graphics to support the briefing and have copies ready for the audience. Be careful of PowerPoint! Do not hide behind PowerPoint slides!

    Visual aids should be used to support your briefing, not detract from it. The most common forms of visual aids are maps, charts, graphs, and photos. If you use visual aids well, they can:

    a.  Make your presentation more persuasive

    b.  Help the audience grasp information quickly

    c.  Add variety and emphasis to what you are saying

    d.  Reinforce your oral comments

    e.  Add organization to your briefing

f.    Help you be concise by removing cumbersome statistics and details from your verbal presentation

g.    Help you stimulate questions

Key points to remember in using visual aids include the following:

1.    Do not use cluttered or complicated graphs that distract from your message

2.    Do not use visual aids as filler. The audience will pick up on that immediately

3.    Do not use outdated visual aids

4.    Do not use a visual aid that does not suit your audience

5.    Do not use a visual aid that is interesting but irrelevant to your topic

Finally, three good rules to keep in mind about oral briefings: First know your material thoroughly; second, be succinct and to the point; and third, answer all questions—or if you cannot, get back to the individual at a later date with the answer.

## A Wrap-up of the Principles of Good Intelligence

Whether you are writing or briefing your intelligence there are three points to remember:

1.    Accuracy—Distinguish between observations, quotations, rumors, hearsay, and opinions. Spell out all abbreviations if you have any concern the reader or listener will not understand. Give full and exact names, addresses, dates, times, and amounts of money involved.

2.    Brevity—Brevity is next to godliness in the production of intelligence. Your written and spoken sentences should be free of unnecessary words and phrases that distract from your message. Avoid information and details that are not necessary for the reader or listener to understand the point(s) you are making. Avoid repetition.

3.    Completeness—Include all relevant information in your written or verbal intelligence that is necessary to make your point(s).

Effective intelligence writing and briefing rely on good organization, which in turn aids clarity and understanding. If drafting an outline for a paper or a briefing helps you, by all means do it. I repeat a word I used earlier: conceptualize. Know what it is you want to say, know why the reader or listener should care, and take the time to make sure the intelligence reporting is easily understandable. Remember, as intelligence officers, we are paid for our brains. We are paid for our ability to take complex situations or problems and bring some sort of meaning or order to them. If your thoughts are muddled, if your writing is confusing, and if your briefings are vague, your credibility is seriously damaged.

# CHAPTER VII

## Odds and Ends
### (OR, WRAPPING IT UP)

We have covered a lot of information in previous chapters of this book, and I think it worthwhile to review and emphasize the main points before concluding with a case study exercise on the Virginia Tech shootings. Let's begin by reviewing what we do as intelligence analysts: we produce intelligence that decisionmakers cannot live without, and we can live with. In order to do our analytic mission:

-- We synthesize.
-- We interpret, we do not describe.
-- We do not pile up details and facts because they are interesting.
-- We write because our analysis has policy relevance.
-- We render the complex simple.
-- We draw conclusions that are greater than the data they're based on.
-- We must have the courage of our analytic conclusions.
-- We must not allow our products to be distorted by individual biases and misplaced assumptions, or from pressures to change judgments.
-- We must submit the best draft we can, and that draft should show that we have spent a great deal of time thinking the problem through logically and planning before we started drafting.
-- We provide sound substantiation for our judgments.
-- We write in clear, concise, precise, and well-structured style.
-- We demonstrate that we have considered other outcomes, rejected them, and why.

For all writing conceptualization is important, but for intelligence writing it is of *paramount* importance. When you conceptualize you establish three things:

– The Contract: We establish a contract with the reader. That contract is the title of your analysis.
– The Focus: Your topic sentence synthesizes the information into an analytic assertion. In other words, you deliver on your contract in your topic sentence. If the reader remembers nothing else, she or he should remember this sentence. It contains the most important intelligence significance of what you have written.
– The Case: You develop your argument in the rest of the paragraph or paragraphs. You advance the line of reasoning that supports your focus.

The conceptualization process then, is the technique we use to crystallize our main judgment or point and lay out the argument for it.

Once an intelligence analyst conceptualizes, he or she writes using the expository style which:
– Requires using precise words and simple language;
– Stresses the importance of clarity, and structure to help stay in control of the argument and the reader stay focused on the analysis;

– Demands clarity, brevity, precision, and structure, which are essential to preparing an effective analysis.

Having said the above, remember there is no cookie-cutter template that fits all intelligence problems or products. Indeed, you can divide the intelligence pies in as many pieces as you want. No matter how many types of intelligence you say there are, they are all difficult, have different characteristics, and draw on different skills. For the purposes of instruction take a look at the four types on the following table:

## FOUR BASIC TYPES OF INTELLIGENCE PROBLEMS

| BASIC: | DETERMINISTIC: | RANDOM: | INDETERMINATE: |
|---|---|---|---|
| Problems are based on facts (The Law-Legal). Usually only one answer | Problems are often based on a formula; one answer possible. | Problems are based on facts, but different answers are possible. | Problems are usually based on few facts, and not all answers can be identified. |

Basic: The name "Basic" is misleading; it is not a value judgment. "Basic" is simply the name most textbooks give to this intelligence category. I suspect the name comes from the fact this type of intelligence is most often associated with law enforcement and much of the intelligence that is done in other categories has its roots in crime and law enforcement.

The major consumers of "Basic" intelligence are members of the legal profession. Lawyers make their living by parsing and defining words; they prefer passive-voice sentences, which are open to greater interpretation. It is the emphasis on the passive voice that sets this category apart. Almost all other categories of intelligence emphasize active voice sentences.

In "Basic" analysis, most often the crime has been committed. The investigation is ongoing and the analysis of the crime, as well as the reactions of people to the crime, may be ongoing. Often the identity of the criminal is not known. The problem is nearly identical to some aspects of intelligence analysis in the international arena. For example, when a terrorist bomb goes off, the analyst needs to know what group was responsible, the names of the terrorists involved, and what we know about the terrorist organization? There is a bit of "Sherlock Holmes" in all aspects of "Basic" intelligence.

Deterministic: "Deterministic" intelligence is usually associated with military intelligence. The sciences—mathematics, chemistry, physics—play key roles in the production of this intelligence. Military intelligence examines problems such as the trajectory of a rocket and the capabilities of a weapons system.

Random: "Random" intelligence refers to the unexpected. Suppose you have a wealth of intelligence sources and you're fairly confident in your conclusions. Then something out-of-the-blue happens—something random. All of your analysis is thrown in doubt, but you must make a judgment.

A good example of "random" intelligence was the election of the Spanish Prime Minister a number of years ago. Spain was an ally of the US in the war in Iraq. Spain's involvement in that war was an issue with the Spanish electorate. All indications were that, while it would be close, the Prime Minister would be returned. Then came the Madrid train bombing. How do you measure the impact of the bombing on the electorate with the election just a few days away? You must; that is what you are paid to do.

Indeterminate: "Indeterminate" intelligence is when you are called on to make an analytic judgment based on one piece of information. You cannot say, "I will wait until I have more information." You may never get that information. The best example I can give is when I was the Yugoslav analyst for the CIA while President Tito was alive. My analysis was that Tito would be succeeded by a collective leadership in both the party and the government (and that is what happened for nearly a decade).

The collective leadership would rotate annually among representatives of the party and the state. But, one day management said that while it was fine for me to write about the collective leadership, I also must identify the one person who would be most likely to succeed Tito if the collective leadership collapsed. I chose a Slovene by the name of Stane Dolanc.

One late Friday afternoon we received a short Belgrade press announcement that Dolanc had been removed from his current position and named to position "x." The problem was that position "x" had never existed before. How do you measure that? I was told to write a short intelligence paragraph telling the President what this change meant. Again, you cannot say, "I will wait for more information." You are paid to make judgments based on what you have. I reviewed the intelligence traffic for the last few weeks and decided to write something like this: "Stane Dolanc's removal from his current job and his appointment to 'x' does not mean he has been purged. He remains the man most likely to succeed President Tito should the collective leadership fail."

As you can see from the above four categories, no two are alike. But, they do not exist mutually exclusive of each other. There is a little of each in all the categories of intelligence. What is important is to remember the differences, be sensitive to change, and cognizant of alternative explanations.

Review and Coordination

Review and coordination are critical to analytic objectivity. Done well, they provide one of the best protections against distorting analysis.

1. Differences are healthy, and analysts should be prepared to discuss how they arrived at their conclusions, the evidence, and what alternatives were examined and rejected—and why.

2. Listen to and try to understand the reviewer's reasons for objecting to your analysis. Don't be arrogant or stubborn, and don't hold a grudge against the person who disagrees with you.

3. Coordination can be a major ingredient to ensure you have considered the widest possible range of information and judgments.

## ALTERNATIVE REVIEW

Customers often want you to lay out different scenarios in your finished intelligence so they can plan for the unexpected. I have not gone into this aspect of intelligence analysis specifically, because I have concentrated on the basic building blocks of intelligence—sentences and paragraphs. Once you have the basics down, it is relatively easy to discuss the alternatives you have considered and why you consider them less likely to be outcome or explanations.

## WHEN TO WRITE

Ask yourself, why have I decided to write now? How does this analysis meet the threshold? Is there a significant departure from the norm or the past? What does it mean? What might happen next? Make your report manageable by using clear and concise vocabulary, and always make your intelligence relevant to the policy or decisionmaker.

## BASIC PRINCIPLES OF ANALYTIC WRITING

1. Put your conclusion(s) first. If the reader reads nothing else, he or she will know from the topic sentence of the first paragraph the main intelligence point or conclusion you want to make.

2. Organize your analysis by your topic sentences. Make sure the topic sentences of each succeeding paragraph ties to, explains, or advances your analysis.

3. Know the formats your intelligence organization uses and know when to use them.

4.  Be precise: pick your words carefully so that you are sure you are conveying the right message.

5.  Be economical in your use of words—avoid adjectives and adverbs.

6.  Clarity trumps all else in intelligence writing. Your intelligence analysis must not leave the reader wondering what you mean or why you decided to write.

7.  Know when to use the active voice and when to use the passive voice. In relation to the Virginia Tech case study at the end of the book, one of the problems is that it is written as a basic, legal-type of document, not an intelligence report, and thus contains the pervasive use of the passive voice.

8.  Self-edit and then welcome the editorial review of others.

9.  Know the reader's needs—know why the reader needs to take the time to read what you have written.

## IMPORTANT REMINDERS ABOUT THE PARAGRAPH

1.  Each paragraph begins with a core assertion—the topic sentence.

2.  The remaining sentences prove, support, or explain the core assertion.

3.  The remaining sentences are in decreasing order of importance (the Inverted Pyramid paragraph).

4.  Facts are sourced as necessary.

5.  Each paragraph has only one main point.

6.  The ideal paragraph is two to five sentences long.

### *Consumers*

The most precious commodity in Washington is time. Frequently, our consumers are pressed for time; their days are often planned in five-minute intervals. They often are looking for intelligence that supports their biases, prejudices, and agendas.

Our consumers do not understand our mission, values, or standards.

They have strong world views and clear policy agendas, and they often assume we have a policy agenda too.

Consumers do not always see how we can help them. The reality is that we must sell them on the need for our services, and demonstrate the value of our intelligence through its timeliness and its sophistication. We must have something to say that they cannot find anywhere else.

There is a misconception in some quarters of intelligence that consumers (particularly policy-makers) do not want to hear "this" or "that." Therefore, there is a reluctance to report "this" or "that." In fact, one of the greatest services intelligence can provide is to deliver analysis that consumers do not want to hear. Frequently, consumers will take bad news and unhappy assessments as long as it is well-reasoned, supported by data and arguments, and presented without rancor, value judgments, or arrogance. They should welcome such intelligence because it may prevent policy-makers from making horrible mistakes.

Once intelligence is in print, there is no taking it back or modifying. Therefore, judgments need to be as precise as we can make them, supported by evidence and argument, and accurately reflect our level of confidence every time.

The public has misconceptions about intelligence—what it is and what it is not. The public forgets successes and remembers failures. Many think intelligence can predict almost anything. In some cases it can predict an event, but in most cases it cannot predict the specific timing of it. Most of the time, the best intelligence can do is to say that the conditions are ripe for a coup or a terrorist attack, for example. Furthermore, unless collectors provide intelligence analysts with information from a source who is in the room when the coup or attack is being planned, it is next to impossible to give a specific time. Some questions are fair; others are not. Those customers who find what we are saying inconvenient or "unhelpful" in advancing a policy position they favor are especially critical.

Nearly everybody believes the CIA failed to predict the collapse of the Soviet Union. But that belief does not match reality. The facts are often far more complex, but this perception of failure has entered into popular mythology.

Take a moment and read the following excerpt from a case study written by Kirsten Lundberg for Professors Ernest May and Philip Zelikow at the Kennedy School of Government, Harvard University, for the Harvard Intelligence and Policy Project, with support from the Central Intelligence Agency.

> *"The Agency before the Coup.* The coup did not surprise the CIA, although it could not foresee the exact timing. SOVA (Office of Soviet Analysis) director George Kolt had taken a short leave in early August during which time he had time to think about the Soviet situation away from the pressure of daily events. The US had already received potent warning, via Ambassador Matlock, of a coup attempt in June. That coup never took place, but plans for it clearly identified those individuals who would be involved in any future takeover attempt.
>
> "On Kolt's return to work, he requested SOVA put together an analysis of the prospects for a coup. The outlook, he recalls, was not encouraging. But the paper did not go so far as to say that Gorbachev's downfall would be linked to signing the controversial union treaty, even though one analyst made this connection. Says Kolt:
>
> "We could have said very clearly that a catalyst is the union treaty. There was one analyst who said they cannot let this be signed. But this thought was brought to my attention only after the coup. We did not pursue it in the piece. We had a hard enough time internally getting it agreed—not with our leadership; we always argued among ourselves.... We said the possibility of a coup was growing. We even said Gorbachev may not go along this time and said it could not succeed in the long run, which was all right. But we couldn't predict it to the exact date."
>
> "On Saturday, Aug. 17, however, signs were growing that action against Gorbachev was imminent. Alexander Yakovlov warned against a Stalinist 'party and state coup.' The President's Daily Brief for that date published SOVA's analysis, which explicitly warned that 'the danger is growing that hardliners will precipitate large-scale violence.'"
>
> The coup began on Sunday, August 18, 1991.

If you look back through the case study, it is correct to say the Intelligence Community was divided on Gorbachev's prospects for success and survival, but it is not correct to say the Intelligence Community gave policy-makers no warning a coup was a distinct possibility. The case study documents numerous warnings of how serious the situation was in the Soviet Union and the precarious nature of Gorbachev's situation. Indeed, in early 1989, the CIA objected to a National Intelligence Estimate saying Gorbachev would probably stay in power for the next three to four years. The CIA said his chances were fifty-fifty. Other Agency intelligence papers contained warnings such as "even Gorbachev realizes…that it is far from certain that he will be able to control the process he has set in motion."

The problem of credibility with the consumer also rests on the adage that if you have not told the consumer within the last twenty-four hours, you have not told them at all. Unfortunately, many consumers of intelligence suffer from acute memory loss. Furthermore, intelligence consumers have their own independent sources of information with which the Intelligence Community is competing—the so-called "Think Tanks."

"Think Tanks" are backed by powerful private interest groups with agendas, and the money to bankroll them. They are paid to produce well documented, well written, and well argued papers. "Think Tanks" frequently cherry-pick the evidence. Their conclusions conform to the agendas of those who have paid for the analysis. This is just as true of some kinds of crime analysis where a panel of experts looks back over evidence in order to play the "blame game" rather than give an objective presentation of events.

## *ETHICS*

*"There are no policy failures. There are only policy successes and intelligence failures." – A senior State Department official only half in jest.*

*"There is no political cost in attacking the CIA." – A senior White House official.*

I know I have repeatedly touched on the ethics of the intelligence profession, but ethical behavior is so important that another look at the subject is justified. Protecting analytic objectivity must remain a paramount goal of any intelligence organization. Without objectivity, our products have no value, and we have no credibility. Every poorly reasoned piece of finished intelligence tarnishes the brand name a bit.

This time let's look at ethics from the prism of what intelligence can do, and what we should expect from intelligence. First, all analysts and consumers must remember that at some point intelligence will be wrong. Therefore, because of the uncertainty that is an everyday part of intelligence, both producers and consumers of intelligence must be ethical in recognizing there is an error rate built into all assumptions, and all intelligence analyses. Intelligence analysis rests on making analytical judgments based on fragmentary evidence and information. As I said earlier, if you have all the information you are writing history.

Intelligence is about discovering others secrets. In the past, examinations of intelligence failures have concentrated solely on the analytic process. This is only half the story. Intelligence successes or failures rest on the information that is gathered, and to ignore this fact is unethical. Unfortunately, many critics do ignore that fact.

It is also unethical for intelligence to tell the policy-maker what course of action should be adopted. That is a political decision. Political decisions must reflect US domestic and international issues. The United States cannot afford an Intelligence Community that is either partisan or defending policy preferences as it goes about collection and analysis.

Both producers and consumers of intelligence must also be candid in recognizing and accepting that intelligence cannot remove risk. There will always be surprises, and sadly some of these will take American lives and property.

What can we expect intelligence to do, and what can we expect of intelligence analysts? The following are some, but not all, of what intelligence can do:

- Intelligence can provide analysis that will lead to more effective US policy and advance US interests.
- Intelligence and crime analysis can identify trends and variables that are shaping decisions by the opposition, and establish relationships between these variables and trends.
- Intelligence can give policy-makers and decisionmakers a better understanding of the situation they face.
- Intelligence and crime analysis can identify risks and point out opportunities.
- Intelligence can identify how the opposition will react to a given policy, and shine light on the consequences of the choices policy-makers are considering—including the option of not choosing.
- Intelligence and crime analysis must warn of threats or consequences of actions and inactions.
- Crime analysis can be (and is) the foundation of bringing criminals to justice.

If we are to be honest and ethical, we must also look at the ways in which intelligence can be abused. Analysts must always write with the consumer in mind, but should never write to the consumer's agenda. For intelligence analysts, this means resisting the temptation to bend facts in order to prop up a consumer's agenda. For crime analysts, this means writing to reveal what really happened, and not to protect any one interested party.

Finally, in order for all parties to be ethical when it comes to intelligence they need to recognize three things:

- Intelligence rests on a set of variables that are continually changing.
- Intelligence products suffer from degradations; no sooner is the product out than the variables start changing.
- Intelligence is always flawed because of the random nature of the variables upon which analytical judgments are made.

Because there are so many variables in the production of intelligence—and because there are so many misunderstandings about what intelligence is and what intelligence can do—it is unconscionable when people in positions of authority deliberately attempt to use intelligence to obscure culpability, deceive the public, or hide a crime. With those thoughts in mind, I have included in this textbook a case study dealing with the shootings at Virginia Tech on April 16, 2007. Students are asked to examine the Governor's Review Panel Report of that crime. That report is an intelligence analysis of the worst mass shooting in this nation's history.

# ANNEX I

# NORTH KOREA EXERCISE

# NORTH KOREA EXERCISE

You are an intelligence analyst at "X" organization. Over the last two weeks there has been some unusual military and intelligence activity in North Korea.

You come into work and are told to write a memorandum of no more than one double-spaced page, explaining what this unusual activity means. Your boss believes the North Koreans are looking for an excuse to invade South Korea. Therefore you are writing for an audience with a strong bias. In your analysis, if you believe the activity is related to something else, you must include a sentence or two to explain why an invasion is not likely at this time.

You must stick to one analytical conclusion as to what the activity means and argue that. You cannot say it could be this or it could be that. The following are conclusions that have been argued successfully in this exercise.

1.  The military and intelligence activity is in preparation to invade South Korea.
2.  The military and intelligence activity is in preparation to quell civil unrest.
3.  The military and intelligence activity is related to problems with China.
4.  The military and intelligence activity is an exercise.
5.  The military and intelligence activity is posturing in preparation for international talks.
6.  The military and intelligence activity is in preparation for a military coup.

All the intelligence sources in this exercise are phony. Information contained in the sources is drawn from actual events over several years, but compressed into a two-week period.

# BACKGROUND

The Democratic Peoples' Republic of Korea was founded on May 1, 1948 in the zone of the Korean peninsula occupied by the Russians after World War II. In 1950, North Korea invaded South Korea and three years of war ensued. Following both Chinese and American interventions, a cease-fire was proclaimed and the border separating the two parts of Korea was established and remains in place today.

North Korea was ruled, from its founding until May 1994, by Kim Il Sung. He was succeeded by his son, Kim Chong Il. North Korea is the only state ever to formally withdraw from the Nuclear Nonproliferation Treaty. This withdrawal took place in March 1993, but was suspended in June because of threats of UN economic sanctions. North Korea is believed to be developing nuclear weapons.

North Korea has suffered from severe food shortages, a deteriorating economy, and a number of high-level defections. U.S. – North Korean relations improved only slightly in September 1999 when Washington agreed to relax travel and trade restrictions on North Korea, and Pyongyang suspended long-range missile tests.

A first-ever summit between North and South Korean leaders took place in June 2000. Since that time, relations between the two Koreas have improved only slightly because of a series of military skirmishes between the two and more high-level defections from the North to the South. Recently, the two did agree to open train service between the two countries—the first in over fifty years.

# FACTS

| | |
|---|---|
| NAME: | Democratic People's Republic of Korea |
| POPULATION: | 22,757,275 |
| PRINCIPAL LANGUAGE: | Korean |
| RELIGIONS: | Activities almost nonexistent. Traditionally Buddhism, Confucianism, Chongdogyo, some Christian, Autonomous religious activity almost non-existent |
| LAND AREA: | 46,400 square miles (Virginia has 42,774 square miles) |
| CAPITAL: | Pyongyang, population 2,878,000 |
| TYPE OF GOVERNMENT: | Communist dictatorship |
| LEADER: | Kim Chong Il |
| LOCAL ADMINISTRATIVE DIVISIONS: | 9 provinces and 3 special cities |
| MILITARY STRENGTH: | 1,106,000 active troops |
| CURRENCY: | Won (143 Won to $1.00) |
| INDUSTRY: | Military products, textiles, chemicals, machinery, food processing, mining, metallurgy |
| CROPS: | Corn, potatoes, soybeans, rice |
| MINERALS: | Coal, lead, tungsten, zinc, graphite, gold, salt, iron, copper |
| GDP: | $40 billion (1999 estimate) |
| PER CAPITA INCOME: | $1,900 |
| LIFE EXPECTENCY: | 68.04 males; 74.15 females |
| LITERACY: | 100% |
| | |
| Note: | The city of Sonjin is Chongjin on the map |

*Figure 1 Central Intelligence Agency World Factbook Map*

**All the intelligence sources in this exercise are phony. Information contained in the sources is drawn from actual events over several years, but compressed into a two-week period.**

# NORTH KOREA AGREES TO TALKS

United Press International

Tokyo (11 July) – Pyongyang has agreed to meet with U.S., Japanese, South Korean and Chinese officials for talks aimed at easing regional tensions. The announcement was made this morning by the North Korean Foreign Ministry. Talks are expected to take place in Geneva in late September or early October.

The announcement came as a surprise. The invitation had been extended three months ago and there had been no indication until today that Pyongyang would accept or decline the invitation. Diplomatic sources in Tokyo are speculating that North Korea's acceptance may mean that Kim Jong-Il is asserting his authority over communist party hard-liners who are known to oppose any talks with the U.S. or South Korea.

# NORTH KOREAN DEFECTOR ANSWERS QUESTIONS

Marvin Mellonmind
*Washington Post* Staff Writer

Washington, 10 July – Kim Hwang Yop, a high-ranking defector from North Korea, is meeting with U.S. policy and intelligence officials, according to an official State Department announcement. The public may never know the full extent of Kim's cooperation with U.S. officials, but in a news conference last week in Seoul, he indicated he was willing to tell all he knows.

Kim Hwang Yop was North Korea's top political theorist before his recent defection. He has hinted that Pyongyang intends to launch an invasion of South Korea, but was cautious during his news conference and gave no details or specifics.

American and South Korean officials were circumspect about whether Kim had told much more than has already been made public. In Seoul, where the news conference was televised, members of President Kim Young Sam's party said that Kim's comments confirmed that North Korea is a military threat and that all in the south should help improve readiness.

In Washington, a senior administration official who is privy to what Kim has told U.S. intelligence experts said the defector "did not have as much information as we had hoped." Kim apparently has no direct knowledge of military matters, nor was he involved in day-to-day decision making.

"Much information is old and dated," and some of it "we know is not true," the official said. Kim's most alarming assertions are hard to evaluate, the official said, because Washington cannot confirm it from other sources. For example, he added, the U.S. believes that North Korea has war plans, but there is no evidence Pyongyang is preparing to carry them out.

There is some speculation in Washington that Kim's defection is too good to be true and that he may be a plant. Still others suggest that he is not an agent of North Korea, but may be acting on behalf of South Korea. Proponents of that theory point out that Kim's statements mirror the official line of Seoul.

# N. KOREANS SEEK REFUGE AT EMBASSY IN BEIJING

The Associated Press

Beijing, 10 July – Two North Koreans have sought refuge in the Canadian Embassy in Beijing. The refugees are asking for safe passage overseas, according to a Canadian embassy spokesperson.

The North Koreans are the latest in a spate of refugees fleeing the hard-line communist state.

The man and the woman appear to be in their late twenties or early thirties and got into the embassy late Saturday, spokesperson Bertha Bomb said. It is unclear if the two are married or otherwise related. Canadian diplomats are negotiating their fate with Chinese officials, Ms. Bomb said.

Last week four North Korean men climbed the wall of the U.S. consulate in the northeastern Chinese city of Shenyang. They are still there. U.S. diplomats are negotiating with Chinese officials.

Five other North Koreans were arrested at the Japanese consulate in Shenyang, prompting strong protests from Tokyo. Japan plans to send a senior envoy to China this week to settle the dispute, according to Japanese Foreign Ministry officials.

Asylum bids by the North Koreans present China's communist government with a diplomatic dilemma because it has a treaty with ally North Korea to send them back. The asylum bids also embarrass Beijing by focusing attention on its refusal to allow UN inspectors permission to screen fleeing North Koreans to see if they deserve political asylum.

Tens of thousands of North Koreans, fleeing hunger and repression, have sought food, work and refuge along China's border with North Korea. China views them as illegal immigrants and often sends back those who get caught.

The five who sought refuge at the Japanese consulate have relatives in the U.S. and were hoping for asylum there, according to a South Korean aid organization, the Citizens' Coalition for the Human Rights of North Korean Defectors and of Peace.

# NORTH KOREANS RIOT FOLLOWING WAGE CUTS, SHORTAGES

United Press International

Tokyo, 12 July – thousands of North Koreans, enraged by wage cuts, energy shortages and failed crops, stormed and burned government buildings in the region of the capital of Sonjin over the weekend, according to news reports and diplomats in Japan. Unconfirmed reports indicate one government official is dead and several were injured – including three policemen.

Most of the violence occurred in Sonjin, but Western diplomats report hearing stories of rioting in at least three other unidentified North Korean cities. News accounts from the Philippines report riots erupted throughout the country, but gave no details.

Diplomats in Pyongyang, reached by telephone, said they have heard over 10,000 rioted in Sonjin and that authorities have imposed an army and police blockade around the city. They also said that it is impossible to reach the city by phone and that all train service north and east of Pyongyang has stopped.

Journalists in Tokyo report stories of rioters rampaging through the streets of Sonjin, looting stores, torching vehicles and chanting: "Down with the party – give us food!" One unconfirmed report indicates a policeman's throat was slit and his body hung upside down on a light pole.

Pyongyang appears calm, according to travelers arriving in Japan, but they report rumors are circulating about disturbances in the city's suburbs. The city's streetcar service has been halted, but officials report that is because of downed power lines. TV and radio broadcasts in Pyongyang give no hint of problems and are broadcasting their regularly scheduled programs.

The daily North Korean Airlines flight arrived in Tokyo on schedule and passengers indicate no problems getting to the airport in Pyongyang. The airport's normal, heavy military presence did not appear to be on heightened alert.

# REGIONAL PRESSURE ON N. KOREA

Bertha Bulge
*Richmond Times-Dispatch* Foreign Affairs Editor

Richmond, 9 July – Washington apparently has concluded that regional powers in Asia, specifically Japan, China and Russia, must take a greater role in resolving problems arising from North Korea's ambitions to become a nuclear power. The U.S. has confirmed that it will not engage in talks with North Korea unless it verifies that it has dismantled a recently discovered nuclear weapons program.

The government in North Korea responded to cuts in U.S. oil deliveries by evicting international weapons inspectors. Pyongyang also announced that it would restart a plutonium reactor that had been shut down since 1994. The U.S. has called an emergency session of the International Atomic Energy Agency—an arm of the United Nations—to address North Korea's actions.

If Pyongyang refuses to back down, the U.S. will raise North Korea's actions with the Security Council. Officials in Washington believe they can get a Security Council resolution condemning North Korea.

The current crisis stems from North Korea's deepening economic crisis, according to Charlie Fern, the acting assistant secretary of state for Eastern Asian and Pacific Affairs. "Although much of the country is now on the brink of starvation," he said, "the few steps toward economic reform they have taken have not led to very much." Mr. Fern also hinted that the confrontation with the U.S. may be part of the North Korean regime's efforts to rally the public behind them and turn their attention away from the economic crisis.

140950Z JUL

FROM BRITISH INTERCEPT SERVICE
TO     DIST RALPH XEROX

MOST DISCREET HUSH TFEX

NORTH KOREAN FLEET PREPARING FOR INCREASED TRAFFIC

1.   BEGINNING ON JULY 10 AND CONTINUING THROUGH 12 JULY DUMMY TRAFFIC HAS BEEN OBSERVED ON THE MAIN NORTH KOREAN SHIP TO SHORE NAVAL COMMUNICATIONS NET.

2.   ON 11 JULY A MSG BROADCAST ON THIS NET ALERTED ALL SHIPS TO CYPHER A KEY CHANGE TO THAT EFFECT AT 1800.

3.   USE OF DUMMY TRAFFIC MAY INDICATE THAT THE TARGET BELIEVED HIS CYPHER TO BE SECURE. TEXT OF THESE MESSAGES DECRYPTS INTO GOOD KOREAN, BUT THE CONTEXT IS GENERALLY ABSURD.

4.   USE OF DUMMY TRAFFIC PRECEDING A KEY CHANGE MAY INDICATE THAT THE TARGET INTENDS TO INCREASE THE FLOW OF OPERATIONAL MESSAGES IN THE NEAR FUTURE.

MOST DISCREET HUSH

END OF MESSAGE

UPI

# CHINESE CANCEL FRIENDSHIP VISIT TO NORTH KOREA

BEIJING (11 JULY) WESTERN DIPLOMATS IN BEIJING ARE REPORTING THAT CHINA HAS QUIETLY CANCELLED AN OFFICIAL FRIENDSHIP VISIT TO PYONGYANG. THE DIPLOMATS, WHO REQUESTED ANONYMITY, SAID A COMBINATION OF FACTORS PLAYED INTO CHINA'S DECISION. NORTH KOREA'S FAILURE TO MEET SCHEDULED LOAN PAYMENTS IS SAID TO BE THE MOST SERIOUS PROBLEM. BUT, BEIJING DOES NOT WANT TO BE EMBARRASSED BY HAVING A HIGH-LEVEL DELEGATION IN THE NORTH KOREAN CAPITAL SHOULD THE GROWING CIVIL UNREST SPREAD TO PYONGYANG.

IN A SEPARATE STORY, CHINESE FOREIGN MINISTRY OFFICIALS REFUSED TO COMMENT ON REPORTS OF CHINESE TROOP MOVEMENTS NEAR THE BORDER WITH NORTH KOREA.

SUPPLEMENTAL

RESTRICTED        WOOP-TEE-DO

FROM:      CIA TOKYO
SUBJECT:   PYONGYANG INTELL LINK
SOURCE:    SPECIAL INTELL

9 JULY

FIELD REP ADVISED STATION UNOFFICIALLY OF NEW COMMO LINK ESTABLISHED BETWEEN PYONGYANG AND SONJIN ON FREQUENCY RESERVED FOR INTELL TRAFFIC. TRANSMISSIONS DETECTED TWICE DAILY SINCE 9 JULY. SOURCE SPECULATES LINK PROBABLY UP FOR TWO WEEKS, BECAUSE INCOMPLETE TRANSMISSIONS WERE DETECTED IN MID-JUNE.

COMMENT:  NONE

OPEN SOURCE CENTER    10 JULY

PRC: BEIJING MAKES NO COMMENT ON TROOP ALERT

(REUTERS) THE CHINESE GOVERNMENT HAS NO COMMENT ON UNCONFIRMED REPORTS THAT IT HAS PLACED ITS MILITARY DIVISIONS ON THE CHINESE-NORTH KOREAN BORDER ON ALERT. TRAVELERS TO MAJOR CHINESE URBAN CENTERS REPORT A LARGE NUMBER OF SOLDIERS IN AND AROUND AIRPORTS AND TRAIN STATIONS. A BRITISH TOUR GROUP REPORTED THAT IT WAS FORCED TO WAIT 48 HOURS AT THE NANKING AIRPORT FOR UNEXPLAINED TECHNICAL REASONS. YET LARGE NUMBERS OF CHINESE CONSCRIPTS BOARDED CIVILIAN AIRCRAFT.

CIA

12 JULY

FROM:       AGENCY
SUBJECT:   NORTH KOREAN ECONOMY
SOURCE:    MID-LEVEL THAI OFFICIAL IN THE MINISTRY OF TRADE WITH EXCELLENT
                    ACCESS. PAST REPORTING – RELIABLE

SOURCE SAYS RAILWAY STRIKES, CENTERING ON COMPLAINTS OVER BACK PAY, PERSIST AND ARE HAVING CRIPPLING CONSEQUENCES. LIGHT BULBS ARE IN SHORT SUPPLY BECAUSE BLACK MARKETEERS CAN PROFIT MORE BY SELLING THEM IN CHINA. INDUSTRIAL PRODUCTION HAS SLUMPED 25 PERCENT IN LAST TWO YEARS.

PYONGYANG'S FAILURE TO MEET EVEN MINIMAL PAYMENTS ON LOANS FROM CHINA IS STRAINING RELATIONS WITH BEIJING. SOURCE BELIEVES CHINA HAS THREATENED TO CUT OFF ALL TRADE IF NORTH KOREA DOES NOT MAKE EVEN A TOKEN PAYMENT ON MONEY OWED.

SOURCE REPORTS HEARING RUMORS OF DISSATISFACTION IN MILITARY, BUT CAUTIONS IT IS ONLY A RUMOR.

12 July

## HEAVY RAINS CONTINUE ON KOREAN PENINSULA

(AP) SEOUL – UNSEASONABLY HEAVY RAINFALL CONTINUES THROUGHOUT MUCH OF THE KOREAN PENINSULA, WITH NO FORESEEABLE LETUP FOR AT LEAST THE NEXT FEW DAYS, ACCORDING TO LOCAL WEATHER REPORTS. THE HEAVIEST HIT AREAS ARE ALONG THE BORDER BETWEEN THE TWO KOREAS, WHERE UP TO TWENTY INCHES OF RAIN HAS FALLEN IN THE PAST THREE DAYS. THE AREA HAS BEEN TURNED INTO A QUAGMIRE. THE RAIN IS MOVING TOWARD THE NORTHERN ISLANDS OF JAPAN.

UPI

VIOLENCE FLARES NEAR YALU RIVER

BY SILVESTER NERFF

CHANGCHUN, CHINA (11 JULY) – TRAVELERS CROSSING INTO CHINA REPORT THAT VIOLENCE HAS FLARED IN SEVERAL SMALL TOWNS JUST INSIDE NORTH KOREA. HUNDREDS OF NORTH KOREAN TROOPS ARE SAID TO BE ENROUTE TO THE REGION TO HELP RESTORE PUBLIC ORDER.

RUMORS OF PUBLIC UNREST IN NORTH KOREA'S BORDER REGION WITH CHINA HAVE BEEN WIDESPREAD FOR SEVERAL YEARS. NORTH KOREA'S FALTERING ECONOMY HAS LED MANY IN THE AREA TO RESORT TO SMUGGLING AND BLACKMARKET ACTIVITY. REFUGEES FROM THE REGION REPORT HUNGER IS WIDESPREAD AND CIVIL DISCONTENT IS GROWING.

IN OCTOBER OF 2001, THERE WERE UNCONFIRMED REPORTS THAT 5,000 NORTH KOREAN ARMY TROOPS WERE RUSHED IN TO RESTORE ORDER IN THE CITY OF HYSEAN. THESE SAME UNCONFIRMED REPORTS INDICATED 20 CIVILIANS WERE KILLED AND SEVERAL HUNDRED WOUNDED BEFORE THE UNREST WAS PUT DOWN.

DISCREET POOP NO FOREIGN DISSEM

12JUL 1020Z CIA

TO INTELLIGENCE COMMUNITY

---

CENTRAL INTELLIGENCE AGENCY

XXXXXXXXXXX

CLASS: DISCREET POOP NO FOREIGN DISSEM

COUNTRY:   IRAN

SUBJECT:    SABOTAGE IN NORTH KOREA

SOURCE:     A RELIABLE SOURCE WHOSE REPORTING HAS BEEN SUBSTANTIATED IN THE PAST. THE SOURCE HAS ACCESS TO INFORMATION ON ARMS SALES BETWEEN IRAN AND NORTH KOREA.

1.   THE NORTH KOREAN SMALL ARMS FIRM, WOO BIG BANG IN CITY OF NAMPO, SUFFERED SEVERE DAMAGES IN A SERIES OF EXPLOSIONS IN EARLY JULY. AN IRANIAN MINISTRY OF DEFENSE DELEGATION WAS TOURING ARMS FACILITY AS PART OF POSSIBLE PURCHASE OF LARGE QUANTITIES OF SMALL ARMS AND AMMUNITION.

2.   DELEGATION WAS IN MIDST OF NEGOTIATIONS WHEN TWO LOUD EXPLOSIONS SERIOUSLY DAMAGED MAIN PLANT BUILDING. SOURCE REPORTS SEEING "DEAD BODIES ALL OVER THE PLACE." MUCH OF MAIN PLANT WAS LEVELED AND SEVERAL SMALLER BUILDINGS WERE DAMAGED.

3.   DELEGATION WAS IMMEDIATELY ESCORTED OUT OF THE AREA, BACK TO AIRPORT AND FLOWN TO PYONGYANG. SOURCE, WHO SPEAKS KOREAN, OVERHEARD HOSTS USE THE WORD "SABOTAGE" SEVERAL TIMES.

## COMMENT: THE KOREAN WORDS FOR "SABOTAGE" AND "ACCIDENT" ARE NEARLY IDENTICAL IN PRONOUNCIATION

12I445Z JUL

FM INTERCEPT SOURCE
TO LISTEN TOO MUCH

DISCREET

ALERT

SPOT REPORT NO. ONE

NORTH KOREAN AIR DEPLOYMENTS

1.   ELEMENTS OF THE 3$^{RD}$ AND 5$^{TH}$ AIR DIVISIONS LOCATED AT PYONGYANG AND HAMHUNG AREAS RESPECTIVELY APPEAR TO BE DEPLOYED TO AIRFIELDS NEAR KAESONG, NEAR THE BORDER WITH SOUTH KOREA.

2.   TACTICAL AIR AUTHORITY DIRECTLY SUBORDINATE TO MINISTRY OF DEFENSE HAS BEEN ACTIVATED AT KAESONG AIR BASE.

DISCREET

OPEN SOURCE CENTER #37

TWO NORTH KOREAN DIPLOMATS SEEK ASYLUM IN PARIS

121141 PARIS AFP IN ENGLISH 1121 12 JUL

(TEXT) PARIS, FRANCE JUL 12 (AFP) – TWO NORTH KOREAN DIPLOMATS SOUGHT ASYLUM TODAY, ACCORDING TO AN OFFICIAL FRENCH FOREIGN MINISTRY ANNOUNCEMENT.

THE FOREIGN MINISTRY DID NOT IDENTIFY THE TWO OR SAY WHEN AND WHERE THEIR ASYLUM REQUEST WAS MADE. PYONGYANG MAINTAINS A SMALL EMBASSY IN PARIS, ONE OF TWO NORTH KOREAN DIPLOMATIC MISSIONS IN WESTERN EUROPE.

FROM: AMEMBASSY SEOUL

TO:     DEPARTMENT OF STATE, WASHINGTON, DC

SUBJECT:     SOUTH KOREAN EXERCISE

DATE:JULY 10

1.   AMBASSADOR ARTHUR (ARTIE) CHOKE MET TODAY WITH SOUTH KOREAN FOREIGN MINISTER KIM DIM DONG TO DISCUSSS UPCOMING SOUTH KOREAN MILITARY EXERCISES.

2.   AMBASSADOR RAISED POSSIBILITY THAT PROCEEDING WITH EXERCISES MIGHT TRIGGER NORTH KOREAN MILITARY ACTION, SPECIFICALLY A STRIKE AGAINST SOUTH KOREAN ISLANDS IN THE YELLOW SEA. FOREIGN MINISTER RESPONDED SAYING SEOUL IS DETERMINED TO PROCEED WITH EXERCISES AND IS PREPARED TO RESPOND IF THE NORTH OPENS UP WITH AN ARTILLERY BARRAGE.

3.   AMBASSADOR CHOKE NOTED THAT A US DELEGATION HEADED BY FORMER NEW MEXICO GOVERNOR RICHARDSON IS DUE TO ARRIVE IN PYONGYANG ON JULY 11. AMBASSADOR EXPRESSED CONCERN THAT MILITARY EXERCISES MIGHT UPSET PROPECTS FOR RICHARDSON'S VISIT SUCCESS IN REDUCING REGIONAL TENSIONS. CHOKE

4.   END OF MESSAGE

# ANNEX II

# VIRGINIA TECH
# CASE STUDY

# VIRGINIA TECH:
# CASE STUDY

On April 16, 2007, Seung Hui Cho, a disgruntled and mentally ill student, shot and killed thirty-two students and faculty members at Virginia Tech University as well as himself. He also wounded seventeen others. This was the second school shooting at an institution of higher learning in the state of Virginia. Five years earlier, on January 16, 2002, Peter Odighizuwa, a former student at the Appalachian School of Law, shot and killed the school's dean, a professor, and a student. He wounded three others. There are striking parallels between the two shootings (profiles of the killers, school attitudes and reactions, and responses to the shootings).

No investigation or analysis was done of the law school shooting. Following the Tech shooting, however, Virginia Governor Kaine appointed a panel to review the tragedy. The following is the panel's mission statement:

> *"The Panel's mission is to provide an independent, thorough, and objective incident review of this tragic event, including a review of educational laws, policies, and institutions, the public safety and health care procedures and responses, and the mental health deliverysystem. With respect to these areas of review, the Panel should focus on what went right, and what went wrong, what practices should be considered best practices, and what practices are in need of improvement. This review should include examination of information contained in academic, health and court records and by information obtained through interviews with knowledgeable individuals. Once that factual narrative is in place and questions have been answered, the Panel should offer recommendations for improvement in light of those facts and circumstances."*

The Governor's Review Panel Report has, however, met with skepticism and criticism from a variety of quarters. The Review Panel Report is a form of crime analysis; it is an analysis of the worst mass shooting to date in U.S. history. How analysis is written and for whom it is written can take on a wide variety of forms, but intelligence must always be accurate and objective. In the case of the Virginia Tech report, it was (and is) imperative that the document not pull any punches.

Many have argued that there were at least five weaknesses in the Review Panel and its report from the outset:

1. The panel was not given subpoena power to force individuals to talk with them, much less talk to the panel under oath. As a result at least three pertinent players did not supply critical documents: the police, the ATF, and the gun dealers.

2. The panel was a state-sponsored investigating body, investigating a major state institution, raising the specter of conflict of interest.

3. The panel chair was a former head of the Virginia State Police, and the Virginia State Police's actions were under investigation. Critics say that at minimum, the chairman should have excused himself from that part of the investigation and the report.

4.   The job of drafting the report was given to TriData, an Arlington, Virginia-based firm with previous business dealings with the state. TriData relies on part of its income from the state of Virginia. Again, a question of conflict of interest (if not objectivity and propriety) arises.

5.   The report was written as an on-going investigation, rather than as an analytical analysis of a major crime designed to draw conclusions.

The report's credibility suffered badly when, after its publication, a large number of factual errors as well as errors of omission became apparent. The first, most glaring problem was with the timeline. There were omissions and inaccuracies when the report was first published. These problems were called to the attention of the Review Panel and TriData. Of the more than forty-eight corrections and clarifications presented to TriData, approximately twelve were accepted.

## THE EXERCISE

Read the Summary of Key Findings and Chapters I through XI of the Governor's Review Panel Report (the Addendum or the Final Report). Once you have finished, write an analysis of the report, keeping the following six points in mind:

1.   What should intelligence/crime analysis do?

2.   Did the Addendum do what it was intended to do? If so, how? If not, why not?

3.   Who was or is the intended audience of the Addendum, the general public, the families, the school administration, the government of Virginia, or the legal community?

4.   Once you determine who the audience is, did the report meet the requirements of that audience?

5.   As you read the Governor's Review Panel Report, note the use of active voice and passive voice sentences. Do the passive-voice sentences add clarity or do they obscure?

6.   Consider the format of the report. Is the format reader-friendly and logical, or does it muddy the picture and confuse rather than clarify?

Below is a list of some of the proposed corrections, additions, and clarifications that were left out of the revised, final report. As part of your analysis, look at the information left out and decide what, if any, difference the inclusion of the information would have made.

Your analysis should be no more than three double-spaced typed pages. Feel free to use charts, graphs, or any graphic (in addition to the text) to support the points you make.

1.   **October 10, 2005**: Professor Giovanni forwards a request and copy of Cho's violent writings to Virginia Tech's student affairs vice president, who sends it to the school's top discipline official. (add to page 23 of timeline)

2.   **October 19, 2005**: The Student Affairs Dean asks English department chair Lucinda Roy to warn Cho that he could face disciplinary action. She offers to tutor him if he leaves Giovanni's class. (add to page 23 of timeline)

3.   **November 2, 2005**: Cho's roommates and dorm residents say they think Cho sets fires in dorm lounge and report it to the police. (add to page 23 of timeline)

4.   **November 27, 2005**: A female student (allegedly harassed by Cho) wants to testify at a disciplinary hearing for Cho, but no hearing is ever held. (add to page 23 of timeline)

5.   **December 6, 2005**: Resident assistant reports that Cho has knives in his room and mentions that the harassment victim is scared. Resident assistant expresses concern that no one has talked to Cho. (add to page 24 of timeline)

6.  **April 16, 2007**: At 0730, a housekeeper in Burruss Hall told the Associate Vice President for Student Affairs and member of the Policy Group, Dr. Ed Spencer, that a Residential Advisor in West Ambler Johnston Hall was murdered. She had received a phone call from a friend who is a housekeeper in that residence hall. (add to page 27 of the timeline)

7.  **April 16, 2007**: 0816-0924: Students Henry Lee and Rachel Hill are cleared to leave West Ambler Johnston Hall for their 0905 class. Both were shot and killed in that class in Norris Hall. (add to page 28 of the timeline)

8.  **April 16, 2007**: 0825: The police cancel bank deposit pickups. (add to page 28 of the timeline)

9.  **April 16, 2007**: 0840: A Virginia Tech Policy Group member notifies the governor's office of the two murders in West Ambler Johnston Hall. (add to page 28 of the timeline)

10. **April 16, 2007**: 0845, a Virginia Tech official reminds a Richmond colleague, "Just try to make sure it doesn't get out." (add to page 28 of the timeline)

11. **April 16, 2007**: 0850: The Virginia Tech Policy Group begins composing a notice to the university about the two murders at West Ambler Johnston one hour and thirty-five minutes earlier at 0715. Larry Hinkler, Associate Vice President for University Relations, is unable to send the message before classes changed at 0905 due to technical difficulties with the wireless LAN connection. The Policy Group decided to wait for more information and hold the notification until the next class change at 0955. (add to page 28 of timeline)

12. **April 16, 2007**: 0924: A Virginia Tech Police Department captain arrives at the Policy Group meeting to act as liaison and provide updates. He reported one gunman is at large possibly on foot (on campus). (add to page 29 of the timeline)

# GOVERNOR'S REVIEW PANEL REPORT– THE ADDENDUM

The Addendum is inserted here in its entirety for your convenience. Copies of the original report and the addendum are available from numerous independent sources on the Internet. The only changes here are that the page numbers for this textbook have been added to the left and right for your reference. The original report page numbers, referenced in the analysis that follows it, are located in the center, as it was originally laid out.

# Mass Shootings at Virginia Tech

*Addendum to the Report of the Review Panel*

**Presented to:**
**Governor Timothy M. Kaine**
**Commonwealth of Virginia**

**November 2009**

# Mass Shootings at Virginia Tech
## *Addendum to the Report of the Review Panel*

Presented to:

Governor Timothy M. Kaine
Commonwealth of Virginia

Presented by:

TriData Division, System Planning Corporation
3601 Wilson Boulevard
Arlington, VA 22201

**November 2009**
**(revised December 2009)**

# INTRODUCTION

On April 16, 2007, Virginia Tech experienced one of the most horrific events in American university history—a double homicide followed by a mass shooting that left 32 students and faculty killed, with many others injured, and many more scarred psychologically. Families of the slain and injured as well as the university community have suffered terribly.

Immediately after the incident Virginia Governor Timothy M. Kaine created a blue ribbon Review Panel, referred to as the Virginia Tech Review Panel, which consisted of nine members selected for their expertise in the areas that were to be investigated. The Review Panel's mission was to assess the events leading to the shooting and how the incident was handled by the university and public safety agencies. Mental health services and privacy laws were examined as well. The Review Panel was to make recommendations that would help college campuses prevent or mitigate such incidents in the future. The Report of the Review Panel was presented to the Governor in late August 2007. It is referred to as the "Report" in this Addendum.

## SCOPE OF THIS REPORT: ADDITIONS AND CORRECTIONS

In the two years since the Review Panel's report was published, additional information has been placed in the public record, including Seung Hui Cho's case file from the Cook Counseling Center and a recent report from the Commonwealth's Inspector General concerning the Cook Counseling Center's handling of Cho's records. Briefings to the victims' families by police and Virginia Tech officials provided additional details of the events In light of the new information presented to the families, and other information they found in the April 16 archive, several family members requested that additions and corrections be made to the Report. Some families had personal knowledge of the events that were not previously shared. Some families requested new interpretations of certain findings or revisions to some of the Review Panel's recommendations in light of the new information. Virginia Tech officials also submitted comments requesting some corrections.

Governor Kaine asked the victims' families and Virginia Tech to submit any corrections or additions they thought important by the end of August, 2009. The time was extended into September after discovery of Cho's missing Cook Counseling Center records.

This Addendum responds to the comments and questions received from the families and Virginia Tech by correcting facts in the original report, including the timeline, and by adding additional information about the events leading to the incidents, the response to the incidents, and the aftermath of April 16. The Addendum also includes corrections to names and titles of people cited in the Report or the list of interviewees. The Addendum does not address opinions or value judgments that were raised, but provides some additional background information that might help address the concerns raised.

## ADDENDUM PROCESS

Governor Kaine engaged the TriData staff that supported the Review Panel to review the additional information and the questions and comments about the Report. TriData was familiar with the research and details of the Report, the sources, and the deliberations behind the Report's original findings and recommendations. All comments received by the Governor's Office were forwarded to TriData for review.

The focus of this Addendum is on correcting and adding to the pertinent facts. Many of the families as well as Virginia Tech submitted corrections or comments and added detailed references to documents now in the public record. After completing an initial review of the comments from all parties, TriData submitted a number of questions to Virginia Tech and also interviewed several family members for clarification of their comments, and to cross-check information and corroborate facts.

There are conflicting opinions on whether the Review Panel should have treated certain issues differently, reached stronger or different conclusions, placed blame on certain individuals, or interviewed additional people. The new and additional information has tended to reinforce the Review Panel's original findings and recommendations. In several instances, emphasis was added to findings where strongly supported by the facts. While some of the findings have been modified slightly and one added, none of the new information merited changes to any of the recommendations in the original Report.

A number of questions and corrections were raised about the timeline in the Report. The timeline was intended to provide an overview of the most important markers in the sequence of events to assist readers as a reference as they went through the details in the text. The Review Panel chose not to include many details in the timeline that were later discussed in the text. This Addendum contains an expanded timeline with virtually all of the additions suggested by the families.

## CLARIFICATION AND CORRECTION OF ADDENDUM

This Addendum was shown to the families of victims, Virginia Tech, and the Review Panel the day before it was published. To maintain independence of the findings they were not asked to review the changes made. Many of the changes but not all had been discussed with various people in these groups, and most of the changes came from comments they had submitted to the Governor, as noted above. Nevertheless, after the initial publication of the Addendum a few errors or unclear points were reported, and they are corrected in this version.

## SCOPE OF ORIGINAL REVIEW PANEL REPORT

As described in the Review Panel's Report, Governor Kaine's executive order directed the Review Panel to accomplish the following:

1. "Conduct a review of how Seung Hui Cho committed these 32 murders and multiple additional woundings, including without limitation how he obtained his firearms and ammunition, and to learn what can be learned about what caused him to commit these acts of violence."

2. "Conduct a review of Seung Hui Cho's psychological condition and behavioral issues prior to and at the time of the shootings, what behavioral aberrations or potential warning signs were observed by students, faculty and/or staff at Westfield High School and Virginia Tech. This inquiry should include the response taken by Virginia Tech and others to note psychological and behavioral issues, Seung Hui Cho's interaction with the mental health delivery system, including without limitation judicial intervention, access to services, and communication between the mental health services system and Virginia Tech. It should also include a review of educational, medical, and judicial records documenting his condition, the services rendered to him, and his commitment hearing."

3. "Conduct a review of the timeline of events from the time that Seung Hui Cho entered West Ambler Johnston Dormitory until his death in Norris Hall. Such review shall in-126ervi an assessment of the response to the first murders and efforts to stop the Norris Hall murders once they began."

4. "Conduct a review of the response of the Commonwealth, all of its agencies, and relevant local and private providers following the death of Seung Hui Cho for the purpose of providing recommendations for the improvement of the Commonwealth's response in similar emergency situations. Such review shall include an assessment of the emergency medical response provided for the injured and wounded, the conduct of post-mortem examinations and release of remains, on-campus actions following the tragedy, and the services and counseling offered to the victims, the victims' families, and those affected by the incident. In so doing, the Review Panel shall to the extent required by federal or state law: (i) protect the confidentiality of any individual's or family member's personal or health information; and (ii) make public or publish information and findings only in summary or aggregate form without identifying personal or health information related to any individual or family member unless authorization is obtained from an individual or family member that specifically permits the Review Panel to disclose that person's personal or health information."

5. "Conduct other inquiries as may be appropriate in the Review Panel's discretion otherwise consistent with its mission and authority as provided herein."

6. "Based on these inquiries, make recommendations on appropriate measures that can be taken to improve the laws, policies, procedures, systems and institutions of the Commonwealth and the operation of public safety agencies, medical facilities, local agencies, private providers, universities, and mental health services delivery system."

"In summary, the Review Panel was tasked to review the events, assess actions taken and not taken, identify lessons learned, and propose alternatives for the future. Included a review of Cho's history and interaction with the mental health and legal systems and of his gun purchases. The Review Panel was also asked to review the emergency response by all parties (law enforcement officials, university officials, medical responders and hospital care providers, and the Medical Examiner). Finally, the Review Panel reviewed the aftermath—the university's approach to helping families, survivors, students, and staff as they dealt with the mental trauma and the approach to helping the university heal itself and function again."

## REVIEW PANEL AND STAFF

The Review Panel consisted of nine highly distinguished members from a variety of relevant backgrounds. Members included a former Governor and Secretary of the U.S. Department of Homeland Security, a judge, a psychiatrist, a professor of emergency medicine, a former FBI official who established the FBI's Center for the Analysis of Violent Crime, a former head of the Virginia State Police, a specialist in university administration, and a specialist in assisting families of crime victims. The Review Panel members volunteered their time for the four month study period.

The Review Panel was supported by staff from the TriData Division, System Planning Corporation of Arlington, Virginia. SPC/TriData specializes in public safety consulting and research, and had undertaken over 50 studies of major disasters to identify the lessons learned. One of those studies reported on the lessons learned from the Columbine High School shootings. These studies were directed by the two TriData managers, Philip Schaenman and Hollis Stambaugh, who served as the Review Panel staff director and deputy director respectively. TriData also completed a review for FEMA of the Northern Illinois University mass shooting and authored this Addendum.

## REVIEW PANEL PROCESS AND CONSTRAINTS

Among questions received from the victims' families was a request for additional information about how the Review Panel approached the investigation into the shooting and arrived at their conclusions, and why certain information was or was not included. Thus, it may be useful to review the process and the constraints within which the Review Panel worked.

Time Constraints – Governor Kaine directed the Review Panel to complete its review of the Virginia Tech shootings before classes resumed the next semester. This meant that the Report had to be published by late August 2007, four months after starting. (Elements of the review started the week immediately following the shooting) The Governor felt it was important to identify any campus safeguards or executive orders needed before students returned to classes at Virginia Tech and other schools across the state. It also was important to identify any changes needed in state legislation with adequate time before the next session of the state legislature. For the families, the Virginia Tech community, and general public, it was important to produce information as soon as possible on the events of April 16.

The Review Panel would have liked to have had more time to interview additional people and to delve further into certain details. However, all understood the importance of getting the main facts and the big picture correct and out to the public as soon as possible. The Review Panel used its best judgment on what to cover in the available time in light of the many issues that were found across many disciplines. As noted above, additional information has become available since the Report was released. The victims' families and Virginia Tech have closely evaluated the Report in light of the new information and have submitted comments to the Governor. These have been thoroughly studied and this Addendum is the product of that work. While some details are added and some corrected, all the original recommendations remain valid.

Authority – The Review Panel benefited from the Governor's authority to collect information but it did not have subpoena power. State and local police and the FBI provided briefings to the Review Panel, but the Panel did not have access to the police investigation files. The police subsequently provided a briefing to the victims' families and that information has been included in this Addendum.)

Breadth of Interviews – In the course of carrying out the Governor's directive, the Review Panel interviewed over 200 individuals, heard presentations from many experts, and listened to comments from the victims' families and the general public at four public hearings held throughout the state. In addition, thousands of other people sent information, opinions, and suggestions to a special website established for that purpose.

The interviewees included many faculty, students, injured victims, victims' families, law enforcement personnel, emergency medical service providers, hospital emergency room personnel, personnel from the Office of the Medical Examiner and the Office of Victim Services, Virginia Tech officials, the Virginia Commissioner of Mental Health and personnel from the Virginia Attorney General's office. Review Panel members also interviewed Cho's family and various health practitioners who had treated him as well as individuals from his high school, including his high school guidance counselor.

Four public hearings were held to help gather information and views from selected key individuals who were close to the events. The Review Panel invited experts in various relevant areas such as university counseling, police procedures, firearm regulations, and mental health to make presentations. Time for public comment was provided at the close of each meeting. Victims' families were present throughout the hearings.

Discretion on Details Included – In addition to interviews, presentations of experts and public hearings, the Review Panel examined and discussed over 1,000 pages of documents. The Review Panel felt it was neither possible nor desirable to publish every fact collected and the Review Panel used its discretion in determining the most relevant information to include in the Report. The Review Panel began by including details of Cho's personal history and the actions taken and decisions made by Virginia Tech and law enforcement on April 16 and then concluded with its findings of what improvements should be made. The Review Panel wanted to avoid obfuscating the major findings in a cloud of lesser important or repetitive details, focusing on the findings and recommendations that were key to improving campus safety. For example, Cho had been a student in over 35 different classes and had written some disturbing material for several English Department faculty members, but only a representative few of his professors were mentioned and only a few of his papers were cited as examples in the Report.

The Review Panel held several 10 and 12-hour Review Panel work sessions in which Review Panel members painstakingly evaluated and discussed the assembled information and drafted recommendations supported by the research.

Independence – The Review Panel operated independently from both Virginia Tech and the Office of the Governor, though numerous Virginia Tech and Commonwealth employees were interviewed during the review. The Report's findings and recommendations were solely those of the Review Panel.

To preserve the Report's objectivity, neither Virginia Tech nor the families of the victims were permitted to comment on drafts of the Report before publication. Families of victims, however, were briefed on the major findings and the nature of the research during the review process.

## ORGANIZATION OF THIS ADDENDUM

Following this introduction are all sections of the original Report and Appendix B. This Addendum presents additions and corrections at the end of each chapter. The additions and corrections are organized by page number of the Report to which the issue was directed. Subject headings and some context are provided to make the corrections self-standing without need to reference the text. A revised timeline is included with additional details and corrections to the original timeline.

A revised interviewee list (Appendix B in the original Report) indicates corrections to names and positions, and some personal preferences expressed to us from some interviewees of how they wished their names to be listed. Some other desired changes to names and descriptions are included in the revised Dedication section.

Specific questions or comments have not been attributed to individuals in order to preserve confidentiality. All comments and concerns submitted to the Governor's office by families and Virginia Tech were reviewed and addressed. In some cases extensive research failed to substantiate a suggested change, but most of the factual comments resulted in changes or clarifications. Comments appear immediately following the corrections and additions on other issues raised that had incorrect factual basis or that missed some information in the Report.

The original Report continues to stand as it was written by the Review Panel. The Review Panel worked hard on crafting the language of its Report and on reaching consensus on its findings and recommendations. The primary intent of this Addendum is to correct the factual record, both for future understanding of the terrible events of April 16, 2007, and to honor and respect those who died or suffered from the attacks.

# Contents

(This page intentionally left blank.)

# DEDICATION

The Virginia Tech Review Panel invited the families of the victims to lend their words as a dedication of this report. The panel is honored to share their words of love, remembrance, and strength.

We dedicate this report not solely to those who lost their lives at Virginia Tech on April 16, 2007, and to those physically and/or psychologically wounded on that dreadful morning, but also to every student, teacher, and institution of learning, that we may all safely fulfill our goals of learning, educating, and enriching humanity's stores of knowledge: the very arts and sciences that ennoble us.*

"Love does not die, people do. So when all that is left of me is love…
Give me away…" – John Wayne Schlatter

"This is the beginning of a new day. You have been given this day to use as you will. You can waste it or use it for good. What you do today is important because you are exchanging a day of your life for it. When tomorrow comes, this day will be gone forever; in its place is something that you have left behind…let it be something good." – Anonymous

"We should consider every day lost on which we have not danced at least once. And we should call every truth false which was not accompanied by at least one laugh."

Friedrich Nietzsche

"Unable are the loved to die, for Love is Immortality." – Emily Dickinson

---

32 candles burning bright for all to see,
Lifting up the world for peace and harmony,
Those of us who are drawn to the lights,
enduringly embedded in our mind, indelibly
ingrained on our heart, forever identifying our spirit,
We call out your name:

Erin, Ryan, Emily, Reema, Daniel, Matthew, Kevin, Brian, Jarrett, Austin, Henry, Liviu, Nicole, Julia, Lauren, Partahi, Jamie, Jeremy, Rachel, Caitlin, Maxine, Jocelyne, Leslie, Juan, Daniel, Ross, G.V., Mary, Matthew, Minal, Michael, Waleed,

and,

hold these truths ever so tight,
your lives have great meaning, your lives have great power, your lives will never be
forgotten, YOU will always be remembered,
–never and always…

– Pat Craig

---

*Neither this dedication nor the use herein of the victims' photos or bios represents an endorsement of the report by the victims' families.

Ross A. Alameddine
Hometown: Saugus, Massachusetts
Sophomore, University Studies
Student since fall 2005

Posthumous degree:
Bachelor of Arts, English and Foreign
Languages/French

Christopher James Bishop
Residence in Blacksburg
Instructor, Foreign Languages
Joined Virginia Tech on
August 10, 2005

Brian Roy Bluhm
Hometown: Cedar Rapids, Iowa
Masters student, Civil Engineering
Student since fall 2000

Posthumous degree:
Master of Science, Civil Engineering

Ryan Christopher Clark
Hometown: Martinez, Georgia
Senior, Psychology
Student since fall 2002

Posthumous degrees:
Bachelor of Science, Biological
Sciences
Bachelor of Arts, English
Bachelor of Science, Psychology

Austin Michelle Cloyd
Hometown: Blacksburg, Virginia
Sophomore, Honors Program,
International Studies
Student since fall 2006

Posthumous degrees:
Bachelor of Arts, Foreign
Languages/French
Bachelor of Arts, International Studies

Kevin P. Granata
Residence in Blacksburg
Professor, Engineering Science and
Mechanics
Joined Virginia Tech on
January 10, 2003

Matthew Gregory Gwaltney
Hometown: Chesterfield, Virginia
Masters student, Environmental
Engineering
Student since fall 2001

Posthumous degree:
Master of Science, Environmental
Engineering

Caitlin Millar Hammaren
Hometown: Westtown, New York
Sophomore, International Studies
Student since fall 2005

Posthumous degree:
Bachelor of Arts, International Studies

Jeremy Michael Herbstritt
Hometown: Blacksburg, Virginia
Masters student, Civil Engineering
Student since fall 2006

Posthumous degree:
Master of Science, Civil Engineering

Rachael Elizabeth Hill
Hometown: Glen Allen, Virginia
Freshman, University Studies
Student since fall 2006

Posthumous degree:
Bachelor of Science, Biological
Sciences

Emily Jane Hilscher
Hometown: Woodville, Virginia
Freshman, Animal and Poultry Sciences
Student since fall 2006

Posthumous degree:
Bachelor of Science, Animal and
Poultry
Sciences

Partahi Mamora Halomoan
Lumbantoruan
Hometown: Blacksburg, Virginia
(originally from Indonesia)
Ph.D. student, Civil Engineering
Student since fall 2003

Posthumous degree:
Doctor of Philosophy, Civil
Engineering

Jarrett Lee Lane
Hometown: Narrows, Virginia
Senior, Civil Engineering
Student since fall 2003

Posthumous degree:
Bachelor of Science, Civil Engineering

Matthew Joseph La Porte
Hometown: Dumont, New Jersey
Sophomore, University Studies
Student since fall 2005

Posthumous degree:
Bachelor of Arts, Political Science

Henry J. Lee
Hometown: Roanoke, Virginia
Sophomore, Computer Engineering
Student since fall 2006

Posthumous degree:
Bachelor of Science, Computer
Engineering

Liviu Librescu
Residence in Blacksburg
Professor, Engineering Science and
Mechanics
Joined Virginia Tech on
September 1, 1985

V. Loganathan
Residence in Blacksburg
Professor, Civil and Environmental
Engineering
Joined Virginia Tech on
December 16, 1981

Lauren Ashley McCain
Hometown: Hampton, Virginia
Freshman, International Studies
Student since fall 2006

Posthumous degree:
Bachelor of Arts, International Studies

Jocelyne Couture-Nowak
Residence in Blacksburg
Adjunct Professor, Foreign Languages
Joined Virginia Tech on
August 10, 2001

Daniel Patrick O'Neil
Hometown: Lincoln, Rhode Island
Masters student, Environmental
Engineering
Student since fall 2006

Posthumous degree:
Master of Science, Environmental
Engineering

Juan Ramon Ortiz-Ortiz
Hometown: Blacksburg, Virginia
Masters student, Civil Engineering
Student since fall 2006

Posthumous degree:
Master of Science, Civil Engineering

Minal Hiralal Panchal
Hometown: Mumbai, India
Masters student, Architecture
Student since fall 2006

Posthumous degree:
Master of Science, Architecture

Daniel Alejandro Perez
Hometown: Woodbridge, Virginia
Sophomore, International Studies
Student since summer 2006

Posthumous degree:
Bachelor of Arts, International Studies

Erin Nicole Peterson
Hometown: Centreville, Virginia
Freshman, International Studies
Student since fall 2006

Posthumous degree:
Bachelor of Arts, International Studies

Michael Steven Pohle, Jr.
Hometown: Flemington, New Jersey
Senior, Biological Sciences
Student since fall 2002

Posthumous degree:
Bachelor of Science, Biological
Sciences

Hometown: Blacksburg, Virginia
Masters student, Biological Systems
Engineering
Student since fall 2001

Posthumous degree:
Master of Science, Biological Systems

Julia Kathleen Pryde
Engineering
Mary Karen Read
Hometown: Annandale, Virginia
Freshman, Interdisciplinary Studies
Student since fall 2006

Posthumous degree:
Bachelor of Arts, Interdisciplinary
Studies

Reema Joseph Samaha
Hometown: Centreville, Virginia
Freshman, University Studies
Student since fall 2006

Posthumous degrees:
Bachelor of Arts, International Studies
Bachelor of Arts, Public and Urban
Affairs

Waleed Mohamed Shaalan
Hometown: Blacksburg, Virginia
(originally from Egypt)
Ph.D. student, Civil Engineering
Student since fall 2006

Posthumous degree:
Doctor of Philosophy, Civil
Engineering

Leslie Geraldine Sherman
Hometown: Springfield, Virginia
Junior, Honors Program, History
Student since fall 2005

Posthumous degrees:
Bachelor of Arts, History
Bachelor of Arts, International Studies

Maxine Shelly Turner
Hometown: Vienna, Virginia
Senior, Honors Program, Chemical
Engineering
Student since fall 2003

Posthumous degree: Bachelor of
Science,
Chemical Engineering

Nicole Regina White
Hometown: Smithfield, Virginia
Sophomore, International Studies
Student since fall 2004

Posthumous degree:
Bachelor of Arts, International Studies

## ADDITIONS AND CORRECTIONS

Two of the above write-ups on the victims have had changes made as requested by their families.

(This page intentionally left blank.)

# FOREWORD

## From Timothy M. Kaine
## Governor, Commonwealth Of Virginia

On April 16, 2007, a tragic chapter was added to Virginia's history when a disturbed young man at Virginia Tech took the lives of 32 students and faculty, wounded many others, and killed himself. In the midst of unspeakable grief, the Virginia Tech community stood together, with tremendous support from friends in all corners of the world, and made us proud to be Virginians.

Over time, the tragedy has been felt by all it touched, most deeply by the families of those who were killed and by the wounded survivors and their families. The impact has been felt as well by those who witnessed or responded to the shooting, the broad Virginia Tech community, and those who are near to Blacksburg geographically or in spirit.

In the days immediately after the shooting, I knew it was critical to seek answers to the many questions that would arise from the tragedy. I also felt that the questions should be addressed by people who possessed both the expertise and autonomy necessary to do a comprehensive review. Accordingly, I announced on April 19 the formation of the Virginia Tech Review Panel to perform a review independent of the Commonwealth's own efforts to respond to the terrible events of April 16. The Panel members readily agreed to devote time, expertise, and emotional energy to this difficult task.

Those who agreed to serve were:

- Panel Chair Col. Gerald Massengill, a retired Virginia State Police Superintendent who led the Commonwealth's law enforcement response to the September 11, 2001, attack on the Pentagon and the sniper attacks that affected the Commonwealth in 2002.

- Panel Vice Chair Dr. Marcus L. Martin, Professor of Emergency Medicine, Assistant Dean of the School of Medicine and Associate Vice President for Diversity and Equity at the University of Virginia.

- Gordon Davies, former Director of the State Council of Higher Education for Virginia (1977–1997) and President of the Kentucky Council on Postsecondary Education (1998–2002).

- Dr. Roger L. Depue, a 20-year veteran of the FBI and the founder, past president and CEO of The Academy Group, Inc., a forensic behavioral sciences services company providing consultation, research, and investigation of aberrant and violent behavioral problems.

- Carroll Ann Ellis, MS, Director of the Fairfax County Police Department's Victim Services Division, a faculty member at the National Victim Academy, and a member of the American Society of Victimology.

- The Honorable Tom Ridge, former Governor of Pennsylvania (1995–2001) and Member of the U.S. House of Representatives (1983–1995) who was also the first U.S. Secretary of Homeland Security (2003–2005).

- Dr. Aradhana A. "Bela" Sood, Professor of Psychiatry and Pediatrics, Chair of Child and Adolescent Psychiatry and Medical Director of the Virginia Treatment Center for Children at VCU Medical Center.

- The Honorable Diane Strickland, former judge of the 23rd Judicial Circuit Court in Roanoke County (1989–2003) and co-chair of the Boyd-Graves Conference on issues surrounding involuntary mental commitment.

These nationally recognized individuals brought expertise in many areas, including law enforcement, security, governmental management, mental health, emergency care, victims' services, the Virginia court system, and higher education.

An assignment of this importance required expert technical assistance and this was provided by TriData, a division of System Planning Corporation. TriData has worked on numerous reports following disasters and tragedies, including a report on the 1999 shooting at Columbine High School. Phil Schaenman and Hollis Stambaugh led the TriData team.

The Panel also needed wise and dedicated legal counsel and that counsel was provided on a pro bono basis by the Washington, D.C., office of the law firm Skadden, Arps, Slate, Meagher & Flom LLP. The Skadden Arps team was led by partners Richard Brusca and Amy Sabrin.

The level of personal commitment by the Panel members, staff and counsel throughout the process was extraordinary. This report is the product of intense work and deliberation and the Commonwealth stands indebted to all who worked on it.

The magnitude of the losses suffered by victims and their families, the Virginia Tech community, and our Commonwealth is immeasurable. We have lost people of great character and intelligence who came to Virginia Tech from around our state, our nation and the world. While we can never know the full extent of the contributions they would have made had their lives not been cut short, we can say with confidence that they had already given much of themselves toward advancing knowledge and helping others.

We must now challenge ourselves to study this report carefully and make changes that will reduce the risk of future violence on our campuses. If we act in that way, we will honor the lives and sacrifices of all who suffered on that terrible day and advance the notion of service that is Virginia Tech's fundamental mission.

## ADDITIONS AND CORRECTIONS

(No changes from original report.)

(This page intentionally left blank.)

# ACKNOWLEDGEMENTS

The Virginia Tech Review Panel thanks the many persons who contributed to gathering information, provided facilities at which the panel held four public meetings around the state, and helped prepare this report. The administration and staff of Virginia Tech, George Mason University, and the University of Virginia hosted public meetings at which speakers presented background information and family members of the victims addressed the panel. The University of Virginia also provided facilities for the panel to meet in three sessions to discuss confidential material related to this report.

The panel is grateful to more than 200 persons who were interviewed or who participated in discussion groups. They are identified in Appendix B.

Finally, the panel is grateful for staff support and legal advice provided by TriData, a Division of System Planning Corporation, and Skadden, Arps, Slate, Meagher & Flom LLP.

## TRIDATA, A DIVISION OF SYSTEM PLANNING CORPORATION

- Philip Schaenman, panel staff director
- Hollis Stambaugh, panel staff deputy director
- Jim Kudla, panel public information officer
- Dr. Harold Cohen
- Darryl Sensenig

- Paul Flippin
- Teresa Copping
- Maria Argabright
- Shania Flagg
- Lucius Lamar III
- Rachel Mershon
- Jim Gray

## SKADDEN, ARPS, SLATE, MEAGHER & FLOM LLP

- Richard Brusca
- Amy Sabrin
- Michael Tierney
- Michael Kelly
- Ian Erickson

- Brad Marcus
- Cory Black, Summer Associate
- Ray McKenzie, Summer Associate
- Colin Ram, Summer Associate

## ADDITIONS AND CORRECTIONS

(No changes from original report.)

(This page intentionally left blank.)

# SUMMARY OF KEY FINDINGS

On April 16, 2007, Seung Hui Cho, an angry and disturbed student, shot to death 32 students and faculty of Virginia Tech, wounded 17 more, and then killed himself.

The incident horrified not only Virginians, but people across the United States and throughout the world.

Tim Kaine, Governor of the Commonwealth of Virginia, immediately appointed a panel to review the events leading up to this tragedy; the handling of the incidents by public safety officials, emergency services providers, and the university; and the services subsequently provided to families, survivors, care-givers, and the community.

The Virginia Tech Review Panel reviewed several separate but related issues in assessing events leading to the mass shootings and their aftermath:

- The life and mental health history of Seung Hui Cho, from early childhood until the weeks before April 16.

- Federal and state laws concerning the privacy of health and education records.

- Cho's purchase of guns and related gun control issues.

- The double homicide at West Ambler Johnston (WAJ) residence hall and the mass shootings at Norris Hall, including the responses of Virginia Tech leadership and the actions of law enforcement officers and emergency responders.

- Emergency medical care immediately following the shootings, both onsite at Virginia Tech and in cooperating hospitals.

- The work of the Office of the Chief Medical Examiner of Virginia.

- The services provided for surviving victims of the shootings and others injured, the families and loved ones of those killed and injured, members of the university community, and caregivers.

The panel conducted over 200 interviews and reviewed thousands of pages of records, and reports the following major findings:

1. Cho exhibited signs of mental health problems during his childhood. His middle and high schools responded well to these signs and, with his parents' involvement, provided services to address his issues. He also received private psychiatric treatment and counseling for selective mutism and depression.

    In 1999, after the Columbine shootings, Cho's middle school teachers observed suicidal and homicidal ideations in his writings and recommended psychiatric counseling, which he received. It was at this point that he received medication for a short time. Although Cho's parents were aware that he was troubled at this time, they state they did not specifically know that he thought about homicide shortly after the 1999 Columbine school shootings.

2. During Cho's junior year at Virginia Tech, numerous incidents occurred that were clear warnings of mental instability. Although various individuals and departments within the university knew about each of these incidents, the university did not intervene effectively. No one knew all the information and no one connected all the dots.

3. University officials in the office of Judicial Affairs, Cook Counseling Center, campus police, the Dean of Students, and others explained their failures to communicate with one another or with Cho's parents by noting their belief that such communications are prohibited by the federal laws governing the privacy of health and education records. In reality, federal laws and their state counterparts afford ample leeway to share information in potentially dangerous situations.

4. The Cook Counseling Center and the university's Care Team failed to provide needed support and services to Cho during a period in late 2005 and early 2006. The system failed for lack of resources, incorrect interpretation of privacy laws, and passivity. Records of Cho's minimal treatment at Virginia Tech's Cook Counseling Center are missing.

5. Virginia's mental health laws are flawed and services for mental health users are inadequate. Lack of sufficient resources results in gaps in the mental health system including short term crisis stabilization and comprehensive outpatient services. The involuntary commitment process is challenged by unrealistic time constraints, lack of critical psychiatric data and collateral information, and barriers (perceived or real) to open communications among key professionals.

6. There is widespread confusion about what federal and state privacy laws allow. Also, the federal laws governing records of health care provided in educational settings are not entirely compatible with those governing other health records.

7. Cho purchased two guns in violation of federal law. The fact that in 2005 Cho had been judged to be a danger to himself and ordered to outpatient treatment made him ineligible to purchase a gun under federal law.

8. Virginia is one of only 22 states that report any information about mental health to a federal database used to conduct background checks on would-be gun purchasers. But Virginia law did not clearly require that persons such as Cho—who had been ordered into out-patient treatment but not committed to an institution—be reported to the database. Governor Kaine's executive order to report all persons involuntarily committed for outpatient treatment has temporarily addressed this ambiguity in state law. But a change is needed in the Code of Virginia as well.

9. Some Virginia colleges and universities are uncertain about what they are permitted to do regarding the possession of firearms on campus.

10. On April 16, 2007, the Virginia Tech and Blacksburg police departments responded quickly to the report of shootings at West Ambler Johnston residence hall, as did the Virginia Tech and Blacksburg rescue squads. Their responses were well coordinated.

11. The Virginia Tech police may have erred in prematurely concluding that their initial lead in the double homicide was a good one, or at least in conveying that impression to university officials while continuing their investigation. They did not take sufficient action to deal with what might happen if the initial lead proved erroneous. The police reported to the university emergency Policy Group that the "person of interest" probably was no longer on campus.

12. The VTPD erred in not requesting that the Policy Group issue a campus-wide notification that two persons had been killed and that all students and staff should be cautious and alert.

13. Senior university administrators, acting as the emergency Policy Group, failed to issue an all-campus notification about the WAJ killings until almost 2 hours had elapsed. University practice may have conflicted with written policies.

14. The presence of large numbers of police at WAJ led to a rapid response to the first 9-1-1 call that shooting had begun at Norris Hall.

15. Cho's motives for the WAJ or Norris Hall shootings are unknown to the police or the panel. Cho's writings and videotaped pronouncements do not explain why he struck when and where he did.

16. The police response at Norris Hall was prompt and effective, as was triage and evacuation of the wounded. Evacuation of others in the building could have been implemented with more care.

17. Emergency medical care immediately following the shootings was provided very 151ervictively and timely both onsite and at the hospitals, although providers from different agencies had some difficulty communicating with one another. Communication of accurate information to hospitals standing by to receive the wounded and injured was somewhat deficient early on. An emergency operations center at Virginia Tech could have improved communications.

18. The Office of the Chief Medical Examiner properly discharged the technical aspects of its responsibility (primarily autopsies and identification of the deceased). Communication with families was poorly handled.

19. State systems for rapidly deploying trained professional staff to help families get information, crisis intervention, and referrals to a wide range of resources did not work.

20. The university established a family assistance center at The Inn at Virginia Tech, but it fell short in helping families and others for two reasons: lack of leadership and lack of coordination among service providers. University volunteers stepped in but were not trained or able to answer many questions and guide families to the resources they needed.

21. In order to advance public safety and meet public needs, Virginia's colleges and universities need to work together as a coordinated system of state-supported institutions.

As reflected in the body of the report, the panel has made more than 70 recommendations directed to colleges, universities, mental health providers, law enforcement officials, emergency service providers, law makers, and other public officials in Virginia and elsewhere.

## ADDITIONS AND CORRECTIONS

Missing Records: p. 2, Finding #4, Addition – Cho's records that were missing from the Cook Counseling Center in 2007 subsequently were found in the summer of 2009. They had been inadvertently removed by the then Director of the Counseling Center, Dr. Robert Miller, who said he found them at his home while looking for records in response to the discovery process related to legal proceedings.

Guns on Campus: p. 2, Finding #9, Addition – Virginia Tech had a "no guns" on campus policy in place in 2007.

Conflicting Policy: p. 3, Finding #13, Correction – Virginia Tech had two different emergency notification policies in effect on April 16, 2007. Their actions followed one of the policies but conflicted with the other regarding police authority to send out an alert. The mechanics of the alert system precluded police from sending an alert directly.

Timely Notification of Families of Double Homicide Victims: p. 3, New Finding #22 – Emily Hilscher (one of the victims of the double homicide at West Ambler Johnston) survived for three hours and was transported from the scene to one hospital and later transferred to another. Despite the fact that her identity was known neither Virginia Tech nor law enforcement nor hospital representatives informed her parents that she had been shot and seriously wounded, or where she had been taken for medical treatment, until after her death.

# Chapter I.

## BACKGROUND AND SCOPE

On April 16, 2007, one student, senior Seung Hui Cho, murdered 32 and injured 17 students and faculty in two related incidents on the campus of Virginia Polytechnic Institute and State University ("Virginia Tech"). Three days later, Virginia Governor Tim Kaine commissioned a panel of experts to conduct an independent, thorough, and objective review of the tragedy and to make recommendations regarding improvements to the Commonwealth's laws, policies, procedures, systems and institutions, as well as those of other governmental entities and private providers. On June 18, 2007, Governor Kaine issued Executive Order 53 reaffirming the establishment of the Virginia Tech Review Panel and clarifying the panel's authority to obtain documents and information necessary for its review. (See Executive Order 53 (2007), Appendix A.)

Each member of the appointed panel had expertise in areas relevant to its work, including Virginia's mental health system, university administration, public safety and security, law enforcement, victim services, emergency medical services, and the justice system. The panel members and their qualifications are specified in the Foreword to this report. The panel was assisted in its research and logistics by the TriData Division of System Planning Corporation (SPC).

In June, the governor appointed the law firm of Skadden, Arps, Slate, Meagher & Flom, LLP, as independent legal counsel to the panel. A team of their lawyers provided their services on a pro bono basis. Their advice helped enormously as they identified the authority needed to obtain key information and guided the panel through many sensitive legal areas related to obtaining and protecting information, public access to the panel and its work, and other issues. Their advice and counsel were invaluable.

The governor requested a report be submitted in August 2007. The panel devoted substantial time and effort from early May to late August to completing its review and preparing the report. All panel members served pro bono. The panel recognizes that some matters may need to be addressed more fully in later research.

## SCOPE

The governor's executive order directed the panel to answer the following questions:

1.  "Conduct a review of how Seung Hui Cho committed these 32 murders and multiple additional woundings, including without limitation how he obtained his firearms and ammunition, and to learn what can be learned about what caused him to commit these acts of violence.

2.  "Conduct a review of Seung Hui Cho's psychological condition and behavioral issues prior to and at the time of the shootings, what behavioral aberrations or potential warning signs were observed by students, faculty and/or staff at Westfield High School and Virginia Tech. This inquiry should include the response taken by Virginia Tech and others to note psychological and behavioral issues, Seung Hui Cho's interaction with the mental health delivery system, including without limitation judicial intervention,

access to services, and communication between the mental health services system and Virginia Tech. It should also include a review of educational, medical and judicial records documenting his condition, the services rendered to him, and his commitment hearing.

3.    "Conduct a review of the timeline of events from the time that Seung Hui Cho entered West Ambler Johnston dormitory until his death in Norris Hall. Such review shall include an assessment of the response to the first murders and efforts to stop the Norris Hall murders once they began.

4.    "Conduct a review of the response of the Commonwealth, all of its agencies, and relevant local and private providers following the death of Seung Hui Cho for the purpose of providing recommendations for the improvement of the Commonwealth's response in similar emergency situations. Such review shall include an assessment of the emergency medical response provided for the injured and wounded, the conduct of post-mortem examinations and release of remains, on-campus actions following the tragedy, and the services and counseling offered to the victims, the victims' families, and those affected by the incident. In so doing, the panel shall to the extent required by federal or state law: (i) protect the confidentiality of any individual's or family member's personal or health information; and (ii) make public or publish information and findings only in summary or aggregate form without identifying personal or health information related to any individual or family member unless authorization is obtained from an individual or family member that specifically permits the panel to disclose that person's personal or health information.

5.    "Conduct other inquiries as may be appropriate in the panel's discretion otherwise consistent with its mission and authority as provided herein.

6.    "Based on these inquiries, make recommendations on appropriate measures that can be taken to improve the laws, policies, procedures, systems and institutions of the Commonwealth and the operation of public safety agencies, medical facilities, local agencies, private providers, universities, and mental health services delivery system."

In summary, the panel was tasked to review the events, assess actions taken and not taken, identify lessons learned, and propose alternatives for the future. Its assignment included a review of Cho's history and interaction with the mental health and legal systems and of his gun purchases. The panel was also asked to review the emergency response by all parties (law enforcement officials, university officials, medical responders and hospital care providers, and the Medical Examiner). Finally, the panel reviewed the aftermath—the university's approach to helping families, survivors, students, and staff as they dealt with the mental trauma and the approach to helping the university itself heal and function again.

## METHODOLOGY

The panel used a variety of research and investigatory techniques and procedures, with the goal of conducting its review in a manner that was as open and transparent as possible, consistent with protecting individual privacy where appropriate and the confidentiality of certain records where required to do so.

Much of the panel's work was done in parallel by informal subgroups on topics such as mental health and legal issues, emergency medical services, law enforcement, and security. The panel was supplemented by SPC/TriData and Skadden staff with expertise in these areas. Throughout the process, panel members identified documents to be obtained and people to be interviewed. The list of interview subjects continued to grow as the review led to new questions and as people came forth to give information and insights to the panel.

From the beginning, the concept was to structure the review according to the broad timeline pertinent to the incidents: pre-incident (Cho's history and security status of the university); the two shooting incidents and the emergency response to them; and the aftermath. This helped ensure that all issues were covered in a logical, systematic fashion.

Openness –The panel's objective was to conduct the review process as openly as possible while maintaining confidential aspects of the police investigation, medical records, court records, academic records, and information provided in confidence. The panel's work was governed by the Virginia Freedom of Information Act, and the requirements of that act were adhered to strictly.

Requests for Documents and Information – An essential aspect of the review was the cooperation the panel received from many institutions and individuals, including the staff of Virginia Tech, Fairfax County Public School officials and employees, the families of shooting victims, survivors, the Cho family, law enforcement agencies, mental health providers, the Virginia Medical Examiner, and emergency medical responders, as well as numerous public agencies and private individuals who responded to the panel's requests for documents and information.

Notwithstanding some difficulties at the outset, the Executive Order of June 18, 2007, and the work of our outside counsel ultimately allowed the panel to obtain copies of, review, or be briefed on all records germane to its review. In this regard, however, a few matters should be noted. First, as explained more fully in the body of the report, the university's Cook Counseling Center advised the panel that it was missing certain records related to Cho that would be expected to be in the center's files.

Second, due to the sensitive nature of portions of the law enforcement investigatory record and due to law enforcement's concerns about not setting a precedent with regard to the release of raw information from investigation files, the panel received extensive briefings and summaries from law enforcement officials about their investigation rather than reviewing those files directly. These included briefings by campus police, Blacksburg Police, Montgomery County Police, Virginia State Police, FBI, and U.S. Bureau of Alcohol, Tobacco, Firearms and Explosives (ATF). The first two such briefings were conducted in private because they included protected criminal investigation information and some material that was deemed insensitive to air in public. Most of the information received in confidence was subsequently released in public briefings and through the media. Although the panel did not have direct access to criminal investigation files and materials in their entirety, the panel was able to validate the information contained in these briefings from the records it did have access to from other sources and from discussions with many of the same witnesses who spoke to the criminal investigators. The panel believes that it has obtained an accurate picture of the police response and investigation.

Finally, with respect to Cho's firearms purchases, the Virginia State Police, the ATF, and the gun dealers each declined to provide the panel with copies of the applications Cho completed when he bought his weapons or of other records relating to any background check that may have occurred in connection with those purchases. The Virginia State Police, however, did describe the contents of Cho's gun purchase applications to members of the panel and its staff.

Virginia Tech Cooperation – An essential aspect of the review was the cooperation of the Virginia Tech administration and faculty. Despite their having to deal with extraordinary problems, pressures, and demands, the university provided the panel with the records and information requested, except for a few that were missing. Some information was delayed until various privacy issues were resolved, but ultimately all records that were requested and still existed were provided. University President Charles Steger appointed a liaison to the panel, Lenwood McCoy, a retired senior university official. Requests for meetings and information went to him. He helped identify the right people to provide the requested information or obtained the information himself. The panel sometimes requested to speak to specific individuals, and all were made available. Many of the exchanges were monitored by the university's attorney, who is a special assistant state attorney general. Overall, the university was extremely cooperative with the panel, despite knowing that the panel's duty was to turn a critical eye on everything it did.

Interviews – Many interviews were conducted by panel members and staff during the course of this review—over 200. A list of persons interviewed is included in Appendix B. A few interviewees wanted to remain anonymous and are not included. Panel members and staff held numerous private meetings with family members of victims and with survivors and their family members.

One group of interviews was to obtain first-hand information about the incidents from victims and responders. This included surviving students and faculty, police, emergency medical personnel and hospital emergency care providers, and coordinators. The police used hundreds of personnel from many law enforcement agencies for their investigation, and the panel did not have nor need the resources to duplicate that effort. Rather, the panel obtained the benefit of much of the investigative information from the law enforcement agencies. Interviews were conducted with survivors, witnesses, and responders to validate the information received and to expand upon it.

To further evaluate the actions taken by law enforcement, the university, and emergency medical services against state and national standards and norms, panel members and staff also conducted interviews with leaders in these fields outside the Virginia Tech community, from elsewhere in Virginia and from other states. The panel also solicited their expert opinions on how things might have been done better, and what things were done well that should be emulated.

Interviews were conducted to understand Cho's history, including his medical and mental health treatment during his early school and university years, and his interactions with the mental health and legal systems. This included interviews with the Cho family, Cho's high school staff and faculty, staff and faculty at the university, many of those involved with the mental health treatment of Cho within and outside the university (including the Cook Counseling Center and his high school counseling), and members of the legal community who had contact with him. The assistance of attorney Wade Smith of Raleigh, NC, was important in dealing with the Cho family. He helped obtain signed releases from the family and arranged an interview with them. Various experts in mental health were consulted on the problems with the mental health and legal system within Virginia that dealt with Cho. They also provided insight on ways to identify and help such individuals in other systems.

In evaluating the aftermath—the attempt to mitigate the damage done to so many families, members of the university community, and the university itself—many interviews were conducted with family members of the victims, survivors and their families, people interacting with the families and survivors, and others. The family members were extended opportunities to speak to the panel in public or private sessions, as were the injured and some other survivors. For these groups, everyone who requested an interview was given one. Not all wanted interviews. Some wanted group interviews. Some were ready to speak earlier or later than others. To the best of the panel's knowledge, and certainly its intent, all were accommodated. The panel learned a great deal about the incident and also confronted directly the indescribable grief and loss experienced by so many. From families and survivors, the panel learned about the positive aspects of the services provided after April 16 and also about the many perceived problems with those services. The panel also considered the many issues that the family members asked to be included in the investigation. This input was invaluable and substantially improved this report.

Most of the formal interviews were conducted by one or two panel members, often with one or two TriData staff present. Some were conducted solely by staff. Generally, they were conducted in private. No recordings or written transcripts were made. All those interviewed were told that the information they provided might be used in the report but if they wished, they would not be quoted or identified. These steps were taken to encourage candor and to protect remarks that were provided with the caveat that they not be attributed to the speaker. The panel believes it was able to obtain more candid and useful information using this approach. Panel members and staff had many informal conversations with colleagues in their fields to obtain additional insights, generally not in formal settings.

Literature Research – Especially toward the beginning of the review but continuing throughout, much research was undertaken on various topics through the Internet and through information sources suggested by panel members and by individuals with whom the panel came into contact. Many useful references were submitted to the panel by the general public and experts.

Public Meetings – A key part of the panel's review process was a series of four public meetings held in different parts of the Commonwealth to accommodate those who wished to contribute information. The first meeting was held in Richmond at the state capitol complex, followed by meetings at Virginia Tech, George Mason University, and the University of Virginia. This facilitated input from the public and officials of various universities on issues they all cared deeply about. Several other universities offered facilities besides those chosen, including some out of state. Each university site was fully supported by their leadership, public relations department, event planning staff, and campus police. The Virginia State Police provided

added protection at the meetings. (The agendas of the public meetings are given in Appendix C.)

In addition to the primary speakers, every public meeting included time for public comment. In some cases the people testifying were representatives of lobbying groups, organizations, and associations, but the panel also heard from victims, family members of victims, independent experts, and concerned citizens. There was even one instance of a cameraman who put his camera down and testified. Generally, the public presenters were expected to restrict themselves to a few minutes, and most did not abuse the opportunity. At one meeting, more people wanted to speak than time available, even though the meeting was extended an hour. Those not able to present information still had the opportunity to submit it to the panel through letters, e-mails, or phone calls, and many did.

Web Site and Post Office Box – Shortly after the panel was formed, its staff created a web site that was used both to inform the public and to receive input from the public. It proved to be very valuable. There was a minimum of spam or inappropriate inputs. The web site was used to post announcements of public meetings and to post presentations made or visual aids used at meetings. More than 400,000 "hits" were recorded, with 26,000 unique visitors. The web site also was advertised as a vehicle for anyone to post information or opinions. As of August 9, 2007, more than 2,000 comments were posted from experts in various fields as well as the general public, victims, families of victims, and others as follows:

| | |
|---|---|
| Parents (self-identified) | 251 |
| General public | 1,547 |
| Educators | 91 |
| EMS | 8 |
| Students | 48 |
| Law enforcement officers | 18 |
| Family members of victims | 12 |
| Health professionals | 102 |
| Virginia Tech staff | 2 |
| Total | 2,079 |

Most persons who submitted information to the web site appeared sincere about making a contribution. Some lobbying groups on issues such as gun control, carrying guns on campus, and the influence of video games on young people clearly urged their members to post comments.

A post office box also was opened for the public to address comments directly to the panel. The number of letters received was much smaller than the number of e-mails but generally with a high percentage of relevancy, especially from experts, families, and victims.

Telephone Calls and E-Mails – Some information was received directly by panel members or staff through phone calls or e-mails. Much of this information was received by one panel member or staff member and was shared with others when thought important.

Panel Interactions – The members of the Virginia Tech Review Panel engaged on a personal level, participating in the majority of interviews conducted and exchanging many e-mails and phone calls among themselves and with the panel staff. The panel was impeded by the FOIA rules that did not allow more than two members to meet together or speak by phone without it being considered a public meeting.

## FINDINGS AND RECOMMENDATIONS

The panel's findings and recommendations are provided throughout the report. Recommendations regarding the methodology used by the panel are presented in Appendix D; they were put in an appendix to avoid having the procedural issues distract the reader from the heart of the main issues.

The findings and related recommendations in this report are of two kinds. The first comes from reviewing actions taken in a time of crisis: what was done very well, and what could have been done better. Almost any crisis actions can be improved, even if they were exemplary.

The second type of finding identifies major administrative or procedural failings leading up to the events, such as failing to "connect the dots" of Cho's highly bizarre behavior; the

missing records at Cook Counseling Center; insensitivity to survivors waiting to learn the fates of their children, siblings, or spouses; and fundraising that appeared opportunistic.

To help in understanding the events, the report begins in Chapter II with a description of the setting of the Virginia Tech campus and its preparedness for a disaster. In Chapter III, a detailed timeline serves as a reference throughout the report—the succinct story of what happened, starting with Cho's background, his treatment, and then proceeding to the events of April 16 and its aftermath. The events are elaborated in subsequent chapters.

## ADDITIONS AND CORRECTIONS

Time for Study: p. 5, Addition – The Report noted that the Governor wanted the Report completed by August 2007. A key motivation for this deadline was to get recommendations for campus security improvements disseminated before the start of the school year in Virginia. Also, the deadline was thought necessary to allow time for developing a legislative agenda (suggested changes to laws and policies) needed to implement some of the Report's recommendations in time for Virginia's annual legislative session in January. Further, the Governor wanted to get information out to the families of victims and to the general public as soon as possible.

Access to Records: p. 7, Clarification – The Report said that…"ultimately all records that were requested [from Virginia Tech] and still existed were provided." At the time, Cho's file at the Cook Counseling Center was missing. An extensive search by Virginia Tech, including contact with the previous CCC director, Dr. Miller, did not turn up the file, and no one knew if it still existed. The file was found two years later by Dr. Miller in his home in response to a discovery request by attorneys involved in a lawsuit.

Cooperativeness of University: pp. 7-8, Clarification – Some victims' families questioned whether Virginia Tech should be characterized as "extremely cooperative" with the Review Panel, and whether having a point of contact to obtain information and arrange interviews was a barrier imposed by Virginia Tech. In fact, it was the Review Panel staff that requested a point of contact to facilitate such things as finding and scheduling Virginia Tech faculty and staff for interviews. Reporters, law enforcement officials, and others were pressing for interviews with many of the same Virginia Tech employees that the Review Panel wanted to interview. Having a point of contact streamlined and prioritized the Review Panel's access.

The person appointed by Virginia Tech to be the contact was highly cooperative and greatly facilitated obtaining information. Not surprisingly there were some Virginia Tech faculty and staff who were guarded in discussions with the Review Panel possibly as a result of being interviewed with other Virginia Tech officials present.

(This page intentionally left blank.)

# Chapter II.

## UNIVERSITY SETTING AND SECURITY

Before describing the details of the events, it is necessary to understand the setting in which they took place, including the security situation at Virginia Tech at the time of the shootings. This chapter focuses on the physical security of the campus and its system for alerting the university community in an emergency. It also gives a brief background on the campus police department and the university's Emergency Response Plan. The prevention aspect of security—including the identification of people who pose safety threats—is discussed in Chapter IV.

### UNIVERSITY SETTING

Virginia Tech occupies a beautiful, sprawling campus near the Blue Ridge Mountains in southwest Virginia. It is a state school known for its engineering and science programs but with a wide range of other academic fields in the liberal arts.

The main campus has 131 major buildings spread over 2,600 acres. The campus is not enclosed; anyone can walk or drive onto it. There are no guarded roads or gateways. Cars can enter on any of 16 road entrances, many of which are not in line of sight of each other. Pedestrians can use sidewalks or simply walk across grassy areas to get onto the campus. Figure 1 shows aerial views of the campus. There is a significant amount of ongoing construction of new buildings and renovation of existing buildings, with associated noise.

On April 16, the campus population was about 34,500, as follows:

| | |
|---|---|
| 26,370 | students (9,000 live in dorms) |
| 7,133 | university employees (not counting student employees) visitors, |
| 1,000 | contractors, transit workers, etc. |
| 34,503 | Total |

### CAMPUS POLICE AND OTHER LOCAL LAW ENFORCEMENT

A key element in the security of Virginia Tech is its police department. It is considered among the leading campus police departments in the state. While many campuses employ security guards, the Virginia Tech Police Department (VTPD) is an accredited police force. Its officers are trained as a full-fledged police department with an emergency response team (ERT), which is like a SWAT team.

The police chief reports to a university vice president.

On April 16, the VTPD strength was 35 officers. It had 41 positions authorized but 6 were vacant. The day shift, which comes on duty at 7 a.m., has 5 officers. Additionally, 9 officers work office hours, 8 a.m. to 5 p.m., including the chief, for a total of 14 on a typical weekday morning. On April 16, approximately 34 of the officers came to work at some point during the day.

The campus police could not handle a major event by themselves with these numbers, and so they have entered into a mutual aid agreement with the Blacksburg Police Department (BPD) for immediate response and assistance. They frequently train together, and had trained for an active shooter situation in a campus building before the incident. As will be seen, this preparation was critical.

The VT campus police also have excellent working relationships with the regional offices of the state police, FBI, and ATF. The high level of cooperation was confirmed by each of the federal, state, and local law enforcement agencies that were involved in the events on April 16, and by the rapidity of coordination of their response to the incident and the investigation that followed. Training together, working cases together, and

*Figure 1. Aerial Views of Virginia Tech Campus*

knowing each other on a first-name basis can be critical when an emergency occurs and a highly coordinated effort is needed.

The purpose of the Virginia Tech campus police is stated in the university's Emergency Response Plan as follows: "The primary purpose of the VTPD is to support the academics through maintenance of a peaceful and orderly community and through provision of needed general and emergency services." Although some do not consider police department mission statements of much importance versus how they actually operate, the mission statement may affect their role by indicating priorities. For example, it may influence a decision as to whether the university puts minimizing disruption to the educational process first and acting on the side of precaution second. There are many crimes and false alarms such as bomb threats on campus, and it is often difficult to make the decision on taking precautions that are disruptive. The police mission statement also may affect availability of student information. Explicitly including the police under the umbrella of university officials may allow them to access student records under Family Educational Rights and Privacy Act (FERPA) regulations.

Several leaders of the campus police chiefs of Virginia commented that they do not always have adequate input into security planning and threat assessment or the authority to access important information on students.

## BUILDING SECURITY

The residence halls on campus require placing a student or staff keycard in an electronic card reader in order to enter between 10:00 p.m. and 10:00 a.m. A student access card is valid only for his or her own dormitory and for the mailbox area of another dormitory if one's assigned mailbox is there.

Many other school buildings are considered public spaces and are open 24 hours a day. The university encourages students to use the facilities for class work, informal meetings, and officially sanctioned clubs and groups.

Most classrooms, such as those in Norris Hall, have no locks. Staff offices generally do have locks, including those in Norris Hall.

There are no guards at campus buildings or cameras at the entrances or in hallways of any buildings. Anyone can enter most buildings. It is an open university.

Some buildings have loudspeaker systems intended primarily for use of the fire department in an emergency. They were not envisioned for use by police. They can only be used by someone standing at a panel in each building and cannot be accessed for a campus-wide broadcast from a central location.

This level of security is quite typical of many campuses across the nation in rural areas with low crime rates. Some universities are partially or completely fenced, with guards at exterior entrances; usually these are in urban areas. Some universities have guards at the entrance to each building and screen anyone coming in without student or staff identification, again usually on urban campuses. Some universities have locks on classroom doors, but they typically operate by key from the hallway. They are intended to keep students and strangers out when they are not in use and often cannot be locked from the inside.

A few universities (e.g., Hofstra University in Nassau County, NY) now have the ability to lock the exterior doors of some or all buildings at the push of a button in a central security office. Most require manual operation of locks. Virginia Tech would have to call people in scores of buildings or send someone to the buildings to lock their outside doors (except for dormitories between 10 p.m. and 10 a.m. when they are locked automatically).

Many levels of campus security existed at colleges and universities across Virginia and the nation on April 16. A basic mission of institutions of higher education is to provide a peaceful, open campus setting that encourages freedom of movement and expression. Different institutions provide more or less security, often based on their locations (urban, suburban, or rural), size and complexity (from research universities to small private colleges), and resources. April 16 has become the 9/11 for colleges and universities. Most have reviewed their security plans since then. The installation of security systems already planned or in progress has accelerated, including those at Virginia Tech.

Although the 2004 General Assembly directed the Virginia State Crime Commission to study campus safety at Virginia's institutions of higher education (HJR 122), the report issued December 31, 2005, did not reflect the need for urgent corrective actions. So far as the panel is aware, there was no outcry from parents, students, or faculty for improving VT campus security prior to April 16. Most people liked the relaxed and open atmosphere at Virginia Tech. There had been concern the previous August about an escaped convict and killer named William Morva whose escape in the VT vicinity unnerved many people. Also, some campus assaults led some students to want to arm themselves. However, if the April 16 incident had not occurred, it is doubtful that security issues would be on the minds of parents and students more than at other universities, where the most serious crimes tend to be rapes, assaults, and dangerous activity related to alcohol or drug abuse by students. These issues were addressed by the State Crime Commission Report and were given an average level of attention at Virginia Tech.

## CAMPUS ALERTING SYSTEMS

Virginia Tech was in the process of upgrading its campus-wide alerting system in spring 2007.

Existing System – Virginia Tech had the capability on April 16 to send messages to the student body, faculty, and other staff via a broadcast e-mail system. The associate vice president for University Relations had the authority and capability to send a message from anywhere that was connected to the web. Almost every student and faculty member on campus has a computer and e-mail address (estimated at 96 percent by the university). Most but not all student computers are portable. Many

are carried to classes. However, an e-mail message sent by the university may not get read by every user within minutes or even hours. The e-mail system had 36,000 registered e-mail addresses. Distribution of an emergency message occurred at a rate of about 10,000 per minute.

The university also has a web site that it uses to post emergency warnings, mostly for weather events. The system has high-volume capacity. (As events unfolded on April 16, the VT web site was receiving 148,000 visits per hour.) An emergency message can be put in a box on the web site that anyone reaching the site would see no matter what they were looking for.

The university also has contacts with every local radio and TV station. The Virginia Tech associate vice president for University Relations has a code by which he can send emergency messages to the stations that could be played immediately. This process could take 20 minutes or so because each station has its own code to validate the sender. The validation codes are necessary because students or members of the public could send spoof messages to the media as a prank. The public media are used for the occasional weather emergencies, and the campus community is trained to tune in to get further information.

An estimated 96 percent of students at Virginia Tech carry cell phones according to the university. Most bring them to classes or wherever else they go. A text message to cell phones probably will reach more students faster than an e-mail message because the devices are more portable and can be rung. But some are forgotten, turned off, or intentionally not carried. The university was still in the process of installing a text messaging system on April 16 and had no way to send a message to all cell phones.

Personal digital assistants (or PDAs) such as Blackberries are used by fewer students and faculty than cell phones because they are more expensive and are not as capable as computers. They have the capacity to receive e-mails and would be treated either as a computer or as a phone or both, depending on how it is ervitered.

The university also has a broadcast phone-mail system that allows it to send a phone message to all phone numbers registered with its messaging system. VT used this system to send messages to all faculty offices and some students on April 16. Students and faculty must voluntarily register their phones with this system if they want to be notified. It takes time to reach all the phones; 11 separate actions are required to send a broadcast message to all registered numbers, said the associate vice president for University Relations. It is not a useful approach when time is critical.

A university switchboard with up to four operators is working during normal business hours. It can handle hundreds of calls per hour.

To augment the range of messaging systems it had available, the university was in the process of installing six outdoor loudspeakers to make emergency announcements. Some are mounted on buildings and others on poles, as shown in Figure 2. They can be used for either a voice message or an audible alarm (such as a siren). Four had been installed and were used on April 16, but they did not play a significant role in this incident. (The announcement was made after the 9:05 a.m. class period in which the mass shooting had already started.)

As part of its emergency planning, the university has another system in place as a last-ditch resort—using resident advisors in dorms and floor wardens in some older classroom and office buildings to personally spread a warning. In Norris Hall, for example, the chairman of the Engineering Mechanics Department, whose office was on the second floor, said he had been issued a bullhorn to make announcements and was instructed to rap on classroom and office doors to alert people if there was an emergency and other notification systems failed, if a personal approach was needed to convey safety information, or if an evacuation or sheltering in place was required

*Figure 2. One of the Six Sirens Being Installed on Virginia Tech Campus*

New Unified Campus Alerting System – In spring 2007, Virginia Tech was in the process of installing a unified, multimedia messaging system to be completed before the next semester. It would allow university officials to send an emergency message that would flow in parallel to computers, cell phones, PDAs, and telephones. The message could be sent by anyone who is registered in the system as having authority to send one, using a code word for validation. The president of the university or associate vice president of University Relations can be anywhere and send a message to everyone—all that is needed is an Internet connection.

Students must be registered with the new system to receive messages. A student can provide a mobile phone number, e-mail address(es), or instant messaging system to be contacted in an emergency. Parents' numbers can be included. All students and staff are encouraged but not required to register with the new system. Each user can set the priority order in which their devices are to be called. The message will cascade through the hierarchy set by each user[1] until it gets answered. This system has the enormous advantage of transmitting a message to the entire university community in less than a minute.

For the Virginia Tech community of about 35,000 users, the system will cost $33,000 a year to operate and no out-of-pocket expense to start. However, it takes considerable staff time to select a system and then oversee its startup. The operating cost is a function of the bandwidth used and the frequency of messages. The more people and devices on the system and the more messages sent per year, the higher the cost. Initially, Virginia Tech is planning to use the system only for emergency messages. Other schools have started using such systems for more routine purposes such as sending information about special events on campus and administrative information, at an extra charge. Virginia Tech was willing to share the criteria it used in its selection of a messaging system (Appendix E). Several competing commercial options have excellent capabilities. Some are only suitable for small schools. Universities and colleges need to balance their needs and the system capability versus costs.

Message Content and Authorization – A critical part of security is not only having the Technical communication capability of reaching students and staff quickly, but also planning what to say and how quickly to say it. Pursuant to its Emergency Response Plan in effect on April 16, the Virginia Tech Policy Group and the police chief could authorize sending an emergency message to all students and staff. Typically, the police chief would make a decision about the timing and content of a message after consultation with the Policy Group, which is comprised of the president and several other vice presidents and senior officials. This process of having the Policy Group decide on the message was used during the April 16 incidents.

However, while the Virginia Tech campus police had the authority to send a message, they did not have the technical means to do so. Only two people, the associate vice president for University Relations and the director of News and Information, had the codes to send a message. The police could not access the alerting system to send a message. The police had to contact the university leadership on the need and proposed content of a message. As a matter of course, the police would usually be consulted if not directly involved in the decision regarding the sending of an alert for an emergency.

There are no preset messages for different types of emergencies, as some public agencies have in order to speed crafting of an emergency message. All VT messages are developed for the particular incident.

The timing and content of the messages sent by the university are one of the major controversies concerning the events of April 16. (Chapter VIII addresses the double homicide at West Ambler Johnston residence hall and the messaging decisions that followed).

**EMERGENCY RESPONSE PLAN**

The university's Emergency Response Plan deals with preparedness and response to a variety of emergencies, but nothing specific to shootings. The version in effect on April 16 was about 2 years old. Emergencies such as weather problems, fires, and terrorism were in the fore of [2]VT emergency planning pre-April 16.

The plan addresses different levels of emergencies, designated as levels 0, I, II, and III. The Norris Hall event was level III, the highest, based on the number of lives lost, the physical and psychological damage suffered by the injured, and the psychological impact on a very large number of people.

The plan calls for an official to be designated as an emergency response coordinator (ERC) to direct a response. It also calls for the

---

[1] A system being developed sends a message to anyone with-in range of a tower or set of towers. It does not matter who you are or whether you have "registered"; if you have a cell phone and are in range, you get the message.

[2] Appendix F has an example of the "active shooter" part of the University of Virginia's plan, and something similar should be included in the Virginia Tech plan.

establishment of an emergency operations center (EOC). Satellite operations centers may be established to assist the ERC. As will be discussed in describing the response to the events, there were multiple coordinators and multiple operations centers but not a central EOC on April 16.

Two key decision groups are identified in the Emergency Response Plan: the Policy Group and the Emergency Response Resources Group. The Policy Group is comprised of nine vice presidents and support staff, chaired by the university president. The Policy Group deals with procedures to support emergency operations and to determine recovery priorities. In the events of April 16, it also decided on the messages sent and the immediate actions taken by the university after the first incident as well as the second mass shooting. The Policy Group sits above the emergency coordinator for an incident. It does not include a member of the campus police, but the campus police are usually asked to have a representative at its meetings.

The second key group, the Emergency Response Resources Group (ERRG), includes a vice president designated to be in charge of an incident, police officials, and others depending on the nature of the event. It is to ensure that the resources needed to support the Policy Group and needs of the emergency are available. The ERRG is organized and directed by the emergency response coordinator. The ERRG is supposed to meet at the EOC. Decisions made by these groups and their members on April 16 are addressed in the remainder of the report, as the event is described.

The VT Emergency Response Plan does not deal with prevention of events, such as establishing a threat assessment team to identify classes of threats and to assess the risk of specific problems and specific individuals. There are threat assessment models used elsewhere that have proven successful. For example, at two college campuses in Virginia, the chief operating officer receives daily reports of all incidents to which law enforcement responded the previous day, including violation of the student conduct code up to criminal activity. This information is then routinely shared with appropriate offices which are responsible for safety and health on campus.

## KEY FINDINGS

The Emergency Response Plan of Virginia Tech was deficient in several respects. It did not include provisions for a shooting scenario and did not place police high enough in the emergency decision-making hierarchy. It also did not include a threat assessment team. And the plan was out of date on April 16; for example, it had the wrong name for the police chief and some other officials.

The protocol for sending an emergency message in use on April 16 was cumbersome, untimely, and problematic when a decision was needed as soon as possible. The police did not have the capability to send an emergency alert message on their own. The police had to await the deliberations of the Policy Group, of which they are not a member, even when minutes count. The Policy Group had to be convened to decide whether to send a message to the university community and to structure its content.

The training of staff and students for emergencies situations at Virginia Tech did not include shooting incidents. A messaging system works more effectively if resident advisors in dormitories, all faculty, and all other staff from janitors to the president have instruction and training for coping with emergencies of all types.

It would have been extremely difficult to "lock down" Virginia Tech. The size of the police force and absence of a guard force, the lack of electronic controls on doors of most buildings other than residence halls, and the many unguarded roadways pose special problems for a large rural or suburban university. The police and security officials consulted in this review did not think the concept of a lockdown, as envisioned for elementary or high schools, was feasible for an institution such as Virginia Tech.

It is critical to alert the entire campus population when there is an imminent danger. There are information technologies available to rapidly send messages to a variety of personal communication devices. Many colleges and universities, including Virginia Tech, are installing such campus-wide alerting systems. Any purchased system must be thoroughly tested to ensure it operates as specified in the purchase contract. Some universities already have had problems with systems purchased since April 16.

An adjunct to a sophisticated communications alert system is a siren or other audible warning device. It can give a quick warning that something is afoot. One can hear such alarms regardless of whether electronics are carried, whether the electronics are turned off, or whether electric power (other than for the siren, which can be self-powered) is available. Upon sounding, every individual is to immediately turn on some communication device or call to receive further instructions. Virginia Tech has installed a system of six audible alerting devices of which four were in place on April 16. Many other colleges and universities have done something similar.

No security cameras were in the dorms or anywhere else on campus on April 16. The outcome might have been different had the perpetrator of the initial homicides been rapidly identified. Cameras may be placed just at entrances to buildings or also in hallways. However, the more cameras, the more intrusion on university life.

Virginia Tech did not have classroom door locks operable from the inside of the room. Whether to add such locks is controversial. They can block entry of an intruder and compartmentalize an attack. Locks can be simple manually operated devices or part of more sophisticated systems that use electromechanical locks operated from a central security point in a building or even university-wide. The locks must be easily opened from the inside to allow escape from a fire or other emergency when that is the safer course of action. While adding locks to classrooms may seem an obvious safety feature, some voiced concern that locks could facilitate rapes or assaults in classrooms and increase university liability. (An attacker could drag someone inside a room at night and lock the door, blocking assistance.) On the other hand, a locked room can be a place of refuge when one is pursued. On balance, the panel generally thought having locks on classroom doors was a good idea.

Shootings at universities are rare events, an average of about 16 a year across 4,000 institutions. Bombings are rarer but still possible. Arson is more common and drunk driving incidents more frequent yet. There are both simple and sophisticated improvements to consider for improving security (besides upgrading the alerting system). A risk analysis needs to be performed and decisions made as to what risks to protect against.

There have been several excellent reviews of campus security by states and individual campuses (for example, the states of Florida and Louisiana, the University of California, and the University of Maryland). The Commonwealth of Virginia held a conference on campus security on August 13, 2007.

The VTPD and BPD were well-trained and had conducted practical exercises together. They had undergone active shooter training to prepare for the possibility of a multiple victim shooter.

The entire police patrol force must be trained in the active shooter protocol, because any officer may be called upon to respond.

It was the strong opinion of groups of Virginia college and university presidents with whom the panel met that the state should not impose required levels of security on all institutions, but rather let the institutions choose what they think is appropriate. Parents and students can and do consider security a factor in making a choice of where to go to school.

Finally, the panel found that the VTPD statement of purpose in the Emergency Response Plan does not reflect that law enforcement is the primary purpose of the police department.

# RECOMMENDATIONS

## EMERGENCY PLANNING

II-1 Universities should do a risk analysis (threat assessment) and then choose a level of security appropriate for their campus. How far to go in safeguarding campuses, and from which threats, need to be considered by each institution. Security requirements vary across universities, and each must do its own threat assessment to determine what security measures are appropriate.

II-2 Virginia Tech should update and enhance its Emergency Response Plan and bring it into compliance with federal and state guidelines.

II-3 Virginia Tech and other institutions of higher learning should have a threat assessment team that includes representatives from law enforcement, human resources, student and academic affairs, legal counsel, and mental health functions. The team should be empowered to take actions such as additional investigation, gathering background information, identification of additional dangerous warning signs, establishing a threat potential risk level (1 to 10) for a case, preparing a case for hearings (for instance, commitment hearings), and disseminating warning information.

II-4 Students, faculty, and staff should be trained annually about responding to various emergencies and about the notification systems that will be used. An annual reminder provided as part of registration should be considered.

II-5 Universities and colleges must comply with the Clery Act, which requires timely public warnings of imminent danger. "Timely" should be defined clearly in the federal law.

## CAMPUS ALERTING

II-6 Campus emergency communications systems must have multiple means of sharing information.

II-7 In an emergency, immediate messages must be sent to the campus community that provide clear information on the nature of the emergency and actions to be taken The initial messages should be followed by update messages as more information becomes known.

II-8 Campus police as well as administration officials should have the authority and capability to send an emergency message. Schools without a police department or senior security official must designate someone able to make a quick decision without convening a committee.

## POLICE ROLE AND TRAINING

II-9 The head of campus police should be a member of a threat assessment team as well as the emergency response team for the university. In some cases where there is a security department but not a police department, the security head may be appropriate.

II-10 Campus police must report directly to the senior operations officer responsible for emergency decision making. They should be part of the policy team deciding on emergency planning.

II-11 Campus police must train for active shooters (as did the Virginia Tech Police Department). Experience has shown that waiting for a SWAT team often takes too long. The best chance to save lives is often an immediate assault by first responders.

II-12 The mission statement of campus police should give primacy to their law enforcement and crime prevention role. They also must to be designated as having a function in education so as to be able to review records of students brought to the attention of the university as potential threats. The lack of emphasis on safety as the first responsibility of the police department may create the wrong mindset, with the police yielding to academic considerations when it comes time to make decisions on, say, whether to send out an alert to the students that may disrupt classes. On the other hand, it is useful to identify the police as being involved in the education role in order for them to gain access to records under educational privacy act provisions.

Specific findings and recommendations on police actions taken on April 16 are addressed in the later chapters.

## ADDITIONS AND CORRECTIONS

Multijurisdictional Police Training: p. 8, Correction – Campus and Blacksburg police had trained together for an active shooter incident as was noted in the Report, but the training was conducted in an empty school building off campus, not on campus.

Mailbox Access and Targeting of Initial Victim: p. 11, Clarification – Some students were assigned mailboxes located in a different dorm from their own. They could access their mailbox after 7:30 a.m. Cho was one of these students. He lived in Harper Hall but his mailbox was in West Ambler Johnston where he committed the first two murders. He had access and reason to be in the mailbox area of WAJ, which may help explain why he chose it. It also was a short walk from his dorm. His motivation for the initial killings still has not been determined. He had no known relationship with Emily Hilscher, nor with her roommate. It is not known and may never be known whether he had targeted Ms. Hilscher beforehand or just happened upon her that fateful morning.

Reason for Closely Held Alert Code: p. 14, Addition – Access codes were required in order to send messages on the campus alerting system and to distribute information to the local media stations at least in part because students had previously sent prank messages about non-existent emergencies. Virginia Tech wanted the alerting system to prevent unauthorized alerts and to validate the emergency messages they broadcast.

Joint Homicide Investigation: p. 18, Addition – While the Virginia Tech and Blacksburg Police Departments had trained and worked well together, including practice for an active shooter, the VTPD had not investigated a homicide since 1984. Its chief and detectives did not have experience as primary investigators for a homicide. Blacksburg investigators had homicide experience, as did the State Police, and VTPD requested immediate assistance from them in the investigation of the shooting.

## OTHER COMMENTS

Frequency of Campus Shootings: Commenter wanted text on page 18 to read that shootings are becoming more frequent, rather than rare, events.

Response: There was no data provided which showed an increasing trend in frequency over recent years compared to earlier years. The data provided did not focus on universities.

On-Duty Psychiatrist at CCC: Commenter claimed that there was no psychiatrist on duty at the CCC after Dr. Miller's departure until the arrival of Dr. Flynn.

Response: There were several psychiatrists on duty during this time period. Dr. Miller was reassigned in January/February 2006. From January through April 2006, Dr. Gary Rooker, a Virginia Tech employee, was the psychiatrist available to assist students. Dr. Brian Bladykus was hired in June of 2006 and worked through February of 2007. Dr. Joseph Frieben was hired half-time August 10, 2006 and full-time on July 1, 2007. Thus, there was a psychiatrist available except for a one-month period in May 2006. When Dr. Flynn started in September 2006, both Dr. Bladykus and Dr. Frieben were at the CCC. Also, throughout this period, Vicki Arbuckle, a psychiatric nurse practitioner, was on staff.

(This page intentionally left blank.)

# Chapter III.

## REVISED TIMELINE OF EVENTS

The modifications to this chapter resulted primarily from additional information identified and made available since the original Report was published.

In constructing both the original and the revised timelines, care was taken to confirm the dates and times through multiple sources where possible. However, even with the newly available information, some of the times provided are approximate, because not every message, phone call and event was time-stamped. In a few cases where no documentation existed it was necessary to rely on individuals' best recollections of times. Many of the interviews for the original timeline were conducted in the weeks immediately after the shootings. Some individuals reported dates and times as they knew them to be true at that time; however, in a few cases they were misinformed. The revised timeline corrects those errors and adds more details.

The original wording of the timeline generally was preserved except where new information required a change or addition.

The following timeline provides highlights of the events leading up to the tragedy on April 16, 2007 the actions taken on April 16, and some subsequent actions. The time scale switches from years to months to days and even to minutes as appropriate. The timeline is an overview and composite of major events, with additional facts and details discussed in the respective chapters. Therefore, the timeline does not include all the details covered later in the chapters, but, rather, is intended to serve as a framework for the reader. The timeline and the Report begin with Seung Hui Cho's childhood and end with Governor Kaine's declaration of a day of mourning, April 20, 2007.

The information here was drawn from numerous interviews, written sources, and briefings. The Cho family and Seung Hui Cho's school administrators, counselors, teachers, and medical and school records are the prime sources for his history prior to attending Virginia Tech.

Information obtained about his Virginia Tech years before the shootings came from interviews with faculty, counselors, administrators, police, courts, psychological evaluators, suitemates,

and others. The panel also had access to many Virginia Tech, medical, and court records and to e-mails and other written materials involving Cho.

The timeline for the events of April 16 relied primarily on Virginia Tech Police Department (VTPD) and Virginia State Police (VSP) reports and interviews, supplemented by interviews with survivors, Virginia Tech officials, emergency medical responders, hospitals, state officials and others.

The information on the aftermath drew on medical examiner records, interviews with families and other sources.

Each aspect of the timeline is discussed further in the following chapters, with an evaluation as well as narration of events.

### PRE-INCIDENTS: CHO'S HISTORY

| 1986–2000 |
|---|
| 1984    Seung Hui Cho is born to a family living in a small two-room apartment in Seoul, South Korea. He is an inordinately shy, quiet child, but no problem to his family. He has serious health problems from 9 |

months to 3 years old, is frail, and after unpleasant medical procedures does not want to be touched.

1992   Cho's family emigrates to Maryland when he is 8 years old.

1993   The Cho family moves to Fairfax County, Virginia, when he is 9 years old. They work long hours in a dry-cleaning business.

1997   Seung Hui in the 6th grade continues to be very withdrawn. Teachers meet with his parents about this behavior. In the summer before he enters 7th grade, he begins receiving counseling at the Center for Multicultural Human Services to address his shy, introverted nature, which is diagnosed as "selective mutism." Parents try to socialize him more by encouraging extracurricular activities and friends, but he remains withdrawn.

1999   During the 8th grade, one of Cho's writings for a teacher depicts suicidal and homicidal ideations. The paper references and celebrates the Columbine shootings in April of this year. The school requests that his parents ask a counselor to intervene, which leads to a psychiatric evaluation at the Multicultural Center for Human Services. He is prescribed antidepressant medication. He responds well and is taken off the medication approximately one year later.

## 2000–2003 (High School)

Fall 2000   Cho starts Westfield High School in Fairfax County as a sophomore, after attending another high school in Centreville for a year. After review by the "local screening committee," he is diagnosed as having an emotional disability and is enrolled in an Individual Educational Program (IEP) to deal with his shyness and lack of responsiveness in a classroom setting. Art therapy (his selective mutism rules out talk therapy as an effective treatment mode) continues with the Multicultural Center for Human Services through his junior year. He has no behavior problems, keeps his appointments, and makes no threats. He gets good grades and adjusts reasonably to the school environment. The guidance office in the school Believes he has been academically successful and the therapist notes he has made limited progress in communicating.

June 2003   Cho graduates from Westfield High School with a 3.5 GPA in the Honors Program. He decides to attend Virginia Tech against the advice of his parents and counselors, who think that it is too large a school for him and that he will not receive adequate individual attention. He is given the name of a contact at the high school if he needs help in college, but never avails himself of it.

## 2003–2004 (Virginia Tech)

August 2003   Cho enters Virginia Tech as a business information systems major. Little attention is drawn to him during his freshman year. He has a difficult time with his roommate over neatness issues and changes rooms. His parents make weekly trips to visit him. His grades are good. He does not see a counselor at school or home. He is excited about college.

Fall 2004   Cho begins his sophomore year. Cho moves off campus to room with a senior who is rarely at home. Cho complains of mites in the apartment, but doctors tell him it is acne and prescribe minocycline. He becomes interested in writing. His grades begin to slip so he decides he will switch his major to English beginning his junior year. His sister notes a growing passion for writing over the winter break, though he is secretive about its content. Cho submits a book idea to a publishing house.

## 2005 (Virginia Tech)

**Spring 2005**   Cho requests a change of major to English. The idea for a book sent to a New York publishing house is rejected. This seems to depress him, according to his family. He still sees no counselor at school or home, and exhibits no behavioral problems other than his quietness.

**Fall 2005**   Cho starts his junior year and moves back into the dorms. Serious problems begin to surface. His sister notes that he is writing less at home, is less enthusiastic, and wonders if the publisher's rejection letter curbed his enthusiasm for writing. At school, Cho is taken to some parties by his suitemates at the start of the semester. On one such occasion he stabs at the carpet in student Margaret Bowman's room with a knife, in the presence of his suitemates.

**October 15**   English Professor Nikki Giovanni writes a letter to Cho expressing her concern about his behavior in her class and about violence in his writing. She offers to help get him into another class.

Professor Giovanni asks department chair Dr. Lucinda Roy to remove Cho from her class.

**October 18**   Dr. Roy informs Mary Ann Lewis, Associate Dean of Liberal Arts and Human Sciences, and others that Cho read a violent and upsetting "poem" in Professor Giovanni's class that day, and that her students said Cho had been surreptitiously taking photos of them. Dr. Roy also says she has contacted Tom Brown (Dean of Student Affairs), Zenobia Hikes (Vice President of Student Affairs), Detective George Jackson at Virginia Tech Police Department (VTPD), and Dr. Robert Miller at the Cook Counseling Center (CCC), to report the incident and seek advice. Tom Brown advises Dr. Roy she can remove Cho from Professor Giovanni's class as long as a viable alternative is offered.

CCC advises that though the "poem" is disturbing, there is no specific threat. They suggest that Cho be referred to the CCC. Frances Keene (Director of Judicial Affairs) and Tom Brown both write to Dr. Roy indicating their concurrence with this plan. Brown tells Dr. Roy to advise Cho that any future similar behavior will be referred [to Judicial Affairs].

**October 19**   Dr. Roy and Cheryl Ruggiero meet with Cho regarding his situation in Professor Giovanni's class, discuss the impact of his writing on the class, and warn that unauthorized picture-taking is inappropriate, and is taken seriously by Virginia Tech. Cho says his writing was intended as satire and agrees not to take any more photos of classmates or professors. Cho is advised of the study alternative available. He is advised to seek counseling. This is reiterated in an e-mail to Cho following the meeting.

Following the above, Dr. Roy removes Cho from Professor Giovanni's class and tutors him one-on-one with assistance from Professor Frederick D'Aguiar. Cho refuses to go to counseling, and Dr. Roy tells this to the Division of Student Affairs, the CCC, the Schiffert Health Center, the Virginia Tech police, and the College of Liberal Arts and Human Sciences. Cho's problems are discussed at a meeting of Virginia Tech's Care Team that reviews students with problems. Care Team members discuss the arrangement worked out to remove Cho from Professor Giovanni's class and tutor him and that Dr. Roy had met with Cho and documented the results. The Care Team considers the problem solved.

November 2   Cho's roommates and dorm residents think Cho set fires in a dorm lounge and say in e-mails that they reported it to police. However, no written police report exists.

November 27   Jennifer Nelson, a resident of West Ambler Johnston (WAJ) resident hall in room 4021, files a report with VTPD indicating that Cho has made "annoying" contact with her on the Internet, by phone, and in person. VTPD interviews Cho, but Nelson declines to press charges, though she says she would testify at a disciplinary hearing. The investigating officer refers the incident to the school's disciplinary system, the Office of Judicial Affairs. The Office of Judiciary Affairs later contacts Nelson, telling her they can only proceed if she files a written complaint. She declines and no hearing is held.

November 30   Cho calls CCC and is triaged (i.e., given a preliminary screening) by phone following his interaction with VTPD.

December 6   E-mails among resident advisors (Ras) reflect complaints by another female student, Christina Lillizu, who lives on the 3rd floor of Cochrane resident hall, regarding derogatory instant messages (Ims) with foul language sent from Cho under various strange aliases. The Ras also report the incidents of Ims Cho to Jennifer Nelson, and his visit in disguise to her dorm room.

Lisa Virga, a resident advisor, sends an e-mail to Rohsaan Settle, a member of the Residence Life staff, detailing a list of complaints about Cho, including a report that he has knives in his room. Virga is concerned that no one in the dorms has confronted Cho directly and she thinks someone should talk to him. Settle responds with an e-mail to Virga saying they should "chat" about the knives.

December 9   Cho sends unwanted IM to a third female student, Margaret Bowman (306 Campbell Hall). Later, he leaves messages on her marker board outside her room.

December 11   Cho leaves a new message, a quote from Shakespeare, on Bowman's marker board.

December 12   Bowman returns from an exam and finds more text added to the message from 12/11. She then files a report with the VTPD complaining of the multiple "disturbing" contacts from Cho. She requests that Cho have no further contact with her. When questioned by students about the notes to Bowman, Cho tells them "Shakespeare did it."

VTPD goes to Cho's room, but he is not there. They leave a message for him with his roommates.

Cho calls and cancels a 2:00 p.m. appointment at CCC but then calls back in the afternoon and is triaged for the second time by phone.

**December 13** VTPD notifies Cho that he is to have no further contact with Margaret Bowman. After campus police leave, Cho's suitemate receives an IM from Cho stating, "I might as well kill myself now." The suitemate alerts VTPD. The police take Cho to the VTPD where a prescreener from the New River Valley Community Services Board (CSB) evaluates him as "an imminent danger to self or others." A magistrate issues a temporary detaining order, and Cho is transported to Carilion St. Albans Psychiatric Hospital for an overnight stay and mental evaluation. No one contacts Cho's parents.

**December 14**

**7 a.m.** The person assigned as an independent evaluator, psychologist Roy Crouse, evaluates Cho and concludes that he does not present an imminent danger to himself.

**Before 11 a.m.** A staff psychiatrist at St. Alban's evaluates Cho, concludes he is not a danger to himself or others, and recommends outpatient counseling. He gathers no collateral information.

**11–11:30 a.m.** Special Justice Paul M. Barnett conducts Cho's commitment hearing and rules in accordance with the independent evaluator, but orders follow-up treatment as an outpatient. Cho then makes an appointment with the CCC and is released.

**Noon** The St. Alban's staff psychiatrist dictates in his evaluation summary that "there is no indication of psychosis, delusions, suicidal or homicidal ideation." The psychiatrist finds that "his insight and judgment are normal…Follow-up and aftercare to be arranged with the counseling center at Virginia Tech; medications, none."

**2:25 p.m.** CCC receives a fax from Carilion Health System with copies of the St. Alban's discharge summary and the Pre-admission Screening Form completed by the CSB evaluator the previous day at police headquarters.

**3:00 p.m.** Cho appears for his appointment and is triaged at the CCC for the third time in 15 days.

Dr. Miller, the CCC director, receives an email notifying him that Cho had been taken to St. Alban's the previous night. Dr. Miller e-mails CCC staff to alert them "in case this student is seen" at the CCC. A CCC staff member e-mails back that Cho already has been seen that afternoon.

## 2006

**January** The CCC receives a psychiatric summary from St. Albans. No action is taken by CCC or the Care Team to follow up on Cho.

February — Dr. Miller is removed from his position following a management study of the CCC. In his hurry to vacate the office, he packs Cho's file and files of several other students in a box and takes them home. (This is only discovered in July, 2009.)

April — Cho's technical writing professor, Carl Bean, suggests that Cho drop his class after repeated efforts to address shortcomings in class and inappropriate choice of writing assignments. Cho follows the 178ervicesor to his office, raises his voice angrily, and is asked to leave. Professor Bean does not report this incident to Virginia Tech officials.

Spring — Cho takes Professor Bob Hicok's creative writing class. Professor Hicok later characterizes Cho's writing as not particularly unique as far as subject matter is concerned, but remarkable for violence.

Fall — Cho enrolls in a playwriting workshop taught by Professor Ed Falco. Cho writes a play concerning a young man who hates the students at his school and plans to kill them and himself. The writing contains parallels to the subsequent events of April 16, 2007, as well as the recorded messages sent to NBC that same day.

Professor Falco confers with Professors Roy and Norris, who tell him that in Fall 2005 and in 2006, Dr. Roy and Dr. Norris, respectively, had alerted Associate Dean Mary Ann Lewis about Cho.

September 6–12 — Professor Lisa Norris, another of Cho's writing professors, alerts Associate Dean Mary Ann Lewis about him, but the dean finds "no mention of mental health issues or police reports" on Cho. Professor Norris encourages Cho to go to counseling with her, but he declines.

September 26–November 4 — Cho writes three more violent stories for an English class.

## 2007

February 2 — Cho orders a .22 caliber Walther P22 handgun online from TGSCOM, Inc.

February 9 — Cho picks up the handgun from J-N-D Pawnbrokers in Blacksburg, across the street from Virginia Tech.

March 12 — Cho rents a van from Enterprise Rent-A-Car at the Roanoke Regional Airport, which he keeps for almost a month. (Cho videotapes some of his subsequently released diatribe in the van.)

March 13 — Cho purchases a 9mm Glock 19 handgun and a box of 50 9mm full metal jacket practice rounds at Roanoke Firearms.

Cho waited the 30 days between gun purchases as required by Virginia law. The store initiates the required background check by police, who find no record of mental health issues.

March 22 — Cho goes to PSS Range and Training, an indoor pistol range, and spends an hour practicing.

March 22 — Cho purchases two 10-round magazines for the Walther P22 on eBay.

| | |
|---|---|
| March 23 | Cho purchases three additional 10-round magazines from another eBay seller. |
| March 31 | Cho purchases additional ammunition magazines, ammunition, and a hunting knife from Wal-Mart and Dick's Sporting Goods. He buys chains from Home Depot. |
| | Cho gets a speeding ticket, his first police contact since December 2005. |
| April 7 | Cho purchases more ammunition |
| April 8 | Cho spends the night at the Hampton Inn in Christiansburg, Virginia, videotaping segments for his manifesto-like diatribe. He also buys more ammunition. |
| April 13 | Bomb threats are made to Torgersen, Durham, and Whittemore halls in the form of an anonymous note. The threats are assessed by the VTPD, and the buildings evacuated. There is no lockdown or cancellation of classes elsewhere on campus. Later, during the investigation of the April 16 murders, no evidence is found linking these threats to Cho's bomb threat note in Norris Hall, based in part on handwriting analysis. |
| April 14 | An Asian male wearing a hooded garment is seen by a faculty member in Norris Hall. The faculty member later (after April 16) tells police that one of her students had told her the doors were chained. This may have been Cho practicing. Cho buys yet more ammunition. |
| April 15 | Cho places his weekly Sunday night call to his family in Fairfax County. They report the conversation as normal and that Cho said nothing that caused them concern. |

## THE INCIDENTS

### April 16, 2007

| | |
|---|---|
| 5:00 a.m. | In Cho's suite in Harper Hall (2121), one of Cho's suitemates notices Cho is awake and at his computer. |
| About 5:30 a.m. | One of Cho's other suitemates notices Cho clad in boxer shorts and a shirt brushing his teeth and applying acne cream. Cho returns from the bathroom, gets dressed, and leaves. |
| About 6:45 a.m. | Cho is spotted by a student loitering in the foyer area of WAJ resident hall, between the exterior door and the locked interior door. He has access to the mailbox foyer, but not to the interior of the building. |
| 7:02 a.m. | Emily Hilscher enters WAJ, her dorm, after being dropped off by her boy-friend, Karl Thornhill. (The time is based on her swipe card record.) |
| About 7:15 a.m. | Cho shoots Hilscher in her room (4040) where he also shoots Ryan Christopher Clark, an RA. Clark, it is thought, most likely came to investigate noises in Hilscher's room, which is next door to his. Both of the victims' wounds ultimately prove to be fatal. Cho exits the scene, leaving behind bloody footprints and shell casings. |
| 7:17 a.m. | Cho's access card is swiped at Harper Hall (his nearby residence hall). He goes to his room to change out of his bloody clothes, cancel his computer account, and make other preparations for what is to come. |
| 7:20 a.m. | The VTPD receives a call on their administrative telephone |

line advising that a female student in room 4040 of WAJ had possibly fallen from her loft bed. The caller was given this information by another WAJ resident near room 4040 who heard the noise.

7:21 a.m.    The VTPD dispatcher notifies the Virginia Tech Rescue Squad that a female student had possibly fallen from her loft bed in WAJ.

7:22 a.m.    A VTPD officer is dispatched to room 4040 at WAJ to accompany the Virginia Tech Rescue Squad, which is also dispatched per standard protocol.

7:24 a.m.    The VTPD officer arrives at WAJ room 4040, finds two people shot inside the room, and immediately requests additional VTPD resources.

7:25 a.m.    Cho accesses his university e-mail account (based on computer records). He erases his files and the account.

7:26 a.m.    Virginia Tech Rescue Squad 3 arrives on-scene outside WAJ.

7:27 a.m.    Police dispatcher is advised of two victims. Officer on scene requests supervisor

7:29 a.m.    Virginia Tech Rescue Squad 3 arrives at room 4040.

7:30 a.m.    Additional VTPD officers begin arriving at room 4040. They secure the crime scene and in effect lock down the dormitory, with police inside and outside. Police start preliminary investigation. Interviews with residents fail to produce a suspect description. No one on Hilscher's floor in WAJ saw anyone leave room 4040 after the initial noise was heard.

A housekeeper in Burruss Hall tells Dr. Ed Spencer, Associate Vice President for Student Affairs and member of the Policy Group, that an RA in WAJ was murdered. (The housekeeper had received a phone call from another housekeeper in WAJ.)

7:35 a.m.    Police on the scene at WAJ say they need a detective.

7:40 a.m.    VTPD Chief Flinchum is notified by phone of the WAJ shootings. Chief Flinchum tries repeatedly to reach the Office of the Executive Vice President.

7:51 a.m.    Chief Flinchum contacts the Blacksburg Police Department (BPD) and requests a BPD evidence technician and BPD detective to assist with the investigation.

7:55 a.m.    Dr. Spencer arrives at WAJ after walking from Burruss Hall. He calls Dr. Zenobia Hikes.

7:57 a.m.    Chief Flinchum finally gets through to the Virginia Tech Office of the Executive Vice President and notifies them of the shootings.

8:00 a.m.    Classes begin. Chief Flinchum arrives at WAJ and finds VTPD and BPD detectives on the scene. A local special agent of the Virginia State Police (VSP) has been contacted and is responding to the scene. The VTPD, BPD, and soon the VSP start to process the crime scene in Hilscher's room (4040) and gather evidence. They then canvass the dorm for possible witnesses, search interior and exterior waste containers and surrounding areas near WAJ for evidence, and canvass rescue squad personnel for additional evidence or information.

About 8:00 a.m. The Virginia Tech Center for Professional and Continuing Education locks down on its own.

8:10 a.m. President Steger is notified by a secretary that there has been a shooting. He tells her to get Chief Flinchum on the phone.

8:11 a.m. Chief Flinchum talks to President Steger via phone and reports one student is critical, one is fatally wounded, and the incident seems to be domestic in nature. He reports no weapon found and there are bloody footprints. President Steger tells Chief Flinchum to keep him informed. A staff member of the Policy Group and President Steger discuss the event, and Steger decides to convene the Policy Group no later than 8:30 a.m.

8:11 a.m. BPD Chief Kim Crannis arrives On scene.

8:13 a.m. Chief Flinchum requests additional VTPD and BPD officers to assist with securing WAJ entrances and with the investigation. He also orders recall of all off-shift personnel.

8:14 a.m. Hilscher's roommate, Heather Hough, arrives at WAJ to go with Hilscher to chemistry class. (Time recorded from swipe card.)

8:15 a.m. Chief Flinchum requests the VTPD Emergency Response Team (ERT) to respond to the scene and then to stage in Blacksburg in the event an arrest is needed or a search warrant is to be executed.

About 8:15 a.m. Two senior officials at Virginia Tech have conversations with family members in which the shooting on campus is related. In one conversation, by phone, the official advised her son, a student at Virginia Tech, to go to class. In the other, in person, the official arranged for extended babysitting.

8:16–8:40 a.m. Hilscher's roommate, Heather Haugh, is interviewed inside WAJ by detectives. She explains that on Monday mornings Hilscher's boyfriend, Karl Thornhill, usually drops her off at WAJ and returns to Radford University where he is a student. She says he owns guns and practices shooting. Police then seek Thornhill as a "person of interest." His vehicle is not found in campus parking lots and officers believe he has left campus. VTPD and BPD officers are sent to his home, but he is not there. The Thornhill home is then put under surveillance until Thornhill is found.

8:16–9:24 a.m. Police continue canvassing WAJ for possible witnesses. VTPD, BPD, and the VSP continue processing Hilscher's room (4040) crime scene and gathering evidence. Investigators secure identification of the victims. Police allow students in WAJ to leave; Some go to 9:00 a.m. classes in Norris Hall.

8:19 a.m.    Chief Crannis requests BPD ERT to respond for the same reason as the VTPD ERT.

8:20 a.m.    A person fitting Cho's description is seen near the Duck Pond on campus.

8:25 a.m.    The Policy Group convenes to plan how to notify students of the double shooting.

Police cancel bank deposit pickups.

8:40 a.m.    Chief Flinchum tells President Steger in a phone update that Hilscher's boyfriend is a person of interest and probably off campus. A Policy Group member notifies the Governor's office of the double shooting.

8:40–8:45 a.m.    Phone calls are made from BPD to its units and to Montgomery County Sheriff's Office and Radford University police to be on the lookout for Thornhill's vehicle.

8:45 a.m.    A Policy Group member e-mails a Richmond colleague saying one student is dead and another critically wounded. "Gunman on the loose," he says, adding "This is not releasable yet."

8:49 a.m.    The same Policy Group member reminds his Richmond colleague, "just try to make sure it doesn't get out."

8:50 a.m.    First period classes end. The Policy Group begins composing a notice to the university about the shootings in WAJ. The Associate Vice President for University Relations, Larry Hincker, is unable to send the message at first due to technical difficulties with the alert system.

8:52 a.m.    Blacksburg public schools lock down until more information is available about the incident at Virginia Tech. School superintendent notifies school board of this by e-mail.

The Executive Director of Government Relations, Ralph Byers, directs that the doors to his office be locked. It is adjacent to the President's suite, but the four doors to the President's suite remain open.

9:00-9:15 a.m.    Virginia Tech veterinary college locks down.

9:01 a.m.    Cho mails a package from the Blacksburg post office to NBC News in New York that contains pictures of himself holding weapons, an 1,800-word rambling diatribe, and video clips in which he expresses rage, resentment, and a desire to get even with oppressors. He alludes to a coming massacre. Cho prepared this material in the previous weeks. The videos are a performance of the enclosed writings. Cho also mails a letter to the English Department attacking Professor Carl Bean, with whom he previously argued.

9:05 a.m.    Classes begin for the second period in Norris Hall.

Virginia Tech trash pickup is cancelled.

9:15 a.m.    Both police ERTs are staged at the BPD in anticipation of

|               |                                                                                                                                                                                                                                                                                                                                                                                             |
|---------------|-------------------------------------------------------------------------------------------------------------------------------------------------------------------------------------------------------------------------------------------------------------------------------------------------------------------------------------------------------------------------------------------|
|               | executing search warrants or making an arrest.                                                                                                                                                                                                                                                                                                                                              |
| 9:15–9:30 a.m. | Cho is seen outside and then inside Norris Hall, an engineering building, by several students. He is familiar with the building because one of his classes meets there. He chains the doors shut on the three public entrances, from the inside. No one reports seeing him do this. A faculty member finds a bomb threat note attached to an inner door near one of the chained exterior doors. She gives it to a janitor to carry to the Engineering School dean's office on the third floor. |

A VTPD police captain joins the Policy Group as police liaison and provides updates as information becomes available. He reports one gunman at large, possibly on foot.

| 9:26 a.m. | Virginia Tech administration sends e-mail to campus staff, faculty, and students informing them of the dormitory shooting. |
| About 9:30 a.m. | Radford University Police had received a request from BPD to look up Thornhill's class schedule and find him in class. Before they can do this they get a second call that he has been found and stopped on the road. |
| 9:30 a.m. | Police pass information to the Policy Group that it is unlikely that Hilscher's boyfriend, Thornhill, is the shooter (though he remains a person of interest). |
| 9:31-9:48 a.m. | A VSP trooper arrives at the traffic stop of Thornhill and |

helps question him. A gunpowder residue test is performed and packaged for lab analysis. (There is no immediate result from this type of test in the field.)

| About 9:40 a.m.-9:51 a.m. | Cho begin shooting in room 206 in Norris Hall, where a graduate engineering class in Advanced Hydrology is underway. Cho kills Professor G. V. Loganathan and other students in the class, killing 9 and wounding 3 of the 13 students. |

Cho goes across the hall from room 206 and enters room 207, an Elementary German class. He shoots teacher Christopher James Bishop, then students near the front of the classroom and starts down the aisle shooting others. Cho leaves the classroom to go back into the hall.

Students in room 205, attending Haiyan Cheng's class on Issues in Scientific Computing, hear Cho's gunshots. (Cheng was a graduate assistant substituting for the professor that day.) The students barricade the door and prevent Cho's entry despite his firing at them through the door.

Meanwhile, in room 211 Madame Jocelyne Couture-Nowak is teaching French. She and her class hear the shots, and she asks student Colin Goddard to call 9-1-1. A student tells the teacher to put the desk in front of the door, which is done, but it is nudged open by Cho. Cho walks down the rows of desks shooting people. Goddard is shot in the leg. Student Emily Haas picks up the cell phone Goddard dropped. She begs the police to hurry. Cho hears Haas and shoots her, grazing her twice in the head. She falls and plays dead, though keeping the phone cradled under her head and the line open. Cho says nothing on entering the room or during the shooting. (Three students who pretend to be dead survive.)

9:41 a.m.    A BPD dispatcher receives a call regarding the shooting in Norris Hall. The dispatcher initially has difficulty understanding the location of the shooting. Once identified as being on campus, the call is transferred to VTPD.

9:42 a.m.    The first 9-1-1 call reporting shots fired reaches the VTPD. A message is sent to all county EMS units to staff and respond.

9:45 a.m.    The first police officers arrive at Norris Hall, a three-minute response time from their receipt of the call. Hearing shots, they pause briefly to check whether they are being fired upon, then rush to one entrance, and then another but find the doors chained shut. An attempt to shoot open the chain or lock on one door fails.

About 9:45 a.m.    The police inform the administration that there has been another shooting. Virginia Tech President Steger hears sounds like gunshots, and sees police running toward Norris Hall.

Back in room 207, the German class, two uninjured students and two injured students go to the door and hold it shut with their feet and hands, keeping their bodies away. Within 2 minutes, Cho returns. He beats on the door and opens it an inch and fires shots around the door handle, then gives up trying to get in.

Cho returns to room 211, the French class, and goes up one aisle and down another, shooting people again. Cho shoots Goddard two more times.

A janitor sees Cho in the hall on the second floor loading his gun; the janitor flees downstairs.

Cho tries to enter room 204 where engineering professor Liviu Librescu is teaching Mechanics. Professor Librescu braces his body against the door yelling for students to head for the window. He is shot through the door. Students push out screens and jump or drop to grass or bushes below the window. Ten students escape this way. The next two students trying to escape are shot. Cho returns again to room 206 and shoots more students.

9:50 a.m.    Using a shotgun, police shoot open the ordinary key lock of a Norris Hall entrance that goes to a machine shop and that could not be chained. These officers hear gunshots as they enter the building.

They immediately follow the sounds to the second floor.

Triage and rescue of victims begin.

A second e-mail is sent by the administration to all Virginia Tech e-mail addresses announcing that "A gunman is loose on campus. Stay in buildings until further notice. Stay away from all windows." Four outside loudspeakers on poles broadcast a similar message.

Virginia Tech and Blacksburg police ERTs arrive at Norris Hall, including one paramedic with each team.

**9:51 a.m.**    Cho shoots himself in the head just as police reach the second floor. Investigators believe that the police shotgun blast alerted Cho to police (starting entry into the building). Cho's shooting spree in Norris Hall lasted about 11 minutes. He fired 174 rounds, and killed 30 people in Norris Hall plus himself, and wounded 17.

The first team of officers begins securing the second floor and aiding survivors from multiple classrooms. They also get a preliminary description of the suspected gunman, and try to determine if there are additional gunmen.

**9:52 a.m.**    The police clear the second floor of Norris Hall. Two tactical medics attached to the ERTs, one medic from Virginia Tech Rescue and one from Blacksburg Rescue, are allowed to enter to start their initial triage.

**9:53 a.m.**    The 9:42 a.m. request for all EMS units is repeated.

**10:08 a.m.**    A deceased male student is discovered by police team and suspected to be the gunman:

- No identification is found on the body.
- He appears to have a self-inflicted gunshot wound to the head.
- He is found among his victims in classroom 211, the French class.
- Two weapons are found near the body.

**10:17 a.m.**    A third e-mail from Virginia Tech administration cancels classes and advises people to stay where they are.

**10:51 a.m.**    All patients from Norris Hall have been transported to a hospital or moved to a minor treatment unit.

**10:52 a.m.**    A fourth e-mail from Virginia Tech administration warns of "a multiple shooting with multiple victims in Norris Hall," saying "the shooter is in custody" and that as routine procedure police are searching for a second shooter.

**10:57 a.m.**    A report of shots fired at the tennis courts near Cassell Coliseum proves false.

**12:42 p.m.**    Virginia Tech President Charles Steger announces that police are releasing people from buildings and that counseling centers are being established.

**1:35 p.m.**    A report of a possible gunshot near Duck Pond proves to be another false alarm.

**4:01 p.m.**    President George W. Bush speaks to the Nation from the White House regarding the shooting.

| | |
|---|---|
| 5:00 p.m. | The first deceased victim is transported to the medical examiner's office. |
| 8:45 p.m. | The last deceased victim is transported to the medical examiner's office. |
| Evening | Police continue investigating whether Karl Thornhill, Emily Hilscher's boyfriend, is linked to her murder and that of Ryan Clark because the ballistics analysis that later ties together the WAJ and the Norris Hall murders (confirming that Cho's guns were used at both incidents) is not yet completed. The Blacksburg ERT, including Virginia Tech and Montgomery County Police, enters Thornhill's home and searches it. The ERT searches his residence. Using standard procedures, ERT members handcuff Thornhill and his family who have come to console him. They are put on the floor while the search is made, because Thornhill is known to own firearms. The search is highly upsetting to Thornhill and his family. |

## POST-INCIDENT

### April 17, 2007

| | |
|---|---|
| 9:15 a.m. | VTPD releases the name of the shooter as Seung Hui Cho and confirms 33 fatalities between the two incidents. |
| 9:30 a.m. | Virginia Tech announces classes will be cancelled "for the remainder of the week to allow students the time they need to grieve and seek assistance as needed." |

| | |
|---|---|
| 11:00 a.m. | A family assistance center is established at The Inn at Virginia Tech. |
| 2:00 p.m. | A convocation ceremony is held for the university community at the Cassell Coliseum. Speakers include President George W. Bush, Virginia Governor Tim Kaine (who had returned from Japan), Virginia Tech President Charles Steger, Virginia Tech Vice President for Student Affairs Zenobia L. Hikes, local religious leaders (representing the Muslim, Buddhist, Jewish, and Christian communities), Provost Dr. Mark G. McNamee, Dean of Students Tom Brown, Counselor Dr. Christopher Flynn, and poet Professor Nikki Giovanni. |
| 8:00 p.m. | A candlelight vigil is held on the Virginia Tech drill field. |
| 11:30 p.m. | The first autopsy is completed. |

### April 18, 2007

| | |
|---|---|
| 8:25 a.m. | A SWAT team enters Burruss Hall, a campus building next to Norris Hall, Responding to a "suspicious event"; this proves to be a false alarm. |
| 4:37 p.m. | Local police announce that NBC News in New York just received by mail a package containing images of Cho holding weapons, his writings, and his video recordings. NBC immediately submitted this information to the FBI. A fragment of the video and pictures are widely broadcast. |

### April 19, 2007

Virginia Tech announces that all students who were killed will be granted posthumous degrees in the fields in which they were studying. The degrees are subsequently awarded to the families at the regular commencement exercises, or privately, or in one case, at a Corps of Cadets event in Fall 2007.

Governor Kaine appoints an independent Virginia Tech Review Panel to review the shootings.

Autopsies on all victims are completed by the medical examiner. The autopsy of Cho found no gross brain function abnormalities and no toxic substances, drugs, or alcohol that could explain the rampage.

## April 20, 2007

Governor Kaine declares a statewide day of mourning.

# Chapter IV.

## MENTAL HEALTH HISTORY OF SEUNG HUI CHO

This chapter is divided into two parts: Part A, the mental health history of Cho, and Part B, a discussion of Virginia's mental health laws.

### Part A – Mental Health History of Seung Hui Cho

One of the major charges Governor Kaine gave to the panel was to develop a profile of Cho and his mental health history. In this chapter, developmental periods of Cho's life are discussed, followed by an assessment and recommendations to address policy gaps or system flaws. The chapter details his involuntary commitment for mental health treatment while at Virginia Tech. It also examines the particular warning signs during Cho's junior year at Virginia Tech and the university's ability to identify and respond appropriately to students who may present a danger to themselves and others.

Information was gleaned from many sources. One of the most significant was a 3-hour interview with Cho's parents and sister. The family stated that they were willing to help in any way with the panel's work, and felt incapable of redressing the loss for other families. They expressed heartfelt remorse, and they apologized to the families whose spouse, son, or daughter was murdered or injured. The Cho's have said that they will mourn, until the day they die, the deaths and injuries of those who suffered at the hands of their son.

Cho's sister, Sun, interpreted the answers to every question posed to Mr. and Mrs. Cho. At the end of the interview, they had portrayed the person they knew as a son and brother, someone who was startlingly different from the one who carried out premeditated murder.

Other sources of information included:

- Hundreds of pages of transcripts and records from Westfield High School, Virginia Tech, and various medical offices and mental health treatment centers.

- Interviews with high school staff and administrators where Cho attended school, faculty and staff at Virginia Tech, and several of Cho's suitemates, roommates, and resident advisors in the dormitories.

- Interviews with staff at the Center for Multicultural Human Services, the Cook Counseling Center, the Carilion Health System, special justices, and Virginia Tech police.

- The tape and written records of Cho's hearing before special justice Barnett.

- The report of the Inspector General for Mental Health, Mental Retardation and Substance Abuse Services, Investigation of April 16, 2007 Critical Incident at Virginia Tech.

### EARLY YEARS

Cho was born in Korea on January 18, 1984, the second child of Sung-Tae Cho and Hyang Im Cho. Both parents were raised in two-parent families that included the paternal grandmother; there was extended family support. The families did not encounter the level of deprivation that many did in post-war Korea. The Chos recall that a paternal uncle in Korea committed suicide. Their first child, daughter Sun Kyung, was born 3 years before Seung Hui.

When he was 9 months old, Cho developed whooping cough, then pneumonia, and was hospitalized. Doctors told the Chos that their son had a hole in his heart (some records say "heart murmur"). Two years later, doctors conducted cardiac tests to better examine the inside of his heart that included a procedure (probably an echocardiograph or a cardiac catherization). This caused the 3-year-old emotional trauma. From that point on, Cho did not like to be touched. He generally was perceived as medically frail. According to his mother, he cried a lot and was constantly sick.

In Korea, Cho had a few friends that he would play with and who would come over to the house. He was extremely quiet but had a sweet nature. In Korea, quietness and calmness are desired attributes—characteristics equated with scholarliness; even so, his introverted personality was so extreme that his family was very concerned.

In 1992, the family moved to the United States to pursue educational opportunities for their children. They were encouraged by Mr. Cho's sister who had immigrated before them. Mrs. Cho began working outside the home for the first time in order to make ends meet. The transition was difficult: none of the family spoke English. Both children felt isolated. The parents began a long period of hard labor and extended work hours at dry cleaning businesses. English was not required to do their work, so both there and at home they spoke Korean.

Sun stated that her brother seemed more withdrawn and isolated in the United States than he had been in Korea. She recalled that at times they were "made fun of," but she took it in stride because she thought "this was just a given." In about 2 years, the children began to understand, read, and write English at school. Korean was spoken at home, but Cho did not write or read Korean.

For the first 6 months in the United States, the Chos lived with family members in Maryland. They moved to a townhouse for 1 year, after which they relocated to Virginia, living in an apartment for 3 years. The move to Virginia occurred in the middle of third grade for Cho. He was 9 years old. Cho's only known friendship was with a boy next door with whom he went swimming.

Sun and her parents recall that Cho seemed to be doing better. He was enrolled in a Tae Kwon Do program for awhile, watched TV, and played video games like Sonic the Hedgehog. None of the video games were war games or had violent themes. He liked basketball and had a collection of figurines and remote controlled cars. Years later when he was in high school, Cho was asked to write about his hobbies and interests. He wrote:

> I like to listen to talk shows and alternative stations, and I like action movies…My favorite movie is X-Men, favorite actor is Nicolas Cage, favorite book is Night Over Water, favorite band is U2, favorite sport is basketball, favorite team is Portland Trailblazers, favorite food is pizza, and favorite color is green.

Transportation to and from extracurricular activities was a problem because both parents worked long hours trying to save money to buy a townhouse, which they accomplished a few years later. The parents recalled that Cho had to wait for transport back and forth all the time.

The parents reported no disciplinary problems with their son. He was quiet and gentle and did not exhibit tantrums or angry outbursts. The family never owned weapons or had any in the house. At one point after Cho was in college, his mother found a pocket knife in one of his drawers, and she expressed her disapproval. He had few duties or responsibilities at home, except to clean his room. He never had a job during summers or over school breaks, either in high school or in college.

The biggest issue between Cho and his family was his poor communication, which was frustrating and worrisome to them. Over the years, Cho spoke very little to his parents and avoided eye contact. According to one record the panel reviewed, Mrs. Cho would get so frustrated she would shake him sometimes. He would talk to his sister a little, but avoided discussing his feelings and reactions to things or sharing everyday thoughts on life, school, and events. If called upon to speak when a visitor came to the home, he would develop sweaty palms, become pale, freeze, and sometimes cry. Frequently, he would only nod yes or no.

Mrs. Cho made a big effort to help Cho become better adjusted, and she would talk to him, urging him to open up, to "have more courage." The parents urged him to get involved in activities and sports. They worried that he was isolating himself and was lonely. Other family members asked why he would not talk. He reportedly resented this pressure. Mr. Cho, having a quiet nature himself, was slightly more accepting of his son's introspective and withdrawn personality, but he was stern on matters of respect. Cho and his father would argue about this. According to one of the records reviewed, Cho's father would not praise his son. Where Cho's later writings included a father-son relationship, the character of the father was always negative. Cho never talked about school and never shared much. His mother and sister would ask how he was doing in school, trying to explore the possibility of "bullying." His sister knew that when he walked down school hallways a few students sometimes would yell taunts at him. He did not talk about feelings or school at all. He would respond "okay" to all questions about his well being.

Cho, as a special needs child, generated a high level of stress within the family. Adaptation to cope with this stress can produce both positive and negative results. The family dynamic which evolved in the Chos' to cope with this stress was that of "rescue" behavior and more coddling of Cho who seemed unreachable emotionally. There was some friction between Cho and his sister, however, nothing that appeared as other than normal sibling rivalry. In fact, Sun was the one to whom Cho spoke the most.

Key Findings of Early Years

- Cho's early development was 65ervice6565rized by physical illness and inordinate shyness.

- Even as a young boy, Cho preferred not to speak, a situation that worried and frustrated his parents.

- He was ostracized by some peers, though he did not discuss this with his family.

- His parents worked very long hours and had financial difficulties. They worried about the effect of this on their children because they had less than optimum time to devote to parenting.

- Medical records did not indicate a diagnosis of mental illness prior to coming to the United States.

## ELEMENTARY SCHOOL IN VIRGINIA

Cho was enrolled in the English as a Second Language (ESL) program in Virginia as soon as he arrived in the middle of third grade. The family at this time was living in a small apartment. School teachers indicated that Cho would not "interact socially, communicate verbally, or participate in group activities." One teacher reported that he did play with one student during recess.

Cho was referred to the school's educational screening committee because teachers believed his communication problems stemmed more from emotional issues than from language barriers. When Cho was in sixth grade, his parents bought a townhouse next to the school so he could easily commute to his classes. The school requested a parent–teacher conference because Cho was not answering any questions in class. Mrs. Cho took an interpreter with her to the parent-teacher conference. She resolved to "find" friends for him and encouraged both their children to go to the church she attended. Because the congregation was small, however, there were few children, so both Cho and his sister lost interest and stopped going to church.

One of Mrs. Cho's friends urged her to look into another church that reportedly had a minister who "could help people with problems like Cho's." She occasionally attended that church over a 6-month period, but decided against reaching out to that pastor to work with her son. Several newspaper articles that appeared after the shooting reported that the pastor from that church had worked directly with Cho. According to Mrs. Cho, those reports are untrue. Mrs. Cho did register her son for a 1-week summer basketball camp sponsored by that church, but she never sought its help on personal matters.

Mrs. Cho tried to be extra nurturing to Cho. He did not reject her attempts at socialization per se, but he disliked talking. Finally, Cho's parents decided to "let him be the way he is" and not force him to interact and talk with others. He never spoke of imaginary friends. He did not seem to be involved in a fantasy world or to be preoccupied by themes in his play or work that caused concern. He never talked of a "twin brother." The parents' characterization of him was a "very gentle, very tender," and "good person."

## MIDDLE SCHOOL YEARS

The summer before Cho started seventh grade, his parents followed up on a recommendation from the elementary school that they seek therapy for Cho. In July 1997, the Cho's took their son to the Center for Multicultural Human Services (CMHS), a mental health services facility that offers mental health treatment and psychological evaluations and testing to low-income, English-limited immigrant and refugee individuals. They told the specialists of their concern about Cho's social isolation and unwillingness to discuss his thoughts or feelings.

Mr. and Mrs. Cho overcame several obstacles to get their son the help he needed. In order for Cho to make his weekly appointments at the center, they had to take turns leaving work early to drive him there. There were cultural barriers as well. In the family's native country, mental or emotional problems were signs of shame and guilt. The stigmatization of mental health problems remains a serious roadblock in seeking treatment in the United States too, but in Korea the issue is even more relevant. Getting help for such concerns is only reluctantly acknowledged as necessary.

After starting with a Korean counselor with whom there was a poor fit, Cho began working with another specialist who had special training in art therapy as a way of diagnosing and addressing the emotional pain and psychological problems of clients. Typically, this form of therapy is used with younger children who do not have sufficient language or cognitive skills to utilize traditional "talk" therapy. Because Cho would not converse and uttered only a couple words in response to questions, art therapy was one way to reach him. The specialist offered clay modeling, painting, drawing, and a sand table at each session. Cho would choose one of the options. As he worked, the therapist could ascertain how he was feeling and what his creations might represent about his inner world. Then she talked to him about what his work indicated and hoped to help him progress in being more socially functional. He modeled houses out of clay, houses that had no windows or doors.

Cho's therapist noted that while explaining the meaning of Cho's artwork to him, his eyes sometimes filled with tears. She never saw anything that he wrote. Eventually, Cho began to make eye contact. She saw this as a start toward becoming healthier.

Cho also had a psychiatrist who participated in the first meeting with Cho and his family and periodically over the next few years. He was diagnosed as having [severe] "social anxiety disorder." "It was painful to see," recalled one of the psychiatrists involved with Cho's case. The parents were told that many of Cho's problems were rooted in acculturation challenges—not fitting in and difficulty with friends. Personnel at the center also noted in his chart that he had experienced medical problems and that medical tests as an infant and as a preschooler had caused emotional trauma. Records sent to Cho's school at the time (following a release signed by his parents) and the tests administered by mental health professionals evaluated Cho to be a much younger person than his actual age, which indicated social immaturity, lack of verbal skills, but not retardation. His tested IQ was above average.

Cho continued to isolate himself in middle school. He had no reported behavioral problems and did not get into any fights. Then, in March 1999, when Cho was in the spring semester of eighth grade, his art therapist observed a change in his behavior. He began depicting tunnels and caves in his art. In and of themselves, those symbols were not cause for alarm, but Cho also suddenly became more withdrawn and showed symptoms of depression. In that context, the therapist felt that the tunnels and caves were red flags. She was concerned and asked him whether he had any suicidal or homicidal thoughts. He denied having them, but she drew up a contract with him anyway, spelling out that he would do no harm to himself or to others, and she told him to communicate with his parents or someone at school if he did experience any ideas about violence. That is just what he did, in the form of a paper he wrote in class.

The following month, April 1999, the murders at Columbine High School occurred. Shortly thereafter, Cho wrote a disturbing paper in English class that drew quick reaction from his teacher. Cho's written words expressed generalized thoughts of suicide and homicide, indicating that "he wanted to repeat Columbine," according to someone familiar with the situation. No one in particular was named or targeted in the words he wrote. The school contacted Cho's sister since she spoke English and explained what had happened. The family was urged to have Cho evaluated by a psychiatrist. The sister relayed this information to her parents who asked her to accompany Cho to his next therapy appointment and report the incident, which she did. The therapist then contacted the psychiatrist for an evaluation.

Cho was evaluated in June 1999 by a psychiatrist at the Center for Multicultural Human Services. There, psychiatric interns from The George Washington University Hospital provide treatment one day a week supervised by other doctors at GWU. Cho was fortunate because the intern who was his psychiatrist was actually an experienced child psychiatrist and family counselor who had practiced in South America prior to coming to the United States. He had to recertify in this country and was in the process of doing that at GWU Hospital when he first met Cho.

Mr. and Mrs. Cho explained to the psychiatrist that they were facing a family crisis since their daughter would be leaving home in the fall to attend college and she was the family member with whom Cho communicated, as limited as that communication was. They feared that once their daughter was no longer home, he would not communicate at all. The psychiatrist also was informed of the disturbing paper Cho had written.

The doctor diagnosed Cho with "selective mutism" and "major depression: single episode." He prescribed the antidepressant Paroxetine 20 mg, which Cho took from June 1999 to July 2000. Cho did quite well on this regimen; he seemed to be in a good mood, looked brighter, and smiled more. The doctor stopped the medication because Cho improved and no longer needed the antidepressant.

Selective mutism is a type of an anxiety disorder that is characterized by a consistent failure to speak in specific social situations where there is an expectation of speaking. The unwillingness to speak is not secondary to speech/communication problems, but, rather, is based on painful shyness. Children with selective mutism are usually inhibited, withdrawn, and anxious with an obsessive fear of hearing their own voice. Sometimes they show passive-aggressive, stubborn and controlling traits. The association between this disorder and autism is unclear.

Major depression refers to a predominant mood of sadness or irritability that lasts for a significant period of time accompanied by sleep and appetite disturbances, concentration problems, suicidal ideations and pervasive lack of pleasure and energy. Major depression typically interferes with social, occupational and educational functioning. Effective treatments for depression and selective mutism include psychotherapy and anti 194ervicesants/anti-anxiety agents such as Selective Serotonin Reuptake Inhibitors (SSRI's).

It should be noted that when the subject of Cho's eighth grade paper and subsequent evaluation was discussed with Mr. and Mrs. Cho and Cho's sister during the interview, they appeared shocked to learn that he had written about violence toward others. They said they knew he had hinted at ideas about suicide, but not about homicide.

School records indicate that an interpreter was provided (sometimes this was Cho's sister) during meetings that involved the parents, as is the policy and required by law.

## HIGH SCHOOL YEARS

In fall of 1999, Cho began high school at Centreville High School. The following year a new school, Westfield High School, opened to accommodate the population growth in that part of Fairfax County. Cho was assigned there for his remaining 3 years. About 1 month after classes began at Westfield, one of Cho's teachers reported to the guidance office that Cho's speech was barely audible and he did not respond in complete sentences. The teacher wrote that he was not verbally interactive at all and was shy and shut down. There was practically no communication with teachers or peers. Those failings aside, teachers also praised Cho for his qualities as a student. He achieved high grades, was always on time for class, and was diligent in submitting well-done homework assignments. Other than failing to speak, he did not exhibit any other unusual behaviors and did not cause problems. When the teacher asked Cho if he would like help with communicating, he nodded yes.

The guidance counselors asked Cho whether he had ever received mental health or special education assistance in middle school or in his freshman year (at the previous high school), and he reportedly indicated (untruthfully) that he had not.

Cho's situation was brought before Westfield's Screening Committee on October 25, 2000, for evaluation to determine if he required special education accommodations. Federal law requires that schools receiving federal funding enable children with disabilities to learn in the least restrictive environment and to be mainstreamed in classrooms. Provisions are made for special services or accommodations after a core evaluation involving a battery of tests is given to diagnose the problems and to guide the school in preparing an Individualized Education Plan (IEP). The high school conducted a special assessment to rule out autism as an underlying factor. Cho also was evaluated in the following domains:

> Psychological
> Sociocultural
> Educational
> Speech/Language
> Hearing Screening
> Medical
> Vision

As part of the assessment process, school personnel met with Cho's parents to find out more about his history and to explain the assessment process. Mrs. Cho expressed concern about how her son would fare later in college given the transition required and his poor social skills. She noted that her son was receiving counseling and gave permission for the school to contact her son's therapist. The therapist, in turn, was encouraged by the fact that the school would be tracking Cho's progress. The committee determined that Cho was eligible for the Special Education Program for Emotional Disabilities and Speech and Language. Mr. and Mrs. Cho were receptive to receiving help for him and so was his older sister who was in college and with whom he had a good relationship. The parents and sister continued to be in contact with the school; Sun usually served as interpreter.

Special accommodations were made to help Cho succeed in class without frustration or intimidation. The school developed an IEP, as required by law that was effective in January 2001. The IEP listed two curriculum and classroom accommodations and modifications:

modification for oral presentations, as needed, and modified grading scale for oral or group participation. In-school language therapy was recommended as well, but Cho only received that service once a month for 50 minutes. His art therapist, who reached out to a few teachers and others at the school with questions or concerns, said she asked why the language therapy was so limited. The school responded that it was reluctant to pull him out of class for this special service because this would interrupt his academic work or negatively impact his grades. Besides, the primary diagnosis was selective mutism, not problems with the mechanics of speaking or an inability to function in English.

Cho was encouraged to join a club and to stay after school for help from teachers. He was permitted to eat lunch alone and to provide verbal responses in private sessions with teachers rather than in front of the whole class where his manner of speaking and accent sometimes drew derision from peers.

With this arrangement, Cho's grades were excellent. He had advanced placement and honors classes. However, his voice was literally inaudible in class, and he would only whisper if pushed (an observation consistent with his behavior later in college). In written responses, at times, his thinking appeared confused and his sentence structure was not fluent. Indeed, his guidance counselor raised the question to the panel: "Why did he change his major to English at Tech?" Why did this student, whose forte appeared to be science and math, switch to humanities?

After the Virginia Tech murders, some newspapers reported that Cho was the subject of bullying. The panel could not confirm whether or not he was bullied or threatened. His family said that he never mentioned being the target of threats or intimidating messages, but then neither did he routinely discuss any details about school or the events of his day. His guidance counselor had no records of bullying or harassment complaints.

Nearly all students experience some level of bullying in schools today. Much of this behavior occurs behind the scenes or off school grounds—and often electronically, through instant messaging, communications on MySpace and, to a lesser extent, on Facebook, a website used by older teenagers. Cho's high school counselor could not say whether bullying might have occurred before or after school, as suggested by other unconfirmed sources.

It would be reasonable, however, to assume that Cho was a victim of some bullying, though to what extent and how much above the norm is not known. His sister said that both of them were subjected to a certain level of harassment when they first came to the United States and throughout their school years, but she indicated that it was neither particularly threatening nor ongoing.

In the eleventh grade, Cho's weekly sessions at the mental health center came to an end because there was a gradual, if slight, improvement over the years and he resisted continuing, according to his parents and therapist "There is nothing wrong with me. Why do I have to go?" he complained to his parents. Mr. and Mrs. Cho were not happy that their son chose to discontinue treatment, but he was turning 18 the following month and legally he could make that decision.

Cho took upper level science and math courses and spent 3 to 4 hours a day on homework. He earned high marks and finished high school with a grade point average of 3.52 in an honors program. That GPA, along with his SAT scores (540 for verbal and 620 for math registered in the 2002 testing year) were the basis for his acceptance at Virginia Tech. What the admission's staff at Virginia Tech did not see were the special accommodations that propped up Cho and his grades. Those scores reflected Cho's knowledge and intelligence, but they did not reflect another component of grades: class participation. Since that aspect of grading was substantially modified for Cho due to the legally mandated accommodations for his emotional disability, his grades appeared higher than they otherwise would have been.

When his guidance counselor talked to Cho and his family about college, she strongly recommended they send him to a small school close to home where he could more easily make the transition to college life. She cautioned that Virginia Tech was too large. However, Cho appeared very self-directed and independent in his decision. He chose Virginia Tech, which had been his goal for some time. He applied and was accepted.

Virginia Tech does not require an essay or letters of recommendation in the freshman application package and does not conduct personal interviews. Acceptance decisions at Virginia Tech are based primarily on grades and SAT scores, though demographics, interests, and some intangibles are also considered. An essay about oneself is optional. Cho included a short writing about rock climbing in his application, which was written in the first person and spoke about human potential that often cannot be achieved because of self-doubt.

Before Cho left high school, the guidance counselor made sure that Cho had the name and contact information of a school district resource who Cho could call if he encountered problems at college. As is now known, Cho never sought that help while at Virginia Tech.

As Cho looked to the fall of 2003, he was preparing to leave home for the first time and enter an environment where he knew no one. He was not on any medication for anxiety or depression, had stopped counseling, and no longer had special accommodations for his selective mutism. Neither Cho nor his high school revealed that he had been receiving special education services as an emotionally disabled student, so no one at the university ever became aware of these pre-existing conditions.

There is a standard cover page that accompanied Cho's transcripts to Virginia Tech called "Pupil Permanent Record, Category 1". The page lists all the types of student records, whether they include information from elementary, middle, or high school, and how long they are to be retained. The lower right corner of the page has a section marked "The Student Scholastic Record" under which are boxes to be checked as they apply. The first six boxes are Clinic, Cumulative, Discipline, Due Process, Law Enforcement, and Legal. Only the first two were checked, indicating Cho had no records pertaining to discipline or legal problems. Then, there is a subheading labeled "Special Services Files" where six additional boxes are presented: Contract Services, ESL, 504 Plan, Gifted and Talented, Homebound, and Special Education. Only the ESL box is checked, even though Cho had special education services. The special education services box was not checked.

As the panel reviewed Cho's mental health records and conducted interviews with persons who had provided psychiatric and counseling services to Cho throughout his public school career, it became evident that critical records from one public institution are not necessarily transferred to the next as a person matures and enters into new stages of development. What are the rules regarding the release of special education records between, for example, high schools and colleges?

It is common practice to require students entering a new school, college, or university to present records of immunization. Why not records of serious emotional or mental problem too? For that matter, why not records of all communicable diseases?

The answer is obvious: personal privacy. And while the panel respects this answer, it is important to examine the extent to which such information is altogether banned or could be released at the institution's discretion. No one wants to stigmatize a person or deny her or him opportunities because of mental or physical disability. Still, there are issues of public safety. That is why immunization records must be submitted to each new institution. But there are other significant threats facing students beyond measles, mumps, or polio.

The panel asked its legal counsel to review the laws pertaining to special education records and the release of that information, specifically as addressed in FERPA and the Americans with Disabilities Act (ADA). Although FERPA generally allows secondary schools to disclose educational records (including special education records) to a university, federal disability law prohibits universities from making what is known as a 'preadmission inquiry" about an applicant's disability status. After admission, however, universities may make inquiries on a confidential basis as to disabilities that may require accommodation.

It should be noted that the Department of Education's March 2007 "Transition of Students with Disabilities to Post Secondary Education: A Guide for High School Educators" clarifies that a high school student has no obligation to inform an institution of post secondary education that he or she has a disability; however, if the student wants an academic adjustment, the student must identify himself or herself as having a disability. Cho did not seek any accommodations from Virginia Tech. The disclosure of a disability is always voluntary.

It is a more subtle question whether Fairfax County Public Schools would have had to remove any indication of special education status or accommodation from Cho's transcript or grade reports as part of his college application.

Because this issue is of such great importance and because much more study is needed, the panel does not make a recommendation here. But the panel hopes that this issue begins to be debated fully in the public realm. Perhaps students should be required to submit records of emotional or mental disturbance and any communicable diseases after they have been admitted but before they enroll at a college or university, with assurance that the records will not be accessed unless the institution's threat assessment team (by whatever name it is known) judges a student to pose a potential threat to self or others.

Or perhaps an institution whose threat assessment team determines that a student is a danger to self or others should promptly contact the student's family or high school, inform them of the assessment, and inquire as to a previous history of emotional or mental disturbance.

This much is clear: information critical to public safety should not stay behind as a person moves from school to school. Students may start fresh in college, but their history may well remain relevant. Maybe there really should be some form of "permanent record."

Key Findings of Cho's School Years

- Both the family and the schools recognized that Cho's problem was not merely introversion and that Cho needed therapy to help with extreme social anxiety, as well as acculturation and communication.

- A depressive phase in the second half of eighth grade led to full blown depression and thoughts of suicide and homicide precipitated by the Columbine shooting. Cho received timely psychiatric assessment and intervention (prescription of Paroxetine and continued therapy). This episode abated within a year, and medications were discontinued.

- Transportation problems interfered with Cho's involvement with sports and extracurricular activities, which may have increased his isolation.

- Intervention for a child suffering from mental illness reduces the burden of illness as well as the risk for severe outcomes such as violence and suicide, as it did for Cho during his precollege years.

- During his high school years, Cho was identified as having special educational needs. His identification as a special education student within the first 9 weeks of enrollment in a new high school and the accommodations accorded him as part of his Individualized Educational Plan led to a high degree of academic success. Indeed, his high school guidance counselor felt that his high school career was a success. With regard to his social skills, however, his progress was minimal at best.

- Clearly, Cho appeared to be at high risk, as withdrawn and inhibited behavior confers risk. This risk seemed mitigated by the interventions and accommodations put in place by the school. This risk also was reduced by involved and concerned parents who were particular in following through with weekly therapy. This risk was further mitigated by 198ervictive therapy that allowed expression (through art therapy) of underlying feelings of inadequacy. These factors as well as an above-average performance in school (buttressed by accommodations) lessened his frustration and anger.

- The school that Cho attended played an important part in reducing the possibility of severe regression in his functioning. The school worked closely with Cho's parents and sister. There was coordination between the school and the therapist and the psychiatrist who were treating Cho. These positive influences ended when Cho graduated from high school. His multifaceted support system then disappeared leaving a huge void.

## COLLEGE YEARS

In August of 2003, Cho began classes at Virginia Tech as a Business Information Technology major. Mr. and Mrs. Cho were concerned about his move away from home and the stress of the new environment, especially when they learned he was unhappy with his roommate. His parents visited him every weekend on Sundays during that first semester, which was a major time commitment since they both worked the other 6 days of the week. They noted that the dorm room trash can was full of beer cans (allegedly, from the interview with Cho's parents, the roommate was drinking) and the room was quite dirty. Cho, in contrast, had kept his room neat at home and had good hygiene. He requested a room change—a move that his parents and sister saw as a positive sign that he was being proactive and taking care of his own affairs. It seemed as though college was working out for him because he seemed excited about it.

Cho settled in, got his room changed by the beginning of the second semester, and seemed to be adjusting. Parental visits became less frequent. According to a routine they established, every Sunday night he spoke with his parents by telephone who always asked how he was doing and whether he needed anything, including money. Mr. and Mrs. Cho said that he never asked for extra money and would not accept any. He was very mindful of the family's financial situation and lived frugally. He would not buy things even though his parents encouraged him occasionally to purchase new clothes or other items. They reported that he did not appear envious or angry about anything.

During his freshman year, Cho took courses in biology, math, communications, political science, business information systems, and introduction to poetry. His grades overall were good, and he ended the year with a GPA of 3.00.

Cho's sophomore year (2004–2005) brought some changes. Cho made arrangements to share the rent on a condominium with a senior at Virginia Tech who worked long hours and was rarely home. His courses that fall leaned more heavily toward science and math. His grades slipped that term. At the same time, he became enthusiastic about writing and decided he would switch his major to English beginning the fall semester of 2005. It is unclear why he made this choice as he disliked using words in school or at home. Moreover, English had not been one of his strongest subjects in high school.

The answer may be found in an exchange of e-mails that Cho had with then-Chair of the English Department, Dr. Lucinda Roy. Cho had taken one of her poetry classes, a large group, entry-level course the previous semester. On Saturday, November 6, 2004, he wrote "I was in your poetry class last semester, and I remember you talking about the books you published. I'm looking for a publisher to submit my novel…I was just wondering if you know of a lot of publishers or agents or if you have a good connection with them." He went on, "My novel is relative[ly] short…sort of like Tom Sawyer except that it's really silly and pathetic depending on how you look at it…." Dr. Roy's first e-mail back said: "Could you send me your name? You forgot to sign your note." "Seung Cho," he wrote. Dr. Roy then recommended two resource books and gave him tips on finding literary agents. She also advised, "If you haven't yet taken a creative writing (fiction) course…you should consider doing so."

University personnel explained to the panel that Virginia Tech's process for changing majors relies on "advisors" who serve to help ensure that students are taking the right number of credits and courses to meet the requirements of their major and to graduate. They do not generally offer counsel on whether a student is making a wise move or examine the reasons behind their class choices. In any given year at Virginia Tech, many students change majors. Over 40 percent of the student body changes their major after the first year or two. Thus this change is not abnormal and not a red flag.

Cho seemed to enjoy the idea of writing, especially poetry. His sister noticed that he would bring home stacks of books on literature and poetry and books on how to become a writer. Writing seemed to have become a passion, and his family was thrilled that he found something he could be truly excited about. He would spend hours at his computer writing, but when his sister asked to see his work, he would refuse. On one rare occasion, she did get to read a story he wrote about a boy and his imaginary friend, which she thought was somewhat strange, but nothing too odd.

Cho's parents never read his compositions, both because he did not offer to show them and because they did not read English, at least not well.

Cho took three English courses in the spring of 2005, plus an economics course, and an introductory psychology course. He did not do particularly well, especially in the literature courses. One of his English professors gave him a D-, another, a C+. He earned a B+ in Introduction to Critical Reading, but also withdrew from the economics class, thus earning only 12 credits and registering a 2.32 for the semester.

Late that sophomore year, in his presence, Cho's sister chanced upon a rejection letter from a New York publishing house on Cho's desk at home. He had submitted a topic for a book describing the book's outline. She encouraged him to continue to write and learn saying that all writers have to work at their craft for a long time before they are published and that he was just at the beginning and not to lose heart.

While living in the off-campus condominium, Cho became convinced that he had mite bites (based on searches he did on the Internet). He went to a local doctor who diagnosed it as severe acne and put him on medication. Other than followup appointments for his acne at home and at the Shiffert Medical Center at Virginia Tech (he continued to believe mites were the problem), he did not have regular appointments with general practitioners, specialists, psychiatrists, or counselors in his hometown during his entire college tenure. His family reported that he came home for all his breaks and would spend the time writing, reading, playing basketball, and riding his bike—alone.

Storm Clouds Gathering, Fall 2005 – The fall semester of Cho's junior year (2005) was a pivotal time. From that point forward, Cho would become known to a growing number of students and faculty not only for his extremely withdrawn personality and complete lack of interest in responding to others in and out of the classroom, but for hostile, even violent writings along with threatening behavior.

He registered for French and four English courses, one of which was Creative Writing: Poetry, taught by Nikki Giovanni. It would seem he selected this course on the basis of Dr. Roy's advice to him the previous fall. His sister began noticing some subtle changes: he was not writing as much in his junior year and he seemed more withdrawn. The family wondered whether he was getting anxious about the future and what he would do after graduation. His father wanted him to go to graduate school, but Cho indicated he did not want to continue with academics after he graduated. His parents then offered to help him find a job after graduation, but he refused.

Cho had moved back to the dormitories that semester. He had a roommate and two suitemates who lived in another room connected by a bathroom—a typical layout in the residence halls. The panel interviewed his roommate and one suitemate who related some events from that year. They described Cho in the same way as he is described throughout this report: very quiet, short responses to questions, and rarely initiating any communication. At the beginning of the school year, the roommate and the other suitemates took Cho to several parties. He would always end up sitting in the corner by himself. One time they all went back to a female student's room. Cho took out a knife ("lock blade, not real large") and started stabbing the carpet. They stopped taking him out with them after that incident.

The three suitemates would invite Cho to eat with them at the beginning of the year, but he would never talk so they stopped asking. They observed him eating alone in the dining hall or lounge. The roommate asked Cho who he hung out with and Cho said "nobody." He would see him sometimes at the gym playing basketball by himself or working out.

Cho's roommate never saw him play video games. He would get movies from the library and watch them on his laptop. The roommate never saw what they were, but they always seemed dark. Cho would listen to and download heavy metal music. Someone wrote heavy metal lyrics on the walls of their suite in the fall, and then in the halls in the spring. Several of the students believed Cho was responsible because the words were similar to the lyrics Cho posted on Facebook.

Several times when the suitemates came in the room, it smelled as though Cho had been burning something. One time they found burnt pages under a sofa cushion. Cho would go to different lounges and call one of the suitemates on the phone. He would identify himself as "question mark"—Cho's twin brother—and ask to speak with Seung. He also posted messages to his roommate's Facebook page, identifying himself as Cho's twin. The roommate saw a prescription drug bottle on his desk. He and the

others in the suite looked it up online and found that it was a medication for "skin fungus."

Cho's actions in the poetry class taught by Nikki Giovanni that semester are widely known and documented. For the first 6 weeks of class, the professor put up with Cho's lack of cooperation and disruptive behavior. He wore reflector glasses and a hat pulled down to obscure his face. Dr. Giovanni reported to the panel that she would have to take time away from teaching at the beginning of each class to ask him to please take off his hat and please take off his glasses. She would have to stand beside his desk until he complied. Then he started wearing a scarf wrapped around his head, "Bedouin-style" according to Professor Giovanni. She felt that he was trying to bully her.

Cho also was uncooperative in presenting and changing the pieces that he wrote. He would read from his desk in a voice that could not be heard. When Dr. Giovanni would ask him to make changes, he would present the same thing the following week. One of the papers he read aloud was very dark, with violent emotions. The paper was titled "So-Called Advanced Creative Writing – Poetry." He was angry because the class had spent time talking about eating animals instead of about poetry, so his composition, which he would later characterize as a satire, spoke of an "animal massacre butcher shop."

In the paper, Cho accused the other students in the class of eating animals, "I don't know which uncouth, low-life planet you come from but you disgust me. In fact, you all disgust me." He made up gruesome quotes from the classmates, then wrote, "You low-life barbarians make me sick to the stomach that I wanna barf over my new shoes. If you despicable human beings who are all disgraces to [the] human race keep this up, before you know it you will turn into cannibals—eating little babies, your friends,. I hope y'all burn in hell for mass murdering and eating all those little animals."

Dr. Giovanni began noticing that fewer students were attending class, which had never been a problem for her before. She asked a student what was going on and he said, "It's the boy...everyone's afraid of him." That was when she learned that Cho also had been using his cell phone to take pictures of students without permission.

Dr. Giovanni talked to Cho, telling him, "I don't think I'm the teacher for you," and offered to get him into another class. He said that he did not want to transfer, which surprised her. She contacted the head of the English Department, Dr. Roy, about Cho and warned that if he were not removed from her class, she would resign. He was not just a difficult student, she related, he was not working at all. Dr. Giovanni was offered security, but declined saying she did not want him back in class, period. She saw him once on campus after that and he just stared at the ground.

Dr. Roy explained to the panel what her actions were once Dr. Giovanni made her aware of Cho's upsetting behavior. She remembered Cho from the previous semester when he took that poetry class she taught (she had given him a B- in the course). Dr. Roy contacted the Dean of Student Affairs, Tom Brown, the Cook Counseling Center, and the College of Liberal Arts with regard to the objectionable writing that Dr. Giovanni showed Dr. Roy. She asked to have it evaluated from a psychological point of view and inquired about whether the picture-taking might have been against the code of student conduct.

Dean Brown sent an e-mail message to Dr. Roy and advised "there is no specific policy related to cell phones in class. But, in Section 2 of the University Policy for Student Life, item #6 speaks to disruption. This is the 'disorderly conduct' section which reads: 'Behavior that disrupts or interferes with the orderly function of the university, disturbs the peace, or interferes with the performance of the duties of university personnel.' Clearly, the disruption he caused falls under this policy if adjudicated."

Dean Brown also said, "I talked with a counselor...and shared the content of the 'poem'... and she did not pick up on a specific threat. She suggested a referral to Cook during your meeting. I also spoke with Frances Keene, Judicial Affairs director and she agrees with your plan." He continued, "I would make it clear to him that any similar behavior in the future will be referred."

Frances Keene noted in her response to Dean Brown and Dr. Roy that she was available if Cho had any further questions about how using his cell phone in class to take photographs could constitute disorderly conduct. She also wrote, "I agree that the content is inappropriate and alarming but doesn't contain a threat to anyone's immediate safety (thus, not actionable under the abusive conduct – threats section of the UPSL)."

During an interview with the panel, Ms. Keene related that she would have needed something in writing to initiate an investigation into the disorderly conduct violation, and reported that she never received anything. The formal request would have come from the English Department.

Ms. Keene recalled that the concern about Cho was brought before the university's "Care Team," of which she is a member, at their regular meeting. The Care Team is comprised of the dean of Student Affairs, the director of Residence Life, the head of Judicial Affairs, Student Health, and legal counsel. Other agencies from the university are occasionally asked to participate; including the Women's Center, fraternities and sororities, the Disability Center, and campus police, though these agencies are not standing members of the Team.

At the Care Team meeting, members were advised of the situation with Cho and that Dr. Roy and Dr. Giovanni wanted to proceed with a class change to address the matter. The perception was that the situation was taken care of and Cho was not discussed again by the Care Team. The team made no referrals of Cho to the Cook Counseling Center. The Care Team did nothing. There were no referrals to the Care Team later that fall semester when Resident Life, and later, VTPD became aware of Cho's unwanted communications to female students and threatening behavior.

Frances Keene said that she received no communications from the female students who had registered complaints about Cho and that she learned of those incidents only through campus police incident reports. However, the assistant director of Judicial Affairs, Rohsaan Settle, received an e-mail communication on December 6 advising her of Cho's "odd behavior" and "stalking." Ms. Keene indicated that it is her office's policy to contact students who have been threatened and advise them of their rights, but one of the students stated that she was never contacted by Judicial Affairs, and there is no documentation that the others were contacted. Ms. Keene indicated that she would have discussed these incidents with the Care Team at the time the incidents occurred had she known about them.

Dr. Roy e-mailed Cho and asked him to contact her for a meeting. He responded with an angry, two-page letter in which he harshly criticized Dr. Giovanni and her teaching, saying she would cancel class and would not really instruct, but just have students read what they wrote and discuss the writings. He agreed to meet with Dr. Roy and said "I know it's all my fault because of my personality…Being quiet, one would think, would repel attention but I seem to get more attention than I want (I can just tell by the way people stare at me)." He said he imagined she was going to "yell at me."

Dr. Roy asked a colleague, Cheryl Ruggiero, to be present for the meeting with Cho. Ms. Ruggiero took notes, the transcription of which provided an exceptionally detailed account of that session with Cho as did e-mails from Dr. Roy to appropriate administration officials after the meeting.

Cho arrived wearing dark sunglasses. He seemed depressed, lonely, and very troubled. Dr. Roy assured him she was not going to yell at him, but discussed the seriousness of what he wrote and his other actions. He replied that he was "just joking" about the writing in Giovanni's class, but agreed that it might have been perceived differently. Dr. Roy asked him if he was offended by the class discussion on eating animals and he said, "I wasn't offended. I was just making fun of it…thought it was funny, thought I'd make fun of it." He was asked if he was a vegetarian or had religious beliefs about eating meat or animals; he answered no to both questions.

Ms. Ruggiero's transcript mentions that Dr. Roy "proposes alternative of working independently with herself and Fred D'Aguiar." The transcript also notes that Cho "doesn't want to lose credits…if not 'kicked out' will stay" [I (Ruggiero) noted some emotion on the words 'kicked out,' a small spark of anger or resentment]. The transcript goes on to document that "Lucinda asked if he would remove his sunglasses." Cho takes a long time to respond, but he does remove them. "It is a very distressing sight, since his face seems very naked and blank without them. It's a great relief to be able to read his face, though there isn't much there." Dr. Roy asks if taking off the sunglasses has been terrible for him…and says "he doesn't seem like himself, like the student she knew in the Intro to Poetry class, and she asks if anything terrible or bad has happened to him." Eventually Cho answers "No."

Twice during the meeting with Cho, Dr. Roy asked him if he would talk to a counselor. She told him she had the name of someone, and asked again if he would consider going. He did not answer for a while, and then said vaguely, "sure."

In her interview with the panel, Dr. Roy stated that the university's policy made the situation difficult. She was obligated to offer Cho an alternative that was equivalent to the instruction he would receive in Giovanni's class. Thus, she offered to tutor him privately. He later agreed. She told Cho that he would have to meet four more times and do some writing. As he left the meeting, Dr. Roy gave him a copy of her book. He took it and "appeared to be crying," she related.

Throughout the deliberations about Cho's writing and behavior and the available options, Dr. Roy communicated widely with all relevant university officers and provided updates on meetings and decisions. On October 19, 2005,

Dr. Roy e-mailed Zenobia Hikes, Tom Brown, George Jackson, and Robert Miller with a report on her meeting with Cho.

> Cheryl and I met with the student we spoke about today. We spoke about 30 minutes. He was very quiet and it took him long time to respond to question; but I think he may be willing to work with me and with Professor Fred D'Aguiar rather than continuing in Nikki's course…h e didn't seem to think that his poem should have alarmed anyone… [But] he also said he understood why people assumed from the piece that he was angry with them. I strongly recommended that he see a counselor, and he didn't commit to that one way or the other. …Both Cheryl and I are genuinely concerned about him because he appeared to be very depressed—though of course only a professional could verify that.

One month later, Dr. Roy wrote to Associate Dean Mary Ann Lewis, Liberal Arts & Human Sciences, who in turn shared it with the dean of Student Affairs and Ellen Plummer, Assistant Provost and Director of the Women's Center. She wrote

> He is now meeting regularly with me and with Fred D'Aguiar rather than with Nikki. This has gone reasonably well, though all of his submissions so far have been about shooting or harming people because he's angered by their authority or by their behavior. We're hoping he'll be able to write inside a different kind of narrative in the future, and we're encouraging him to do so…I have to admit that I'm still very worried about this student. He still insists on wearing highly reflective sunglasses and some responses take several minutes to elicit. (I'm learning patience!) But I am also impressed by his writing skills, and by what he knows about poetry when he opens up a little. I know he is very angry, however, and I am encouraging him to see a counselor—something he's resisted

so far. Please let me and Fred know if you see a problem with this approach.

For the remainder of the semester, Dr. Roy focused on William Butler Yeats and Emily Dickinson to help him develop empathy toward others and redirect his writing away from violent themes. They worked on a poem together where she went over technical skills. She saw no overt threats in the writings he did for her. He was stiff, sad, and seemed deliberately inarticulate, but gradually he opened up and wrote well. She repeatedly offered to take him to counseling. She eventually gave him an "A" for a grade.

Cho did not go home for Thanksgiving, according to his roommate and resident advisor, though he thought that Cho may have gone home for a few days at Christmas. When Cho's parents were asked about this they indicated that he came home at every break, but that sometimes he would have to wait a day or so until their day off work so they could come pick him up at school.

According a VTPD incident report, on Sunday, November 27, the police, following a complaint from a female student who lived on the fourth floor of West Ambler Johnston, came to Cho's room to talk to him. The roommate went to the lounge and then returned after the police left. Cho said "want to know why the police were here?" He then related that "he had been text messaging a female student and thought it was a game". He went to her room wearing sunglasses and a hat pulled down and said "I'm question mark." He said that "the student freaked out," and the resident advisor came out and called the police. According to the police record, the officer warned Cho not to bother the female student anymore, and told him they would refer the case to Judicial Affairs.

The resident advisor told the panel about Cho, "He was strange and got stranger." She said that Cho's roommate and one of the other suitemates found a very large knife in Cho's desk and discarded it.

On Wednesday, November 30, at 9:45 am, Cho called Cook Counseling Center and spoke with

Maisha Smith, a licensed professional counselor. This is the first record of Cho's acting upon professors' advice to seek counseling, and it followed the interaction he had had with campus police three days before. She conducted a telephone triage to collect the necessary data to evaluate the level of intervention required. Ms. Smith has no independent recollection of Cho and her notes from the triage are missing from Cho's file. A note attached to the electronic appointment indicates that Cho specifically requested an appointment with Cathye Betzel, a licensed clinical psychologist, and indicated that his professor had spoken with Dr. Betzel. The appointment was scheduled for December 12 at 2:00 pm, but Cho failed to keep the appointment. However, he did call Cook Counseling after 4:00 pm that same afternoon and was again scheduled for telephone triage.

According to the Cook scheduling program documents, Cho was again triaged by telephone at 4:45 on December 12. This triage was conducted by Dr. Betzel who has no recollection of the specific content of the "brief triage appointment." Written documentation that would have typically been completed at that time is missing. The "ticket" completed to indicate the type of contact indicates that the telephone appointment was kept, that no diagnosis was made (consistent with Cook's procedure to not make a diagnosis until a clinical intake interview is completed) and that no referral was made for follow-up services either at Cook or elsewhere. Dr. Betzel did recall at the time of her interview with the panel that she had a conversation with Dr. Roy concerning a student whose name she did not recall, however the details were so similar that she believes it was Cho. She recalls that Dr. Roy was concerned about disturbing writings submitted by Cho in class, and that Dr. Roy detailed her plans to meet with the student individually. The date of Dr. Betzel's consultation with Dr. Roy is unknown and any written documentation that would typically have been associated with the consultation is missing from Cho's file.

## CHO'S HOSPITALIZATION AND COMMITMENT PROCEEDINGS

(The law pertaining to these proceedings is discussed in Part B of this chapter.)

On December 12, 2005, the Virginia Tech Police Department (VTPD) received a complaint from a female sophomore residing in the East Campbell residence hall regarding Cho. She knew Cho through his roommate and suitemate. The students had attended parties together at the beginning of the semester and it was at this young woman's room that Cho had produced a knife and stabbed the carpet. While the student no longer saw Cho socially, she had received instant messages and postings to her Facebook page throughout the semester that she believed were from him. The messages were not threatening, but, rather, self-deprecating. She would write back in a positive tone and inquire if she were responding to Cho. The reply would be "I do not know who I am." In early December, she found a quote from Romeo and Juliet written on the white erase board outside her dorm room. It read:

> By a name
> I know not how to tell thee who I am
> My name, dear saint is hateful to myself
> Because it is an enemy to thee
> Had I it written, I would tear the word

The young woman shared with her father her concerns about the communications that she believed were from Cho. The father spoke with his friend, the chief of police for Christiansburg, who advised that the campus police should be informed.

The following day, December 13, a campus police officer met with Cho and instructed him to have no further contact with the young woman. She did not file criminal charges. No one spoke with her regarding her right to file a complaint with Judicial Affairs. Records document that there were multiple e-mail communications regarding the incident among Virginia Tech residential staff, the residence life administrator on call, and the president's & upper quad area coordinator, the director of Residence Life, and the assistant director of

Judicial Affairs. The matter was not, however, brought before the Virginia Tech multidisciplinary Care Team.

Following the visit from the police, Cho sent an instant message to one of his suitemates stating "I might as well kill myself." The suitemate reported the communication to the VTPD.

Police officers returned around 7:00 p.m. that same day to interview Cho again in his dorm room. The suitemate was not present, but they spoke to Cho's roommate out of his presence. The officers took Cho to VTPD for assessment, and a pre-screen evaluation was conducted there at 8:15 p.m. by a licensed clinical social worker for New River Valley Community Services Board (CSB). The pre-screener interviewed Cho and the police officer, and then spoke with both Cho's roommate and a suitemate by phone. She recorded her findings on a five-page Uniform Pre-Admission Screening Form, checking the findings boxes indicating that Cho was mentally ill, was an imminent danger to self or others, and was not willing to be treated voluntarily. She recommended involuntary hospitalization and indicated that the CSB could assist with treatment and discharge planning. She located a psychiatric bed, as required by state law at St. Albans Behavioral Health Center of the Carilion New River Valley Medical Center (St. Albans) and contacted the magistrate by phone to request that a temporary detention order (TDO) be issued.

The magistrate considered the pre-screen findings and issued a TDO at 10:12 p.m. Police officers transported Cho to St. Albans where he was admitted at 11:00 p.m. Cho did not speak at all with the officer during the trip to the hospital. He was noted to be cooperative with the admitting process. The diagnosis on the admission orders was "Mood Disorder, NOS" [non specific]. On the Carilion Health Services screening form for the potential for violence, it was marked that Cho denied any prior history of violent behavior, but that he did have access to a firearm. (The panel inquired about this, and checking the box for firearm access may have been an error.) He was on no medication at the time of admission, but Ativan was prescribed

for anxiety, as needed. One milligram of Ativan was administered at 11:40 p.m. (The records do not show that he ever received another dose.) Cho passed an uneventful night according to the nursing notes.

On the morning of December 14, at approximately 6:30 a.m., the Clinical Support Representative for St. Albans met with Cho to give him information about the mental health hearing. Around 7:00 a.m., the representative escorted Cho to meet with a licensed clinical psychologist, who conducted an independent evaluation of Cho pursuant to Virginia law.

The independent evaluator reported to the panel that he reviewed the prescreening report, but that due to the early hour, there were no hospital records available for his review. He did not speak with the designated attending psychiatrist who had not yet seen Cho. The evaluator has no specific recollection, but believes that the independent evaluation took approximately 15 minutes.

The evaluator completed the evaluation form certifying his findings that Cho "is mentally ill; that he does not present an imminent danger to (himself/others), or is not substantially unable to care for himself, as a result of mental illness; and that he does not require involuntary hospitalization." The independent evaluator did not attend the commitment hearing; however, both counsel for Cho and the special justice signed off on the form certifying his findings.

Shortly before the commitment hearing, the attending psychiatrist at St. Albans evaluated Cho. When he was interviewed by the panel, the psychiatrist did not recall anything remarkable about Cho, other than that he was extremely quiet. The psychiatrist did not discern dangerousness in Cho, and, as noted, his assessment did not differ from that of the independent evaluator—that Cho was not a danger to himself or others. He suggested that Cho be treated on an outpatient basis with counseling. No medications were prescribed, and no primary diagnosis was made.

The psychiatrist's conclusion was based in part on Cho's denying any drug or alcohol problems or any previous mental health treatment. The psychiatrist acknowledged that he did not gather any collateral information or information to refute the data obtained by the pre-screener on the basis of which the commitment was obtained. He indicated that this is standard practice and that privacy laws impede the gathering of collateral information. (Chapter V discusses these information privacy laws in detail.) The psychiatrist also said that the time it takes to gather collateral information is prohibitive in terms of existing resources.

Freer access to clinical information among agencies is imperative so that a rational plan for treatment can be developed. As for the relationship between the independent evaluator and the staff psychiatrist, they rarely see each other and they function independently. The role of the independent evaluator is to provide information to the court and the job of the attending psychiatrist is to provide clinical care for the patient.

As for counseling services at Virginia Tech and the other area universities from which St. Albans Hospital receives patients, according to the psychiatrist they are all stretched for mental health resources. The lack of outpatient providers who can develop a post-discharge treatment plan of substance is a major flaw in the current system. The lack of services is common in both the public and the private outpatient sectors.

The psychiatrist noted his recommendation for outpatient counseling on the Initial Consent Form for TDO Admissions. The clinical support representative then escorted Cho and other TDO patients to meet with their attorney prior to their hearings. There were four hearings that morning, and the attorney has no specific recollection of Cho.

A special justice designated by the Circuit Court of Montgomery County presided over the commitment hearing for Cho held shortly after 11:00 a.m. on December 14. Neither Cho's suitemate nor his roommate nor the detaining police officer nor the pre-screener nor the independent evaluator nor the attending

psychiatrist attended the hearing. The prescreening report was read into the record by Cho's attorney. The special justice reviewed the independent evaluation form completed by the independent evaluator and the treating psychiatrist's recommendation. He heard evidence from Cho. The special justice ruled that Cho "presents an imminent danger to himself as a result of mental illness" and ordered "O-P" (outpatient treatment) "—to follow all recommended treatments."

The clinical support representative (CSR) contacted Cook Counseling Center at Virginia Tech to make an appointment for Cho. The Cook Counseling Center required that Cho be put on the phone (a practice begun shortly before this hearing according to the CSR) to make the appointment, which he did. The appointment was scheduled for 3:00 p.m. that afternoon, December 14. The CSR does not recall whether this phone call was made prior to or following the hearing.

The clinical support representative recalls making his customary phone call to New River Valley CSB to advise them of the outcome of the morning's hearings. It was not the hospital's practice at that time to send copies of the orders from the commitment hearings.

Due to the rapidly approaching outpatient appointment for Cho, the CSR urged the treating psychiatrist to expedite the dictation and transcription of his discharge summary. It was transcribed shortly before noon and the physical evaluation findings and recommendation about an hour later. The clinical support representative recalls faxing the records to Cook Counseling Center, but he did not place a copy of the transmittal confirmation in the hospital records. Cook Counseling Center, however, has no record of having received any hospital records until January 2006. The physical evaluation report indicated that Cho was to be treated by the psychiatrist at St. Albans "and hopefully have some intervention in therapy for treatment of his mood disorder." The discharge summary, which was not part of the records received by the panel from Cook Counseling Center, indicated "followup and aftercare to be arranged with counseling center at Virginia Tech. Medications none."

Cho was discharged from St. Albans at 2:00 p.m. on December 14. No one the panel interviewed could say how Cho got back to campus. However, the electronic scheduling program at the Cook Counseling Center indicates that Cho kept his appointment that day at 3:00 p.m. He was triaged again, this time face-to-face, but no diagnosis was given. The triage report is missing (as well as those from his two prior phone triages), and the counselor who performed the triage has no independent recollection of Cho. It is her standard practice to complete appropriate forms and write a note to document critical information, recommendations, and plans for followup.

It is unclear why Cho would have been triaged for a third time rather than receiving a treatment session at his afternoon appointment following release from St. Albans. The Collegiate Times had run an article at the beginning of the fall semester expressing "concern about the diminished services provided by the counseling center" and the temporary loss of its only psychiatrist.

It was the policy of the Cook Counseling Center to allow patients to decide whether to make a followup appointment. According to the existing Cook Counseling Center records, none was ever scheduled by Cho. Because Cook Counseling Center had accepted Cho as a voluntary patient, no notice was given to the CSB, the court, St. Albans, or Virginia Tech officials that Cho never returned to Cook Counseling Center.

## AFTER HOSPITALIZATION

Cho's family did not realize what was happening with him at Blacksburg that fall 2005 semester: his dark writings, stalking, and other odd and unsettling behavior that worried roommates, resident advisors, teachers and eventually, campus police. They were unaware that their son had been committed for a time to St. Albans Hospital or that he had appeared in court before a special justice. This is corroborated by documents and interviews relating that Cho refused to notify his parents when campus police responded to his threat of suicide. The university did not inform the parents either.

According to Virginia Tech records, there was a "home town" doctor or counselor who Cho could see when he was home. The panel did not discover what led to this assumption. However, it is known that the university did not contact the family to ascertain the veracity of home town followup for counseling and medication management.

When Cho's parents were asked what they would have done if they had heard from the college about the professors', roommates, and female students' complaints, their response was, "We would have taken him home and made him miss a semester to get this looked at ...but we just did not know... about anything being wrong." From their history during the high school years, we do know that they were dedicated to getting him to therapy consistently and also consented to psychopharmacology when the need arose.

More Problems, Spring 2006 – The trend of disturbing themes continued to be apparent in many of Cho's writings, along with his selective mutism.

Robert Hicok had Cho in his Fiction Workshop class that semester. Hicok described his class as a mid-level fiction course with about 20 students. He told the panel that there was no participation from Cho and that Cho's stories and work were violent. He said Cho was a very cogent writer, but his creativity was not that good. Cho was open to suggestions and he made some edits, but he was "not very unique" in his writing. The combination of the content of Cho's stories and his not talking raised red flags for Hicok. He consulted with Dr. Roy, but then decided to keep Cho in the class and just deal with him. Hicok scheduled two meetings with Cho, but he did not show up, and Hicok never saw Cho again after the semester ended. Cho received a D+ in this class.

Professor Hicok shared none of Cho's writings with the panel. However, based on a question to a panel member by a reporter, further inquiry was made as this report was about to go to press. Several writings by Cho in Hicok's class were produced, one of which is of particular significance. It tells the story of a morning in the life of Bud "who gets out of bed unusually early…puts on his black jeans, a strappy black vest with many pockets, a black hat, a large dark sunglasses [sic] and a flimsy jacket…." At school he observes "students strut inside smiling, laughing, embracing each other….A few eyes glance at Bud but without the glint of recognition. I hate this! I hate all these frauds! I hate my life….This is it….This is when you damn people die with me…." He enters the nearly empty halls "and goes to an arbitrary classroom…." Inside "(e)veryone is smiling and laughing as if they're in heaven-on-earth, something magical and enchanting about all the people's intrinsic nature that Bud will never experience." He breaks away and runs to the bathroom "I can't do this….I have no moral right…." The story continues by relating that he is approached by a "gothic girl." He tells her "I'm nothing. I'm a loser. I can't do anything. I was going to kill every god damn person in this damn school, swear to god I was, but I…couldn't. I just couldn't. Damn it I hate myself!" He and the "gothic girl" drive to her home in a stolen car. "If I get stopped by a cop my life will be forever over. A stolen car, two hand guns, and a sawed off shotgun." At her house, she retrieves "a .8 caliber automatic rifle and a M16 machine gun." The story concludes with the line "You and me. We can fight to claim our deserving throne."

Cho encountered problems in another English class that semester, Technical Writing, taught by Carl Bean. The professor told the panel that Cho was always very quiet, always wore his cap pulled down, and spoke extremely softly. Bean opined that "this was his power." By speaking so softly, he manipulated people into feeling sorry for him and his fellow students would allow him to get credit for group projects without having worked on them. Bean noted that Cho derived satisfaction from learning "how to play the game—do as little as he needed to do to get by." This profile of Cho stands in contrast to the profile of a pitiable, emotionally disabled young man, but it may in fact represent a true picture of the other side of Cho—the one that murdered 32 people.

Bean allowed that Cho was very intelligent. He could write with technical proficiency and could read well. However, his creative writing skills were limited and his command of the English language was "very impoverished." He had trouble with verb tenses and use of articles. On two or three occasions early in the semester, Bean had spoken to Cho after class regarding the fact that he was not participating orally nor working collaboratively on group assignments. By late March or early April, the class was given a writing assignment to do a technical essay about a subject within their major. Cho suggested George Washington and the American Revolution, but Bean advised him that this was not within his major. Cho next suggested the April 1960 revolution in Korea—again rejected because the topic was not in his major. Cho then decided to write "an objective real-time" experience based on Macbeth and corresponding to serial killings.

On April 17, 2006, one school year prior to the shooting to the day (because it was also a Monday), Bean asked Cho to stay after class again. The professor explained to Cho that his work was not satisfactory and that his topic was not acceptable. He recommended that Cho drop the class and that he would recommend that a late drop be permitted. Cho never said a word, just stared at him. Then, without invitation, Cho followed Bean to his office. The professor offered for him to sit down, but Cho refused and proceeded to argue loudly that he did not want to drop the class. Bean was surprised because he had never heard Cho speak like that before nor engage in that type of conduct. He asked Cho to leave his office and return when he had better control of himself. Cho left and subsequently sent an e-mail advising that he had dropped the course.

Bean did not discuss the matter with Dr. Roy and he was not aware that Nikki Giovanni had encountered problems with Cho the prior semester. After the massacre of April 16, it was discovered that Cho had mailed a letter to the English Department on that same day. Bean stated he knew Cho was antisocial, manipulative, and intelligent. Cho, he said, had obviously "researched" Bean after dropping Bean's course, because in the April 16 letter Cho wrote numerous times that Bean "went holocaust on me." Bean has a great interest in the Holocaust.

Fall 2006 – Cho enrolled in Professor Ed Falco's playwriting workshop in the fall semester. During the first class when each student was asked to introduce him/herself to the class, Cho got up and left before his turn. When he returned for the second class, Professor Falco informed him that he would have to participate; Cho did not respond. In his interview with the panel, Professor Falco described Cho's writing as juvenile with some pieces venting anger.

Post April 16, 2007 students from this class were quoted in the campus newspaper as saying that some class members had joked that they were waiting for Cho to do something. One student reportedly had told a friend that Cho "was the kind of guy who might go on a rampage killing".

According to an article in the August 10, 2007 edition of The Roanoke Times, Professor Falco, director of Virginia Tech's creative writing program, recently proposed and participated in the drafting of written guidelines for dealing with students who submit disturbing and violent work. The guidelines suggest that faculty concerned about a student's writing pursue a series of actions including speaking to the student, encouraging the student to seek counseling, and involving university administrators.

Cho also took a class called "Contemporary Horror" in the fall of 2006. His final exam paper which appears to analyze a horror film is reasonable and cogent. The professor awarded Cho a B for the course.

Cho's senior year roommate explained to the panel that he tried speaking to Cho at the beginning of the semester, but Cho barely responded. "I hardly knew the guy; we just slept in the same room." Cho went to bed early and got up early, so his roommate just left him alone and gave him his space. The only activities Cho engaged in were studying, sleeping, and downloading music. He never saw him play a video game, which he thought strange since he and most other students play them. One of the suitemates mentioned that he saw Cho working out at McCommis Hall and saw him return to the room from time to time in workout attire. Cho kept his side of the room very neat. Nothing appeared to be abnormal—no knives, guns, chains, etc. The only reading material the roommate saw on Cho's side was a paperback copy of the New Testament, which he thought may have been for a class. (Cho took a course in the spring 2007 semester: The Bible as Literature.)

The resident advisor for the section of Harper Hall where Cho resided had been forewarned by the previous year's RA that "there were issues" with Cho. She knew about his unwanted advances toward female students and that he was suspected of writing violent song lyrics on the dorm walls that also were posted on his web site. However, she did not encounter a single problem with him.

That fall semester, Cho enrolled in Professor Norris' Advanced Fiction Workshop—a small class of only about 10 students. Cho had taken one of her classes the previous spring, on contemporary fiction, so she knew how little he participated in class. Norris realized that the workshop class would be a problem for Cho because there would be discussions and readings. Cho appeared in class with a ball cap pulled low and making no eye contact. Norris checked with the dean's office to see if it was safe—if Cho was okay—and she asked to have someone intervene on his behalf.

The English Department did not know about Cho's dealings with campus police and the communications generated from Residence Life about his stalking behavior.

Norris told Cho that he had to come see her if he was going to able to make it through this particular class. She ascertained that Cho had trouble speaking in both English and Korean, and she offered to connect him with the Disability Services Office.

After meeting with Cho, she e-mailed him to reiterate her offers to go with him for counseling or for other services. He did not pursue those offers. His written work was on time and he was on time for class, but he missed the last 2 weeks of class. Cho earned a B+ in Norris's class that semester.

The following semester, spring 2007, Cho began to buy guns and ammunition. His class attendance began to fall off shortly before the assaults. There were no outward signs of his deteriorating mental state. In their last phone call with him the night of April 15, 2007, Mr. Cho and Mrs. Cho had no inkling that anything was the matter. Cho had called per their usual Sunday night arrangement. He appeared his "regular" self. He asked how his parents were, and other standard responses: "No I do not need any money." His parents said, "I love you."

## MISSING THE RED FLAGS

The Care Team at Virginia Tech was established as a means of identifying and working with students who have problems. That resource, however, was ineffective in connecting the dots or heeding the red flags that were so apparent with Cho. They failed for various reasons, both as a team and in some cases in the individual offices that make up the core of the team.

Key agencies that should be regular members of such a team are instead second tier, non-permanent members. One of these, the VTPD, knew that Cho had been cautioned against stalking—twice, that he had threatened suicide, that a magistrate had issued a temporary detention order, and that Cho had spent A night at St. Albans as a result of such detention order. The Care Team did not know the details of all these occurrences.

Residence Life knew through their staff (two resident advisors and their supervisor) that there were multiple reports and concerns expressed over Cho's behavior in the dorm, but this was not brought before the Care Team. The academic component of the university spoke up loudly about a sullen, foreboding male student who refused to talk, frightened classmate and faculty with macabre writings, and refused faculty exhortations to get counseling. However, after Judicial Affairs and the Cook Counseling Center opined that Cho's writings were not actionable threats, the Care Team's one review of Cho resulted in their being satisfied that private tutoring would resolve the problem. No one sought to revisit Cho's progress the following semester or inquire into whether he had come to the attention of other stakeholders on campus.

The Care Team was hampered by overly strict interpretations of federal and state privacy laws (acknowledged as being overly complex), a decentralized corporate university structure, and the absence of someone on the team who was experienced in threat assessment and knew to investigate the situation more broadly, checking for collateral information that would help determine if this individual truly posed a risk or not. (The interpretation of FERPA and HIPAA rules is discussed in a later chapter.)

There are particular behaviors and indicators of dangerous mental instability that threat assessment professionals have documented among murderers. A list of red flags, warning signs and indicators has been compiled by a member of the panel and is included as Appendix M.

## KEY FINDINGS – CHO'S COLLEGE YEARS TO APRIL 15, 2007

The lack of information sharing among academic, administrative, and public safety entities at Virginia Tech and the students who had raised concerns about Cho contributed to the failure to see the big picture. In the English Department alone, many professors encountered similar difficulties with Cho—non-participation in class, limited responses to efforts to personally interact, dark writings, reflector glasses, hat pulled low over face. Although to any one professor these signs might not necessarily raise red flags, the totality of the reports would have and should have raised alarms.

Cho's aberrant behavior of pathological shyness and isolation continued to manifest throughout his college years. He shared very little of his college life with his family, had no friends, and engaged in no activities outside of the home during breaks and summer vacations. While he was an adult, he was a member of the household and receiving parental support, but he did not hold a job to help earn money for college. Unusual by U.S. standards, a high, sometimes exclusive focus on academics is common among parents from eastern cultures.

Cho's roommates and suitemates noted frequent signs of aberrant behavior. Three female residents reported problems with unwanted attention from Cho (instant messages, text messages, Facebook postings, and erase board messages). One of Cho's suitemates combined many of these instances of concern into a report shared with the residence staff. The residence advisors reported these matters to the hall director and the residence life administrator on call. These individuals in turn, communicated by e-mail with the assistant director of Judicial Affairs.

Notwithstanding the system failures and errors in judgment that contributed to Cho's worsening depression, Cho himself was the biggest impediment to stabilizing his mental health. He denied having previously received mental health services when he was evaluated in the fall of 2005, so medical personnel believed that their interaction with him on that occasion was the first time he had showed signs of mental illness. While Cho's emotional and psychological disabilities undoubtedly clouded his ability to evaluate his own situation, he, ultimately, is the primary person responsible for April 16, 2007; to imply otherwise would be wrong.

## RECOMMENDATIONS

IV-1 Universities should recognize their responsibility to a young, vulnerable population and promote the sharing of information internally, and with parents, when significant circumstances pertaining to health and safety arise.

IV-2 Institutions of higher learning should review and revise their current policies related to—

a) recognizing and assisting students in distress

b) the student code of conduct, including enforcement

c) judiciary proceedings for students, 211erviceing enforcement

d) university authority to appropriately intervene when it is believed a distressed student poses a danger to himself or others IV-3 Universities must have a system that links troubled students to appropriate medical and counseling services either on or off campus, and to balance the individual's rights with the rights of all others for safety.

IV-4 Incidents of aberrant, dangerous, or threatening behavior must be documented and reported immediately to a college's threat assessment group, and must be acted upon in a prompt and effective manner to protect the safety of the campus community.

IV-5 Culturally competent mental health services were provided to Cho at his school and in his community. Adequate resources must be allocated for systems of care in schools and communities that provide culturally competent services for children and adolescents to reduce mental-illness-related risk as occurred within this community.

IV-6 Policies and procedures should be implemented to require professors encountering aberrant, dangerous, or threatening behavior from a student to report them to the dean. Guidelines should be established to address when such reports should be communicated by the dean to a threat assessment group, and to the school's counseling center.

IV-7 Reporting requirements for aberrant, dangerous, or threatening behavior and incidents for resident hall staff must be clearly established and reviewed during annual training.

IV-8 Repeated incidents of aberrant, dangerous, or threatening behavior must be reported by Judicial Affairs to the threat assessment group. The group must formulate a plan to address the behavior that will both protect other students and provide the needed support for the troubled student.

IV-9 Repeated incidents of aberrant, dangerous, or threatening behavior should be reported to the counseling center and reported to parents. The troubled student should be required to participate in counseling as a condition of continued residence in campus housing and enrollment in classes.

IV-10 The law enforcement agency at colleges should report all incidents of an issuance of temporary detention orders for students (and staff) to Judicial Affairs, the threat assessment team, the counseling center, and parents. All parties should be educated about the public safety exceptions to the privacy laws which permit such reporting.

IV-11 The college counseling center should report all students who are in treatment pursuant to a court order to the threat assessment team. A policy should be implemented to address what information can be shared with family and roommates pursuant to the public safety exceptions to the privacy laws.

IV-12 The state should study what level of community outpatient service capacity will be required to meet the needs of the commonwealth and the related costs in order to adequately and appropriately respond to both involuntary court-ordered and voluntary referrals for those services. Once this information is available it is recommended that outpatient treatments services be expanded statewide.

The panel's report deals with facts. Sometimes, however, police investigation requires educated guesses and speculation—such as in instances where a "profile" of an unknown killer is generated by FBI profilers, who are specially trained in this area. Set forth in Appendix N is such a work, written by panel member Dr. Roger Depue, who is, among many other qualifications, a former FBI profiler. While no member of the panel can definitively ascertain what was in Cho's mind, this profile offers one theory.

## Part B – Virginia Mental Health Law Issues

The Commonwealth of Virginia Commission on Mental Health Law Reform was appointed in October 2006, by Virginia Chief Justice Leroy R. Hassell, Sr. The 26-member commission, chaired by Professor Richard J. Bonnie, Director of the Institute of Law, Psychiatry and Public Policy at the University of Virginia, is charged to "conduct a comprehensive examination of Virginia's mental health laws and services" and to "study ways to use the law more effectively to serve the needs of people with mental illness, while respecting the interests of their families and communities."

The commission has held four meetings with another scheduled for November 2007 and is working through five task forces with more than 200 participants. The Task Force on Civil Commitment is addressing criteria for inpatient and outpatient commitment, transportation, and the emergency evaluation process, procedures for hearings, training, and compensation for participants in the process, and oversight.

The Task Force on Civil Commitment will submit its final report to the commission in November 2007. The commission intends to prepare a preliminary report during the winter and to submit a final report by the fall of 2008 for consideration by the 2009 General Assembly.

The discussion that follows constitutes an abridged effort, due to constraints of time and manpower, to address some of the issues that will be dealt with by the commission in a far more comprehensive manner. Many of the panel's recommendations are framed in general terms with the expectation that the commission will formulate specific proposals.

Throughout the panel's work, there was close collaboration with Professor Bonnie and James Stewart, the Inspector General for the Department of Mental Health and Mental Retardation and Substance Abuse Services. The inspector general released a report in June 2007 detailing his findings concerning Cho's interaction with mental health services in Virginia.

## TIME CONSTRAINTS FOR EVALUATION AND HEARING

Va. Code 37.2-808 establishes the procedures for involuntary temporary detention of persons who are mentally ill, present an imminent danger to self or others, and are in need of hospitalization but unwilling or unable to volunteer for treatment. Subsection H provides that no person shall remain in custody for longer than 4 hours without a temporary detention order issued by a magistrate. In Cho's case, the New River Valley CSB was able to provide a pre-screener in a timely manner, and she was able to conduct the screening and locate an available bed in order to present the matter to the magistrate within the required 4-hour period.

However, mental health service providers and special justices interviewed for this report set forth numerous arguments as to why this period should be lengthened to either 6 hours or to permit one renewal of the 4-hour period for good Cause. The concerns raised included that it is often difficult to promptly secure qualified personnel to perform the prescreening evaluation given staff resources and required travel time, particularly in rural jurisdictions. It is often even more difficult to locate the available bed required for a temporary detention order (TDO) to issue. Four hours do not allow sufficient time to gather meaningful collateral information from family, friends, or other health care providers nor to secure proper evaluations for medical clearance. Some noted, however, that an extension of the 4-hour period may require police departments to spend more time

with a person in emergency custody in those locales where hospital security are unable to assume responsibility.

The American College of Emergency Physicians (ACEP) has recommended that emergency physicians trained in psychiatric evaluation be given more authority in the involuntary hold process. Since emergency departments are 24-hour facilities, resources are already in place. Because the CSB serves an independent "gatekeeper" role under the Virginia TDO process, emergency physicians and CSB staff are generally expected to work collaboratively in determining whether a TDO is needed for those patients screened in emergency departments. However, where CSB pre-screeners are not immediately available, properly trained emergency physicians can effectively screen patients under an emergency custody order and communicate with the magistrate to obtain the TDO when needed. If such a gate keeping responsibility were to be conferred on emergency physicians, further questions would have to be addressed regarding the respective roles of the emergency physicians and the CSB staff in exploring alternatives to hospitalization and in participating in the commitment hearing.

Under current Virginia law, the duration of temporary detention may not exceed 48 hours prior to a hearing (or the next day that is not a Saturday, Sunday, or legal holiday). The mental health service providers in Cho's case were able to comply with the 48-hour requirement; however, the information available to the special justice was extremely limited. There was no history regarding prior treatment; there were no lab or toxicology reports, nor the report regarding access to a firearm. At the hearing, there were no witnesses present such as family, roommate/suitemates, the CSB pre-screener, the independent evaluator, or the treating psychiatrist.

Mental health professionals interviewed reported that 48 hours is one of the shortest detention periods in the nation and recommended that it be lengthened. Reasons cited for expanding this period included the need to contact family or friends and to explore the person's prior history. Also cited was the need for a more comprehensive independent evaluation and the difficulty in securing a complete report of the treating psychiatrist in time for the hearing. It was suggested that a psychiatric "workup" as well as a toxicology screen be available to the independent examiner. A further concern was that often psychiatric inpatient bed space is not available within the 48 hours. As a financial consideration, it was argued that a longer period would allow patients an opportunity to stabilize or recognize the need for voluntary treatment, thereby reducing the number of commitment hearings and the costs associated with special justices and appointed counsel.

## STANDARD FOR INVOLUNTARY COMMITMENT

The judge or special justice ordering commitment must find by clear and convincing evidence that the person presents (1) an imminent danger to himself or others or is substantially unable to care for himself, and (2) less restrictive alternatives to involuntary inpatient treatment have been investigated and are deemed unsuitable. Cho was found to be an imminent danger to himself by the pre-screener who also found that he was "unable to come up with a safety plan to adequately ensure safety." He was unwilling to contact his parents to pick him up. However, Cho was found not to be an imminent danger to self or others by both the independent examiner and the treating psychiatrist at St. Albans, and accordingly neither recommended involuntary admission. At the commitment hearing, the special justice did find Cho to be an imminent danger to himself; however, he agreed with the independent examiner and treating psychiatrist that a less restrictive alternative to involuntary admission, outpatient treatment, was suitable. Perhaps Cho presented himself differently at various stages of the commitment process or perhaps the professionals had differing evaluations of someone who did not speak much or perhaps they had differing interpretations of the standard set forth in the Virginia Code.

Mental health professionals advised the panel that the standard "imminent danger to self or others" is not clearly understood and is subject to differing interpretations. They recommend that the criteria for commitment be revised to achieve a more consistent application. Service providers and special justices suggest that the "imminent danger" criterion should be replaced by language requiring "a substantial likelihood" or "significant risk" that the person will cause serious injury to himself or others "in the near future." A few disagreed on the basis that personal rights of liberty should be paramount, and that changing the standard would lower the threshold for admission. Proponents for modifying the criteria respond that Virginia's commitment standard is one of the most restrictive of all the states. They contend that the threshold finding prevents intervention in cases of severe illness accompanied by substantial impairment of cognition, emotional stability, or self-control.

## PSYCHIATRIC INFORMATION

Many of those interviewed expressed serious concerns regarding the paucity of psychiatric information available to the independent valuator and judge/special justice. As noted above, the independent evaluator for Cho had only the report from the CSB pre-screener and no collateral information or medical records. The independent evaluator plays a key role in the commitment process in many jurisdictions. In Cho's case, notwithstanding the finding from the independent evaluator that Cho did not pose an imminent threat, the special justice, nevertheless convened the hearing and actually made a finding that differed from that of the independent evaluator. He did, however, agree with the independent evaluator that inpatient treatment was not required. The panel was advised that in many jurisdictions, absent a finding by the independent evaluator that an individual poses an imminent danger or is substantially unable to care for himself, many special justices will decline to hold a hearing.

It is unclear under existing law whether the independent evaluator is intended to serve as a gate keeper. If the opinion of the independent evaluator is to be given great weight, then it is critical that sufficient psychiatric information be available upon which an informed judgment may be made. Background information 215erviceing records from the current hospitalization must be assembled for review. The Cho case calls attention to the need to assure that the independent evaluator has both sufficient time and information to conduct an adequate evaluation.

At Cho's hearing, the only documents available to the special justice were the Uniform Pre-Admission Screening Form, a partially completed Proceedings for Certification form recording the findings of the independent evaluator and a physician's examination form containing the findings of the treating psychiatrist. No prior patient history was presented; no toxicology, lab results, or physical evaluation from the treating psychiatrist were available. The admitting form indicating that Cho had access to a firearm was not presented.

Panel members have been advised by mental health providers and special justices from other locales in Virginia that it is not unusual for the evidence presented at commitment hearings to be minimal. Due to the time constraints and limitations of resource personnel, the information available to the judge/special justice is often very limited. Witnesses cannot be located quickly and hospital records have often not been transcribed. Additionally, conflicting interpretations of the constraints of the Health Insurance Portability and Accountability Act (HIPAA) and Virginia Code 32.1-127.1:03 Health Records Privacy (VaHRP) often make it difficult to acquire background medical/psychiatric information on a patient previously treated elsewhere. Legal experts from a research advisory group for the Commission on Mental Health Law Reform participated in the development of a questionnaire for judges and special justices to complete following civil commitment hearings in the month of May 2007. More than 1400 questionnaires were returned. They reflected that approximately 60 percent of the May

hearings lasted no more than 15 minutes and only 4 percent required more than 30 minutes.

Cho was the only person to testify at his commitment hearing, and he was not very communicative. The pre-screener was not present nor was any representative from the CSB. The independent evaluator was not present. The officer who detained Cho was not present. Cho's roommate, suitemates, and Cho's family were all absent. This apparently is not an unusual scenario for commitment hearings in Virginia. Often the pre-screener is off duty by the time of the hearing. CSBs with limited staff frequently do not send a substitute. (The commission's survey reflected that the CSB representatives attended only half of the hearings held in May, 2007). Independent evaluators, paid $75 per commitment evaluation, often feel compelled to return to their private practice rather than waiting for hearings that may be held hours after the evaluation is complete. (The responses to the questionnaires indicated that the independent evaluators were present at approximately two-thirds of Mays hearings.) Due to time constraints and concerns regarding HIPAA and VaHRP restrictions, friends and family are often not notified.

HIPAA and VaHRP generally require that no health care entity disclose an individual's health records or information. However, permitted exceptions are information necessary for the care of a patient and information concerning a patient who may present a serious threat to public health or safety. Therefore, a treating physician at the facility where a patient is detained should be granted access to all prior psychiatric history. These exceptions, however do not clearly permit these records be shared with the judge or special justice at the commitment hearing. Although a person may consent to the release of information to any person or entity, detained individuals are often unable or disinclined to do so.

Because interpretation of HIPAA and FERPA were key in stopping adequate exchange of information concerning Cho, the panel requested that its legal council research the interpretation and exceptions under these laws, which is presented in the next chapter.

## INVOLUNTARY OUTPATIENT ORDERS

In conducting the investigation, the panel encountered many questions concerning involuntary outpatient orders. What specificity should be required of outpatient orders? To whom should notice of outpatient orders be given? How should compliance with outpatient orders be monitored? What procedures should be available to address noncompliance and what resources are needed?

The special justice ordered that Cho receive outpatient treatment; however, the order provided no information regarding the nature of the treatment other than to state "to follow all recommended treatments." The order did not specify who was to provide the outpatient treatment or who was to monitor the treatment.

There was considerable support among those interviewed by panel members for greater guidance in the Virginia Code regarding outpatient treatment orders. Some felt that the order should track recommendations from the treating physician as to the frequency and duration of treatment and whether medication was required. Others observed that often physician's evaluations and orders were not available and the special justice/substitute judge did not have the expertise to order specific treatment. However, all agreed that more specificity in outpatient treatment orders is essential.

New River Valley CSB did not have a representative at Cho's hearing due to financial constraints. Va. Code 37.2-817I currently requires the CSB to recommend a specific course for involuntary outpatient treatment and to monitor compliance. However, the Code does not specify how or by whom the CSB will be notified that outpatient treatment has been ordered if a representative is not present at the hearing. There exists a disagreement as to whether the CSB was advised of the entry of the outpatient order in Cho's case. The clinical support representative for St. Albans advised

that he always calls the CSB following commitment hearings to report the results. The CSB reports that they have no record of having been notified. If the CSB is represented at the hearing, there can be no reason for confusion. However, if Virginia Code is not amended to require the presence in person or telephonically, it must be amended to designate who has responsibility for certifying a copy of the outpatient order to the CSB. There should also be clear guidance provided in the Virginia Code as to who has responsibility for notification if a private mental health practitioner is to provide the mandated outpatient treatment.

No notice of the hearing or the order issued by the special justice was given to Cho's family, his roommate/suitemates, the VTPD, or the Virginia Tech administration. The Code of Virginia authorizes no such notice. The recordings of the hearing must be kept confidential pursuant to Va. Code 37.2-818(A). The records, reports and court documents pertaining to the hearing are kept confidential if so requested by the subject of the hearing under 37.2-818(B) and are not subject to the Virginia Freedom of Information Act. HIPAA and VaHRP restrictions may further limit dissemination of certain information as no person to whom health records are disclosed may redisclose beyond the purpose for which disclosure was made. Concerns were raised by many interviewees and speakers at panel hearings that family members, those residing with the subject of a commitment hearing, the police department and school officials should all be notified of the hearing and its outcome in the interest of public safety.

In Cho's case, there are conflicting reports regarding the issue of notice to the treatment provider, Cook Counseling Center. An appointment had been scheduled by Cho with the assistance of the clinical support representative for St. Albans. The representative reports that he faxed a copy of the discharge summary to Cook. Cook, however, contends that they did not receive any written documentation until January, and even then it was the physical examination which indicated that Cho would be treated by the St. Alban's psychiatrist. Following Cho's in-person triage appointment on December 14, the Cook Counseling Center left it to Cho's discretion whether to return for follow up treatment. When he did not, it was not reported to the special justice, St. Alban's, or the CSB. The Virginia Code imposes no legal obligation for Cook Counseling Center to do so, and Cook counselors question whether they have the right to do so given the restrictions of HIPAA and VaHRP.

Furthermore, there exists the question of whether Cho was noncompliant given the general language of the involuntary treatment order; and if Cho were considered noncompliant, how was that to be addressed. There is no contempt provision in the Virginia Code for those noncompliant with involuntary outpatient orders. There is no guidance as to the nature of the hearing to be held for noncompliance; nor is there a basis for compensating the special justice/substitute judge or attorney for followup proceedings. Many questions are raised. If a form is created to report noncompliance, can a treatment provider file the report without violating HIPAA and VaHRP? If the noncompliance report is filed, how does the special justice secure the presence of the individual for a followup hearing? If the noncompliant individual does not pose an imminent danger to himself or others at the time of the followup hearing, an emergency custody order cannot be issued; nor can the special justice order involuntary inpatient treatment. Should there be a Code provision allowing for a short period of inpatient treatment for those not compliant with the outpatient order yet not an "imminent danger" at the time returned for noncompliance? Will commitment for noncompliance pose yet another burden on the already overcrowded inpatient facilities?

On June 22, 2007, the Commission on Mental Health Law Reform released the final report of its study of the current commitment process. This study, undertaken for the commission by Dr. Elizabeth McGarvey of the University of Virginia School of Medicine, involved intensive interviews with 64 professional participants in the process, 60 family members of persons with serious mental illness, and 86 people who have had the experience of being committed. According to Dr. McGarvey's report, professional participants and family stakeholders are uniformly frustrated by almost every aspect of the civil commitment process in Virginia. Among the most common complaints were a shortage of beds in willing detention facilities, insufficient time for adequate evaluation, the high cost and inefficiency of transporting people for evaluation, inadequate compensation for professional participants in the process, inadequate reimbursement for hospitals, inconsistent interpretation of the statute by different judges, and lack of central direction and oversight.

## CERTIFICATION OF ORDERS TO THE CENTRAL CRIMINAL RECORDS EXCHANGE

Va. Code 37.2-819 requires the clerk to certify, on a form provided, any order for involuntary admission to the Central Criminal Records Exchange. The section does not specify who bears responsibility for completion of the form. The failure of Va. Code 37.2-819 to specify responsibility for preparation of the order furnished by the Central Criminal Records Exchange was noted to be a problem. It is reported that in some jurisdictions, if the clerk is not furnished the completed form, no form is forwarded to the exchange. There is lack of consistency throughout the Commonwealth regarding who prepares the forms. In some jurisdictions, the forms are completed by the special justice/substitute judge, in others by the clerk of court, and reportedly in others, the forms are often not completed at all.

Of further concern was the issue of under what circumstances the forms are to be completed. Mental health and legal professionals interviewed by panel members felt that there was no reasonable distinction to be drawn between persons ordered for involuntary inpatient treatment and those ordered for involuntary out-patient treatment when a finding has been made that the individual poses an imminent danger to self or others. If firearms restrictions apply, they should be based upon the fact that an individual poses a danger, not on the basis of the type of treatment ordered; therefore, both involuntary inpatient and involuntary outpatient treatment orders should be certified. While the governor has addressed this matter by executive order, it was felt that legislation should be enacted embodying the certification requirement. Mental health and legal experts also raised the question of whether persons electing voluntary admission upon being advised of their right to do so during the commitment hearing should also be reported. (The commission's survey indicated that 30 percent of the commitment hearings in May resulted in voluntary admission.)

It was also noted with concern by the mental health and legal experts interviewed that the reporting requirement does not apply to orders for juveniles found to pose an imminent danger, regardless of whether inpatient or outpatient treatment was ordered. They further expressed concern regarding the absence of any provision in the Virginia Code requiring the clerk to certify orders pertaining to persons found not guilty by reason of insanity.

## KEY FINDINGS

Statutory time constraints for temporary detention and involuntary commitment hearings significantly impede the collection of vital psychiatric information required for risk assessment.

The Virginia standard for involuntary commitment is one of the most restrictive in the nation and is not uniformly applied.

The fact that a CSB representative did not attend the commitment hearing and the failure to certify a copy of the outpatient commitment Order to the CSB resulted in an absence of oversight for Cho's outpatient treatment.

The lack of a requirement in the Virginia Code to certify outpatient commitment orders to the CCRE resulted in Cho's name not being entered in the database, which could have prevented his purchase of firearms.

There was a lack of doctor-to-clinician contact between St. Albans Hospital and the Cook Counseling Center.

In the wake of the Virginia Tech tragedy, much of the discussion regarding mental health services has focused on the commitment process. However, the mental health system has starting from the lack of short-term crisis stabilization units to the outpatient services and the highly important case management function, which strings together the entire care for an individual to ensure success. These gaps prevent individuals from getting the psychiatric help when they are getting ill, during the need for acute stabilization, and when they need therapy and medication management during recovery.

## RECOMMENDATIONS

IV-13 Va. Code 37.2-808 (H) and (I) and 37.2-814 (A) should be amended to extend the time periods for temporary detention to permit more thorough mental health evaluations.

IV-14 Va. Code 37.2-809 should be amended to authorize magistrates to issue temporary detention orders based upon evaluations conducted by emergency physicians trained to perform emergency psychiatric evaluations.

IV-15 The criteria for involuntary commitment in Va. Code 37.2-817(B) should be modified in order to promote more consistent application of the standard and to allow involuntary treatment in a broader range of cases involving severe mental illness.

IV-16 The number and capacity of secure crisis stabilization units should be expanded where needed in Virginia to ensure that individuals who are subject to a temporary detention order do not need to wait for an available bed. An increase in capacity also will address the use of inpatient beds for moderately to severely ill patients that need longer periods of stabilization.

IV-17 The role and responsibilities of the independent evaluator in the commitment process should be clarified and steps taken to assure that the necessary reports and collateral information are assembled before the independent evaluator conducts the evaluation.

IV-18 The following documents should be presented at the commitment hearing:

- The complete evaluation of the treating physician, including collateral information.
- Reports of any lab and toxicology tests conducted.
- Reports of prior psychiatric history.
- All admission forms and nurse's notes.

IV-19 The Virginia Code should be amended to require the presence of the prescreener or other CSB representative at all commitment hearings and to provide adequate resources to facilitate CSB compliance.

IV-20 The independent evaluator, if not present in person, and treating physician should be available where possible if needed for questioning during the hearing.

IV-21 The Virginia Health Records Privacy statute should be amended to provide a safe harbor provision which would protect health entities and providers from liability or loss of funding when they disclose information in connection with evaluations and commitment hearings conducted under Virginia Code 37.2-814 et seq.

IV-22 Virginia Health Records Privacy and Va. Code 37.2-814 et seq. should be amended to ensure that all entities involved with treatment have full authority to share records with each other and all persons involved in the involuntary commitment process while providing the legal safeguards needed to prevent unwarranted breaches of confidentiality.

IV-23 Virginia Code 37.2-817I should be amended to clarify—

- The need for specificity in involuntary outpatient orders.
- The appropriate recipients of certified copies of orders.
- The party responsible for certifying copies of orders.
- The party responsible for reporting non-compliance with outpatient orders and to whom noncompliance is reported.
- The mechanism for returning the non-compliant person to court.
- The sanction(s) to be imposed on the non-compliant person who does not pose an imminent danger to himself or others.
- The respective responsibilities of the detaining facility, the CSB, and the outpatient treatment provider in assuring effective implementation of involuntary outpatient treatment orders.

IV-24 The Virginia Health Records Privacy statute should be clarified to expressly authorize treatment providers to report noncompliance with involuntary outpatient orders.

IV-25 Virginia Code 37.2-819 should be amended to clarify that the clerk shall immediately upon completion of a commitment hearing complete and certify to the Central Criminal Records Exchange, a copy of any order for involuntary admission or involuntary outpatient treatment.

IV-26 A comprehensive review of the Virginia Code should be undertaken to determine whether there exist additional situations where court orders containing mental health findings should be certified to the Central Criminal Records Exchange.

## ADDITIONS AND CORRECTIONS

Ruling on Cho's Poem: p. 43, Clarification – To be clear, it was the content of the poem written by Cho to which Director of Judicial Affairs Frances Keene was referring in the second paragraph, second column, which might have been confusing because the immediately preceding issue discussed in the paragraph is Cho's secret photos in the classroom.

Name and Title: p. 44, Correction – Rohsaan Settle should have been identified as a member of the Residence Life staff and not the Assistant Director of Judicial Affairs. The reference to Settle as "she" also is incorrect.

E-mail to Rohsaan Settle: p. 44, Addition – The email Settle received on December 6 concerning Cho's behavior was sent by an RA, Lisa Virga. She advised Settle of Cho's "odd behavior" and described Cho's "stalking" of a student, Christina Lillizu, who lived in Cochrane residence hall on the other side of the third floor where Cho lived. Cho had a class with Lillizu. He harassed her online, talked to her on IM, and went to her room twice, once in disguise. Lillizu reportedly did not confront Cho because she was afraid to but did contact VTPD after Cho appeared at her door in disguise. (The exact date and time of the VTPD contact are not known because there is no incident report at VTPD on that contact.) Ms. Virga also explained to Settle that Cho had two knives in the dorm room, though she did not specify the size of the knives. Mr. Settle responded to the RA that they should "chat" about the knives. There are no records indicating that Mr. Settle followed up with VTPD to report the possession of knives – which, if of a certain size, was a violation of the Code of Conduct – and the pattern of Cho's aberrant behavior. Mr. Settle has said he is not sure if he responded to the information in Virga's email but he thought VTPD was handling it.

Nature of Complaint: p. 45, Addition – The text says "…on Sunday, November 27, the police, following a complaint from a female student who lived on the fourth floor of West Ambler Johnston, came to Cho's room to talk to him." To elaborate, it was about 11:30 p.m. when a VTPD officer responded to 4021 West Ambler Johnston due to a harassment complaint from student Jennifer Nelson. She reported that she had received multiple Ims from someone who gave a false address and false email address. He also had called her. Nelson had no idea who he was, though he said they went to the same high school; she had identified him through Facebook. He had just come to her room, calling himself "The Question Mark Kid." Nelson and her roommate told him to leave and said they were calling police.

The officer investigated the moniker "question mark" on Facebook and confirmed Cho's identification and address after speaking with one of the individuals listed as Cho's friend. The 220ervicer immediately went to Cho's dorm room, read him his Miranda rights, and questioned him. The officer told Cho not to have any contact with Nelson by any means. Cho also was told there could be a judicial referral filed, but no criminal charges were being placed at that time.

The officer then returned to West Ambler Johnston to speak with Nelson. Nelson read Cho's statement, said she did not want to press criminal charges but would be comfortable testifying if there were a judicial hearing. The officer advised Nelson he would file a judicial referral, which he did. According to Virginia Tech policy, either a law enforcement officer or a victim can make a judicial referral. However, when Judicial Affairs followed up with Nelson they told her that in addition to the VTPD referral, she, too, would have to make a referral for them to pursue the matter. She declined.

Cho's CCC File: p. 46, Corrections and Clarification – There are several corrections to the text in the second paragraph of the left column. First the written documentation of Dr. Betzel's December 12 triage of Cho is no longer missing as it is part of the file found in Dr. Miller's home, as discussed previously. Second, the consultation between Dr. Betzel and Dr. Roy is misplaced in the chapter and should appear on page 43 as it relates to the activities surrounding Cho's removal from Dr. Giovanni's class. Moreover, the last sentence of that paragraph should be deleted and replaced with this text:

Dr. Roy's consultation with Dr. Betzel occurred around October 18, 2005 during the course of handling and following up on Dr. Giovanni's alarm about Cho's writings and behavior in class. This consultation predated Cho's triage appointments at CCC. There should have been a Triage Report on this consultation somewhere in the CCC records, but it would not typically have been part of a file on Cho unless it was connected to him after his visit to CCC and his subsequent case file. There were no formal procedures for what to do with these forms after they were reviewed by the CCC Director and returned to the front desk.

According to the Virginia Inspector General's report #179-09, Investigation-Records, Virginia Tech Cook Counseling Center, p. 9, issued November 9, 2009, the practice at CCC in the fall of 2005 was as follows:

"CCC counselors periodically had contact with faculty, university staff and parents who sought consultation regarding students about whom they were concerned. This occurred both for students who were being served by the Center and for students who had had no contact with the Center. It was expected that each consultation was to be documented on a separate Triage Form."

The Triage Forms were then to be placed in Dr. Miller's inbox for review and later filing in the front office "where all Triage Forms on students whose cases have not yet been opened are filed." To the extent that Triage Forms were completed for the consultations between faculty and the CCC and between administrators and the CCC concerning Cho they would not have been saved in a file with Cho's name because he was not an established patient there at that time. (Most of these communications were e-mails, not Triage Forms). Moreover, when a student is not identified during a consultation (as was the case with at least one about Cho) the Triage Form would likely not be linked to the student in question if he or she were to seek CCC services later and have a file started at that time. It was not a requirement to name the individual in question during a consultation.

Female Student Complaints About Cho: p. 46, Addition – More details are available about the call to VTPD on December 12, 2005. The complaint was from Margaret Bowman, 306 East Campbell residence hall, and regarded harassment by Cho. Bowman was upset over a series of unwanted communications over several days. Cho had sent her an IM on December 9. Then, on December 11 in the evening, she discovered an excerpt from Shakespeare written on the whiteboard outside her door. Returning from an exam the following morning, she found that a continuation of the quotation from Shakespeare had been added. She believed Cho was responsible because mutual friends told her that when they mentioned the situation to Cho he commented that "Shakespeare wrote it."

One of the responding officers went to Cho's room and left a message with Cho's roommate for Cho to contact the officers; they also sent an email to Cho requesting the same.

Discharge Summary to CCC: pp. 48–49, Correction – The last sentence of page 48 states that Cook Counseling Center has "no record of having received any hospital records until January 2006," which is what had been reported to the Review Panel. It is now known that on December 14, 2005 at 2:25 p.m., 35 minutes before Cho was seen at CCC, the CCC received a fax from Diane Turner at Carilion Health System in Radford. The fax included a discharge summary by Dr. Migliani which was transcribed on 12/14/05 at 11:57. The fax also included the New River Valley Community Services Uniform Pre-admission Screening Form of 12/13/05 completed by Kathy Godbey. Full hospital records were mailed, but not received (or marked as received) until 1/06.

Cho Writings and Professor Hicok's Class: p. 50, Corrections and Clarification – The Review Panel's concern over not receiving from Professor Hicok a copy of Cho's writing and of that writing not being mentioned by Professor Hicok was largely unwarranted. Professor Hicok had turned over some of Cho's writings in his class to an FBI agent acting on behalf of the Virginia State Police just two days after the April 16 shootings. Hicok thought the VSP would share the documents with the Review Panel, but they did not, apparently because they considered Cho's writings part of their investigation file.

Professor Hicok told the Review Panel that Cho's responses to writings by other students (not Cho's own writing as stated in the Report) were surprisingly cogent, but that Cho was not a good creative writer. Cho was open to suggestions and made some edits in response to suggestions. Professor Hicok noted that Cho's writing was "not unique in terms of subject matter," and though "remarkable for violence," he added, "I have seen worse."

Lack of Further Police Contact – Virginia Tech police noted that Cho had no further contact with law enforcement after they took him for evaluation on Dec 13-14 2005 until he received a speeding ticket on March 31, 2007, and they were not informed about his additional problems.

More Lack of Attention to Red Flags: p. 53, Addition – The finding that there was lack of adequate attention by Virginia Tech to the red flags raised by Cho's actions is reinforced by further examination of communications among faculty and Virginia Tech staff. The Review Panel faulted Virginia Tech for not connecting the dots. Since then, more unconnected "dots" have come to light. Members of the Virginia Tech administration and campus police failed to adequately heed warnings and take the initiative to investigate more fully a long list of frightening writings and aberrant behaviors leading up to the shootings, especially those reported by the resident advisors and English Department faculty. Examples are given in the various addenda here, such as the discussion of the email to Settle above.

## OTHER COMMENTS

VIII    File on Cho at the CCC and the Relative Importance of Counseling for Cho: Some of the comments that related to the CCC's file on Cho, placed a heavy emphasis on the importance of that file and what impact counseling at CCC would have had on Cho. One individual stated that those records "were the linchpin that could have connected the dots." Another comment was that the Review Panel saw only some of Cho's records, but not crucial records.

Response: The papers in the file on Cho provided very little information that the Review Panel did not already have. The Review Panel sought and received a huge amount of crucial records, both academic and medical, from Cho's middle school, high school, and Virginia Tech years. The Review Panel also interviewed Cho's high school counselor, doctors and therapists in Northern Virginia, plus professors and health/mental health practitioners at the CCC and at the CSB. The records from practitioners who treated Cho before he attended Virginia Tech are far more informative and relevant than the intake forms in Cho's file from CCC. We also had his court records and met with Special Justice Paul M. Barnett who conducted Cho's commitment hearing. Additional factors to consider with regard to Cho and counseling include the following:

> Cho would not talk much. He was a poor candidate for traditional talk therapy because he would not communicate, did not want to be in therapy, and was not legally required to go for counseling. For therapy to have any effect and value to a patient the person must truly want to participate in the sessions and work with the therapist. Cho contacted CCC because he was getting into trouble with Virginia Tech police and then because it was required prior to his discharge from St. Albans. Since he lied about previous mental health problems, (including his ideas of suicide and homicide, prior years in art therapy, and medication for depression), to all medical personnel, evaluators, and court officials who dealt with him, he likely would have continued denying problems, much like he denied being serious about his suicide threat.

Cho's parents initiated therapy for Cho the summer before he started 7th grade because they were concerned about his social isolation and unwillingness to discuss his thoughts or feelings. The only therapy that could be used with Cho was art therapy, typically used for very young children, because it did not require him to talk. His art therapist told the Review Panel that through clay, drawings, and other media, she was able to diagnose his extreme loneliness and isolation. Some limited progress was made in connecting with him and getting him to make eye contact, though he remained unwilling to respond verbally in a significant way.

There is an extremely relevant note in the psychological evaluation of Cho contained in Cho's high school files. The psychologist wrote: "The quality of any diagnosis made or care delivered will depend, to a large extent, on the quality of information exchanged in both (emphasis added) directions…. Psychological therapy in the form of counseling is likely to be difficult and of limited effectiveness given Seung-Hui's extreme reticence and apparent anxiety. There are reports that Seung-Hui resents his participation in therapy and attends only grudgingly."

VIII- Availability of Home Town Doctor: One commenter asked, "Why did the panel not check into why Virginia Tech records indicate that there was a "home town" doctor or counselor that Cho could see when he was home? What written document led the panel to make their decision that Cho had a "home town" doctor or counselor?

Response: During Cho's interactions with medical personnel on December 13-14, he had nodded a "yes" to having doctors available at home, and that was noted on the record. Additionally, the Review Panel interviewed various health and mental health providers that had treated Cho in Northern Virginia.

VIII- Dr. Roy's Warning to Cho Regarding Referral to Judicial Affairs: A commenter claimed that Dr. Roy and others failed to address or discuss that Cho was guilty of violating the Code of Student Conduct and that Dr. Roy did not tell Cho that he had violated the CSC and that similar behavior in the future would be referred to Judicial Affairs.

Response: Chapter IV, page 43, discusses the Code of Student Conduct, that Dr. Roy had asked Dean Brown about it, and that he had responded that Cho's cell phone picture-taking would "clearly" fall under "disorderly conduct, if adjudicated." Brown also spoke with Frances Keene who agreed with Dr. Roy's plan to meet with Cho and propose individual work with her and Professor Fred D'Aguiar. Keene communicated to Roy and Brown she was available if Cho had questions. Moreover, detailed notes of the meeting with Cho, Dr. Roy, and Cheryl Ruggiero (serving as assistant chair in the English Department at the time) document the following exchange:

L: [Lucinda Roy] asks about Cho's taking photos of the students in the class

Cho: says it is "just a hobby," that he takes pictures of "trees, sky…"

L: explains that taking unauthorized photographs, without permission from the subjects, and especially publishing them on a website, is something the University is taking very seriously, and that is could be something that could get a student into trouble."…asks if Seung understands

Cho: "Yeah"

VIII- Dr. Roy and Attempt to Get Cho to Seek Counseling: A commenter noted that the Report states that Dr. Roy tells others she will try to get Cho to go to counseling, "but she does not mention it in her last email to Cho, or future communication."

Response: Dr. Roy urged Cho to get counseling multiple times and personally called CCC to see if Cho could be required to get counseling. The counselor informed Dr. Roy of CCC's then-existing rules that CCC only saw students who voluntarily sought counseling. Dr. Roy pleaded with the counselor to come to Shanks Hall to meet Cho, and the counselor declined due to then-existing CCC policy to only counsel students at the CCC. Dr. Roy writes in No Right to Remain Silent (Chapter Two) about how often she brought up the subject of counseling and Cho's response was always noncommittal. She even offered to go with him to CCC, and she recommended a particular counselor by name. Page 46 of the Report discusses Dr. Betzel's recollection of Dr. Roy contacting her regarding a student Dr. Betzel believes was Cho, his writing, and Dr. Roy's plans to meet with Cho individually.

VIII- Notification to VTPD Regarding Cho's Writings: There was an objection that the Report did not discuss that Dr. Roy and Mary Ann Lewis failed to notify VTPD of the content of Cho's writings, and that Cho's writings were not forwarded to a counselor.

Response: The Report discusses that Cho's "poem" written in Dr. Giovanni's class was sent to the CCC for review and the CCC responded that Cho's wirings, while disturbing, did not seem threatening since he did not specify a target. He had not committed a crime therefore contacting police and naming Cho would not have been appropriate. VTPD were informed that security might be needed due to a concern in Dr. Giovanni's classroom; however, since Cho did not return to that class, the security was cancelled.

VIII- Criminal Charges Against Cho: The comment was that the report fails to reveal if criminal charges were filed by Margaret Bowman regarding Cho's message on her white board and Facebook/emails.

Response: Page 46 of the Report states: "She [Bowman] did not file criminal charges."

VIII- Discrepancies Between the Inspector General's Report, Investigation of April 16, 2007 Critical Incident at Virginia Tech and the Panel Report: A commenter charged that information was intentionally omitted and misleading.

Response: There were two minor discrepancies between the two reports, both of which covered an enormous amount of detailed information. The two discrepancies are:

IG's report notes that Cho harassed Margaret Bowman on 3 occasions. The Review Panel Report documents one. The Review Panel did not have the VTPD incident reports which now are available, and which show the three dates. This addendum reflects the additional incidents.

IG's report notes that the father of Cho's suitemate called VTPD at 3:42 concerning Cho's suicide threat. Commenter says the Review Panel Report is incorrect and that Cho's suitemate [Andy Koch] did not call VTPD. However, a VTPD Incident/ Investigation Report dated 12/13/05 states: "On 12-13-05 at approximately 1909 hours, I, Officer Lucas received a phone call from [suitemate]Andy Koch... Andy advised that Mr. Seung Hui Cho had sent him an instant message earlier today saying that he was thinking about killing himself." Andy Koch's father also may have contacted police independently.

VIII- Interviews of Ras: Commenter states the Review Panel only interviewed one RA, Melissa Troutman and that other RA's should have been interviewed.

Response: Appendix B, page 9, of the original Report indicates the Review Panel interviewed three Ras: Troutman, Chandler Douglas (the RA during Cho's senior year) and Austin Moron.

VIII- Events of December 12, 2005 on: Commenter states that the Report lacks an accurate account of what really happened from December 12th on, but that the IG's report covers more details, so the Review Panel either was not given pertinent information or the Review Panel wrote the Report so as to omit the accurate accounts.

Response: The Report devotes three pages to describe the events of December 12-13. Part B of Chapter IV) describes in great detail the legal and mental health process involving Cho and the implications for future improvements. Part B alone contains 12 recommendations.

VIII- Cho's emergency custody and transport to St. Albans: Commenter states: the Report says officers transported Cho to St. Albans for admission at 11:00. Stewarts' (the IG) report says he was admitted at 11:15. It took VTPD 4 hours to take Cho into emergency custody after the magistrate issued the TDO.

Response: VTPD immediately took Cho to police headquarters for evaluation by a mental health prescreener who arrived shortly after being called. The prescreener took time interviewing Cho, the police, and Cho's roommates by phone, and found a psychiatric bed at St. Albans – then contacted the magistrate to request a TDO. The TDO was issued at 10:12 p.m. Cho was in custody at the Virginia Tech police station during this time. Police then left with Cho at 11:00 p.m. to travel to St. Albans. The hospital admitted Cho at 11:15.

VIII- Screening form and box for "access to firearms" and finding of error: Commenter states that the screening form released on 8/19/09 does not include a form with a box for firearm access and asks why it was not released and on what the Review Panel based its finding that the marked box was an error. Claims it is very likely that Cho had possession of a gun at that time.

Response: Several intake and screening forms were used for Cho's evaluation and treatment process and release from Carillion St. Albans. The form completed by the CSB evaluator Kathy Godbey during her preliminary screening of Cho at VTPD includes the question on access to a firearm. The Review Panel was provided with a copy of that, and all other intake and screening forms. The Review Panel members interviewed Ms. Godbey who indicated that she might have inadvertently checked the wrong box, because if the "Yes" box is checked, then the evaluator must describe the access and the firearm, and she had not written anything on that line. There are no indications that Cho had possession of any gun until his purchase in early 2007.

VIII- Information sent to CCC and staff emails: Commenter notes there was an email between Emily Conway, a member of the CCC support staff and Dr. Miller at 4:24 on December 14, 2005, less than 45 minutes after Cho was seen and maintains the email was deliberately omitted.

Response: The Report includes discussion of this email. There were two relevant communications at CCC on December 14, 2005. The first was the fax with the St. Albans discharge summary and CSB evaluator's report received shortly before Cho was seen at 3:00. The second was an email sent to Dr. Miller from Sandra Ward, the Director of Residence Life, which described the events of the previous night and Cho's transfer to St. Albans. Dr. Miller immediately forwarded this to CCC staff as an alert in case Cho came to CCC.

(This page intentionally left blank.)

# Chapter V.

## INFORMATION PRIVACY LAWS

While Cho was a student at Virginia Tech, his professors, fellow students, campus police, the Office of Judicial Affairs, the Care Team, and the Cook Counseling Center all had dealings with him that raised questions about his mental stability. There is no evidence that Cho's parents were ever told of these contacts, and they say they were unaware of his problems at school. Most 227ervicecantly, there is no evidence that Cho's parents, his suitemates, and their parents were ever informed that he had been temporarily detained, put through a commitment hearing for involuntary admission, and found to be a danger to himself. Efforts to share this information was impeded by laws about privacy of information, according to several university officials and the campus police. Indeed, the university's attorney, during one of the panel's open hearings and in private meetings, told the panel that the university could not share this information due to privacy laws.

The panel's review of information privacy laws governing mental health, law enforcement, and educational records and information revealed widespread lack of understanding, conflicting practice, and laws that were poorly designed to accomplish their goals. Information privacy laws are intended to strike a balance between protecting privacy and allowing information sharing that is necessary or desirable. Because of this difficult balance, the laws are often complex and hard to understand.

The widespread perception is that information privacy laws make it difficult to respond effectively to troubled students. This perception is only partly correct. Privacy laws can block some attempts to share information, but even more often may cause holders of such information to default to the nondisclosure option—even when laws permit the option to disclose. Sometimes this is done out of ignorance of the law, and sometimes intentionally because it serves the purposes of the individual or organization to hide behind the privacy law. A narrow interpretation of the law is the least risky course, notwithstanding the harm that may be done to others if information is not shared.

Much of the frustration about privacy laws stems from lack of understanding. When seen clearly, the privacy laws contain many provisions that allow for information sharing where necessary. Also, FERPA and HIPAA are not consistent (Cook Counseling Center records come under FERPA, Carilion's under HIPAA), which causes difficulties, as explained below.

This chapter addresses federal and state law concerning four key categories of information that may be useful in evaluating and responding to a troubled student:

> Law enforcement records
> Court records
> Medical information and records
> Educational records.

The report also examines a Virginia law that regulates the process of disclosing information. These laws are discussed in the context of Cho's conduct leading to the shootings of April 16.

Appendix G summarizes the privacy laws as background for this chapter, for those unfamiliar with them.

### LAW ENFORCEMENT RECORDS

Law enforcement agencies must disclose certain information to anyone who [3] requests it. They must disclose basic information about

---

[3] Va. Code § 2.2-3706

felony crimes: the date, location, general description of the crime, and name of the investigating officer. Law enforcement agencies also have to release the name and address of anyone arrested and charged with any type of crime. All records about noncriminal incidents are available upon request. When they close noncriminal incident records, law enforcement agencies must withhold personally identifying information, such as names, [4]addresses, and social security numbers.

Universities with campus police departments have additional responsibilities. They are required to maintain a publicly available log that lists all [5]crimes. The log must give the time, date, and location of each offense, as well as the disposition of each case. Under Virginia law, campus police departments must also ensure that basic [6]information about crimes is open to the public. This includes the name and address of those arrested for felony crimes against people or property and misdemeanor crimes involving assault, battery, or [7]moral turpitude.

Most of the detailed information about criminal activity is contained in law enforcement investigative files. Under Virginia's Freedom of Information Act, law enforcement agencies are allowed to keep these records confidential. The law also gives [8]agencies the discretion to release the records. However, law enforcement agencies across the state typically have a policy against disclosing such records.

## JUDICIAL RECORDS

As a general matter, court records are public and can be widely disclosed. For the purposes of responding to troubled students, two types of Court proceedings do not fit the general rule: juvenile hearings and commitment hearings [9]for involuntary admission.

A commitment hearing for involuntary admission is a hearing where a judicial officer makes a determination as to whether an individual will be committed to a mental health facility involuntarily. Records of these hearings, which consist of any medical records, reports of evaluations, and all court documents, must be sealed when the subject of the hearing requests it. Tape recordings are made of the proceedings. The tapes are sealed and held by court clerks. These records can only be [10]released by court order.

Although their records are confidential, the hearings themselves must be open to the public and certain information about the hearing [11]is, at least in theory, publicly available. This would include the name of the subject and the time, date, and location of the hearing. Of course, there is no central location where this information is stored so, as a practical matter, unless an interested party knew where the hearing was being held or who was presiding over it, that person would have a difficult time uncovering such information. For example, Cho's commitment hearing occurred approximately 12 hours after he was detained. Logistical difficulties also make it difficult to visit psychiatric facilities, which are common locations for commitment hearings. The key, though, is that the information is public. In

---

[4] Law enforcement records regarding juveniles (persons under 18) have special restrictions regarding disclosure. Normally, they can only be released to other parts of the juvenile justice system or to parents of an underaged suspect. However, Virginia law also authorizes, but does not require, law enforcement to share information with school principals about offend ers who commit a serious felony, arson, or weapons offense. Police can tell principals when they believe a juvenile is a suspect or when a juvenile is charged with an offense. After the case is finished, law enforcement officials can tell principals the outcome. Va. Code § 16.1-301
[5] 20 U.S.C. § 1092(f)(4)(A)
[6] Va. Code § 23-232.2(B)
[7] Va. Code § 23-232.2(B)
[8] Va. Code § 2.2-3706

[9] Va. Code § 17.1-208 (circuit court records open to the public). Regarding juvenile court records: under Virginia law, juvenile court records are even more tightly restricted than juvenile law enforcement records. Court records can only be used within the juvenile justice system unless a judge orders the records released. Va. Code § 16.1-305
[10] Va. Code § 37.2-818. Cho was the subject of a commitment hearing for involuntary admission on December 14, 2005. The panel obtained the tape recording and records of this hearing through court order.
[11] Va. Code § 37.2-820

Cho's case, the Virginia Tech Police Department (VTPD) was aware that he had been detained pending a commitment hearing. VTPD could have shared this information with university administration or Cho's parents, though they did not.

## MEDICAL INFORMATION

Both state and federal law govern privacy of medical information. The federal Health Insurance and Portability and Accountability Act of 1996 and regulations by the Secretary of Health and Human Services establish the federal standards. Together, the law and regulations are commonly known as "HIPAA." Virginia law on medical information privacy is found in the Virginia Health Records Privacy Act (VHRPA).

HIPAA and Virginia law have similar standards. They both state that health information is private and can only be disclosed for certain reasons. When specific provisions conflict, HIPAA can preempt a state law, making the state law ineffective. Generally, this occurs when a state law attempts to be less protective of privacy than the federal law or rules.

Both laws apply to all medical providers and billing entities. They define "provider" broadly to include doctors, nurses, therapists, counselors, social workers, and health organizations such as HMOs and insurance companies, among others.

Three basic types of disclosures are permitted under these medical information privacy laws:

- Requests made or approved by the person who is the subject of the records. These exceptions are based on the idea that the privacy laws are for the benefit of the person being treated. If the patient asks for his or her records from a health care provider or provides written authorization, the provider must release them.

- Disclosure when information must be shared in order to make medical treatment effective. Medical privacy laws allow providers to share information with each other when necessary for treatment

[12]purposes. If a medical provider needs to disclose information to a family member, the provider can do so in two ways. The provider can gain permission from the patient. Or, in an emergency where the patient is unable to make such a decision, the provider can [13]proceed without explicit permission.

- Situations where privacy is out-weighed by certain other interests. For example, providers may sometimes disclose information about a person who presents an imminent threat to the health and safety of individuals [14]and the public. Providers can also disclose information to law enforcement in order to locate a fugitive or [15]suspect. Providers also are authorized to disclose information when [16]state law requires it.

Disclosure of information is required by state law in some situations and is permissible by HIPAA. An example under Virginia state law is that Virginia health care providers must report evidence of child abuse or neglect. Another type of required disclosure is when freedom of information laws require public agencies to disclose their records. If a freedom of information law requires a public hospital to disclose information, the disclosure is [17]authorized under HIPAA.

## EDUCATIONAL RECORDS

Privacy of educational records is primarily governed by federal law, The Family Educational Rights and Privacy Act of 1974 and regulations issued by the Secretary of Education

---

[12] 45 C.F.R. § 164.506I(2); Va. Code § 32.1-127.1:03(D)(7)

[13] 45 C.F.R. § 164.510(b)

[14] 45 C.F.R. § 164.512(j)

[15] Va. Code § 32.1-127.1:03(D)(28)

[16] 45 C.F.R. § 164.512(a), (c)

[17] If, however, a state law merely permits disclosure, HIPAA usually will override state law and prevent disclosure. For example, Virginia's Freedom of Information Act gives public agencies the discretion to release information, but does not require information to be released. Because the decision is left to the discretion of the agency, HIPAA would prohibit disclosure.

that interpret the law. This law and the regulations are commonly known as "FERPA."

FERPA applies to all educational institutions that accept federal funding. As a practical matter, this means almost all institutions of higher learning, including Virginia Tech. It also includes public elementary and secondary schools. Like HIPAA, FERPA's basic rule favors privacy. Information from educational records cannot be shared unless authorized by law or with consent of a parent, or if the student is enrolled in college or is 18 or older, with that student's consent.

FERPA has special interactions for medical and law enforcement records. HIPAA also makes an [18]exception for all records covered by FERPA. Therefore, records maintained by campus health[19] clinics are not covered by HIPAA. Instead, FERPA and state law restrictions apply to these[20] records. FERPA provides the basic requirements for disclosure of health care records at campus health clinics, and state law cannot require [21]disclosure that is not authorized by FERPA. However, if FERPA authorizes disclosure, a campus health clinic would then have to look to state law to determine whether it could disclose records, including state laws on confidentiality of medical records.

For example, Virginia Tech's Cook Counseling Center holds records regarding Cho's mental health treatment. On a request for those records, the center must determine whether the disclosure is authorized under both FERPA and the Virginia Health Records Privacy Act. It is important to note that FERPA was drafted to apply to educational records, not medical records. Though it has a small number of provisions about medical records, FERPA does not enumerate the different types of disclosures authorized by HIPAA.

FERPA also has a different scope than HIPAA. Medical privacy laws such as HIPAA apply to all information—written or oral— gained in the course of treatment. FERPA applies only to information in student records. Personal observations and conversations with a student fall outside FERPA. Thus, for example, teachers or administrators who witness students acting strangely are not restricted by FERPA from telling anyone— school officials, law enforcement, parents, or [22]any other person or organization. In this case, several of Cho's professors and the Residence Life staff observed conduct by him that raised their concern. They would have been authorized to call Cho's parents to report the behavior they witnessed.

Many records kept by university law enforcement agencies also fall outside of FERPA. For example, it does not apply to records created and maintained by campus law enforcement[23] for law enforcement purposes. If campus law enforcement officers share a record with the school, however, the copy that is shared becomes subject to FERPA. For example, in fall 2005, VTPD received complaints from female students about Cho's behavior. Their records of investigation were created for the law enforcement purpose of investigating a potential crime. Accordingly, the police could have told Cho's parents of the incident. When the university's Office of Judicial Affairs requested the records, FERPA rules applied to the copies held in that office but not to any record retained by the VTPD.

Law enforcement performs various other functions that promote public order and safety.

---

[18] C.F.R. § 160.103, definition of "protected health information."

[19] U.S. Department of Education, FERPA General Guidance for Parents, available at http://www.ed.gov/policy/gen/guid/fpco/ferpa/parents.html (attached as Appendix H) ("June 2007 ED Guidance").

[20] The nature of FERPA's application to treatment records has not been uniformly interpreted (discussed in the "Recommen- dations" section). The analysis in this section is based in part on an official letter sent to the University of New Mexico by the Family Policy Compliance Office (FPCO). The FPCO is the part of the Department of Education that officially interprets FERPA. The letter is included in Appendix G.

[21] Letter from LeRoy S. Rooker, Director, Family Compliance Policy Office, U.S. Department of Education, to Melanie P. Baise, Associate University Counsel, The University of New Mexico, dated November 29, 2004 (enclosed as Appendix G).

[22] June 2007 ED Guidance (Appendix H)

[23] 20 U.S.C. § 1232g(a)(4)(B)(ii)

For example, law enforcement officers are usually responsible for transporting people who are under temporary detention orders to mental health facilities. No privacy laws apply to this law enforcement function. In the Cho case, the VTPD was not prohibited from contacting the university administration or Cho's parents to inform them that Cho was under a temporary detention order and had been transported to Carilion St. Albans Behavioral Health.

FERPA authorizes release of information to parents of students in several situations. First, it authorizes disclosure of any record to parents who claim adult students as dependents for tax purposes[24]. FERPA also authorizes release to parents when the student has violated alcohol or drug[25] laws and is under 21.

FERPA generally authorizes the release of information to school officials who have been determined to have a legitimate educational interest in[26] receiving the information. FERPA also authorizes unlimited disclosure of the final result of a disciplinary proceeding that concludes a student violated university rules for an incident involving a crime of violence (as defined under federal law)[27] or a sex offense. Finally, some FERPA exceptions regarding juveniles are governed by state[28] law.

FERPA also contains an emergency exception. Disclosure of information in educational records is authorized to any appropriate person in connection with an emergency "if the knowledge of such information is necessary to protect the health or[29] safety of the student or other persons." Although this exception does authorize sharing to a potentially broad group of parties, the regulations specifically state that it is to be narrowly construed. HIPAA, too, contains

exceptions that allow disclosure in emergency situations[30]. For both laws, the exceptions have been construed to be limited to circumstances involving imminent, specific threats to health or safety. Troubled students may present such an emergency if their behavior indicates they are a threat to themselves or others. The Department of Education's Family Compliance Policy Office (FCPO) has advised that when a student makes suicidal comments, engages in unsafe conduct such as playing with knives or lighters, or makes threats against another student, the student's conduct can amount to an emergency (see letter in[31] Appendix G). However, the boundaries of the emergency exceptions have not been defined by privacy laws or cases, and these provisions may discourage disclosure in all but the most obvious cases.

## GOVERNMENT DATA COLLECTION AND DISSEMINATION PRACTICES ACT

One other law on information disclosure applies to most Virginia government agencies. The Government Data Collection and Dissemination Practices Act establishes rules for collection, maintenance, and dissemination of individually-identifying data. The act does not apply to police departments or courts. Agencies that are bound by the act can only disclose information when permitted or[32] required by law. The attorney general of Virginia has interpreted "permitted by law" to include any official request made by a government agency for a lawful function of the agency. An agency must inform people who give it personal information how it will ordinarily use and share that information. An agency can disclose personal information outside of these ordinary uses. When it does, however, it must give notice to the people who provided the information[33]. This act was

[24] 20 U.S.C. § 1232g(b)(1)(H); 34 C.F.R. § 99.31(a)(8)
[25] 20 U.S.C. § 1232g(i)
[26] 20 U.S.C. § 1232g(b)(1)(A); 34 C.F.R. § 99.31(a)(1)
[27] 20 U.S.C. § 1232g(b)(6)(B)
[28] U.S.C. § 1232g(b)(1)(E); Va. Code § 22.1-287. Virginia law authorizes disclosure to law enforcement officers seeking information in the course of his or her duties, court services units, mental health and medical health agencies, and state or local children and family service agencies.
[29] 20 U.S.C. § 1232g(b)(1)(I)

[30] 20 U.S.C. § 1232g(b)(1)(I)
45 C.F.R. § 164.512(j); Va. Code § 32.1-127.1:03(D)(19);
[31] Letter from LeRoy S. Rooker, Director, Family Compliance Policy Office, U.S. Department of Education, to Superintendent, New Bremen Local Schools, dated September 24, 1994 (enclosed as Appendix G).
[32] Va. Code § 2.2-3803(A)(1)
[33] Va. Code § 2.2-3806(A)(2)

initially used as a reason for not providing information to the panel until its authenticity was strengthened by the governor's executive order.

## KEY FINDINGS

Organizations and individuals must be able to intervene in order to assist a troubled student or protect the safety of other students. Information privacy laws that block information sharing may make intervention ineffective.

At the same time, care must be taken not to invade a student's privacy unless necessary. This means there are two goals for information privacy laws: they must allow enough information sharing to support effective intervention, and they must also maintain privacy whenever possible.

Effective intervention often requires participation of parents or other relatives, school officials, medical and mental health professionals, court systems, and law enforcement. The problems presented by a seriously troubled student often require a group effort. The current state of information privacy law and practice is inadequate to accomplish this task. The first major problem is the lack of understanding about the law. The next problem is inconsistent use of discretion under the laws. Information privacy laws cannot help students if the law allows sharing but agency policy or practice forbids necessary sharing. The privacy laws need amendment and clarification. The panel proposes the following recommendations to address immediate problems and chart a course for an effective information privacy system.

## RECOMMENDATIONS

V-1 Accurate guidance should be developed by the attorney general of Virginia regarding The application of information privacy laws to the behavior of troubled students. The lack of understanding of the laws is probably the most significant problem about information privacy. Accurate guidance from the state attorney general's office can alleviate this problem. It may also help clarify which differences in practices among schools are based on a lack of understanding and which are based on institutional policy. For example, a representative of Virginia Tech told the panel that FERPA prohibits the university's administrators from sharing disciplinary records with the campus police department. The panel also learned that the University of Virginia has a policy of sharing such records because it classifies its chief of police as an official with an educational interest in such records.

The development of accurate guidance that signifies that law enforcement officials may have an educational interest in disciplinary records could help eliminate discrepancies in the application of the law between two state institutions. The guidance should clearly explain what information can be shared by concerned organizations and individuals about troubled students. The guidance should be prepared and widely distributed as quickly as possible and written in plain English. Appendix G provides a copy of guidance issued by the Department of Education in June 2007, which can serve as a model or starting point for the development of clear, accurate guidance.

V-2 Privacy laws should be revised to include "safe harbor" provisions. The provisions should insulate a person or organization from liability (or loss of funding) for making a disclosure with a good faith belief that the disclosure was necessary to protect the health, safety, or welfare of the person involved or members of the general public. Laws protecting good-faith disclosure for health, safety, and welfare can help combat any bias toward nondisclosure.

V-3 The following amendments to FERPA should be considered:

FERPA should explicitly explain how it applies to medical records held for treatment purposes. Although the Department of Education interprets FERPA as applying to all[34] such records, that interpretation has not been universally accepted. Also, FERPA does not address the differences between medical records and ordinary educational records such as grade

---

[34] June 2007 ED Guidance (Appendix H).

transcripts. It is not clear whether FERPA preempts state law regarding medical records and confidentiality of medical information or merely adds another requirement on top of these records.

FERPA should make explicit an exception regarding treatment records. Disclosure of treatment records from university clinics should be available to any health care provider without the student's consent when the records are needed for medical treatment, as they would be if covered under HIPAA. As currently drafted, it is not clear whether off-campus providers may access the records or whether students must consent. Without clarification, medical providers treating the same student may not have access to health information. For example, Cho had been triaged twice by Cook Counseling Center before being seen by a provider at Carilion St. Albans in connection with his commitment hearing. Later that day, he was again triaged by Cook. Carilion St. Albans's records were governed by HIPAA. Under HIPAA's treatment exception, Carilion St. Albans was authorized to share records with Cook. Cook's records were governed by FERPA. Because FERPA's rules regarding sharing records for treatment are unclear about outside entities or whether consent is necessary, Carilion St. Albans could not be assured that Cook would share its records. This situation makes little sense.

V-4 The Department of Education should allow more flexibility in FERPA'a "emergency" exception. As currently drafted, FERPA contains an exception that allows for release of records in an emergency, when disclosure is necessary to protect the health or safety of either the student or other people. At first, this appears to be an exception well-suited to sharing information about seriously troubled students. However, FERPA regulations also state that this exception is to be strictly construed. The "strict construction" requirement is unnecessary and unhelpful. The existing limitations require that an emergency exists and that disclosure is necessary for health or safety. Further narrowing of the definition does not help clarify

when an emergency exists. It merely feeds the perception that non-disclosure is always a safer choice.

V-5 Schools should ensure that law enforcement and medical staff (and others as necessary) are designated as school officials with an educational interest in school records. This FERPA-related change does not require amendment to law or regulation. Education requires effective intervention in the lives of troubled students. Intervention ensures that schools remain safe and students healthy. University policy should recognize that law enforcement, medical providers, and others who assist troubled students have an educational interest in sharing records. When confirmed by policy, FERPA should not present a barrier to these entities sharing information with each other.

V-6 The Commonwealth of Virginia Commission on Mental Health Reform should study whether the result of a commitment hearing (whether the subject was voluntarily committed, involuntarily committed, committed to outpatient therapy, or released) should also be publicly available despite an individual's request for confidentiality. Although this information would be helpful in tracking people going though the system, it may infringe too much on their privacy.

As discussed in Chapter IV, and its recommendations to revise Virginia law regarding the commitment process, the law governing hearings should explicitly state that basic information regarding a commitment hearing (the time, date, and location of the hearing and the name of the subject) is publicly available even when a person requests that records remain confidential. This information is necessary to protect the public's ability to attend commitment hearings.

V-7 The national higher education associations should develop best practice protocols and associated training for information sharing. Among the associations that should provide guidance to the member institutions are:

- American Council on Education (ACE)
- American Association of State Colleges and Universities (AASCU)
- American Association of Community Colleges (AACE)
- National Association of State and Land Grant Universities and Colleges (NASLGUC)
- National Association of Independent Colleges and Universities (NAICU)
- Association of American Universities (AAU)
- Association of Jesuit Colleges and Universities

If the changes recommended above are implemented, it is possible that no further changes to privacy laws would be necessary, but guidance on their interpretation will be needed. The unknown variable is how entities will choose to exercise their discretion when the law gives them a choice on whether to share or withhold information. How an institution uses its discretion can be critically important to whether it is effectively able to intervene in the life of a troubled student. For example, FERPA currently allows schools to release information in their records to parents who claim students as dependents. Schools are not, however, required to release that information. Yet, if a university adopts a policy against release to parents, it cuts off a vital source of information.

The history of Seung Hui Cho shows the potential danger of such an approach. During his formative years, Cho's parents worked with Fairfax County school officials, counselors, and outside mental health professionals to respond to episodes of unusual behavior. Cho's parents told the panel that had they been aware of his behavioral problems and the concerns of Virginia Tech police and educators about these problems, they would again have become involved in seeking treatment. The people treating and evaluating Cho would likely have learned something (but not all) of his prior mental health history and would have obtained a great deal of information germane to their evaluation and treatment of him. There is no evidence that officials at Virginia Tech consciously decided not to inform Cho's parents of his behavior; regardless of intent, however, they did not do so. The example demonstrates why it may be unwise for an institution to adopt a policy barring release of information to parents.

The shootings of April 16, 2007, have forced all concerned organizations and individuals to reevaluate the best approach for handling troubled students. Some educational institutions in Virginia have taken the opportunity to examine the difficult choices involved in attempts to share necessary information while still protecting privacy. Effort should be made to identify the best practices used by these schools and to ensure that these best practices are widely taught. All organizations and individuals should be urged to employ their discretion in appropriate ways, consistent with the best practices. Armed with accurate guidance, amended laws, and a new sense of direction, it is an ideal time to establish best practices for intervening in the life of troubled students.

# ADDITIONS AND CORRECTIONS

(No changes from original report.).

(This page intentionally left blank.)

# Chapter VI.

## GUN PURCHASE AND CAMPUS POLICIES

In investigating the role firearms played in the events of April 16, 2007, the panel encountered strong feelings and heated debate from the public. The panel's investigation focused on two areas: Cho's purchase of firearms and ammunition, and campus policies toward firearms. The panel recognizes the deep divisions in American society regarding the ready availability of rapid fire weapons and high capacity magazines, but this issue was beyond the scope of this review.

### FIREARMS PURCHASES

Every person killed at Cho's hands on April 16 was shot with one of two firearms, a Glock 19 9mm pistol or a Walther P22 .22 caliber pistol. Both weapons are semiautomatic, which meant that once loaded, they fire a round with each pull of the trigger, rather than being able to fire continuously by holding the trigger down. Cho purchased the Walther P22 first—by placing an online order with the TGSCOM, Inc., a company that sells firearms over the Internet. Cho then picked up the pistol on February 9, 2007, at J-N-D Pawn-brokers in Blacksburg, which is located just across Main Street from the Virginia Tech campus.

Cho purchased the Glock a month later, on March 13, from Roanoke Firearms in Roanoke. Virginia law limits handgun purchases to one every 30 days, which he may have known judging[35] by this spacing. Cho made his purchases using a credit card. Although his parents gave him money to pay for his expenses, they said they did not receive his credit card bills and did not know what he purchased. They stated that the only time they received an actual billing statement was after his death, and at that point the total bill was over $3,000.

On March 22, 2007, shortly after purchasing the Glock, Cho went to PSS Range and Training, an indoor pistol range in Roanoke. Cho practiced shooting for about an hour.

Cho was not legally authorized to purchase his firearms, but was easily able to do so. Gun purchasers in Virginia must qualify to buy a firearm under both federal and state law. Federal law disqualified Cho from purchasing or possessing a firearm. The federal Gun Control Act, originally passed in 1968, prohibits gun purchases by anyone who has "has been adjudicated as a mental defective or who has been committed to a mental[36] institution." Federal regulations interpreting the act define "adjudicated as a mental defective" as "[a] determination by a court, board, commission, or other lawful authority that a person, as a result of …mental illness …[i]s a danger to himself[37] or to others." Cho was found to be a danger to himself by a special justice of the Montgomery County General District Court on December 14, 2005. Therefore, under federal law, Cho could not purchase any firearm.

The legal status of Cho's gun purchase under Virginia law is less clear. Like federal law, Virginia law also prohibits persons who have been adjudged incompetent or committed to[38] mental institutions from purchasing firearms. However, Virginia law defines the terms differently. It defines incompetency by referring to the section of Virginia Code for declaring a

---

[35] Va. Code § 18.1-308.2:2(P)

[36] 18 U.S.C. § 922(g)(4)
[37] 27 C.F.R. § 478.11
[38] Va. Code §§ 18.2-308.1:2 and 3

person[39] incapable of caring for himself or herself. It does not specify that a person who had been found to be a danger to self or others is "incompetent." Because he had not been declared unable to care for himself, it does not appear that Cho was disqualified under this provision of Virginia law.

Virginia law also prohibits "any person who has been involuntarily committed pursuant to Article 5 (§ 37.2-814 et seq.) of Chapter 8 of Title 37.2"[40] from purchasing or possessing a firearm. This section authorizes a court to order either in-patient or outpatient treatment. When a person is ordered into a hospital, the law is relatively straightforward—the person has been "involuntarily committed." What is not clear from the statute, however, is whether a person such as Cho, who was found to be a danger to self or others and ordered to receive outpatient treatment, qualifies as being involuntarily committed. Among the mental health community, "involuntary outpatient commitment" is a recognized term for an order for outpatient treatment. In practical terms, a person who is found to be an imminent danger to self or others and ordered into outpatient treatment is little different than one ordered into inpatient treatment. However, the statute does not make clear whether out-patient treatment is covered. Thus, Cho's right to purchase firearms under Virginia law was not clear.

This uncertainty in Virginia law carries over into the system for conducting a firearms background check. In general, nationally, before purchasing a gun from a dealer a person must go through a background check. A government agency runs the name of the potential buyer through the databases of people who are disqualified from purchasing guns. If the potential purchaser is in the database, the transaction is stopped. If not, the dealer is instructed to proceed with the sale. The agency performing the check varies by state. Some states rely on the federal government to conduct the checks. In others, the state and the federal

government both do checks. In yet other states, such as Virginia, the state conducts the check of both federal and state databases. In Virginia the task is given to the state police.

Because purchasers have to be eligible under both state and federal law, potential buyers in Virginia have to fill out two forms: the federal "Firearms Transaction Record" (ATF 4473) and the Virginia Firearms Transaction Record (SP 65.) (Copies of the forms are provided in Appendix I.) The forms collect basic information about the potential buyer, such as name, age, and social security number. Each form also asks questions to determine whether a buyer is eligible to purchase a weapon. Form 4473 asks 11 questions, such as whether the buyer has been convicted of a felony. SP 65 contains questions and information regarding Virginia law, such as whether restraining orders were issued that disqualify purchasers. Firearms dealers initiate the background check by transmitting information from the forms to the state police's Firearms Transaction Program.

Certain firearms transfers do not require background checks at all. Virginia law does not require background checks for personal gifts or sales by private collectors, including transactions by collectors that occur at gun shows.

In Virginia, the Central Criminal Records Exchange (CCRE), a division of the state police, is tasked with gathering criminal records and other court information that is used for the background checks. Information on mental health commitment orders "for involuntary admission to a facility" is supposed to be sent to the CCRE by court clerks, who must send all copies of the orders along with a copy of form SP 237 that provides basic information about the person who is[41] the subject of the order. As currently drafted, the law only requires a clerk to certify a form, and does not specify who should complete the form. Because of the lack of clarity, it was reported to the panel that clerks in some jurisdictions do not send the information unless they receive a completed

---

[39] Va. Code § 18.2-308.1:2, citing Va. Code 37.2-1000 et seq.
[40] Va. Code § 18.2-308.1:3

[41] Va. Code § 37.2-819

form. Recommendations to improve this aspect of the law were given in Chapter IV.

The meaning of the term "admission to a facility" is less clear than it might seem. The law appears on an initial reading to only include orders requiring a person to receive inpatient care. This reading seems to have support from the Virginia involuntary commitment statute. That law uses "admission to a facility" when describing[42] inpatient treatment, not outpatient treatment. But the law is actually more complex. Laws about mental health commitment and sending orders to CCRE all appear in Title 37.2 of the Virginia Code. The definitions for that title state that facility "means a state or licensed hospital, training center, psychiatric hospital, or other type of residential or outpatient mental health or[43] mental retardation facility." So while the most obvious reading of the law is that only inpatient orders should be sent to CCRE, the actual requirement is unclear.

At the time Cho purchased his weapons, the general understanding was that only inpatient orders had to be sent to CCRE. Probably due to this understanding, the special justice's December 14, 2005, order finding Cho to be a danger to himself was not reported to the firearms background check system. Although the law may have been ambiguous, the checking process was not. Either you are or are not in the database when a gun purchase request form is submitted, and Cho was not.

There does not seem to have been an appreciation in setting up this process that the federal mental health standards were different than those of the state or that the practice deprived the federal database of information it needed in order to make the system effective. Thus on February 9 and March 13, 2007, Cho, a person disqualified under federal law from purchasing a firearm, walked into two licensed firearms dealers. He filled out the required forms. The dealers entered his information into the background check system. Both checks told the dealers to proceed with the transaction. Minutes after both checks, Cho left the stores in possession of semiautomatic pistols.

The FBI indicated in a press release dated April 19, 2007, that just 22 states reported any mental health information to the federal database. Ironically, the FBI cited Virginia as the state that provided the most information on people disqualified due to mental deficiency.[44]

In the days following the killings at Virginia Tech, Governor Kaine moved to clarify the law regarding inclusion of outpatient treatment into the database. Executive Order 50 now requires executive branch employees, including the state police, to collect information on outpatient orders and to treat such orders as disqualifications to owning a firearm. The state police revised SP 237 to ensure that they receive information regarding out-patient orders. Copies of the older and revised versions of SP 237 are presented in Appendix J. As previously discussed in Chapter IV, the panel recommends that the General Assembly clarify the relevant laws in this regard to permanently reflect the interpretation of Executive Order 50.

It is not clear whether Cho knew that he was prohibited from purchasing firearms. ATF 4473 asks each potential purchaser "[h]ave you ever been adjudicated mentally defective (which includes having been adjudicated incompetent to manage your own affairs) or have you ever been committed to a mental institution?" The state and federal forms that Cho filled out are currently held by the Virginia state police in their case investigation file, but were destroyed in the CCRE file, as required after 30 days. The state police did not permit the panel to view copies of the forms in their investigation file but indicated that Cho answered "no" to this question on both forms. It is impossible to know whether Cho understood that the proper response was "yes" and whether his answers

[42] Va. Code § 37.2-817. Paragraph B describes inpatient orders and uses the term "admitted to a facility"; paragraph C authorizes outpatient commitment but does not use the term "admitted to a facility."
[43] Va. Code. § 37.2-100

[44] The panel notes that the federal law terminology referring to mentally ill persons as "mentally defective" is outmoded based on current medical and societal understanding of mental health.

were mistakes or deliberate falsifications. In any event, the fact remains that Cho, a person disqualified from purchasing firearms, was readily able to obtain them.

## AMMUNITION PURCHASES

Cho purchased ammunition on several occasions in the weeks and months leading up to the shootings. On March 13, 2007, he purchased a $10 box of practice ammunition from Roanoke Firearms at the same time he bought his Glock 9mm pistol. On March 22 and 23, he purchased a total of five 10-round magazines for the Walther on the Internet auction site eBay. In addition, Cho purchased several 15-round magazines along with ammunition and a hunting knife on March 31 and April 1 at local Wal-Mart and Dick's Sporting Goods stores. With these magazines loaded, Cho would be able to fire 15 rounds, eject the magazine, and load a fresh one in a matter a moments. By the time he walked into Norris Hall, Cho had almost 400 bullets in magazines and loose ammunition.

Federal law prohibited Cho from purchasing ammunition. Just as it prohibits anyone from purchasing a gun who has been found to be a danger to self or others, it prohibits the same[45] individuals from buying ammunition. However, unlike firearms, there is no background check associated with purchasing ammunition. Neither does Virginia law place any restrictions on who can purchase ammunition. It does prohibit the use of some types of ammunition while committing a crime, but does not regulate the purchase[46] of such ammunition. Cho did not use any special types of ammunition that are restricted by law.

The panel also considered whether the previous federal Assault Weapons Act of 1994 that banned 15-round magazines would have made a difference in the April 16 incidents. The law lapsed after 10 years, in October 2004, and had banned clips or magazines with over 10 rounds. The panel concluded that 10-round magazines

that were legal would have not made much difference in the incident. Even pistols with rapid loaders could have been about as deadly in this situation.

## GUNS ON CAMPUS

Virginia Tech has one of the tougher policy constraints of possessing guns on campus among schools in Virginia. However, there are no searches of bags or use of magnetometers on campus like there are in government offices or airports. Cho carried his weapons in violation of university rules, and probably knew that it was extremely unlikely that anyone would stop him to check his bag. He looked like many others.

Virginia universities and colleges do not seem to be adequately versed in what they can do about banning guns on campus under existing interpretations of state laws. The governing board of colleges and universities can set policies on carrying guns. Some said their understanding is that they must allow anyone with a permit to carry a concealed weapon on campus. Others said they thought guns can be banned from buildings but not the grounds of the institution. Several major universities reported difficulty understanding the rules based on their lawyers' interpretation. Most believe they can set rules for students and staff but not the general public. Virginia Tech, with approval of the state Attorney General's Office, had banned guns from campus altogether.

This issue came to a head at one of the panel's public meetings held at George Mason University. It was known that many advocates of the right to carry concealed weapons on campus were planning to attend the meeting carrying weapons to make a point. GMU did not know they could have established a policy to stop the weapons from being carried into their buildings.

The Virginia Tech total gun ban policy was instituted a few years ago when it was accidentally discovered that a student playing the role of a patient in a first aid drill was carrying a concealed weapon. That student, now a Virginia Tech graduate with a master's degree

[45] 18 U.S.C § 922(d)(4)
[46] Va. Code § 18.2-308.3

in engineering, stated to the panel that he started carrying a weapon after witnessing assaults and hearing about other crimes on the Virginia Tech campus. He and other students told the panel that they felt it was safer for responsible people to be armed so they could fight back in exactly the type of situation that occurred on April 16. They might have been able to shoot back and protect themselves and others from being injured or killed by Cho. The guns-on-campus advocates cited statistics that overall there are fewer killings in environments where people can carry weapons for self-defense. Of course if numerous people had been rushing around with handguns outside Norris Hall on the morning of April 16, the possibility of accidental or mistaken shootings would have increased significantly. The campus police said that the probability would have been high that anyone emerging from a classroom at Norris Hall holding a gun would have been shot.

Data on the effect of carrying guns on campus are incomplete and inconclusive. The panel is unaware of any shootings on campus involving people carrying concealed weapons with permits to do so. Likewise, the panel knows of no case in which a shooter in campus homicides has been shot or scared off by a student or faculty member with a weapon. Written articles about a campus shooting rarely if ever comment on permits for concealed weapons, so this has been difficult to research. It may have happened, but the numbers of shootings on campuses are relatively few—about 16 a year at approximately 4,000 colleges and universities, according to the U.S. Department of Education Campus Crime Statistics for 2002–2004. It could be argued that if more people carried weapons with permits, the few cases of shootings on campus might be reduced further.

On the other hand, some students said in their remarks to the panel that they would be uncomfortable going to class with armed students sitting near them or with the professor having a gun. People may get angry even if they are sane, law-abiding citizens; for example, a number of police officers are arrested each year for assaults with weapons they carry off duty, as attested to by stories in daily newspapers and other media.

Campus police chiefs in Virginia and many chief-level officers in the New York City region who were interviewed voiced concern that as the number of weapons on campuses increase, sooner or later there would be accidents or assaults from people who are intoxicated or on drugs who either have a gun or interact with someone who does. They argued that having more guns on campus poses a risk of leading to a greater number of accidental and intentional shootings than it does in averting some of the relatively rare homicides. (See Appendix K for an article about the recent discharge of a gun by someone intoxicated in a fraternity house. Although a benign incident, it illustrates the concern.)

The panel heard a presentation from Dr. Jerald Kay, the chair of the committee on college mental health of the American Psychiatric Association about the large percentage of college students who binge drink each year (about 44 percent), and the surprisingly large percentage of students who claim they thought about suicide (10 percent). College years are full of academic stress and social stress. The probability of dying from a shooting on campus is smaller than the probability of dying from auto accidents, falls, or alcohol and drug overdoses.

## KEY FINDINGS

Cho was able to purchase guns and ammunition from two registered gun dealers with no problem, despite his mental history.

Cho was able to kill 31 people including himself at Norris Hall in about 10 minutes with the semiautomatic handguns at his disposal. Having the ammunition in large capacity magazines facilitated his killing spree.

There is confusion on the part of universities as to what their rights are for setting policy regarding guns on campus.

# RECOMMENDATIONS

VI-1 All states should report information necessary to conduct federal background checks on gun purchases. There should be federal incentives to ensure compliance. This should apply to states whose requirements are different from federal law. States should become fully compliant with federal law that disqualifies persons from purchasing or possessing firearms who have been found by a court or other lawful authority to be a danger to themselves or others as a result of mental illness. Reporting of such information should include not just those who are disqualified because they have been found to be dangerous, but all other categories of disqualification as well. In a society divided on many gun control issues, laws that specify who is prohibited from owning a firearm stand as examples of broad agreement and should be enforced.

VI-2 Virginia should require background checks for all firearms sales, including those at gun shows. In an age of widespread information technology, it should not be too difficult for anyone, including private sellers, to contact the Virginia Firearms Transaction Program for a background check that usually only takes minutes before transferring a firearm. The program already processes transactions made by registered dealers at gun shows. The practice should be expanded to all sales. Virginia should also provide an enhanced penalty for guns sold without a background check and later used in a crime.

VI-3 Anyone found to be a danger to themselves or others by a court-ordered review should be entered in the Central Criminal Records Exchange database regardless of whether they voluntarily agreed to treatment. Some people examined for a mental illness and found to be a potential threat to themselves or others are given the choice of agreeing to mental treatment voluntarily to avoid being ordered by the courts to be treated involuntarily. That does not appear on their records, and they are free to purchase guns. Some highly respected people knowledgeable about the interaction of mentally ill people with the mental health system are strongly opposed to requiring voluntary treatment to be entered on the record and be sent to a state database. Their concern is that it might reduce the incentive to seek treatment voluntarily, which has many advantages to the individuals (e.g., less time in hospital, less stigma, less cost) and to the legal and medical personnel involved (e.g., less time, less paperwork, less cost). However, there still are powerful incentives to take the voluntary path, such as a shorter stay in a hospital and not having a record of mandatory treatment. It does not seem logical to the panel to allow someone found to be dangerous to be able to purchase a firearm.

VI-4 The existing attorney general's opinion regarding the authority of universities and colleges to ban guns on campus should be clarified immediately. The universities in Virginia have received or developed various interpretations of the law. The Commonwealth's attorney general has provided some guidance to universities, but additional clarity is needed from the attorney general or from state legislation regarding guns at universities and colleges.

VI-5 The Virginia General Assembly should adopt legislation in the 2008 session clearly establishing the right of every institution of higher education in the Commonwealth to regulate the possession of firearms on campus if it so desires. The panel recommends that guns be banned on campus grounds and in buildings unless mandated by law.

VI-6 Universities and colleges should make clear in their literature what their policy is regarding weapons on campus. Prospective students and their parents, as well as university staff, should know the policy related to concealed weapons so they can decide whether they prefer an armed or arms-free learning environment.

## ADDITIONS AND CORRECTIONS

Testimony on Shooting Incidence on Campuses: p. 75, Clarification – A question was received on the relevancy of testimony by Dr. Jerald Kay on the frequency of shootings on campuses—whether its inclusion was an attempt to downplay the seriousness of the Virginia Tech shootings in light of other dangers to students such as drunk driving.

The Review Panel invited Dr. Kay's presentation for two reasons: First to consider the risk from guns as part of the larger picture of campus emergency planning. The Review Panel wanted colleges and universities to consider, as part of emergency planning, the whole range of threats and their likelihood, not just guns. Second, this testimony was of interest as part of the discussion of whether guns should be allowed to be carried on campuses. The frequency and nature of shootings on campus was very relevant to the deliberations of the Review Panel in making recommendations regarding these issues. It also was relevant in understanding the risk of a further shooting faced by the Policy Group after the double homicide.

This page intentionally left blank.)

# Chapter VII.

## DOUBLE MURDER AT WEST AMBLER JOHNSTON

This chapter discusses the double homicide at West Ambler Johnston (WAJ) residence hall and the police and university actions taken in response. It covers the events up to the shootings in Norris Hall, which are presented in the next chapter.

### APPROACH AND ATTACK

Cho left his dormitory early in the morning of April 16, 2007 and went to the WAJ, about a 2-minute walk. He was seen outside WAJ by a student about 6:45 a.m. Figure 3 shows the exterior of WAJ and Figure 4, a typical hallway inside WAJ.

*Figure 4. Hallway Outside Dorm Rooms in West Ambler Johnston*

*Figure 3. Exterior of West Ambler Johnston*

Because Cho's student mailbox was located in the lobby of WAJ, he had access to that dormitory with his pass card, but only after 7:30 a.m.

Cho somehow gained entrance to the dormitory, possibly when a student coming out let him in or by tailgating someone going in. (No one remembers having done so, or admits it.)

Cho went to the fourth floor by either stairway or elevator to the room of student Emily Hilscher.

She had just returned with her boyfriend, a student at Radford University who lived in Blacksburg. He drove her back to her dorm, saw her enter, and drove away. She entered at 7:02 a.m., based on swipe card records, which also showed that she used a different entrance than Cho did. Although it is known that Cho previously stalked female students, including one in WAJ on her floor, the police have found no connection between Cho and Hilscher from any written materials, dorm mates, other friends of his or hers, or any other source.

As of this writing, the police still had found no motive for the slaying.

 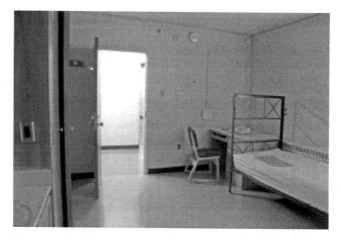

*Figure 5. Typical Dorm Room in Ambler Johnston Hall*

Not long after 7:15 a.m., noises emanating from Hilscher's room were loud enough and of such a disturbing nature that resident advisor Ryan Clark, who lived next door, checked to see what was happening. The presumption is that he came to investigate, saw Cho, and was killed to stop any interference with the shooter and his identification. Both Hilscher and Clark were shot by Cho at close range. (Figure 5 shows a typical dorm room in WAJ.)

The sounds of the shots or bodies falling were misinterpreted by nearby students as possibly someone falling out of a loft bed, which had happened before. A student in a nearby room called the Virginia Tech Police Department (VTPD), which dispatched a police officer and an emergency medical service (EMS) team—standard protocol for this type of call. The police received the call at 7:20 a.m. and arrived outside at 7:24 a.m. (an EMS response under 5 minutes for dispatch plus travel time is better than47 average, even in a city). The EMS team arrived on scene at 7:26 and at the dorm room at 7:29. As soon as the police officer arrived and saw the gunshot wounds, he called for additional police assistance. Hilscher was transported to Montgomery Regional Hospital where she received care, and then transferred to

Carilion Roanoke Memorial Hospital where she died. Clark was treated en route to Montgomery Regional Hospital, but could not be resuscitated by the emergency medical technicians (EMTs) and was pronounced dead shortly after arrival at the hospital. Their wounds were considered nonsurvivable at the time and in retrospect.

In the meantime, Cho somehow exited the building. No one reported seeing him leaving, according to police interviews of people in the dorm at the time. His clothes and shoes were bloodied, and he left bloody footprints in and coming out of the room. His clothes were found later in his room. Students were getting ready for 8:00 a.m. classes, but no one reported seeing Cho. Figure 6 shows the door to Hilscher's dorm room, with a peephole typical of others on that floor.

When Chief Wendell Flinchum of the VTPD learned of the incident at 7:40 a.m., he called for additional resources from the Blacksburg Police Department (BPD). A detective for investigation and an evidence technician headed for the scene. Chief Flinchum notified the office of the executive vice president at 7:57 a.m., after obtaining more information on what was found.

Immediately after they arrived, police started interviewing students in the rooms near Hilscher's room, and essentially locked down the building, with police inside and outside. (The exterior dorm doors were still locked from

---

[47] This is based on data from 150 TriData studies of fire and EMS departments over 25 years. The National Fire Protec- tion Association standard calls for a fire or EMS response in 5 minutes (1 minute turnout time, 4 minutes travel time) in 90 percent of calls, but few agencies meet that objective. 78

*Figure 6. Emily Hilscher's Door With Peephole*

usual nighttime routine.) A female friend of Hilscher came to the dorm to accompany her to class, as was their common practice, and she was immediately questioned by the police. She reported that Hilscher had been visiting her boyfriend, knew of no problems between them, and that Hilscher's boyfriend owned a gun and had been practicing on a target range with it. She knew his name and the description of his vehicle and that he usually drove her back to the dorm. The boyfriend was immediately considered[48] a "person of interest." Because he had been the last known person to see her before the shooting, he was the natural starting point for an investigation. No one had seen him drop her off. (The fact that he had dropped her off was established more than an hour later, after he was questioned.) The police then sent out a BOLO (be on the lookout) alert for his pickup truck and searched for it in the campus parking lots but could not find it. This implied that the only known person of interest had likely left the campus. There were no other leads at that time.

___

[48] "Person of interest" means someone who might be a sus- pect or might have relevant information about a crime.

The police had no evidence other than shell casings in the room, the footprints, and the victims. The VTPD police chief said that this murder might have taken a long time to solve, if ever, for lack of evidence and witnesses. After the second incident occurred, the gun was identified by ATF as having been the same one used in the first shooting, but that was hindsight. If Cho had stopped after the first two shootings, he might well have never been caught.

## PREMATURE CONCLUSION?

AT this point, the police may have made an error in reaching a premature conclusion that their initial lead was a good one, or at least in conveying that impression to the Virginia Tech administration. While continuing their investigation, they did not take sufficient action to deal with what might happen if the initial lead proved false. They conveyed to the university Policy Group that they had a good lead and that the person of interest was probably not on campus. (That is how the Policy Group understood it, according to its chair and other members who were interviewed by the panel and who presented information at one of its open hearings.) After two people were shot dead, police needed to consider the possibility of a murderer loose on campus who did a double slaying for unknown reasons, even though a domestic disturbance was a likely possibility. The police did not urge the Policy Group to take precautions, as best can be understood from the panel's interviews.

It was reasonable albeit wrong that the VTPD thought this double murder was most likely the result of a domestic argument, given the facts they had initially, including the knowledge that the last person known to have been with the female victim was her boyfriend who owned a gun and cared greatly for her, according to police interviews, plus the fact that she was shot with a young man in her room under the circumstances found.

There are very few murders each year on campuses—an average of about 16 across 4,000 universities and colleges, as previously noted. The only college campus mass murder in the

United States in the past 40 years was the University of Texas tower sniper attack, though there have been occasional multiple murders. Based on past history, the probability of more shootings following a dormitory slaying was very low. The panel researched reports of multiple shootings on campuses for the past 40 years, and no scenario was found in which the first murder was followed by a second elsewhere on campus. (See Appendix L for a summary of the multiple criminal shootings on campus.) The VTPD had the probabilities correct, but needed to consider the low-probability side as well as the most likely situation.

Both the VTPD and the BPD immediately put their emergency response teams (ERTs) (i.e., SWAT teams) on alert and staged them at locations from which they could respond rapidly to the campus or city. They also had police on campus looking for the gunman while they pursued the boyfriend. The ERTs were staged mainly in case they had to make an arrest of the gunman or serve search warrants on the shooting suspect.

## DELAYED ALERT TO UNIVERSITY COMMUNITY

The VTPD chief and BPD chief both responded to the murder scene in minutes. Chief Flinchum of the VTPD arrived at 8:00 a.m. and Chief Crannis of the BPD arrived at 8:13 a.m. As noted above, the VTPD chief had notified the university administration of the shootings at 7:57 a.m., just before he arrived at the scene.

Once informed, the university president almost immediately convened the emergency Policy Group to decide how to respond, including how and when to notify the university community. In An interview with President Steger, members of the panel were told that the police reports to the Policy Group first described a possible "murder– suicide" and then a "domestic dispute," and that the police had identified a suspect. After the area parking lots had been searched, the police reported the suspect probably had left the campus.

The police did not tell the Policy Group that there was a chance the gunman was loose on campus or advise the university of any immediate action that should be taken such as canceling classes or closing the university. Also, the police did not give any direction as to an emergency message to be sent to the students. The police were very busy at WAJ investigating what had happened, gathering evidence, and managing the scene. They were conveying information by phone to the Policy Group at this point. Not until 9:25 a.m. did the police have a representative sitting with the Policy Group, a police captain.

The VTPD has the authority under the Emergency Response Plan and its interpretation in practice to request that an emergency message be sent, but as related in Chapter II, the police did not have the capability to send a message themselves. That capability was in the hands of the associate vice president for University Affairs and one other official. As stated earlier, the VTPD is not a member of the Policy Group but is often invited to attend Policy Group meetings dealing with the handling of emergencies.

One of the factors prominent in the minds of the Policy Group, according to the university president and others who were present that day, was the experience gained the previous August when a convict named William Morva escaped from a nearby prison and killed a law enforcement officer and a guard at a local hospital. Police reported he might be on the VT campus. The campus administration issued an alert that a murderer was on the loose in the vicinity of the campus. Then a female employee of the bank in the Squires Student Activities Center reportedly called her mother on a cell phone, and the mother incorrectly inferred that people were being held hostage in the student center. The mother called the police, who responded with a SWAT team. News photos of the event show students rushing out of the building with their hands up while police with drawn automatic weapons and bulletproof vests were charging into the building, a potentially dangerous situation. It was a false alarm. Morva was captured off campus, but this situation was fresh in the minds of the Policy Group as it met to decide what to do on the report of the double homicide at WAJ. It is questionable whether there was any panic among the students in the Morva incident, as some reports had it, and how dangerous that situation really was, but the Policy Group remembered it as a highly charged and dangerous situation. In the eyes of the Policy Group, including the university president, a dangerous situation had been created by their warning in that August 2006 event coupled with the subsequent spread of rumors and misinformation. The Policy Group did not want to cause a repeat of that situation if the police had a suspect and he was thought to be off campus.

Even with the police conveying the impression to campus authorities that the probable perpetrator of the dormitory killings had left campus and with the recent past history of the "panic" caused by the alert 9 months earlier, the university Policy Group still made a questionable decision. They sent out a carefully worded alert an hour and half after they heard that there was a double homicide, which was now more than 2 hours after the event.

Vice Provost of Student Affairs David Ford presented a statement to the panel on May 21, 2007. He was a member of the university Policy Group that made the decisions on what to do after hearing about the shootings.

> Shortly after 8:00 a.m. on Monday, April 16, I was informed that there had been a shooting in West Ambler Johnston hall and that President Steger was assembling the Policy Group immediately. By approximately 8:30 a.m., I and the other members of the group had arrived at the Burruss Hall Boardroom and Dr. Steger convened the meeting. I learned subsequently that as he awaited the arrival of other group members, President Steger had been in regular communication with the police, had given direction to have the governor's office notified of the shooting, and had called the head of University Relations to his office to begin planning to activate the emergency communication systems.

> When he convened the meeting, President Steger informed the Policy Group that Virginia Tech police had received a call at approximately 7:20 a.m. on April 16, 2007, to investigate an incident in a residence hall room in West Ambler Johnston. Within minutes of the call, Virginia Tech police and Virginia Tech Rescue Squad members responded to find two gunshot victims, a male and a female, inside a room in the residence hall. Information continued to be received through frequent telephone conversations with Virginia Tech police on the scene. The Policy Group was informed that the residence hall was being secured by Virginia Tech police, and students within the hall were notified and asked to remain in their rooms for their safety. We were further informed that the room containing the gunshot victims was immediately secured for evidence collection, and Virginia Tech police began questioning hall residents and identifying potential witnesses. In the preliminary stages of the investigation, it appeared to be an isolated incident, possibly domestic in nature. The Policy Group learned that Blacksburg police and Virginia state police had been notified and were also on the scene.

> The Policy Group was further informed by the police that they were following up on leads concerning a person of interest in relation to the shooting. During this 30-minute period of time between 8:30 and 9:00 a.m., the Policy Group processed the factual information it had in the context of many questions we asked ourselves. For instance, what information do we release without causing a panic? We learned from the Morva incident last August that speculation and misinformation spread by individuals who do not have the facts cause panic. Do we confine the information to students in West Ambler Johnston since the information we had

focused on a single incident in that building? Beyond the two gunshot victims found by police, was there a possibility that another person might be involved (i.e., a shooter), and if so, where is that person, what does that person look like, and is that person armed? At that time of the morning, when thousands are in transit, what is the most effective and efficient way to convey the information to all faculty, staff, and students? If we decided to close the campus at that point, what would be the most effective process given the openness of a campus the size of Virginia Tech? How much time do we have until the next class change?

And so with the information the Policy Group had at approximately 9 a.m., we drafted and edited a communication to be released to the university community via e-mail and to be placed on the university web site. We made the best decision we could based upon the information we had at the time. Shortly before 9:30 a.m., the Virginia Tech community—faculty, staff, and students—were notified by e-mail as follows:

"A shooting incident occurred at West Ambler Johnston earlier this morning. Police are on the scene and are investigating. The university community is urged to be cautious and are asked to contact Virginia Tech Police if you observe anything suspicious or with information on the case. Contact Virginia Tech Police at 231–6411. Stay tuned to the www.vt.edu. We will post as soon as we have more information"

The Virginia Tech Emergency/Weather Line recordings were also transmitted and a broadcast telephone message was made to campus phones. The Policy Group remained in session in order to receive additional updates about the West Ambler Johnston case and to consider further actions if appropriate.

No mention was made in the initial message sent to the students and staff of a double murder, just a shooting, which might have implied firing a gun and injuries, possibly accidental, rather than two murdered. Students and faculty were advised to be alert. The message went out to e-mails and phones. Some students and faculty saw the alert before the second event but many, if not most, did not see it, nor did most in Norris Hall classes. Those who had 9:05 a.m. classes were already in them and would not have seen the message unless checking their computers, phone, or Blackberries in class. If the message had gone out earlier, between 8:00 and 8:30 a.m., more people would have received it before leaving for their 9:05 a.m. classes. If an audible alert had been sounded, even more might have tuned in to check for an emergency message.

Few anywhere on campus seemed to have acted on the initial warning messages; no classes were canceled, and there was no unusual absenteeism. When the Norris Hall shooting started, few connected it to the first message.

The university body was not put on high alert by the actions of the university administration and was largely taken by surprise by the events that followed. Warning the students, faculty, and staff might have made a difference. Putting more people on guard could have resulted in quicker recognition of a problem or suspicious activity, quicker reporting to police, and quicker response of police. Nearly everyone at Virginia Tech is adult and capable of making decisions about potentially dangerous situations to safeguard themselves. So the earlier and clearer the warning, the more chance an individual had of surviving.

## DECISION NOT TO CANCEL CLASSES OR LOCK DOWN

Many people have raised the question of whether the university should have been locked down. One needs to analyze the feasibility of doing this for a campus of 35,000 people, and what the results would have been even if feasible. Most police chiefs consulted in this review believe that a lockdown was not feasible.

When a murder takes place in a city of 35,000 population, the entire city is virtually never shut down. At most, some in the vicinity of the shooting might be alerted if it is thought that the shooter is in the neighborhood. People might be advised by news broadcast or bullhorns to stay inside. A few blocks might be cordoned off, but not a city of 35,000. A university, however, in some ways has more control than does the mayor or police of a city, so the analogy to a city is not entirely fitting. The university is also considered by many as playing a role in loco parentis for at least some of its students, even those who are legally adults, a view shared by several victims' families.

President Steger noted that closing the university in an emergency presents another problem, traffic congestion. In the Morva incident, when the school was closed, it took over an hour and a half for the traffic to clear despite trying to stage the evacuation. Numerous people also stood waiting for buses. Those evacuating were very vulnerable in their cars and at bus stops.

Some people suggested that the university should have closed out of respect for the two students who were killed. However, the general practice at most large universities is not to close when a student dies, regardless of the cause (suicide, homicide, traffic accident, overdose, etc.). Universities and colleges need to make that decision based on individual criteria.

Feasibility – A building can be locked down in the sense of locking the exterior doors, barring anyone from coming or going. Elementary schools practice that regularly, and so do some intermediate and high schools. At least some schools in Blacksburg were locked down for a while after the first shootings. Usually, a lock-down also implies locking individual classrooms. Virginia Tech does not have locks on the inside of classroom doors, as is the case for most universities and many high schools.

The analogy to elementary or high schools, however, is not very useful. The threat in elementary schools usually is not from students, the classrooms have locks, they have voice communication systems to teachers and students, and the people at risk are in one building, not 131 buildings. High schools usually have one building and some of the other characteristics too.

A message could theoretically be sent to all buildings on campus to lock their doors, but there was no efficient way to do this at Virginia Tech. It would have required calls or e-mails to individuals who had the ability to lock the doors for at least 131 buildings or sending people on foot to each building. E-mails might have been used, but one could not be sure they would be read promptly. Even if people in the buildings received a message by phone or e-mail, the university had no way of knowing who received the message without follow up calls or requesting returned responses to the calls and e-mails. The process was complicated and would have taken considerable time.

Some university campuses, mostly urban ones, have guards at every entrance to their build ings. Virginia Tech does not. It would take approximately 450–500 guards to post one at all entrances of all major buildings on the VT campus.[49] The VTPD at full strength has 41 officers, of which only 14 are on-duty at 8:00 a.m. on a weekday, 5 on patrol and 9 in the office[49] erviceing the chief. It is unlikely all VT buildings could be guarded or closed within 1–2 hours after the first shooting.

Closing all of the roads into the school would also be a problem. The large campus includes 16 vehicle entrances separated in some cases by a mile from each other. More police can be brought in from Blacksburg and other areas. Without a clear emergency, however, it is inconceivable that large numbers of police would rush to the campus, leaving non-campus areas at risk from the same gunman and all other crimes when it was not expected to be more than an isolated incident.

---

[49] There are about 30 dorm-type buildings with an average of about two entrances each, and 100 class-room/administration buildings with an average of about four entrances each, for an estimated total of about 460.

There are no barriers to pedestrians walking across lawns into the campus. It would have taken hundreds of police, National Guard troops, or others to truly close down the campus, and they could not have arrived in time.

Messages might have been prioritized to reach the buildings with the most people and to guard them first, but it still was impractical and not seriously considered. All police with whom the panel consulted felt that a lockdown for a campus like Virginia Tech was not feasible on the morning of April 16.

More feasible would have been canceling classes and asking everyone to stay home or stay indoors until an all-clear was given, although even getting that message to everyone quickly was problematical with the new emergency alerting system not totally in place. Students could have been asked to return to their dormitories or to housing off campus. However, many might have gone to other public buildings on campus unless those buildings also were ordered to close. Canceling classes and getting a message out to students off campus would have stopped some from coming onto the campus. But students still could congregate vulnerably in dorms or other places.

Furthermore, the police and university did not know whether the gunman was inside or outside WAJ or other buildings. People not in buildings, typically numbering in the thousands outdoors on the campus at a given time, may seek refuge in buildings in the face of an emergency. Without knowing where the gunman is, one might be sending people into a building with the gunman, or sending them outside where a gunman is waiting. The shooters at the Jonesboro Middle School massacre in Arkansas in 1998 planned to create an alarm inside their school building and get students and faculty to go outside where the shooters were set up.

Cho, too, could have shot people in the open on campus, after an alert went out, waiting for them outside. Although he was armed with only handguns, no one knew that at the time. The Texas tower shooter sniped at people with a rifle outdoors.

Impact of Lockdown or Closedown – In this event, the shooter was a member of the campus community, an insider with a pass card to get into his dorm, able to receive whatever message was sent to the university community, and able to go anywhere that students were allowed to go. He would have received an alert, too.

It might be argued that the total toll would have been less if the university had canceled classes and announced it was closed for business immediately after the first shooting; or if the earlier alert message had been stronger and clearer. Even with the messaging system that was in place on April 16, many could have received messages before they left for class by e-mail or phone before 9 a.m., and the message probably would have quickly spread mouth to mouth as well. Even if it only partially reduced the university population on campus, it might have done some good. It is the panel's judgment that, all things considered, the toll could have been reduced had these actions been taken. But none of these measures would likely have averted a mass shooting altogether. There is a possibility that the additional measures would have dissuaded Cho from acting further, but he had already killed two people and sent a tape to NBC that would arrive the following morning with all but a confession. From what we know of his mental state and commitment to action that day, it was likely that he would have acted out his fantasy somewhere on campus or outside it that same day.

This was a single-shooter scenario; Columbine High School had two shooters, and that scenario was quite different. Emergency planners have to anticipate various high-risk scenarios and how to prepare for them. They must be aware that what happens will rarely be just like the scenario planned for. The right thing for one scenario might be just the wrong thing to do for another, such as whether to tell people to stay inside buildings or get outside.

## CONTINUING EVENTS

To continue the story of April 16, there was not an event, a pause for 2 hours, and then a second event. The notion that there was a 2-hour gap as mentioned in some news stories and by many who sent questions to the panel is a misconception. There was continuous action and deliberations from the first event until the second, and they made a material difference in the results of the second event.

Police Actions – The VTPD and the other law enforcement agencies involved did a professional job in pursuing the investigation of the WAJ incident with the one large and unfortunate exception of having conveyed the impression to the university administration that they probably had a solid suspect who probably had left the campus. These agencies did not know that with certainty. A stronger patrol of the campus and random checking of bags being carried might have found Cho carrying guns. Cho, however, was one of tens of thousands of students on campus, did not stand out in appearance, and carried his weapons in a backpack like many other backpacks. The police had no clues pointing to anyone other than the boyfriend, and it would not have been reasonable to expect them to be able to check what each person on campus was carrying.

The VTPD and BPD mobilized their emergency response teams after the first shooting. They did not know what the followup would bring, but they wanted to be ready for whatever occurred. The VTPD had not investigated a homicide in recent memory, and properly called on the resources of the BPD, state police, and ultimately ATF and FBI to assist in the investigation.

Boyfriend Questioning – At 9:30 a.m., the boyfriend of Emily Hilscher was stopped in his pickup truck on a road. He was cooperative and shocked to hear that his girlfriend had just been killed. He passed a field test for the presence of gunpowder residue. While he remained a person of interest, it appeared unlikely that he was the shooter, with the implication that the real shooter was probably still at large. The police passed this information to the university leadership through the police captain who was interacting with the university staff.

This negative finding on the boyfriend raised the urgency of the situation, and the university Proceeded to send out more alerts of the changing situation, but by then it was too late.

Even after they realized he was not a likely suspect and had been traumatized by the news of his girlfriend's death, the police agencies involved in stopping and questioning Emily Hilscher's boyfriend did not treat him sympathetically; he deserved better care.

Cho's Next Actions – After shooting the two students in WAJ, Cho went back to his own dormitory, arriving at 7:17 a.m. (based on the record of his swipe card). He changed out of his blood-stained clothing, which was later found in his room. He accessed his university computer account at 7:25 a.m. and proceeded to delete his e-mails and wipe out his account. He then removed the hard drive of his computer and later disposed of it and his cell phone. Cho apparently also had planned to dispose of his weapons after using them in a different scenario because he had filed down the serial numbers on the guns.[50] Mentally disturbed killers often make one plan and then change it for some reason. The motivation may never be known for why he partially obscured his identity and did not carry any identification into Norris Hall, but then sent his manifesto to a national news network with his pictures.

Between 8:10 and 8:20 a.m., an Asian male thought now to be Cho was seen at the Duck Pond. (The pond has been searched unsuccessfully for the whereabouts of his phone and hard drive, which are still missing.)

Before 9:00 a.m., Cho went to the Blacksburg post office off campus, where he was recognized by a professor who thought he looked frightening. At 9:01 a.m., he mailed a package to NBC News in New York and a letter to the university's English Department.

Diatribe – The panel was allowed to view the material Cho sent to NBC. The package was signed "A. Ishmael," similar to the "Ax

---

[50] The ATF laboratory was able to raise the numbers and identify the weapons collected after the shootings.

Ishmael" name he had written on his arm in ink at the time he committed suicide and also the name he used to sign some e-mails. The significance of this name remains to be explained, but it may tie to his self-view as a member of the oppressed.

Inside the package was a CD with a group of about 20 videos of himself presenting his extreme complaints against the world, two rambling, single-spaced letters with much the same information that were used as the scripts for the videos, and pictures of himself with written captions. The pictures showed him wielding weapons, showing his preparations for a mass murder, and railing against society that had ill-treated him. He seemed to be trying to look powerful posing with weapons, the "avenger" for the mistreated and downtrodden of the world, and even its "savior", in his words.

The videos and pictures in the package appear to have been taken at various times in a motel, a rented van, and possibly his dorm room over the previous weeks. It is likely that he alone took the photos; he can be seen adjusting the camera.

His words to the camera were more than most people had ever heard from him. He wanted his motivation to be known, though it comes across as largely incoherent, and it is unclear as to exactly why he felt such strong animosity. His diatribe is filled with biblical and literary references and references to international figures, but in a largely stream of consciousness manner. He mentions no one he knew in the videos. Rather, he portrays a grandiose fantasy of becoming a significant figure through the mass killing, not unlike American assassins of presidents and public figures. The videos are a dramatic reading or "performance" of the writings he enclosed. He read them several minutes at a time, then reached up to turn off the camera, changed the script he had mounted near the camera, and continued again. They clearly were[51] not extemporaneous. Intentionally or accidentally, he even provided two takes of reading one portion of his written diatribe.

After the mailings, Cho's exact path is unknown until he gets to Norris Hall.

## MOTIVATION FOR FIRST KILLINGS?

NO one knows why Cho committed the first killings in the dormitory. He ran a great risk of being seen and having any of a number of things go wrong that could have thwarted his larger plan. One line of speculation is that he might have been practicing for the later killings, since he had never shot anyone before (some serial killers have been known to do this). He may have thought he would create a diversion to draw police away from where his main action would later be, though in fact it worked the opposite way. Many more police were on campus than would have been there without the first shootings, which allowed the response to the second incident to be much faster and in greater force. There is also a possibility that he considered attacking a woman as part of his revenge—he was known to have stalked at least three women in the previous year and had complaints registered against him, one from WAJ. Although there is a small possibility he knew the victim, no evidence of any connection has been found. In fact, he did not really know any of his victims that day, not faculty, roommates, or classmates. None of the speculative theories as to motive seem likely. The state and campus police have not closed their cases yet, in part trying to determine his motives.

## KEY FINDINGS

Generally the VTPD and BPD officers responded to and carried out their investigative duties in a professional manner in accordance with accepted police practices. However, the police conveyed the wrong

---

[51] NBC News in New York has the package Cho sent to them and has released only a small amount of the material. There is a balance between the public interest and the harm this material can do to families of victims, the potential for giving incentive to future shooters, and the possibility of hidden messages triggering actions of others. NBC spent much time wrestling with what was the responsible thing to do journalistically. It was a difficult set of decisions. They did not delay at all in getting the information package to the FBI well before they released any of it.

impression to the university Policy Group about the lead they had and the likelihood that the suspect was no longer on campus.

The police did not have the capability to use the university alerting system to send a warning to the students, staff, and faculty. That is, they were not given the keyword to operate the alerting system themselves, but rather they had to request a message be sent from the Policy Group or at least the associate vice president for University Relations, who did have the keyword. The police did have the authority to request that a message be sent, but did not request that be done. They gave the university administration the information on the incident, and left it to the Policy Group to handle the messaging.

The university administration failed to notify students and staff of a dangerous situation in a timely manner. The first message sent by the university to students could have been sent at least an hour earlier and been more specific. The university could have notified the Virginia Tech community that two homicides of students had occurred and that the shooter was unknown and still at large. The administration could have advised students and staff to safeguard themselves by staying in residences or other safe places until further notice. They could have advised those not en route to school to stay home, though after 8 a.m. most employees would have been en route to their campus jobs and might not have received the messages in time.

Despite the above findings, there does not seem to be a plausible scenario of university response to the double homicide that could have prevented a tragedy of considerable magnitude on April 16. Cho had started on a mission of fulfilling a fantasy of revenge. He had mailed a package to NBC identifying himself and his rationale and so was committed to act that same day. He could not wait beyond the end of the day or the first classes in the morning. There were many areas to which he could have gone to cause harm.

## RECOMMENDATIONS

VII-1 In the preliminary stages of an investigation, the police should resist focusing on a single theory and communicating that to decisionmakers.

VII-2 All key facts should be included in an alerting message, and it should be disseminated as quickly as possible, with explicit information.

VII-3 Recipients of emergency messages should be urged to inform others.

VII-4 Universities should have multiple communication systems, including some not dependent on high technology. Do not assume that 21st century communications may survive an attack or natural disaster or power failure.

VII-5 Plans for canceling classes or closing the campus should be included in the university's emergency operations plan. It is not certain that canceling classes and stopping work would have decreased the number of casualties at Virginia Tech on April 16, but those actions may have done so. Lockdowns or cancellation of classes should be considered on campuses where it is feasible to do so rapidly.

## ADDITIONS AND CORRECTIONS

Cho's Access to WAJ: p. 77, Clarification and Addition – Cho had access to his mailbox in the foyer of West Ambler Johnston residence hall, but only after 7:30 a.m. Cho did not have key access to the rest of the residence hall. At about 6:45 a.m. he was seen loitering in the foyer area, between the exterior and interior doors. He may have entered the foyer and then the interior residential area when other students entered or exited, but no one remembered facilitating his entry.

Motive for Homicides: p. 77, Addition – As of October 2009 no motive has been established for the double homicide at WAJ. There have been speculations that it was a rehearsal and test of nerve for the later actions, or a diversion, but the risk of being caught before committing the mass murders was high. There was no mention in Cho's writings or videotapes that suggested a motive or link to the victims at WAJ. Cho had harassed a female student on the same floor as Emily Hilscher, but neither Emily's roommate nor anyone else interviewed knew of any connection between Emily and Cho.

Time of Shootings: p. 78, Addition – The exact time of the double shooting is not known. The Report stated "not long after 7:15 a.m." Emily Hilscher had swiped her card upon entry to WAJ at 7:02 a.m. and Cho swiped his entry card back at his dorm at 7:17 a.m. So Hilscher and Clark were shot sometime between a few minutes after 7:02 and a few minutes before 7:17 a.m., depending on the path and speed of Hilscher as she went to her room, the interaction in her room, and the path and speed of Cho as he returned to his room after the murders. The first call to police was at 7:20 a.m., approximately 5 minutes after the shooting, after two students had discussed whether to report the noise they heard.

Failure of Timely Notice to Emily Hilscher's Family: p. 78, Addition – No one from Virginia Tech or from the hospitals contacted the Hilscher family before she died to let them know Emily had been shot and was severely wounded. The VTPD knew Emily's identity from information provided by Heather Haugh, Emily Hilscher's roommate, around 8:15 a.m. The Hilschers learned their daughter was a victim from the mother of Emily's boyfriend, Karl Thornhill, and the Thornhills did not know where Emily had been taken. The Hilschers exerted every effort to locate Emily but ran into problems with hospital personnel not wanting to disclose information over the phone. The family lived about a 3 ½ hour drive from campus, but had the family received a timely call and been told where Emily was being treated they would have had a chance to at least place a call and talk to Emily's doctors and to her even if she could not respond. Moreover, the Hilschers would not have had to go through the stress of not knowing Emily's condition. Notification of family should have been an immediate priority and should have been verified as having been performed by the Virginia Tech administrators, VTPD, and/or Virginia State Police.

Additional Officials at WAJ: pp. 78–79, Addition – Dr. Spencer, Associate VP for Student Affairs, arrived at WAJ at 7:55 a.m., and then called the VP for Student Affairs, Dr. Zenobia Hikes with information on the events.

Emily's Roommate: p. 79, Addition – The "girlfriend" of Emily Hilscher who was interviewed by the police was Emily's roommate, Heather Haugh. The boyfriend of Emily referred to in the text was Karl Thornhill. (The review panel chose to minimize use of student names to focus on the lessons learned, and maintain privacy, but some victims' families have asked that these names be noted.)

Time of Roommate Interview: p. 79, Addition – Emily's roommate Heather Haugh swiped her card at WAJ at 8:14 a.m. and was then interviewed by the police. (She was interviewed inside the residence, so the interview time was after 8:14.) Police did not know about Emily's boy-friend until that point. Immediately following the interview he became a "person of interest." The Policy Group did not know this fact until police updated them at 8:40 a.m. Until then the Policy Group just knew there was a double shooting with both student victims critically wounded, the shooter was unknown and at large, and that the initial police impression was that it was probably a domestic issue.

Lockdown of WAJ: p. 79, Addition – Police in effect locked down WAJ residence hall after the shootings to process the crime scene and interview witnesses. Police were inside and outside the residence hall. No one was allowed to leave. The shooter was unknown and possibly still present. Some time before 9:00 a.m. students in the dorm were allowed to exit and go to class. Tragically, two of them were later killed during the mass shootings at Norris Hall. As was normally the case, doors on all dormitories remained locked and required a resident's scan card to get in until 10:00 a.m.

Solution to Initial Homicides: p. 79, Clarification – The Report states: "If Cho had stopped after the first two shootings, he might well have never been caught." That was the opinion of VTPD Chief Flinchum reflecting on the paucity of evidence. There were shell casings, which could help identify a gun once it was found, and bloody footprints, which could help identify a shoe, but the gun and shoe had to be found and linked to a suspect. As a side note, at least three states at the time, including Maryland and New York, required gun dealers to test-fire each gun sold and send the results to the state, which maintained a registry and database of this information. The gun purchaser could be identified from a shell casing found at a crime scene. California went further, and required guns to have a chip inserted that marked each casing with an identification number by which a gun purchaser could be rapidly identified. In those states it is likely that the registered owner of the gun used in the shooting would have been identified even if no other evidence were found.

Victim Still Alive: p. 79, Correction – When the Policy Group was first informed about the shootings, Emily Hilscher was still alive. The Report should not have referred to both victims as homicides at that point in time. Emily survived for three hours while she was treated at two hospitals.

Chief Flinchum Calls to BPD and Executive Vice President: p. 80, Clarification – The Report Stated Chief Flinchum was notified about the shootings at 7:40 a.m. and then contacted Blacksburg PD. The latter occurred at 7:51 a.m. He also tried to reach the Office of the Executive Vice President but did not get through until 7:57 a.m.

Delayed Alert: pp. 80-81, Correction and Addition – President Steger first spoke directly with Virginia Tech Police Chief Flinchum at 8:11 a.m., and then convened the Policy Group, which met at 8:25 am. According to a police briefing for victims' families, Chief Flinchum told President Steger that two students were critically wounded, that no weapon was found, that there were bloody footprints, and that the incident seemed to be domestic in nature. Chief Flinchum did not offer a recommendation about an alert or closing the campus at that time nor was he asked his opinion about doing so. Essentially, the police focused on the investigation and hunt for the killer, and the Policy Group was left to handle the alert.

The Review Panel had been told that the Policy Group was informed early on that there was a person of interest. However, the first calls to the Policy Group and President could not have mentioned a person of interest because it was not until at least a few minutes after the 8:14 A.M arrival of Emily Hilscher's roommate at WAJ that the police learned of Emily's boy-friend and that he owned a gun.

Under the provisions of Virginia Tech's policy document called "Campus Safety: A Shared Responsibility," the VTPD is given the responsibility and authority to send an emergency alert. That document, formulated as part of Virginia Tech's compliance with the Clery Act, required issuing a timely warning. It stated in pertinent part:

i.      (Page 1) "Virginia Tech has designed policies and regulations in order to create a safer and more harmonious environment for the members of its community. All campus community members and visitors of the university are required to obey these regulations. These policies not only reflect the university's high standards of conduct, but also local, state and federal laws. Observed and enforced, they create a high degree of safety for the university community."

ii.     (Page 6) "At time it may be necessary for "timely warnings" to be issued to the university community. If a crime(s) occur [sic] and notification is necessary to warn the University of a potential[sic] dangerous situation then the Virginia Tech Police Department should be notified. The police department will then prepare a release and the information will be disseminated to all students, faculty and staff and to the local community."

However, Virginia Tech's Emergency Management Plan also contained formal emergency alert procedures and these assigned authority for releasing a warning to the Policy Group only. The two documents and policies were inconsistent. The one that VTPD and the Policy Group followed on April 16th was the Emergency Management Plan because that Plan was the one with which they were familiar and historically had used as their basis of operations. Under the Emergency Management Plan, the VTPD could request or develop, but not send, an alert because they did not have the computer code needed to send out a warning. Only two Virginia Tech officials had the code, and the police chief was not one of them. The code was needed to ensure that any message was authorized, and was not a false alarm – which had occurred previously in some messages to the local media.

Pre-Alert Actions to Protect: p. 83, Addition – The Report stated that few on campus acted on the first warning message sent, and that still appears to be generally correct. However, there were a growing number of actions taken even before the first official warning message from Virginia Tech was sent, as word of the shootings spread by word of mouth and media and other means. Some people who had information about the double shooting acted to protect their safety and the safety of others for whom they had responsibility, even before receiving an "official" message. For example, the Center for Professional and Continuing Education, and the Veterinary College, locked down on their own accord. The VT Governmental Affairs Director ordered the President's office to be locked. VTPD cancelled bank deposit pickups and trash collection. The Blacksburg schools also made the decision to lock down.

Field Test for Gunpowder Residue: p. 86, Correction – The Report said that Emily Hilscher's boyfriend had passed a gunpowder residue test when he was stopped on the road. In fact, Thornhill was given the Primer Residue Test, but unlike some other gunpowder tests this one does not give a preliminary result in the field. Rather, the sample requires analysis in a crime lab. The sample was packaged for submission to a lab but the analysis was never done as events overtook the need to do so.

The Report also said that information on the results of the gunpowder test was passed on to the Policy Group. Since no analysis was performed no results could have been provided to the Policy Group. The Policy Group was informed of the roadside stop and test. Thus at no time on April 16 did the Policy Group have information that the person of interest was cleared for the initial double shooting. Police doubted Thornhill was a suspect after interviewing him, but he was kept as a person of interest until the next day.

When stopped by the police, Thornhill was only told that his girlfriend Emily Hilscher was shot, not that she was severely wounded. He did not know whether she was in a hospital or anything else about her situation. Police left him immediately upon receiving word about the Norris Hall attack, and Thornhill continued searching for Emily.

Search of Thornhill Apartment: p. 86, Correction and Addition – In the evening of the shooting, a police ERT (SWAT team) entered the residence of Karl Thornhill, Emily Hilscher's boyfriend. They handcuffed him and put him on the floor while they searched his apartment. They also handcuffed and put on the floor his family members who had arrived to console him. The police had a search warrant, but did not present it until they were leaving. Thornhill and his family were cooperative but felt they had been treated with a heavy hand unnecessarily, especially since police had released Thornhill after the traffic stop that morning, and did not bring him in for questioning later in the day. They did not realize he was still considered a suspect. However, it should be noted that the link between the double shooting and the mass shooting had not yet been proven, and police knew Thornhill had a gun, so they were exercising caution in the interest of everyone's safety, even though unpleasant and traumatic for the Thornhill family.

Comments of Senior VT Staff to Their Families: Addition – At about 8:15 a.m. two senior officials at Virginia Tech had conversations with family members in which the shooting on campus was mentioned. In one conversation, by phone, the official advised her son, a student at Virginia Tech, to go to class. In the other, in person, the official arranged for extended baby-sitting because she knew she would be tied up for more of the day as a result of the shootings.

## OTHER COMMENTS

Page 81 of the Report discusses reasons why Virginia Tech delayed sending an alert. One family member commented that police informed families in a 2009 briefing that another reason for not immediately informing the campus was to avoid making the police work and investigation more difficult. Police Chief Flinchum has denied making this remark and it may or may not have been made by others or correctly understood. Nevertheless, there are indeed tradeoffs between informing a community of what has happened so they have context in which to take actions for their own safety, and possibly informing the perpetrator(s) of police knowledge and action, potentially making the investigation more difficult. The consensus of the Review Panel and many others in hindsight was that early warning should have received the higher priority in this situation. With the events at Virginia Tech as an example, early warning with the known facts now is the widely adopted practice in numerous colleges and universities as well as other venues.

Page 87 of the Report contains a discussion of what might have happened had there been earlier warning sent to Virginia Tech students and staff about a shooter on the loose. The Report spoke of Cho "fulfilling a fantasy of revenge" which he had articulated in the videos he sent to NBC and that it was likely he would have found some variation on his plan, since he had already essentially committed himself by mailing the videotaped message at 9:00 a.m. and was probably of a mind to complete his "mission." The question was asked by a victim family member: what would have resulted if the warning went out prior to 9:00 a.m., and Cho heard about or saw evidence of a manhunt and preventive measures such as additional police patrols, buildings being locked down, etc. before he sent out the videos? Might he have not sent the tape and aborted his "mission?"

There are many "what if" questions that can be raised, and no one knows the answers for certain. The forensic psychologist on the Review Panel thought that most likely Cho was committed to his mission: he had purchased and trained with his weapons, had obtained chains for the doors and rehearsed using them, and had thought out the scenario. When Cho returned to his dorm room, he erased his hard drive and deleted his Virginia Tech account, a sign he was starting a departure process. If not implementing his scheme as originally planned, he could have staged a variation that day in a residence hall, dining hall, or out in the open, or waited another day.

Another family member asked why the Virginia Tech Emergency Plan was not updated after the Morva incident the previous year, in which the gunman was (incorrectly) thought to be on campus. Though the plan was not revised, and no annex written specifically for handling a shooting incident or a shooter loose on campus, some major changes in preparedness were in process. The whole emergency alerting system was being upgraded significantly at the time of the April 16, 2007 incidents. The police departments in the region practiced how to handle a shooting incident. The VT Rescue Squad practiced handling mass casualty incidents. These police and EMS preparations undoubtedly saved lives on April 16.

A third question was why Virginia Tech did not conduct exercises for sending out an alert. Virginia Tech sent actual alerts for weather emergencies and other events from time to time, and was testing parts of the new emergency response system as they came on-line. Once the system was completed, it was tested again.

# Chapter VIII.

## MASS MURDER AT NORRIS HALL

Many police were on campus in the 2 hours following the first incident, most at West Ambler Johnston residence hall but others at a command center established for the first incident. Two emergency response teams (ERTs) were positioned at the Blacksburg Police Department (BPD) headquarters, and a police captain was with the Virginia Tech Policy Group acting as liaison.

Cho left the post office about 9:01 a.m. (the time on his mailing receipt). He proceeded to Norris Hall wearing a backpack with his killing tools. He carried two handguns, almost 400 rounds of ammunition most of which were in rapid loading magazines, a knife, heavy chains, and a hammer. He wore a light coat to cover his shooting vest. He was not noticed as being a threat or peculiar enough for anyone to report him before the shooting started.

In Norris Hall, Cho chained shut the pair of doors at each of the three main entrances used by students. Figure 7 shows one such entrance. The chaining had the dual effect of delaying anyone from interrupting his plan and keeping victims from escaping. After the Norris Hall incident, it was reported to police that an Asian male wearing a hooded garment was seen in the vicinity of a chained door at Norris Hall 2 days before the shootings, and it may well have been Cho practicing. Cho may have been influenced by the two Columbine High School killers, whom he mentioned in his ranting document sent to NBC News and previously in his middle school writings. He referred to them by their first names and clearly was familiar with how they had carried out their scheme.

On the morning of April 16, Cho put a note on the inside of one set of chained doors warning that a bomb would go off if anyone tried to

remove the chains. The note was seen by a faculty member, who carried it to the Engineering School dean's office on the third

*Figure 7. One of the Main Entrances to Norris Hall*

floor. This was contrary to university instructions to immediately call the police when a bomb threat is found. A person in the dean's office was about to call the police about the bomb threat when the shooting started. A handwriting comparison revealed that Cho wrote this note, but that he had not written bomb threat notes found over the previous weeks in three other buildings. Those threats, which led to the evacuation of the three buildings, proved to be false. That may have contributed to the Cho note not being taken seriously, even though found on a chained door.

The usual VTPD protocol for a bomb threat that is potentially real is to send officers to the threatened building and evacuate it. Had the Cho bomb threat note been promptly reported prior to the start of the shooting, the police might have arrived at the building sooner than they did.

A female student trying to get into Norris Hall shortly before the shooting started found the entrance chained. She climbed through a window to get where she was going on the first floor. She did not report the chains, assuming they had something to do with ongoing construction. Other students leaving early from an accounting exam on the third floor also saw the doors chained before the shooting started, but no one called the police or reported it to the university.

Prior to starting the shootings, Cho walked around in the hallway on the second floor poking his head into a few classrooms, some more than once, according to interviews by the police and panel. This struck some who saw him as odd because it was late in the semester for a student to be lost. But no one raised an alarm. Figure 8 shows the hallway in Norris Hall.

*Figure 8. Hallway in Norris Hall*

## THE SHOOTINGS

The occupants of the first classroom that Cho attacked had little chance to call for help or take cover. After peering into several classrooms, Cho walked into the Advanced Hydrology engineering class of Professor G. V. Loganathan in room 206, shot and killed the instructor, and continued shooting, saying not a word. In fact, he never uttered a sound during his entire shooting spree—no invectives, no rationale, no comments, Nothing. Even during this extreme situation at the end of his life, he did not speak to anyone. Of 13 students present in the classroom, 9 were killed and 2 injured by shooting, and only 2 survived unharmed. No one in room 206 was able to call the police.

Occupants of neighboring classrooms heard the gunshots but did not immediately recognize them as gunfire. One student went into the hallway to investigate, saw what was happening, and returned to alert the class.

First Alarm to 9-1-1 – Cho started shooting at about 9:40 a.m. It took about a minute for students and faculty in room 211, a French class, to recognize that the sounds they heard in the nearby room were gunshots. Then the instructor, Jocelyne Couture-Nowak, asked student Colin Goddard to call 9-1-1.

Cell phone 9-1-1 calls are routed according to which tower receives them. Goddard's call was routed to the Blacksburg police. Another call by cell phone from room 211 was routed first to the Montgomery County sheriff. The call-taker at the BPD received the call at 9:41 a.m. and was not familiar with campus building names. But it took less than a minute to sort out that the call was coming from Virginia Tech and it was then transferred to the Virginia Tech Police Department (VTPD).

At 9:42 a.m., the first call reached the Virginia Tech police that there was shooting in Norris Hall. Other calls later came from other classrooms and offices in Norris Hall and from other buildings.

Students and faculty in other nearby rooms also heard the first shots, but no one immediately realized what they were. Some thought they were construction noises. Others thought they could be the popping sounds sometimes heard from chemistry lab experiments on the first floor. One professor told his class to continue with the lesson after some raised questions about the noise. When the noise did not stop, some people went into the hallway to investigate. One student from an engineering class was shot when he entered the hallway. At that point, terror set in among the persons in the classrooms who realized that what they were hearing was gunfire.

Continued Shooting – This section portrays the sense of the key action rather than trace the exact path of Cho. It is based on police presentations to the panel, police news releases, and interviews conducted by the panel.

After killing Professor Loganathan and several students in room 206, Cho went across the hall to room 207, a German class taught by Christopher James Bishop. Cho shot Professor Bishop and several students near the door. He then started down the aisle shooting others. Four students and Bishop ultimately died in this room, with another six wounded by gunshot. One student tried to wrench free the podium that was fastened securely to the floor in order to build a barricade at the door. She was unsuccessful and injured herself in the process.

As Goddard called 9-1-1 from classroom 211, Couture-Nowak's class tried to use the instructor's table to barricade the door, but Cho pushed his way in, shot the professor, and walked down the aisle shooting students. Cho did not say anything. Goddard was among the first to be shot. Another student, Emily Haas, picked up Goddard's cell phone after he was shot. She stayed on the line for the rest of the shooting period. She was slightly wounded twice in the head by bullets, spoke quietly as long as she could to the dispatcher, heard that the police were responding, closed her eyes, and played dead. She said she did not open her eyes again for over 10 minutes until the police arrived. During her ordeal, she was concerned that the shooter would hear the 9-1-1 dispatch operator over the cell phone. But by keeping the line open she helped keep police apprised of the situation. She kept the phone hidden by her head and hair so she could appear dead but not disconnect. Although the dispatcher at times asked her questions and at other times told her to keep quiet, she spoke only when Cho was out of the room, which she could tell by the proximity of the shots.

Students in room 205 attending a class in scientific computing heard Cho's gunshots and barricaded the door to prevent his entry, mainly with their bodies kept low, holding the door with their feet. Cho never did succeed in getting into this room though he pushed and fired through the door several times. No one was injured by gunshot in this room.

Back in room 207, the German class, two uninjured students and two injured students rushed to the door to hold it shut with their feet and hands before Cho returned, keeping their bodies low and away from the center of the door. Within 2 minutes, Cho returned and beat on the door. He opened it an inch and fired about five shots around the door handle, then gave up trying to reenter and left.

Cho returned to room 211, the French class, and went around the room, up one aisle and down another, shooting students again. Cho shot Goddard two more times. Goddard lay still and played dead. This classroom received the most visits by Cho, who ultimately killed 11 students and the instructor, and wounded another 6, the entire class. A janitor saw Cho reloading his gun in the hall on the second floor and fled downstairs.

Cho tried to enter the classroom of engineering professor Liviu Librescu (room 204), who was teaching solid mechanics. Librescu braced his body against the door and yelled for students to head for the window. Students pushed out the screens and jumped or dropped onto bushes or the grassy ground below the window. Ten of the 16 students escaped this way. The next two students trying to leave through the window were shot. Librescu was fatally shot through the door trying to hold it closed while his students escaped. A total of four students were shot in this class, one fatally.

Cho returned to most of the classrooms more than once to continue shooting. He methodically fired from inside the doorways of the classrooms, and sometimes walked around inside them. It was very close range. Students had little place to hide other than behind the desks. By taking a few paces inside he could shoot almost anyone in the classroom who was not behind a piece of overturned furniture. The classrooms were all roughly square, with no obstructions. Figure 9 shows the interior of a typical classroom, seen from the corner furthest from the door. Table 1 shows the dimensions of the rooms with the shootings.

*Figure 9: Interior of Typical Classroom*

Table 1. Dimensions of the Classrooms Attacked

| Room # | Dimensions |
| --- | --- |
| 204 | 28' x 25' |
| 205 | 24' x 25' |
| 206 | 22' x 25' |
| 207 | 24' x 25' |
| 211 | 22' x 25' |

The rooms were furnished with lightweight desk–chair combinations, single units combining both functions. Each instructor had a table desk and a podium, the latter bolted to the floor. The doors were not lockable from the inside. Unlike many lower grade schools and typical of most colleges, the instructors had no university-furnished messaging system for receiving or sending an alarm. Emergency communications from classrooms were limited to any phone or electronic devices carried by students or instructors. The offices had standard telephones, but they were on the third floor.

The massacre continued for 9 minutes after the first 9-1-1 call was received by the VTPD, and about 10–12 minutes in total, including a minute for processing and transferring the call to VTPD, and the time to comprehend that shots were being fired and to make the call. From the first call, shots can be heard continuously on the dispatch tapes, until they stopped with the suicide shot.

Within that period, Cho murdered 25 students and 5 faculty of Virginia Tech at Norris Hall. Another 17 were shot and survived, and 6 were injured when they jumped from classroom windows to escape.

Cho expended at least 174 bullets from two semiautomatic guns, his 9mm Glock and .22 caliber Walther, firing often at point-blank range. The police found 17 empty magazines, each capable of holding 10–15 bullets. Ammunition recovered included 203 live cartridges,122 for the Glock and 81 for the Walther. The unexpended ammunition included two loaded 9mm magazines with 15 cartridges each and many loose bullets.

Cho committed suicide by shooting himself in the head, probably because he saw and heard the police closing in on him. With over 200 rounds left, more than half his ammunition, he almost surely would have continued to kill more of the wounded as he had been doing, and possibly others in the building had not the police arrived so quickly. Terrible as it was, the toll could have been even higher.

## DEFENSIVE ACTIONS

According to survivors, the first reaction of the students and faculty was disbelief, followed rapidly by many sensible and often heroic actions. One affirmative judgment in reflecting on this event is that virtually no one acted irrationally. People chose what they thought was the best option for their survival or to protect others, and many tried to prevent the shooter from gaining access to their room. Unfortunately, a shooter operating at point-blank range does not offer many options.

Escaping – Professor Librescu's class was the only one where students escaped by jumping from windows. This classroom's windows face a grassy area. (Figure 10 is the view from outside and Figure 11 shows the structure of the windows. The view from inside looking out is shown in Figure 12.)

*Figure 10. Norris Hall Classroom Windows, Grassy Side*

*Figure 11. Typical Set of Windows in Norris Hall*

The window sills are 19 feet high from the ground, two stories up. In order to escape through the window, the first jumper, a male student, had to take down a screen, swing the upper window outward, climb over the lower portion of the window that opened into the classroom, and then jump. He tried to land on

the bushes. Following his example, most of the rest of the class formed groups behind three windows and started jumping. All who jumped survived, some with broken bones, some uninjured except for scratches or bruises. Some survivors did the optimum window escape, lowering themselves from the window sill to drop to the ground, reducing the fall by their body length.

*Figure 12. To Escape, They Had to Climb Over the Low Window*

The other classes faced out onto concrete walks or yards, and jumping either did not seem a good idea or perhaps did not even enter their minds. No one attempted to jump from any other classroom.

Some attempts were made by a few students to escape out of the classroom and down the hall in the earliest stage of the incident. But after some people were shot in the hall, no one else tried that route.

Attempting to Barricade – In three of the four classrooms that Cho invaded and one more that resisted invasion, the instructor and students attempted to barricade the door against Cho entering either on his first attempt or on a later try. They tried to use the few things available—the teacher's table, the desk–chair combinations, and their bodies. Some attempts to barricade succeeded and others did not. Cho pushed his way in or shot through some doors that were being barricaded. In the German class, two wounded students and two non-wounded students managed to hold the door closed against the return entry by Cho. They succeeded in staying out of the line of fire through the door. Two other rooms did the same. In one, Cho never did get in. At least one effort was made to use the podium, but it failed (it was bolted to the floor). Cho was not a strong person—his autopsy noted weak musculature—and these brave students and faculty helped reduce the toll.

Playing Dead – Several students, some of whom were injured and others not, successfully played dead amid the carnage around them, and survived. Generally, they fell to the ground as shots were fired, and tried not to move, hoping Cho would not notice them. Cho had erviceycally shot several of his victims a second time when he saw them still alive on revisiting some of the rooms, so the survivors tried to hold still and keep quiet. This worked for at least some students.

## POLICE RESPONSE

Within 3 minutes of the Virginia Tech police receiving the 9-1-1 call, two officers arrived outside of Norris Hall by squad car. They were Virginia Tech officer H. Dean Lucas and Blacksburg Sgt. Anthony Wilson. A few seconds later, three more officers arrived by car: Blacksburg Police Department officers John Glass, Scott Craig, and Brian Roe. More continued to arrive throughout the incident.

By professional standards, this was an extraordinarily fast police response. The officers had been near WAJ as part of the investigation and security following the first incident, so they were able to respond much faster than they otherwise would have. The two police forces trusted each other, had trained together, and did not have to take time sorting out who would go

from which organization in which car. They just went together as fast as they could.

The five officers immediately proceeded to implement their training for dealing with an active shooter. The policy is to go to the gunfire as fast as possible, not in a careless headlong rush, but in a speedy but careful advance. The first arriving officers had to pause several seconds after exiting their cars to see where the gunfire was coming from, especially whether it was being directed toward them. They quickly figured out that the firing was inside the building, not coming from the windows to the outside. Because Cho was using two different caliber weapons whose sounds are different, the assumption had to be made that there was more than one shooter.

The officers tried the nearest entrance to Norris Hall, found it chained, quickly proceeded to a second and then a third entrance, both also chained. Attempts to shoot off the padlocks or chains failed. They then moved rapidly to a fourth entrance—a maintenance shop door that was locked but not chained. They shot open the conventional key lock with a shotgun. Five police officers entered and rapidly moved up the stairs toward the gunfire, not knowing who or how many gunmen were shooting.

The first team of five officers to enter Norris Hall after the door lock was shot were:

> VT Officer H. Dean Lucas (patrol)
> Blacksburg Officer Greg Evans (patrol)
> Blacksburg Officer Scott Craig (SWAT)
> Blacksburg Officer Brian Roe (SWAT)
> Blacksburg Officer Johnny Self (patrol)

They were followed seconds later by a second team of seven officers:

> VT Lt. Curtis Cook (SWAT)
> VT Sgt Tom Gallemore (SWAT)
> VT Sgt Sean Smith (SWAT)
> VT Officer Larry Wooddell (SWAT)
> VT Officer Keith Weaver (patrol)
> VT Officer Daniel Hardy (SWAT)
> Blacksburg Officer Jeff Robinson (SWAT)

Both teams had members from more than one police department. The first police team got to the second floor hallway leading to the classrooms as the shooting stopped. The second police team that entered went upstairs to the opposite end of the shooting hallway on the second floor. They saw the first team at the opposite end of the hall and held in place to avoid a crossfire should the shooter emerge from a room. They then went to clear the third floor.

The first team of officers arriving on the second floor found it eerily quiet. They approached cautiously in the direction from which the shots were fired. They had to clear each classroom and office as they passed it lest they walk past the shooter or shooters and get fired upon from the rear. They saw casualties in the hallway and a scene of mass carnage in the classrooms, with many still alive. Although the shooter was eventually identified, he was not immediately apparent, and they were not certain whether other shooters lurked. This seemed a distinct possibility. As one police sergeant later reflected: "How could one person do all this damage alone with handguns?"

Some people have questioned why the police could not force entry into the building more quickly. First, most police units do not carry bolt cutters or other entry devices; such tools would rarely be used by squad car officers. They usually are carried only in the vans of special police units. Second, the windows on the first floor are very narrow, as on all floors of Norris Hall. A thin student could climb through them; a heavily armed officer wearing bulletproof vest could not. Knocking down a door with a vehicle was not possible given the design and site of the building.

The auditorium connecting Norris Hall with Holden Hall and shared by both could have been used as an entry path, but it would have taken longer to get in by first running into Holden Hall, going through it, and then up the stairs to Norris Hall. The police ERT had the capability of receiving plans of the buildings by radio from the fire department, but that would have taken too long and was not needed in the event.

During the shooting, a student took pictures from his cell phone that were soon broadcast on television. They showed many police outside of Norris Hall behind trees and cars, some with guns drawn, not moving toward the gunfire. Most of them were part of a perimeter established around the building after the first officers on the scene made entry. The police were following standard procedure to surround the building in case the shooter or shooters emerged firing or trying to escape. What was not apparent was that the first officers on the scene already were inside.

Once the shooting stopped, the first police on the scene switched modes and became a rescue team. Four officers carried out a victim using a diamond formation, two actually doing the carrying and two escorting with guns drawn. At this point, it still was not known whether there was a second shooter. The police carried several victims who were still alive to the lawn outside the building, where they were turned over to a police-driven SUV that took the first victims to emergency medical treatment. (The emergency medical response is discussed in Chapter IX.)

A formal incident commander and emergency operations center was not set up until after the shooting was over mainly because events unfolded very rapidly. A more formal process was used for the follow-up investigation.

## UNIVERSITY MESSAGES

When university officials were apprised of the Norris Hall shootings, they were horrified. Vice Provost Ford explained the events as follows (continuing his statement presented to the panel from the previous chapter):

At approximately 9:45 a.m., the Policy Group received word from the Virginia Tech police of a shooting in Norris Hall. Within five minutes, a notification was issued by the Policy Group and transmitted to the university community which read:

"A gunman is loose on campus. Stay in buildings until further notice. Stay away from all windows."

Also activated was the campus emergency alert system. The voice message capability of that system was used to convey an emergency message throughout the campus. Given the factual information available to the Policy Group, the reasonable action was to ask people to stay in place. The Policy Group did not have evidence to ensure that a gunman was or was not on the loose, so every precaution had to be taken. The Virginia Tech campus contains 153 major buildings[52], 19 miles of public roads, is located on 2,600 acres of land, and as many as 35,000 individuals might be found on its grounds at any one time on a typical day. Virginia Tech is very much like a small city. One does not entirely close down a small city or a university campus.

Additionally, the Policy Group considered that the university schedule has a class change between 9:55 a.m. and 10:10 a.m. on a MWF schedule. To ensure some sense of safety in an open campus environment, the Policy Group decided that keeping people inside existing buildings if they were on campus and away from campus if they had not yet arrived was the right decision. Again, we made the best decision we could based on the information available. So at approximately 10:15 a.m. another message was transmitted which read:

"Virginia Tech has cancelled all classes. Those on campus are asked to remain where they are, lock their doors, and stay away from windows. Persons off campus are asked not to come to campus."

At approximately 10:50 a.m., Virginia Tech Police Chief Flinchum and Blacksburg Police Chief Crannis arrived to inform the Policy Group about what they had witnessed in the aftermath of the shootings in Norris Hall.

Chief Flinchum reported that the scene was bad; very bad. Virginia state police was handling the crime scene. Police had one shooter in custody and there was no evidence at the time to confirm or negate a second shooter, nor was there evidence at the time to link the shootings in

West Ambler Johnston to those in Norris Hall. The police informed the Policy Group that these initial observations were ongoing investigations.

Based upon this information and acting upon the advice of the police, the Policy Group immediately issued a fourth transmittal which read:

"In addition to an earlier shooting today in West Ambler Johnston, there has been a multiple shooting with multiple victims in Norris Hall. Police and EMS are on the scene. Police have one shooter in custody and as part of routine police procedure, they continue to search for a second shooter.

"All people in university buildings are required to stay inside until further notice. All entrances to campus are closed."

Information about the Norris Hall shootings continued to come to the Policy Group from the scene. At approximately 11:30 [a.m.], the Policy Group issued a planned faculty–staff evacuation via the Virginia Tech web site which read:

"Faculty and staff located on the Burruss Hall side of the drill field are asked to leave their office and go home immediately. Faculty and staff located on the War Memorial/ Eggleston Hall side of the drill field are asked to leave their offices and go home at 12:30 p.m."

At approximately 12:15 p.m., the Policy Group released yet another communication via the Virginia Tech web site which further informed people as follows:

"Virginia Tech has closed today Monday, April 16, 2007. On Tuesday, April 17, classes will be cancelled. The university will remain open for administrative operations. There will be an additional university statement presented today at noon.

"All students, faculty and staff are required to stay where they are until police execute a planned evacuation. A phased closing will be in effect today; further information will be forthcoming as soon as police secure the campus.

"Tomorrow there will be a university convocation/ceremony at noon at Cassell

---

[52] From another university source, we identified 131 major buildings and several more under construction. In any event, it is a large number of structures.

Coliseum. The Inn at Virginia Tech has been designated as the site for parents to gather and obtain information."

A press conference was held shortly after noon on April 16, 2007, and President Charles W. Steger issued a statement citing "A tragedy of monumental proportions." Copies of that statement are available on request.

The Policy Group continued to meet and strategically plan for the events to follow. A campus update on the shootings was issued at another press conference at approximately 5:00 p.m.

It should be noted that the above messages were sent after the full gravity of what happened at Norris Hall had been made known to the Policy Group. They were too late to be of much value for security. The messages still were less than full disclosure of the situation. There may well have been a second shooter, and the university community should have been told to be on the lookout for one, not that the continued search was just "routine police procedure." When almost 50 people are shot, what follows is hardly "routine police procedure." The university appears to have tempered its messages to avoid panic and reduce the shock and fright to the campus family. But a more straightforward description was needed. The messages still did not get across the enormity of the event and the loss of life. By that time, rumors were rife. The events were highly disturbing and there was no way to sugarcoat them. Straight facts were needed.

## OTHER ACTIONS ON THE SECOND AND THIRD FLOORS

While the shootings were taking place in classrooms on the second floor of Norris Hall, people on the other floors and in offices on the second floor tried to flee or take refuge—with one exception. Professor Kevin Granata from the third floor guided his students to safety in a small room, locked the room and went to investigate the gunfire on the second floor. He was shot and killed. People who did take refuge in locked rooms were badly frightened by gunfire and the general commotion, but all of them survived.

In the first minutes after they arrived, the police could not be sure that all of the shooters were dead. The police had to be careful in clearing all rooms to ensure that there was not a second shooter mixed in with the others. In fact, perpetrators can often blend with their victims, Groups of police went through the building clearing each office, lab, classroom, and closet. When they encountered a group of people hiding in a bathroom or locked office, they had to be wary. The result was that many people were badly frightened a second time by the police clearing actions. Some were sent downstairs accompanied by officers and others were left to make their own way out. Although quite a few officers were in the building at this time, they still did not have sufficient members to clear all areas and simultaneously escort out every survivor. It also appears that there was inadequate communication between the police who were clearing the building and those outside guarding the exits.

For example, one group of professors and staff was hiding behind the locked doors of the Engineering Department offices on the third floor. When they were cleared by police to evacuate, they were directed down a staircase toward an exit where they found a chained door with police outside pointing guns at them. One of them remembered that there was an exit through the auditorium to Holden Hall and they left that way.

The group of students from Professor Granata's third-floor class that hid in a small locked office were frightened by officers approaching with guns at the ready, but then were escorted safely out of the building.

The police had their priorities straight. Although many survivors were frightened, the police understandably were focused on clearing the building safely and quickly. Had there been a second shooter not found quickly, the police would have wasted manpower escorting people out instead of searching for and neutralizing the shooter.

## ACTION ON THE FIRST FLOOR

According to VTPD Chief Flinchum: When officers entered Norris Hall, two stayed on the first floor to secure it. One officer said one or two people came out of rooms and were evacuated. Officers on the second floor took survivors down to the first floor on the Drillfield side of Norris, but they had to shoot the lock on the chained door to get out. When they did this, other officers entered Norris and began initial clearing of the first floor while the other teams were clearing the third and second floors. The first floor was cleared again by SWAT after the actions on the second floor were completed.

This all was appropriate, thorough police procedure.

## THE TOLL

In about 10 minutes, one shooter armed with handguns shot 47 students and faculty, of whom 30 died. The shooter's self-inflicted wound made the toll 48.

Of the seven faculty conducting classes, five were fatally shot. Three were standing in the front of their classrooms when the gunman walked in. One was shot barricading the door, and one shot while investigating the sounds after getting his class to safety on the third floor. They were brave and vulnerable.

Based on university records, 148 students were on the rolls of classes held at 9:05 a.m. in Norris Hall on April 16. At least 31 and possibly a few more missed classes or had classes cancelled that day. So at least 100 students were in the building, possibly as many as 120, including a few not enrolled in the classes. (The statistics are inexact because not all Norris Hall students responded to a university survey of their whereabouts that day.) Of the students present, 25 were killed, 17 were shot and survived, 6 were injured jumping from windows, and 4 were injured from other [53] causes.

---

[53] There are small inconsistencies in the tallies of injuries among police, hospitals, and university because some students sought private treatment for minor injuries, and the definition of "injury" used.

Room 211 suffered the most student casualties (17). The other rooms with casualties were 207 (11), 206 (11), 204 (10), 205 (1), and 306 (1).

In addition to the classes, there were many other people in the building at the time of the shootings, including staff of the dean's office, other faculty members with offices in the building, other students, and janitorial staff. None of them was injured.

When the shooting stopped, about 75 students and faculty were uninjured, some still in classroom settings and others in offices or hiding in restrooms. With over 200 rounds left, the toll could have been higher if the police had not arrived when they did, as noted earlier.

Table 2 and Table 3 at the end of this chapter show the numbers of students and faculty who were killed and injured, by room, based on the university's research.

## KEY FINDINGS

Overall, the police from Virginia Tech and Blacksburg did an outstanding job in responding quickly and using appropriate active-shooter procedures to advance to the shooter's location and to clear Norris Hall.

The close relationship of the Virginia Tech Police Department and Blacksburg Police Department and their frequent joint training saved critical minutes. They had trained together for an active shooter incident in university buildings. There is little question their actions saved lives. Other campus police and security departments should make sure they have a mutual aid arrangement as good as that of the Virginia Tech Police Department.

Police cannot wait for SWAT teams to arrive and assemble, but must attack an active shooter at once using the first officers arriving on the scene, which was done. The officers entering the building proceeded to the second floor just as the shooting stopped. The sound of the shotgun blast and their arrival on the second floor probably caused Cho to realize that attack by the police was imminent and to take his own life.

Police did a highly commendable job in starting to assist the wounded, and worked closely with the first EMTs on the scene to save lives.

Several faculty members died heroically while trying to protect their students. Many brave students died or were wounded trying to keep the shooter from entering their classrooms. Some barricading doors kept their bodies low or to the side and out of the direct line of fire, which reduced casualties.

Several quick-acting students jumped from the second floor windows to safety, and at least one by dropping himself from the ledge, which reduced the distance to fall. Other students survived by feigning death as the killer searched for victims.

People were evacuated safely from Norris Hall, but the evacuation was not well organized and was frightening to some survivors. However, being frightened is preferable to being injured by a second shooter. The police had their priorities correct, but they might have handled the evacuation with more care.

## RECOMMENDATIONS

VIII-1 Campus police everywhere should train with local police departments on response to active shooters and other emergencies.

VIII-2 Dispatchers should be cautious when giving advice or instructions by phone to people in a shooting or facing other threats without knowing the situation. This is a broad recommendation that stems from reviewing other U.S. shooting incidents as well, such as the Columbine High School shootings. For instance, telling someone to stay still when they should flee or flee when they should stay still can result in unnecessary deaths. When in doubt, dispatchers should just be reassuring. They should be careful when asking people to talk into the phone when they may be overheard by a gunman. Also, local law enforcement dispatchers should become familiar with the major campus buildings of colleges and universities in their area.

VIII-3 Police should escort survivors out of buildings, where circumstances and manpower permit.

VIII-4 Schools should check the hardware on exterior doors to ensure that they are not subject to being chained shut.

VIII-5 Take bomb threats seriously. Students and staff should report them immediately, even if most do turn out to be false alarms.

Table 2. Norris Hall Student Census for April 16, 2007 9:05 a.m. Classes

| Room No. | Killed or Total Students Later on Class Roll Died | Total Students Accounted For: | | | | | | Students Injured** by Not Gunshot Injured | Used Windows To Escape | |
| --- | --- | --- | --- | --- | --- | --- | --- | --- | --- | --- |
| | | Injured | Not Physically Injured | Did Not Attend Class | Status Not Verified | Total | | | Injured* | |
| 200 | 14* | 0 | 0 | 0 | 14** | 0 | 14 | 0 | | |
| 204 | 23 | 1 | 9 | 6 | 5 | 2 | 23 | 3 | 6 | 4 |
| 205 | 14 | 0 | 1 | 8 | 3 | 2 | 14 | 0 | | |
| 206 | 14 | 9 | 2 | 2 | 1 | 0 | 14 | 2 | | |
| 207 | 15 | 4 | 7 | 1 | 3 | 0 | 15 | 6 | | |
| 211 | 22 | 11 | 6 | 0 | 4 | 1 | 22 | 6 | | |
| 306 | 37 | 0 | 1 | 20 | 1 | 15 | 37 | 0 | | |
| Labs | 9 | 0 | 0 | 9 | 0 | 0 | 9 | 0 | | |
| Totals | 148 | 25 | 26 | 47 | 31 | 20 | 148 | 17 | 6 | 4 |

VIII- Included in "Total Students Accounted For"

** Class was cancelled that day

Table 3. Norris Hall Faculty Census

| Room # | Total Faculty Scheduled | Total Faculty Accounted For | | | | | |
|---|---|---|---|---|---|---|---|
| | | Killed or Later Died | Injured | Not Physically Injured | Did Not Attend Class | Status Not Verified | Total |
| 200 | 1 | 0 | 0 | 0 | 1** | | 1 |
| 204 | 1 | 1 | 0 | 0 | | | 1 |
| 205 | 1 | 0 | 0 | 1 | | | 1 |
| 206 | 1 | 1 | 0 | 0 | | | 1 |
| 207 | 1 | 1 | 0 | 0 | | | 1 |
| 211 | 1 | 1 | 0 | 0 | | | 1 |
| 306 | 1 | 0 | 0 | 1 | | | 1 |
| 225/hallway | 1 | 1 | 0 | 0 | | | 1 |
| Total | 8 | 5 | 0 | 2 | | | 8 |

Class was cancelled that day

These tables were provided by the Virginia Tech administration

## ADDITIONS AND CORRECTIONS

Cho Surveillance of Norris Hall: Addition – In Spring 2007, Cho had a class at Norris Hall. Between February and April 2007 he was seen numerous times in and around Norris Hall at times other than when he had class, possibly casing the building. He picked a Monday for his attack, a day when his class was not in session, which lessened the chance of confronting students and faculty whom he knew and who knew him.

Handling of Bomb Threat Note: p. 89, Correction – Cho left a note saying there was a bomb in Norris Hall not on the inside of one of the chained doors as was stated in the Report, but rather on the inside of an interior door leading to the vestibule where the exit door was chained. Also, that note was found by a faculty member and given to a custodian on the second floor to take to the Dean's Office, not carried there by the faculty member herself. Virginia Tech bomb threat policy required that anyone discovering or receiving a bomb threat should immediately report the threat to the VTPD.

Doors Shot At: p. 94, Correction – Cho had chained all three public entrances to Norris Hall, using a lock and chain on each. Police tried to get into one of the chained entrances and then a second. They shot at the lock on the second door but could not break it. The metal chain was on the inside and there was little play in the door. Police successfully shot open the conventional lock on an exterior door leading to a maintenance shop, from which they gained entrance to the rest of Norris Hall. They did not shoot at all three chained doors as reported in the text.

Student Victim Status: p. 100, Addition – The one student in Room 211 of Norris Hall who was listed in Table 2 as "status not verified" was later identified as Clay Violand, the only student unharmed in that classroom. The total number of people present but unharmed during the shootings in Norris Hall increases by one, to 47.

(This page intentionally left blank.)

# Chapter IX.

## EMERGENCY MEDICAL SERVICES RESPONSE

The tragic scenes that occurred at Virginia Tech are the worst that most emergency medical service (EMS) providers will ever see. Images of so many students and faculty murdered or seriously injured in such a violent manner and the subsequent rescue efforts can only be described by those who were there. This chapter discusses the emergency medical response on April 16 to victims including their pre-hospital treatment, transport, and care in hospitals.

Interviews were conducted with first responders, emergency managers, and hospital personnel (physicians, nurses, and administrators) to determine:

- The on-scene EMS response.
- Implementation of hospital multicasualty plans and incident command systems.
- Pre-hospital and in-hospital initial patient stabilization.
- Compliance with the National Incident Management System (NIMS).
- Communications systems used.
- Coordination of the emergency medical care with police and EMS providers.

Evaluating patient care subsequent to the initial pre-hospital and hospital interventions was beyond the scope of this investigation. Fire department personnel were not interviewed because there were no reports of their involvement in patient care activities.

Although there is always opportunity for improvement, the overall EMS response was excellent and the lives of many were saved. The challenges of systematic response, scene and provider safety, and on-scene and hospital patient care were effectively met. Responders are to be commended. The results in terms of patient care are a testimony to their medical education and training for mass casualty events, dedication, and ability to perform at a high level in the face of the disaster that struck so many people.

The Virginia Tech Rescue Squad and Blacksburg Volunteer Rescue Squad were the primary agencies responsible for incident command, triage, treatment, and transportation. Many other regional agencies responded and functioned under the Incident Command System (ICS). The Blacksburg Volunteer Rescue Squad (BVRS) personnel and equipment response was timely and strong. Virginia Tech Rescue Squad (VTRS), the lead EMS agency in this incident, is located on the Virginia Tech campus and is the oldest collegiate rescue squad of its kind nationwide. It is a volunteer, student-run organization with 38 [54]members. Their actions on April 16 were heroic and demonstrated courage and fortitude.

### WEST AMBLER JOHNSTON INITIAL RESPONSE

The first EMS response was to the West Ambler Johnston (WAJ) residence hall incident. At 7:21 a.m., VTRS was dispatched to 4040 WAJ for the report of a patient who had fallen from a loft. In 3 minutes, at 7:24 a.m., VT Rescue 3 was en route. While en route, dispatch advised that a resident assistant reported a victim lying against a dormitory room door and that bloody footprints and a pool of blood were seen on the floor. VT Rescue 3 arrived on scene at 7:26 a.m., 5 minutes from the time of

---

[54] VTRS. (2007). April 16, 2007: EMS Response. Presentation to the Virginia Tech Review Panel. May 21, 2007, The Inn at Virginia Tech.

dispatch. This response time falls within the nationally [55]accepted range.

At 7:29 a.m., Rescue 3 accessed the dorm room to find two victims with gunshot wounds, both obviously in critical condition. At 7:31 a.m., it requested a second advanced life support (ALS) unit and ordered activation of the all-call tone requesting all available Virginia Tech rescue personnel to respond to the scene. The "all-call" request is a normal procedure for VTRS to respond to an incident with multiple patients. Personnel from BVRS responded to WAJ as well.

At 7:48 a.m., VT Rescue 3 requested that Carilion Life-Guard helicopter be dispatched and was informed that its estimated time of arrival was 40 minutes. It was decided to dispatch the helicopter to Montgomery Regional Hospital (MRH). Carilion Life-Guard then advised that they were grounded due to weather and never began the mission.

One of the victims in 4040 WAJ was a 22-year-old male with a gunshot wound to the head. He was in cardiopulmonary arrest. CPR was initiated, and he was immobilized using an extrication collar and a long spine board. VT Rescue 3 transported him to MRH. During communications with the MRH online physician, CPR was ordered to be discontinued. He arrived at the [56]hospital DOA.

The second victim was an 18-year-old female with a gunshot wound to the head. She was treated with high-flow oxygen via mask, two Ivs were established, and cardiac monitoring was initiated. She was immobilized with an extrication collar and placed on a long spine board. At 7:44 a.m., she was transported by VT Rescue 2 to MRH. During transport, her level of consciousness began to deteriorate and her radial pulse [57]was no longer palpable. Upon

arrival at MRH, endotracheal intubation was performed. At 8:30 a.m., she was transferred by ground ALS unit to Carilion Roanoke Memorial Hospital (CRMH), a [58]Level I trauma center in Roanoke, Virginia.

Following CPR that occurred en route she was [59]pronounced dead at CRMH.

Based on the facts known, the triage, treatment, and transportation of both WAJ victims appeared appropriate. The availability of helicopter transport likely would not have affected patient outcomes. Their injuries were incompatible with survival.

## NORRIS HALL INITIAL RESPONSE

At 9:02 a.m., VT Rescue 3 returned to service following the WAJ incident. VT Rescue 2 continued equipment cleanup at MRH when the call for the Norris Hall shootings came in. At approximately 9:42 a.m., VTRS personnel at their station overheard a call on the police radio advising of an active shooter at Norris Hall. Many EMS providers were about to respond to the worst mass shooting event on a United States college campus.

Upon hearing the police dispatch of a shooting at Norris Hall, the VTRS officer serving as EMS commander immediately activated the VTRS Incident Action Plan and established an incident command post at the VTRS building. VT Rescue 3, staffed with an ALS crew, stood by at their station. At about 9:42 a.m., VTRS requested the Montgomery County emergency services coordinator to place all county EMS units on standby and for him to respond to the VTRS Command Post. "Standby" means that all agency units should be staffed and ready to respond. Each agency officer in charge is supposed to notify the appropriate dispatcher when the units are staffed.

The Montgomery County Communications Center immediately paged out an "all call" alert

---

[55] NFPA (2004). NFPA 1710: Standard for the Organization and Deployment of Fire Suppression Operations, Emergency Medical Operations, and Special Operations to the Public by Career Fire Departments. National Fire Protection Association: Battery March Park, MA.

[56] EMS Patient Care Report Q0669603.

[57] EMS Patient Care Report Q0669604.

[58] Turner, K. N., and Davis, J. (2007). Public Safety Timeline for April 16, 2007. Unpublished Report. Montgomery County Department of Emergency Services, p. 4.

[59] EMS Patient Care Report Q0019057.

(9:42 a.m.) advising all units to respond to the scene at Norris Hall.

The EMS responses to West Ambler Johnston and Norris halls occurred in a timely manner. However, for the shootings at Norris Hall, all EMS units were dispatched to respond to the scene at once contrary to the request. Subsequently, the Montgomery County emergency services coordinator requested dispatch to correct the message in time to allow for most of the incoming squads to proceed to the secondary staging area at the BVRS station.

At 9:46 a.m., VTRS was dispatched by police to Norris Hall for multiple shootings—4 minutes after VTRS monitored the incident (9:42 a.m.) on the police radio. The VTRS EMS commander advised VT dispatch that the VTRS units would stand by at the primary staging site until police secured the shooting area. At 9:48 a.m., the EMS commander also requested the VT police dispatcher to notify all responding EMS units from outside Virginia Tech to proceed to the secondary staging area at BVRS instead of responding directly to Norris Hall.

The VTPD and the Montgomery County Communications Center issued separate dispatches for EMS units, which led to some confusion in the EMS response.

## EMS INCIDENT COMMAND SYSTEM

At the national level, Homeland Security Presidential Directives (HSPDs) 5 and 8 require all federal, state, regional, local, and tribal governments, including EMS agencies, to [60]adopt the NIMS, including a uniform ICS. The Incident Management System is defined by Western Virginia EMS Council in their Mass Casualty Incident (MCI) Plan as:

> A written plan, adopted and utilized by all participating emergency response agencies, that helps control, direct and coordinate emergency personnel, equipment and other resources from the scene of an MCI or evacuation, to

the transportation of patients to definitive care, to the conclusion of the [61]incident.

Overall, the structure of the EMS ICS was 277ervictive. The ICS as implemented during the incident is compared in Figure 13 and Figure 14 to NIMS ICS guidelines. Figure 13 shows the Virginia Tech EMS ICS structure as [62]implemented in the incident. Although it did not strictly follow NIMS guidelines, it included most of the necessary organization. Figure 14 shows the Model ICS structure based on the NIMS guidelines.

EMS Command – An EMS command post was established at VTRS. The BVRS officer-in-charge who arrived at Norris Hall reportedly was unable to determine if an EMS ICS was in place. Since each agency has its own radio frequency, the potential for miscommunication of critical information regarding incident command is possible. To enhance communications, EMS command reportedly switched from the VTRS to the BVRS radio frequency. In addition, to shift routine communications from the main VT frequency, EMS command requested units to switch to alternate frequency, VTAC 1. Some units were confused by the term VTAC 1. Eventually, all units switched to the Montgomery County Mutual Aid frequency.

The fact that BVRS was initially unaware that VTRS had already established an EMS command post could have caused a duplication of efforts and further organizational challenges. Participants interviewed stated that once a BVRS 277ervicer reported to the EMS command post, communications between EMS providers on the scene improved. The Montgomery County emergency management coordinator was on the scene and served as a liaison between the police tactical command

---

[60] Bush, G. W. (2003). December 17, 2003 Homeland Security Presidential Directive/HSPD–8.

[61] WVEMS. (2006). Mass Casualty Incident Plan: EMS Mutual Aid Response Guide: Western Virginia EMS Council, Section 2.1.7, p. 2.

[62] VTRS. (2007). April 16, 2007: EMS Response. Presentation to the Virginia Tech Review Panel. May 21, 2007, The Inn at Virginia Tech.

post and the EMS incident command post, which also helped with communications.

Because BVRS and VTRS are on separate primary radio frequencies, BVRS reportedly did not know where to stage their units. In addition, BVRS units reportedly did not know when the police cleared the building for entry.

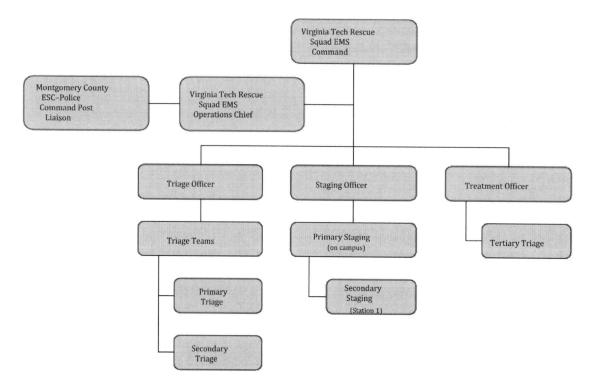

*Figure 13. Virginia Tech EMS ICS as Implemented in the Incident*

Another issue concerned the staging of units and personnel. EMS command correctly advised dispatch that assignments and staging would be [63]handled by EMS command.

Triage – The VTPD arrived at Norris Hall at 9:45 a.m. At 9:50 a.m., the VTPD and Blacksburg police emergency response teams (ERTs) arrived at Norris Hall, each with a tactical medic. At 9:50 a.m., two ERT medics entered Norris Hall where they were held for about 2 minutes inside the stairwell before being allowed to proceed. At 9:52 a.m., the two medics, one from VTRS and one from BVRS, began triage. Medics initially triaged those victims brought to the stairwells while police were moving them out of the building. As victims exited the building, some walked and some were carried out and transported by police SUV's and other mobile units to the safer EMS treatment areas.

The triage by ERT medics inside the Norris Hall classrooms had two specific goals: first, to identify the total number of victims who were alive or dead; and second, to move ambulatory victims to a safe area where further triage and treatment could begin. The tactical medics employed the START triage system (Simple Triage and Rapid Treatment) to quickly assess a victim and determine the overall incident status. The START triage is a "method whereby patients in an MCI are assessed and evaluated on the basis of the severity of injuries and assigned to [64]treatment priorities." Patients are classified in one of four categories (Figure 15). Colored tags are affixed to patients corresponding to these categories.

---

[63] Turner, K.N., & Davis, J. (2007). Public Safety Timeline for April 16, 2007. Unpublished Report. Montgomery County Department of Emergency Services, p. 6.

[64] WVEMS. (2006). Mass Casualty Incident Plan: EMS Mutual Aid Response Guide: Western Virginia EMS Council, Section 2.1.8, p. 2.

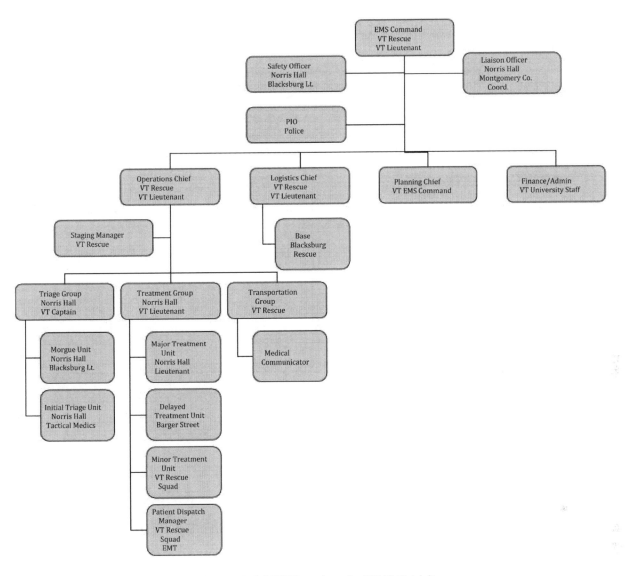

*Figure 14. Model ICS Based on the NIMS Guidelines*

In an incident of this nature, the triage team must concentrate on the overall situation instead of focusing on individual patient care. Patient care is limited to quick interventions that will make the difference between life and death. The medics systematically approached the initial triage, with one assessing victims in the odd-numbered rooms on the second floor of Norris Hall while the other assessed victims in the even-numbered rooms. The medics were able to quickly identify those victims who were without vital signs and would likely not benefit from medical care. This initial triage by the two tactical medics accompanying the police was appropriate in identifying patient viability. The medics reported "a tough time with radio communications traffic" while triaging in Norris Hall.

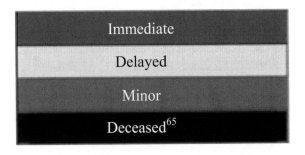

*Figure 15. START Triage Patient Classifications*

---

[65] Critical Illness and Trauma Foundation, Inc. (2001). START—Simple Triage and Rapid Treatment. http://www.citmit.org/start/default.htm

The triage medics identified several patients who required immediate interventions to save their lives. Some victims with chest wounds were treated with an Asherman Chest Seal (Figure 16). It functions with a flutter valve to prevent air from entering the chest cavity during inhalation and permits air to leave the chest cavity during exhalation. This is a noninvasive technique that can be applied quickly with low risk. It was reported that a female victim with chest wounds benefited by the immediate application of the seal. Since the scene was not yet secured at this point to allow other EMS providers to enter, the tactical medics quickly instructed some police officers how to use the seal.

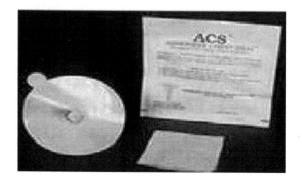

*Figure 16. Asherman Chest Seal[66]*

A decision was quickly made to treat a 22-year-old male victim who exhibited a profuse femoral artery bleed by applying a commercial-brand tourniquet (Figure 17) to control the bleeding. The patient was transported to MRH, where surgical repair was performed and he survived. The application of a tourniquet was likely a lifesaving event.

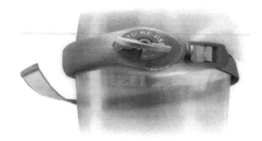

*Figure 17 Tourniquet[67]*

At approximately 10:09 a.m., VTPD dispatch notified EMS command that the "shooter was down" and that EMS crews could enter Norris Hall. EMS command assigned a lieutenant from VTRS to become the triage unit leader. Triage continued inside and in front of Norris Hall. Some critical patients at the Drillfield side and others at the secondary triage (critical treatment unit) Old Turner Street side of Norris Hall were placed in ambulances and transported directly to hospitals. Noncritical patients were moved to a treatment area at Stanger and Barger Streets.

A BVRS officer and crew arrived at Norris Hall and began to retriage victims. Their reassessment confirmed that 31 persons were dead. Based on the evidence available, the decision not to attempt resuscitation on those originally triaged as dead was appropriate. No one appeared to have been mistriaged. A medical director (emergency physician) for a Virginia State Police Division SWAT team responded with his team to the scene. He was primarily staged at Burress Hall and was available to care for wounded officers if needed. There were no reports of injuries to police officers.

Interviews of prehospital and hospital personnel revealed that triage ribbons or tags were not consistently used on victims. The standard triage tags were used on some patients but not on all. These triage tags, shown in Figure 18, are part of the Western Virginia EMS Trauma Triage Protocol and can assist with record keeping and [68]patient follow-up. Not using the tags may have led to some confusion regarding patient identification and classification upon arrival at hospitals.

Treatment – Patients were moved to the treatment units based on START guidelines. The treatment group was divided into three units: a critical treatment unit, a delayed treatment unit and a minor treatment unit. The critical treatment unit was located at the Old

---

[66] ACS (2007). Asherman Chest Seal. http://www.compassadvisors.biz

[67] Medgadget (2007). http://www.medgadget.com
[68] WVEMS. (2006). Mass Casualty Incident Plan: EMS Mutual Aid Response Guide: Western Virginia EMS Council., Section 22.3, p. 13.

Turner Street Side of Norris Hall where patients with immediate medical care needs (red tag) received care. Patients who were classified as less critical (yellow tag) were moved to the delayed treatment unit at Stanger and Barger Streets. Patients with minor injuries, including walking wounded/worried well (green tag) were moved to a minor treatment unit at VTRS (Figure 19). "Worried well" are those who may not present with injuries but with psychological or safety issues.

Patients were moved to the treatment units in various ways. Some critical patients were carried out of Norris Hall by police and EMS personnel. Others were moved via vehicles, while those less critical walked to the delayed treatment or minor treatment units. EMS command assigned leaders to each of the units.

The weather was a significant factor with wind gusts of up to 60 mph grounding all aeromedical services and hampering the use of EMS equipment. This included tents, shelters, and treatment area identification flags that could not be set up or maintained. Large vehicles such as trailers and mobile homes, often used for temporary shelter, had difficulty responding as high winds made interstate driving increasingly hazardous. The incident site was close to ongoing construction. High winds blew debris, increasing danger to patients and providers and impeding patient care. To protect the walking wounded/worried well from the environment, patients were moved to the minor treatment unit at the VTRS building.

Twelve EMS patient care reports (PCRs) were available for review. In some cases PCRs were not completed, and in other cases not provided upon request. In multiple casualty incident situations, EMS providers can use standard triage tags in place of the traditional PCR; however, no triage tag records were provided, as noted earlier.

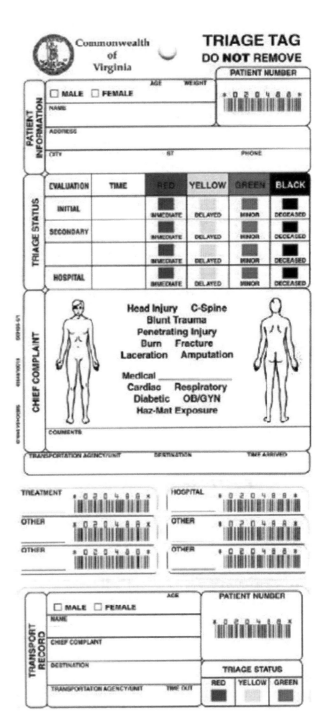

*Figure 18. Virginia Triage Tag*

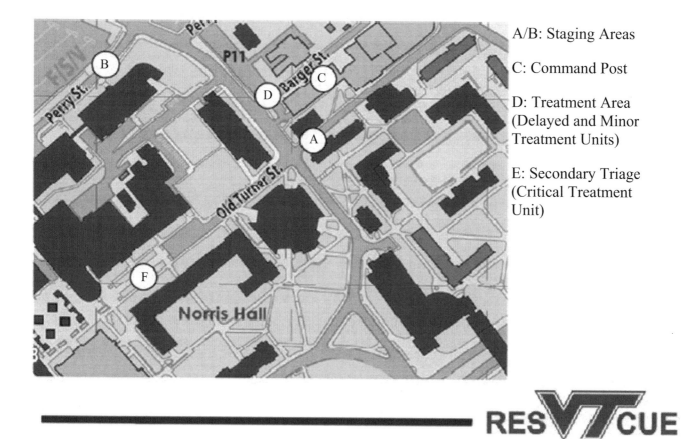

A/B: Staging Areas

C: Command Post

D: Treatment Area (Delayed and Minor Treatment Units)

E: Secondary Triage (Critical Treatment Unit)

RES**VT**CUE

*Figure 19. Initial Location of Treatment Units*

Twelve EMS patient care reports (PCRs) were available for review. In some cases PCRs were not completed, and in other cases not provided upon request. In multiple casualty incident situations, EMS providers can use standard triage tags in place of the traditional PCR; however, no triage tag records were provided, as noted earlier.

Based on the PCRs available and the interviews of EMS and hospital personnel, it appears that the patient care rendered to Norris Hall victims was appropriate.

Transportation – EMS command appointed a transportation group leader who assigned patients to ambulances and specific hospital destinations. Christiansburg Rescue Squad (CRS) responded with BLS and ALS units and was among the first in line at Norris Hall. CRS, BVRS, CPTS, and Longshop–McCoy Rescue Squad transported critical patients to area hospitals. CPTS ambulances from Giles, Radford, and Blacksburg as well as some of

their Roanoke-based units, including Life-Guard flight and ground critical care crews, responded in mass to the incident either at Norris Hall or by interfacility transport of critical victims. By 10:51 a.m., all patients from Norris Hall were either transported to a hospital, or moved to the delayed or minor treatment units. In addition to VTRS, 14 agencies responded to the incident with 27 ALS ambulances and more than 120 EMS personnel (Table 4). Some agencies delayed routine interfacility patient transports or "back filled" covering neighboring communities through preset mutual aid agreements. Agency supervisors and administrators were working effectively behind the scenes procuring

Table 4. EMS Response[69]

14 Assisting Agencies

> Montgomery County Emergency Services Coordinator
> Blacksburg Volunteer Rescue Squad
> Christiansburg Rescue Squad
> Shawsville Rescue Squad
> Longshop-McCoy Rescue Squad
> Carilion Patient Transportation Services
> Salem Rescue Squad
> Giles Rescue Squad
> Newport Rescue Squad
> Lifeline Ambulance Service
> Roanoke City Fire and Rescue
> Vinton First Aid Crew
> Radford University EMS
> City of Radford EMS

The necessary resources and supporting the response of their EMS crews. These agencies demonstrated an exceptional working relationship, likely an outcome of interagency training and drills.

False Alarm Responses – At 10:58 a.m., EMS command was notified of a reported third shooting incident at the tennis court area on Washington Street that proved to be a false alarm. At 11:18 a.m., EMS command was notified of a bomb threat at Norris and Holden Halls that also proved to be false. Due to safety concerns, EMS command ordered the staging area moved from Barger St. to Perry St. Post-Incident Transport of the Deceased – At 4:03 p.m., the medical examiner authorized removal of the deceased from Norris Hall to the medical examiner's office in Roanoke. Due to another rescue incident in the Blacksburg area, units were not available until 5:15 p.m. to begin transport of the deceased. Several options were considered including use of a refrigeration truck, funeral coaches, or EMS units. EMS command, in consultation with the medical examiner's representative, determined that EMS units from several companies would transport the deceased to Roanoke. In general, frontline EMS units are not used to transport the deceased. In this instance, however, the use of EMS units was acceptable because emergency coverage was not neglected and the rescuers felt that the sight of a refrigeration truck and funeral coaches on campus would be undesirable.

The decedents were placed two to a unit for transport. A serious concern raised by EMS providers was an order given by an unidentified police official that the decedents be transported to Roanoke under emergency conditions (lights and sirens). Due to safety considerations, EMS command modified this order.

The police order to transport the deceased under emergency conditions from Norris Hall to the medical examiners office in Roanoke was inappropriate for several reasons:

- It is not within law enforcement's scope of practice to order emergency transport (red lights and siren) of the deceased.
- There was no benefit to anyone by transporting under emergency conditions.
- A 30-minute or longer drive to Roanoke, during bad weather, with winds gusting above 60 mph, exposes EMS personnel to unnecessary risks.
- Transporting under emergency conditions increases the possibility of vehicle crashes with risk to civilians.

Critical Incident Stress Management – Although no physical injuries were reported, psychological and stress-related issues can subsequently manifest in EMS providers. Local and regional EMS providers participated in critical incident stress management activities such as defusings and debriefings immediately postincident.

## HOSPITAL RESPONSE

Patients from Virginia Tech were treated at five area hospitals:

- Montgomery Regional Hospital
- Carilion New River Valley Hospital
- Lewis–Gale Medical Center

[69] VTRS. (2007). April 16, 2007: EMS Response. Presentation to the Virginia Tech Review Panel. May 21, 2007, The Inn at Virginia Tech.

- Carilion Roanoke Memorial Hospital
- Carilion Roanoke Community Hospital

Twenty-seven patients are known to have been treated by local emergency departments. Some others who were in Norris Hall may have been treated at other hospitals, medical clinics, or doctor's offices including their own primary care providers; but there are no known accounts.

Overall, the local and regional hospitals quickly implemented their hospital ICS and mobilized resources. Aggressive measures were taken to postpone noncritical procedures, shift essential personnel to critical areas, reinforce physician staffing, and prepare for patient surge. Three hospitals initiated their hospital-wide emergency plans. One hospital, a designated Level I trauma center, did not feel that a full-scale, hospital-wide implementation of their emergency plan was necessary.

The most significant challenge early on was the lack of credible information about the number of patients each expected to receive. The emergency departments did not have a single official information source about patient flow. Likely explanations for this were (1) an emergency operations center (EOC) was not opened at the university, and (2) the Regional Hospital Coordinating Center did not receive complete information that it should have under the MCI [70] plan.

Preparedness, patient care/patient flow, and patient outcomes were reviewed for each of the receiving hospitals.

Montgomery Regional Hospital – The MRH emergency department, a Level III trauma center, received 17 patients from the Virginia Tech incident; two from West Ambler Johnston and 15 from Norris Hall. The patients from WAJ arrived at 7:51 and 7:55 a.m. The first patient from WAJ was the 22-year-old male with a gunshot wound to the head who was DOA. No further attempts at resuscitation were made in the emergency department.

The second patient from WAJ was the 18-year-old female who arrived in critical condition with a gunshot wound to the head. Upon arrival to the emergency department, she was unable to speak and her level of consciousness was deteriorating. Airway control via endotracheal intubation was achieved using rapid sequence induction. At 8:30 a.m., she was transported by ALS ambulance to Carilion Roanoke Memorial Hospital, the Level I trauma center for the region. She died shortly after arrival at CRMH.

HOSPITAL PREPAREDNESS: At 9:45 a.m., MRH was notified of shots fired somewhere on the Virginia Tech campus. Because they were unsure of the number of shooters or whether the incident was confined to campus, MRH initiated a lockdown procedure. Since the killing of a hospital guard at MRH in August 2006 (the Morva incident mentioned in Chapter VII), there has been heightened awareness at MRH regarding security procedures. At 10:00 a.m., information became available confirming multiple gunshot victims. A "code green" (disaster code) was initiated and the following actions were taken:

- The hospital incident command center was opened and preassigned personnel reported to command.

- The hospital facility was placed on a controlled access plan (strict lockdown). Only personnel with appropriate identification (other than patients) could enter the hospital and then only through one entrance.

- All elective surgical procedures were postponed.

- Day surgery patients with early surgery times were sent home as soon as possible.

- The emergency department was placed on divert for all EMS units except those arriving from the Norris Hall incident. The emergency department was staffed at full capacity. A rapid emergency department discharge plan was instituted. Stable patients were transferred from the emergency department to the outpatient surgery suite.

---

[70] Personal communications, Morris Reece, Near Southwest Preparedness Alliance, June 15, 2007.

At 10:05 a.m., the first patient from Norris Hall arrived via self-transport. This patient was injured escaping from Norris Hall. MRH was unable to determine the extent of the Norris Hall incident based on the history and minor injuries of this patient. The Regional Hospital Coordinating Center (RHCC) was notified of the incident and asked to open. Although the RHCC had early notification of the incident, they too were not able to ascertain the extent of the crisis initially.

At 10:14 and 10:15 a.m., two EMS-transported patients from Norris Hall arrived. It was evident that MRH might continue to receive expected and unexpected patients. In preparation for the surge, MRH took the following additional actions:

- The Red Cross was alerted and the blood supply reevaluated.

- Additional pharmaceutical supplies and a pharmacist were sent to the emergency department.

- A runner was assigned to assist with bringing additional materials to and from the emergency department and the pharmacy.

- Disaster supply carts were moved to the hallways between the emergency [71]department and outpatient surgery.

At 10:30 a.m. as the above actions were being taken, four more gunshot victims arrived via EMS transport from Norris Hall. Between 10:45 and 10:55 a.m., five additional patients arrived via EMS. Command designated a public information officer and, by 11:00 a.m., a base had been established where staff and counselors could assist family and friends of patients.

By 11:15 a.m., MRH was still unclear about how many additional patients to expect. (They had a total of 12 by this time.) The operations chief instructed an emergency administrator to respond to the Virginia Tech incident as an onscene liaison to determine how many more

patients would be transported to MRH. At 11:20 a.m., the emergency department administrator reported to the Virginia Tech command center. MRH said that the face-to-face communications were helpful in determining how many additional patients to expect.

At 11:40 a.m., MRH received its last gunshot victim from the incident. By 11:51 a.m., its onscene liaison confirmed that all patients had been transported. At 12:12 p.m., the EMS divert was lifted. At 13:04 and 13:10 p.m., however, two additional patients from the incident arrived by private vehicle. At 13:35 p.m., the code green was lifted.

Patient Care/Patient Flow/Patient Outcomes: In all, 15 patients arrived at MRH from the Norris Hall incident (Table 5) and were managed well.

An emergency department (ED) nurse/EMT-C was assigned to online medical direction and assisted with directing patients to other hospitals. EMS was instructed to transport four patients to Carilion New River Valley Hospital and five patients to Lewis–Gale Medical Center. One patient from the Norris Hall incident was transferred from MRH to CRMH in Roanoke.

The hospital representatives reported that there were problems with patient identification and tracking. As noted earlier:

Table 5. Norris Hall Victims Treated by Montgomery Regional Hospital

| Injuries | Disposition |
| --- | --- |
| GSW left hand – fractured 4th finger | OR and admission |
| GSW to right chest – hemothorax | Chest tube in OR and admission |
| GSW to right flank | OR and admission to ICU |
| GSW left elbow, right thigh | Admitted |
| GSW x 2 to left leg | OR and admission |
| GSW right bicep | Treated and discharged |

---

[71] Montgomery Regional Hospital. (2007). Montgomery Regional Hospital VT Incident Debriefing. April 23, 2007, p. 1.

| | |
|---|---|
| GSW right arm, grazed chest wall; abrasion to left hand | Admitted |
| GSW right lower extremity; laceration to femoral artery | OR and ICU |
| GSW right side abdomen and buttock | OR and ICU |
| GSW right bicep | Treated and discharged |
| GSW to face/head | Intubated and transferred to CRMH |
| Asthma attack precipitated by running from building | Treated and discharged |
| Tib/fib fracture due to jumping from a 2nd-story window | OR and admission |
| First-degree burns to chest wall | Treated and discharged |
| Back pain due to jumping from a 2nd-story window | Treated and discharged |

- An EOC was not activated at Virginia Tech. Establishing an EOC can enhance communications and information flow to hospitals.

- Triage tags were not used for all patients. This would have provided a discrete number for identifying and tracking each patient.

MRH activated its ICS as shown in Figure 20.

ACCOMMODATIONS FOR PATIENTS' FAMILIES AND FRIENDS: MRH accommodated families and friends of patients they treated in their emergency department. MRH was challenged by the need to provide assistance to those who were unsure of the status or location of persons they were trying to find (possibly victims). An open space on the first floor was used for family and friends to gather. Since Virginia Tech had not yet opened an EOC or family assistance center, some victims' family and friends chose to proceed to the closest hospital. Several family members and friends of victims came to MRH even though their loved ones were never transported there.

A psychological crisis counseling team was assembled at MRH to provide services to victims, their families and loved ones, and hospital [72]staff. Virginia State Police troopers were assigned to the hospital and were helpful in maintaining security.

At 11:30 a.m., a surgeon arrived from Lewis–Gale Hospital and was emergently credentialed by the medical staff office. This is notable as Lewis–Gale and MRH are not affiliated.

Police departments often rely on hospitals to help preserve evidence and maintain a chain of custody. MRH was able to gather evidence in the emergency department and operating rooms, including bullets, clothing, and patient identification. At 1:45 p.m., the Virginia State Police notified the hospital that all bullets and fragments were to be considered evidence. Internal communications issues included:

- The Nextel system was overwhelmed. Clinical directors were too busy to retrieve and respond to messages.

- Monitoring EMS radio communications was difficult due to noise and chatter.

- There was deficient communications between the university and MRH.

- An EOC could have been helpful with communications

---

[72] Heil, J. et al. (2007). Psychological Intervention with the Virginia Tech Mass Casualty: Lessons Learned in the Hospital Setting. Report to the Virginia Tech Review Panel.

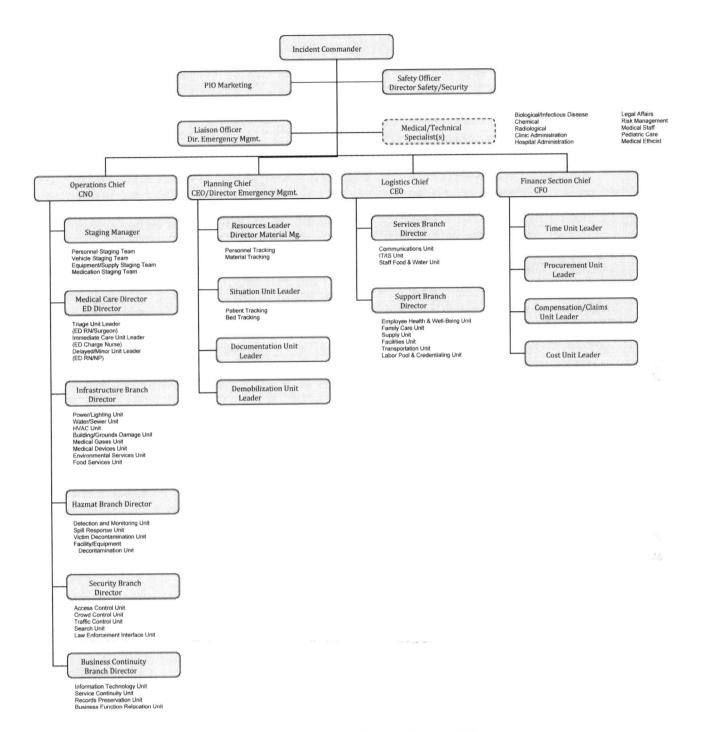

*Figure 20. Montgomery Regional Hospital ICS*

Carilion New River Valley Hospital – CNRVH is a Level III trauma center that received four patients with moderate to severe injuries.

Hospital Preparedness: CNRVH initially heard unofficial reports of the WAJ shootings. They heard nothing further for over 2 hours until they received a call from MRH and also from an RN/medic who was on scene. They were called again later by MRH and advised that they would be receiving patients with "extremity injuries." They were also notified that MRH was on EMS divert.

While waiting for patients to arrive, the emergency department (ED) physician medical director assumed responsibility for the "regular" ED patients while the on-duty physicians were preparing to treat patients from Norris Hall. The on-duty hospitalist (a physician who is hired by the hospital to manage in-patient care needs) reported to the ED to make rapid decisions on whether current patients would be admitted or discharged.

The hospital declared a "code green" and their EOC was opened at 11:50 a.m. The incident commander was a social worker who had special training in hospital ICS. Security surveyed all patients with a metal detection wand because they were unsure who may be victims or perpetrators. A SWAT team from Pulaski County responded to assist with security.

PATIENT CARE/PATIENT FLOW/PATIENT OUTCOMES:
Four patients were transported by EMS to CNRVH, each having significant injuries. The hospital managed the patients well and could have handled more. Table 6 lists the patient injuries and dispositions.

Accommodations for Patients' Families and Friends: The hospital received many phone calls concerning the whereabouts of Virginia Tech shooting victims. Communications issues, particularly the lack of accurate information, were a big concern for the hospital; while providing accommodations for patients' families and friends and assisting others who were looking for their loved ones.

Table 6. Norris Hall Victims Treated by Carilion New River Valley Hospital

| Injuries | Disposition |
| --- | --- |
| GSW to face, preauricular area, bleeding from external auditory canal, GCS of 7, poor airway, anesthesiologist recommended surgical airway | Surgical cricothyrotomy Transferred to CRMH by critical care ALS ambulance |
| GSW to flank and right arm, hypotensive | Immediately taken to OR; small bowel injury/resection |
| GSW to posterior thorax (exit right medial upper arm), additional GSWs to right buttock, and left lateral thigh | To OR for surgical repair of left femur fracture |
| GSW to right lateral thigh, exit thru right medial thigh, lodged in left medial thigh | Admitted in stable condition and observed; no vascular injuries |

Lewis–Gale Medical Center – LGMC, a community hospital, received five patients from the Norris Hall shootings. The ICS structure used and their emergency response to the incident were appropriate. Multiple casualty incidents and use of the ICS were not new to LGMC. Their ICS had been recently tested after an outbreak of food poisoning at a local college.

Hospital Preparedness: LGMC first became aware of the Norris Hall incident when a call was received requesting a medical examiner. They were unable to fulfill the request. At 11:10 a.m., they received a call from Montgomery Regional Hospital advising them of the incident. LGMC immediately declared a "code aster," which is their disaster plan.

The code aster was announced throughout the hospital, the EOC was opened, and the ICS was initiated. At 11:16 a.m., they were notified that MRH was on EMS diversion. At 11:32 a.m., they were notified that they were receiving their first patient suffering from a gunshot wound. In addition to preparing for the patients to arrive at their own hospital, LGMC sent a surgeon to MRH to assist with the surge of surgical patients there.

PATIENT CARE/PATIENT FLOW/PATIENT OUTCOMES: EMS transported five patients from the Norris Hall shootings to LGMC. Table 7 lists the patient injuries and dispositions. These patients were well managed.

Table 7. Norris Hall Victims Treated by Lewis–Gale Medical Center

| Injuries | Disposition |
|---|---|
| GSW grazed shoulder and lodged in occipital area, did not enter the brain | Patient taken to surgery by ENT for debridement |
| GSW in back of right arm, bullet not removed | Patient admitted for observation |
| GSW to face, bullet fragment in hair, likely secondary to shrapnel spray | Treated in ED and released |
| Jumped from Norris Hall, 2nd floor, shattered tib/fib | Admitted, taken to surgery the next day |
| Jumped from Norris Hall, 2nd floor, soft tissue injuries, neck and back sprain, reportedly was holding hands with another jumper | Treated in ED and released |

Accommodation for Patients' Family and Friends: No specific information was obtained from LGMC about accommodations for patients' families and friends. However, the hospital's needs for accurate information while accommodating patient families' and friends and assisting others in attempting to locate loved ones are similar for all emergency departments in times of mass casualty incidents.

Carilion Roanoke Memorial Hospital – This Level I trauma facility located in Roanoke received three critical patients transferred from local hospitals. Two patients were transported from MRH (one from the WAJ incident and one from the Norris Hall incident). The third patient was transferred from CNRVH (from the Norris Hall incident).

HOSPITAL PREPAREDNESS: CRMH did not initiate its hospital-wide disaster plan since standard procedures allowed for effective incident management with the relatively small number of patients received. They did initiate a "gold trauma alert" that brings to the ED three nurses, one trauma attending physician, one trauma fellow physician, one radiologist, one anesthesiologist, and a lab technician.

In addition to the patient transfers, CRMH received a trauma patient from another incident. The ED had three other emergency physicians physically present with others on standby. A neurosurgeon was also in the ED awaiting the arrival of transfer patients.

CRMH's concerns echoed those of the other hospitals who received patients from the Virginia Tech incident, including lack of clarity as to expected patient surge and the need for better regional coordination. It was suggested that the RHCC Mobile Communications Unit could have been dispatched to the scene.

Patient Care/Patient Flow/Patient Outcomes: CRMH appropriately triaged and managed well the patients they received. Adequate staffing and operating rooms were immediately available. Table 8 lists WAJ and Norris Hall victims treated at CRMH.

Table 8. WAJ and Norris Hall Victims Treated by Carilion Roanoke Memorial Hospital

| Injuries | Disposition |
|---|---|
| Transfer from MRH, severe head injury | Pronounced dead in ED |
| Transfer from MRH, head and significant facial/jaw injuries, subsequent orotracheal intubation | Patient taken to OR for surgery, subsequently transferred to a facility closer to home |
| Transfer from CNRVH, GSW to face, subsequent cricothyrotomy | Patient taken to OR for surgery |

Carilion Roanoke Community Hospital

VIII-CRCH is a community hospital located near and associated with CRMH. CRCH treated a self-transported student who was injured by jumping from Norris Hall. Table 9 lists the injuries and disposition of this patient.

Table 9. Norris Hall Victim Treated by Carilion Roanoke Community Hospital

| Injuries | Disposition |
|---|---|
| Ankle contusion and sprain secondary to jumping | Treated and released |

## EMERGENCY MANAGEMENT

Multicasualty incidents often require coordination among state, regional, and local authorities. This section reviews the interrelationships of these authorities.

Virginia Department of Health – In 2002, the Virginia Department of Health (VDH) was awarded funding from the Health Resources and Services Administration (HRSA) National Bioterrorism Hospital Preparedness Program (NBHPP) for enhancement of the health and medical response to bioterrorism and other emergency events. As part of this process, VDH developed a contract with the Virginia Hospital and Healthcare Association (VHHA) to manage the distribution of funds from the HRSA grant to state acute care hospitals and other medical facilities and to monitor compliance. A small percentage of the HRSA funds were used within VDH to fund a hospital coordinator position, as well as to partially fund a deputy commissioner and other administrative positions. Substantially more than 85 percent of this HRSA grant funding was distributed to hospitals or used for program enhancement, including development of a web-based hospital status monitoring system, multidisciplinary training activities, behavioral health services, and poison control centers.

At the same time, VDH received separate funding from the Centers for Disease Control and Prevention (CDC) for the enhancement of public health response to bioterrorism and other emergency events. The position of VDH Deputy Commissioner for Emergency Preparedness and Response was created, with responsibility for both CDC and HRSA emergency preparedness funds. The physician in this position reports directly to the state health commisioner, who serves as the state health officer for Virginia.[73] The Virginia Department of Health regional planning approach aligns hospitals with health department planning regions. In collaboration with the 88 acute care hospitals in the Commonwealth, six hospital and healthcare planning regions were established, closely corresponding with five health department planning regions. Each of the six hospital planning regions has a designated Regional Hospital Coordinating Center (RHCC) located at or near the Level I trauma facility in the region as well as a regional hospital coordinator funded through the HRSA cooperative agreement.

Near Southwest Preparedness Alliance

VIII- The Near Southwest Preparedness Alliance (NSPA), which covers the Virginia Tech area, was developed under the auspices of the Western Virginia EMS Council pursuant to a memo-290ervic of understanding between the Virginia Department of Health, the Virginia Hospital and Healthcare Association, and the NSPA. NSPA is organized to facilitate the development of a regional healthcare emergency response system and to support the development of a statewide healthcare emergency response system. Regional hospital preparedness and coordination will foster collaborative planning efforts between the several medical care facilities and local emergency response agencies in the established geographically and demographically diverse region.[74]

The "Near Southwest" region is defined as:

- 4th Planning District (New River area), which includes Floyd, Giles, Montgomery, and Pulaski counties and the City of Radford.

---

[73] Kaplowitz, L, Gilbert, C. M., Hershey, J. H., and Reece, M. D. (2007). Health and Medical Response to Shooting Episode at Virginia Tech, April, 2007: A Successful Approach. Unpublished Manuscript. Virginia Department of Health, p. 2.
[74] Ibid.

- 5th Planning District (Roanoke and Alleghany area), which includes Alleghany, Botetourt, Craig, and Roanoke counties as well as the cities of Covington, Roanoke, and Salem.

- 11th Planning District, which includes Amherst, Appomattox, Bedford, and Campbell counties; the cities of Lynchburg and Bedford; and the towns of Altavista, Amherst, Appomattox, and Brookneal.

- 12th Planning District (Piedmont area), which includes Franklin, Henry, Patrick and Pittsylvania counties and the cities of Danville and Martinsville

The region covers 7,798 square miles and houses a population of 910,900. It has 24 local governments and 16 hospitals.

Regional Hospital Coordinating Center

VIII-  At the regional level, hospital emergency response coordination during exercises and actual events is provided by RHCCs that have been established to facilitate emergency response, communication, and resource allocation within and among each of the six hospital regions. These centers serve as the contact among healthcare facilities within the region and with RHCCs in other state regions. RHCCs are also linked to the statewide response system through the hospital representative seat at the VDH Emergency Coordinating Center (ECC) in Richmond, Virginia. The hospital seat at the ECC serves as the contact between the healthcare provider system and the statewide emergency response system. It provides a communication link to the Virginia Emergency [75]Operations Center (VEOC).

The primary responsibilities of the RHCC include:

- Provide a single point of contact between hospitals in the region and the VDH ECC.

- Collect and disseminate initial event notification to hospitals and public safety partners.

- Collect and disseminate ongoing situational awareness updates and warnings, including the management of the current bed availability in hospitals.

- Establish and manage WebEOC and [76]communications systems for the duration of the incident.

- Serve as the single point of contact and collaboration point for Virginia fire/EMS agencies for the purposes of hospital diversion management, movement of patients from an incident scene to receiving hospitals, and input/guidance with respect to hospital capabilities, available services, and medical transport decisions.

- Coordinate interhospital patient movement, transfers, and tracking

- Provide primary resource management to hospitals for:

  Personnel
  Equipment
  Supplies
  Pharmaceuticals.

- Coordinate regional expenditures for reimbursement.

- Coordinate regional medical treatment and infection control protocols during the incident as needed.

- Coordinate Virginia hospital requests for the Strategic National Stockpile through the local jurisdiction EOC.

The RHCC complements but does not replace the relationships and coordinating channels established between individual healthcare facilities and their local emergency operations centers and health department officials. The regional structure is intended to enhance the communication and coordination of specific issues related to the healthcare component of the emergency response system at both regional and state levels.

---

[75] Ibid.

[76] WebEOC is a web-based information management system that provides a single access point for the collection and dissemination of emergency or event-related information

At 10:05 a.m. on April 16, MRH requested that the RHCC be activated. At 10:19 a.m., it was activated under a standby status and signed on to WebEOC. By [77]10:25 a.m., the Virginia Department of Health also had signed on to WebEOC and monitored the event. At 10:40 a.m., the RHCC requested that all hospitals provide an update of bed status and diversion status for their facility. By 10:49 a.m., LGMC was the only hospital that signed on to WebEOC of the hospitals that had received patients from the Norris Hall incident. Pulaski County Hospital also signed on and provided their status. At 11:49 a.m. (1 hour later), MRH signed on [78]followed by CNRVH at 12:33 p.m.

The WebEOC boards (the RHCC Events Board and the Near Southwest Region Events Board) were used for a variety of communications between the RHCC, hospitals, and other state agencies. Some hospitals spent considerable time attempting to post information on the WebEOC boards. None of the EMS jurisdictions signed on to either of the boards. Not all hospitals or EMS agencies are confident in using WebEOC and require regular training drills for familiarity.

The hospitals and public safety agencies should have used the RHCC and WebEOC expeditiously to gain better control of the situation. Considering the many rumors and unconfirmed reports concerning patient surge, the incident could have been better coordinated. If the RHCC was kept informed as per the MCI plan, it could have acted as the one official voice for information concerning patient status and hospital availability.

Western Virginia EMS Mass Casualty Incident Plan – The Western Virginia EMS region encompasses the 7 cities and 12 counties of Virginia Planning Districts 4, 5, and 12. The region extends from the West Virginia border to the north and to the North Carolina border to the south. The region encompasses the urban and suburban areas of Roanoke and Danville, as

well as many rural and remote areas such as those in Patrick, Floyd, and Giles counties. The region's total population (based on 1998 estimates) is 661,200. The region encompasses 9,643 square miles.

The region encompasses the counties of Alleghany, Botetourt, Craig, Floyd, Franklin, Giles, Henry, Montgomery, Patrick, [79]Pittsylvania, Pulaski, and Roanoke (Figure 21).

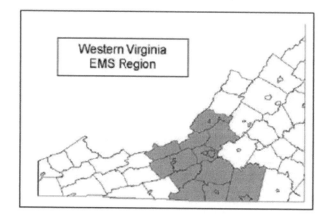

*Figure 21. Map Showing Counties in the [80]Western Virginia EMS Region*

Multicasualty Incidents – The Western Virginia EMS Mass Casualty Incident Plan (WVEMS MCI) plan defines a multiple casualty incident as "an event resulting from man-made or natural causes which results in illness and/or injuries that exceed the emergency medical services capabilities of a hospital, locality, [81]jurisdiction and/or region." Online medical direction is the responsibility of the MCI Medical Control, defined as:

> That medical facility, designated by the hospital community, which provides remote overall medical direction of the MCI or evacuation scene according to predetermined

---

[77] Baker, B. (2007). VA Tech 4-16-2007: RHCC Events Board, p. 1.

[78] Baker, B. (2007). April 16, 2007: Near Southwest Region Events Board, p. 1.

[79] WVEMS. (2006). Trauma Triage Plan. Western Virginia EMS Council, Appendix E.

[80] Ibid.

[81] WVEMS. (2006). Mass Casualty Incident Plan: EMS Mutual Aid Response Guide: Western Virginia EMS Council, Section 2.1.1, p. 1.

guidelines for the distribution of [82]patients throughout the community.

Access to online physician medical direction should be available. In MCI situations, modern EMS systems rely more on standing orders and protocols and less on online medical direction. Therefore, it may be more logical to have the RHCC coordinate these efforts, including patching in providers to online physician medical direction as needed.

The MCI plan identifies three levels of incidents based on the initial EMS assessment using the Virginia START Triage System:

- Level 1 – Multiple-casualty situation resulting in less than 10 surviving victims.
- Level 2 – Multiple casualty situation resulting in 10 to 25 surviving victims.
- Level 3 – Mass casualty situation [83]resulting in more than 25 surviving victims.

The Virginia Tech incident clearly fits into the definition of a Level 3 MCI, since at least 27 patients were treated in local emergency departments.

Frustrating communications issues and barriers occurred during the incident. Every service operated on different radio frequencies making dispatch, interagency, and medical communications difficult. These issues included both onscene and in-hospital situations that could be avoided. Specific communications challenges included the following:

- The radios used by responding agencies consisted of VHF, UHF, and HEAR frequencies. This led to on-scene communications difficulties and the inability for EMS command or Virginia Tech dispatch to assure that all units were aware of important information.
- Communications between the scene and the hospitals were too infrequent. Hospitals were unable to understand exactly what was going on at the scene. They were unable to determine the appropriate level of preparation.

- In several instances, on-scene providers called hospitals or other resources directly instead of through the ICS. This included relaying incorrect information to hospitals.
- Cell phones and blackberries worked intermittently and could not be relied upon. Officials did not have time to return or retrieve messages left on cell phones. A mobile cell phone emergency operating system was not immediately available to EMS providers.

Interviews with EMS and hospital personnel reiterated a well-known fact: face-to-face communications, when practical, is the preferred method.

From a technological standpoint, the NIMS requirement for interoperability is critical. Local communities must settle historical issues and move forward toward an efficient communications system.

Lack of a common communications system between on-scene agencies creates confusion and could have caused major safety issues for responders. Each jurisdiction having its own frequencies, radio types, dispatch centers, and procedures is a sobering example of the lack of economies of scale for emergency services. Local political entities must get past their inability to reach consensus and assure interoperability of their communications systems. In this case, the most reasonable and prudent action probably would be to expand the Montgomery County Communications System to handle all public safety communications within the county. Cooperation, consensus building, and the provision of adequate finances are required by emergency service leaders and governmental entities. Failure to accomplish this goal will leave the region vulnerable to a similar situation in the future with potentially tragic results.

Unified Command – There is little evidence that there was a unified command structure at the Virginia Tech incident. Command posts were established for EMS and law enforcement at the

---

[82] Ibid., Section 2.1.4, p. 1.
[83] Ibid., Section 7, p. 4.

Norris Hall scene and for law enforcement at another location. Separate command structures are traditional for public safety agencies. The 9/11 attack in New York City exemplified the need for public safety agencies to step back and reconsider these traditions. At Norris Hall, a unified command structure could have led to less confusion, better use of resources, better direction of personnel, and a safer working environment. Figure 22 depicts a proposed model unified command structure that could have been utilized.

The unified command post would be staffed by those having statutory authority. During the Virginia Tech incident, those personnel would likely have been the police chiefs for VTPD and the BPD, a university official, a VT EMS officer, a BVRS EMS officer, the FBI special agent-in-charge, the state police superintendent, and the ranking elected official for the City of Blacksburg. The operations section chief would have received operational guidelines from the unified command post and assured their implementation.

The unified command team would be in direct communications with the EOC and policymaking group. Command and general staff members would have communicated with their counterparts in the EOC. The policymaking group would have transmitted their requests to the EOC and the unified command post.

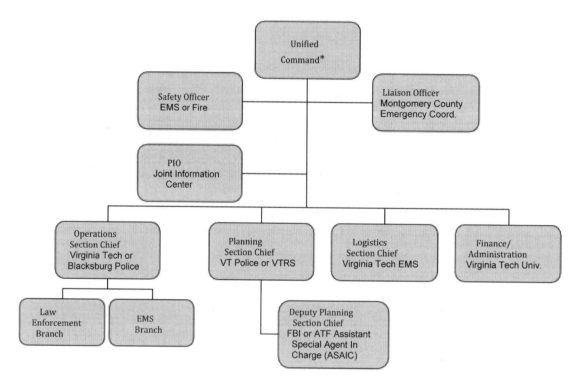

*For this incident, law enforcement would have been the lead agency. The unified command post would be staffed by those having statutory authority. During the Virginia Tech Incident, those personnel would likely have been the police chiefs for the VTPD and BPD, a university official, a VT EMS officer, the FBI special agent-in-charge, the Virginia State Police superintendent, and the ranking elected official for the City of Blacksburg.

*Figure 22. Proposed Model Unified Command Structure for an April 16-Like Incident*

Emergency Operations Center – The lack of an EOC activated quickly as the incident unfolded led to much of the confusion experienced by hospitals and other resources within the community. An EOC should have been activated at Virginia Tech. The EOC is usually located at a pre-designated site that can be quickly activated. Its main goals are to support emergency responders and ensure the continuation of operations within the community. The EOC does not become the incident commander but instead concentrates on assuring that necessary resources are available.

A policy-making group would function within the EOC. Virginia Tech had assembled a policy making group that functioned during the incident.

Another responsibility of the EOC is the establishment of a joint information center (JIC) that acts as the official voice for the situation at hand. The JIC would coordinate the release of all public information and the flow of information concerning the deceased, the survivors, locations of the sick and injured, and information for families of those displaced. By not immediately activating an EOC, hospitals or the RHCC did not receive appropriate or timely information and intelligence. There was also a delay in coordinating services for families and friends of victims who needed to be identified or located. Although Virginia Tech eventually set up a family assistance center, it was not done immediately.

## KEY FINDINGS

Positive Lessons

The EMS responses to the West Ambler Johnston residence hall and Norris Hall occurred in a timely manner.

Initial triage by the two tactical medics accompanying the police was appropriate in identifying patient viability.

The application of a tourniquet to control a severe femoral artery bleed was likely a life-saving event.

Patients were correctly triaged and transported to appropriate medical facilities.

The incident was managed in a safe manner, with no rescuer injuries reported.

Local hospitals were ready for the patient surge and employed their NIMS ICS plans and ma

295ervic patients well.

All of the patients who were alive after the Norris Hall shooting survived through discharge from the hospitals.

Quick assessment by a hospitalist of emergency department patients waiting for disposition helped with preparedness and patient flow at one hospital.

The overall EMS response was excellent, and the lives of many were saved.

EMS agencies demonstrated an exceptional working relationship, likely an outcome of interagency training and drills.

Areas for Improvement

All EMS units were initially dispatched by the Montgomery County Communications Center to respond to the scene; this was contrary to the request.

There was a 4-minute delay between VTRS monitoring the incident (9:42 a.m.) on the police radio and its being dispatched by police (9:46 a.m.).

Virginia Tech police and the Montgomery County Communications Center issued separate dispatches. This can lead to confusion in an EMS response.

BVRS was initially unaware that VTRS had already set up an EMS command post. This could have caused a duplication of efforts and further organizational challenges. Participants interviewed noted that once a BVRS officer reported to the EMS command post, communications between EMS providers on the scene improved.

Because BVRS and VTRS are on separate primary radio frequencies, BVRS reportedly did not know where to stage their units. In addition, BVRS units were reportedly unaware of when the police cleared the building for entry.

Standard triage tags were used on some patients but not on all. The tags are part of the Western Virginia EMS Trauma Triage Protocol. Their use could have assisted the hospitals with patient tracking and record management. Some patients were identified by room number in the emergency department and their records became difficult to track.

The police order to transport the deceased under emergency conditions from Norris Hall to the medical examiners office in Roanoke was inappropriate.

The lack of a local EOC and fully functioning RHCC may lead to communications and operational issues such as hospital liaisons being sent to the scene. If each hospital sent a liaison to the scene, the command post would have been overcrowded.

A unified command post should have been established and operated based on the NIMS ICS model.

Failure to open an EOC immediately led to communications and coordination issues during the incident.

Communications issues and barriers appeared to be frustrating during the incident.

## RECOMMENDATIONS

IX-1 Montgomery County, VA should develop a countywide emergency medical services, fire, and law enforcement communications center to address the issues of interoperability and economies of scale.

IX-2 A unified command post should be established and operated based on the National Incident Management System Incident Command System model. For this incident, law enforcement would have been the lead agency.

IX-3 Emergency personnel should use the National Incident Management System procedures for nomenclature, resource typing and utilization, communications, interoperability, and unified command.

IX-4 An emergency operations center must be activated early during a mass casualty incident.

IX-5 Regional disaster drills should be held on an annual basis. The drills should include hospitals, the Regional Hospital Coordinating Center, all appropriate public safety and state agencies, and the medical examiner's office. They should be followed by a formal postincident evaluation.

IX-6 To improve multi-casualty incident management, the Western Virginia Emergency Medical Services Council should review/revise the Multi-Casualty Incident Medical Control and the Regional Hospital Coordinating Center functions.

IX-7 Triage tags, patient care reports, or standardized Incident Command System forms must be completed accurately and retained after a multi-casualty incident. They are instrumental in evaluating each component of a multi-casualty incident.

IX-8 Hospitalists, when available, should assist with emergency department patient dispositions in preparing for a multicasualty incident patient surge.

IX-9 Under no circumstances should the deceased be transported under emergency conditions. It benefits no one and increases the likelihood of hurting others.

IX-10 Critical incident stress management and psychological services should continue to be available to EMS providers as needed.

**ADDITIONS AND CORRECTIONS**

(No changes from original report.)

**COMMENT**

One family member noted that the Report states that at 10:51 a.m. all patients from Norris Hall had either been transported to the hospital or to a minor treatment area and that at 11:40 a.m. Montgomery Regional Hospital received the last patient. The question was why it took 49 minutes to transport the last gunshot victim to the hospital.

Response: As noted in the Report, Norris Hall patients were triaged at the scene using the Simple Triage and Rapid Treatment system. The most seriously injured victims, who were denoted with a red tag as requiring immediate treatment, were transported to the hospital first. Those whose injuries were less severe (yellow tag) were attended to first at the delayed treatment unit set up at Stanger and Barger Streets and then transported to a hospital shortly afterward. This is standard, acceptable practice during a mass casualty incident. The overall EMS process received high marks from the professor of emergency medicine on the panel, and the staff member who is an instructor at the National Fire Academy on EMS management.

(This page intentionally left blank.)

# Chapter X.

## OFFICE OF THE CHIEF MEDICAL EXAMINER

On April 16, 2007, after the gunfire ceased on the Virginia Tech campus and the living had been triaged, treated, and transported, the sad job of identifying the deceased and conducting autopsies began. Since these were deaths associated with a crime, autopsies were legally required. The Office of the Chief Medical Examiner (OCME) had to scientifically identify each victim and conduct autopsies to determine with specificity the manner and cause of death. Autopsy reports help link the victim to the perpetrator and to a particular weapon. The OCME also has a role in providing information to victims' families.

To assess how these responsibilities were met, the panel interviewed:

- The parents and family members of the deceased victims

- Dr. Marcella F. Fierro, Chief Medical Examiner and her staff

- Colonel Steven Flaherty, Superintendent of Virginia State Police

- Mandie Patterson, Chief of the Victim Service Section, Virginia Department of Criminal Justice Services

- Jill Roark, Terrorism and Special Jurisdiction, Victim Assistance Coordinator, Federal Bureau of Investigation

- Mary Ware, Director of the Criminal Injuries Compensation Fund

- Numerous victim service providers.

The panel also reviewed the report issued by the OCME on areas for improvement, lessons learned, and recommendations.

## LEGAL MANDATES AND STANDARDS OF CARE

The Office of the Chief Medical Examiner incorporates a statewide system with headquarters in Richmond and regional offices in Fairfax, Norfolk, and Roanoke. Commonwealth law requires the OCME to be notified and to [84]investigate deaths from violence.

Autopsies are used to collect and document evidence to link the accused with the victim of the crime. In the Virginia Tech cases, this was ballistic evidence—bullets and fragments of bullets. The autopsies provided scientific evidence on the types and numbers of bullets that caused the fatal injuries.

The OCME also must ensure that there is complete, accurate identification of the human remains presented for examination. When there are multiple fatalities, the possibility exists that there could be a misidentification, which would result in the release of the wrong body to at least two families. Though a rare occurrence, there are examples of this type of error in recent history. The National Association of Medical Examiners (NAME) has adopted Forensic Autopsy Performance Standards, which are considered minimal consensus standards. The most recent version was approved in October 2006. Dr. Fierro is a member of the standards committee of NAME.

The NAME standards require several procedures to be performed if human remains are presented that are unidentified. A major issue with some of the families of those who were murdered, however, was that they felt they

---

[84] Sec. 32.1-283 Investigations of deaths. Section A, Code 1950

were capable of identifying the body of their family member; in other words, from their viewpoint, the remains were not unidentifiable.

Family members of homicide victims are generally unaware that the medical examiner is required to complete a thorough, scientific investigation in order to identify a body, determine the cause of death, and collect evidence. For the family members of victims, the experience is focused on immediacy. Is my loved one dead? When can I see my loved one? As happened at Virginia Tech, a difference in perspectives can cause deep hurt and misunderstanding. A separate matter in some of the cases was whether it was advisable for a family to view the remains.

The Virginia Tech incident presented the potential for misidentification. Bodies were presented with either inconsistent identification or none at all. This is not uncommon in mass fatality scenes due to the amount of confusion that generally exists. In order to prevent misidentification, medical examiners have established a rigorous set of practices based on national standards to ensure that identification is irrefutable. The Virginia OCME followed these standards as well as Commonwealth law in identifying the deceased.

## DEATH NOTIFICATION

The death notification process is the opening portal to the long road of painful experiences and varying reactions that follow in the wake of the life-altering news that a loved one has met with death due to homicide. This news that someone intentionally murdered a family member is the critical point of trauma and often inflicts its own wounds to the body, mind, and spirit of the survivors. From a psychological and mental health perspective, trauma is an emotional wounding that affects the will to live and one's beliefs, assumptions, and values.

A homicide affects victims' families differently than other crimes due to its high-profile nature, intent, and other factors. The act of informing family members of a homicidal death requires a

responsible, well-trained, and sensitive individual who can manage to cope with this mutually traumatizing experience. Family members of deceased victims have a wide range of needs and reactions to the sudden and untimely death of their loved ones. Consequently, the individuals who deliver the death notifications and the manner in which they carry out this duty factor significantly in the trauma experienced by the family. Death notifications must be delivered with accuracy, sensitivity, and respect for the deceased and their families. Ideally, death notification should be delivered in private, in person, and in keeping with a specific protocol adopted from one of the effective models.

## EVENTS

Monday, April 16 – The closest OCME office to Virginia Tech is located in Roanoke. All remains from the western part of the commonwealth that require an autopsy are taken there.

In addition to their full-time employees, the OCME has part-time and per-diem investigators to help conduct death investigations and refer cases to the regional offices.

The first news about the Virginia Tech shootings came to the OCME from the Blacksburg Police Department at 7:30 a.m. A police evidence technician there, who also is a per-diem employee for the ME, called to say he would not be able to attend a scheduled post-mortem exam (autopsy) because there had been a shooting at the Virginia Tech campus. At this time, six cases were awaiting examination in the western regional office, an average caseload.

By 11:30 a.m., another per-diem medical examiner, who was a member of a local rescue squad, notified the regional OCME office of a multiple fatality incident at Norris Hall with upwards of 50 victims. It was at this time that one of the decedents from West Ambler Johnston (WAJ) residence hall was transported to Carillion Roanoke Memorial Hospital. The western office notified the central office in

Richmond that additional assistance would be needed to handle the surge in caseload.

At 1:30 p.m., representatives from the Roanoke office arrived on campus and attended an incident management team meeting with the public safety agencies that had responded. OCME representatives attended the operations section briefing. The activities in Norris Hall were organized by areas (classrooms and a stairway). Investigation teams of law enforcement and OCME employees were assigned specific tasks.

The OCME requested resources from the northern regional office in Fairfax and the central office in Richmond. They, along with Dr. Fierro, departed for Blacksburg by 3:00 p.m. The western office had two vacancies in forensic pathologist positions, so additional staff clearly was needed.

The first autopsy that of one of the dormitory victims, began at 3:15 p.m. No autopsy could begin until after the crime scene had been thoroughly documented and investigated. As each decedent was transported from campus, the Roanoke regional office was notified so that a case number could be assigned.

By 5:00 p.m., the first victim from Norris Hall had been transported to the Roanoke office. Volunteer rescue squads were transporting the victims from campus to the regional office, a 45-minute trip.

At 6:30 p.m., Dr. Fierro and additional staff from Richmond arrived and met with representatives from state police and the Departments of Health and Emergency Management. The methods for identification were discussed, as was the process of documenting personal effects. The last victim was removed from Norris Hall and transported to Roanoke by 8:45 p.m. By 11:30 p.m., the first autopsy was completed; 301ervice301-cation made, next of kin notified, and the remains released to a funeral home.

Tuesday, April 17 – In the early morning hours of the first day after the shooting, additional pathologists departed the Tidewater and central regional offices for Roanoke. A staff meeting was held at 7:00 a.m. to formulate the OCME portion of the incident action plan (IAP). Key points addressed for the morgue operations sections included:

- All victims were to be forensically identified prior to release.
- A second-shooter theory was still under consideration by law enforcement. As such, all ballistic evidence had to be collected and documented. The distribution of gunshot wounds was:

VIII-    One victim with nine
VIII-    One victim with seven
VIII-    Five victims with six
VIII-    One victim with five
VIII-    Five victims with four

The remainder of the victims had three or fewer gunshot wounds. The complexity of tracking bullet trajectories and retrieving fragments would be especially time consuming for the multiple wounds.

It was decided to use fingerprints as the primary identification method and dental records as the secondary. The reasons for this decision were:

- Fingerprints were able to be taken from all of the victims.
- Foreign students had prints on file with Customs and Border Protection.
- There was an abundance of latent prints on personal effects in dorm rooms and apartments and on personal effects recovered on site.
- The Department of Forensic Services had adequate staff available to assist in the collection and comparison of the fingerprints. (The police reported that nearly 100 law enforcement officers from local, state, and federal agencies volunteered or were assigned to assist in gathering prints and other identification.)

The alternative method for identification, dental examination, required the name of the decedent's dentist to obtain dental records, and families were asked to provide the contact information in case that method was needed.

DNA was excluded as a means of identification because the collection and processing of samples would have taken weeks.

In addition to being short-staffed by two vacancies and one injured pathologist, the ME's office had to respond to the concerns and demands of a religious group that contested one of the autopsies. By the end of the first day of operations, all of the deceased, 33, had been transported to the western region office. Thirteen post-mortem examinations had been completed, two positive identifications had been made, and two families were notified and the remains released and picked up by next of kin or their representative.

Wednesday, April 18 – On the second day of morgue operations, the process of forensic identification continued. Procedures began at 7:45 a.m. and continued until 8:00 p.m.

At 10:00 a.m., the chief medical examiner gave a press conference where she discussed forensic procedures and the methods employed.

At 11:00 a.m., a representative from OCME assisted in collecting ante-mortem data from the families who had gathered at the family assistance center at The Inn at Virginia Tech.

"VIP" AND MISUNDERSTANDINGS: The primary form OCME uses to collect ante-mortem data is called a Victim Identification Protocol (VIP) form. This form, used by many medical examiners and federal response teams, documents information on hair and eye color, medical history (such as an appendectomy), and other distinguishing marks such as scars or tattoos. During a post-mortem examination, the pathologist conducting the autopsy comments on his or her findings and each identifier and that information is entered into a case file. Forensic odontology (dental) and fingerprint findings may also be incorporated. Both profiles can be compared electronically and possible matches or exclusions made. The pathologist then reviews these findings as part of the scientific identification.

As case files were compiled, a designation was made as to whether a VIP form was available and included in the file. Some state officials, seeing the VIP acronym, mistakenly concluded that OCME had designated some victims as "VIPs" (very important persons), singling them out for special consideration. As it happened, several embassies did contact state officials to demand preferential treatment for their nationals who were among the victims. However, the OCME did not provide any preferential or "VIP" treatment.

MEDIA MISINFORMATION: Radio station K-92 announced that the "coroner" would be releasing all of the human remains on Wednesday, April 18. The origin of this incorrect report is unknown.

TRACKING INFORMATION: At the request of the governor's office, a spreadsheet that detailed specific information for each victim was developed. During this process, members of the governor's staff became concerned that the OCME had prioritized some cases. But in fact, cases were handled without a specific plan or intent to prioritize them.

Staff members from the OCME went to the Inn to assist in the operation of the FAC. The Virginia State Police and the OCME established a process and team to notify families that their loved ones had been positively identified.

IDENTIFICATION AND VIEWING: Family members of the deceased victims were anxious for the formal identification and release of the bodies to be completed. In response to the concerns of family members regarding the length of time involved in the identification process, some state officials suggested that the families should be permitted to go to the morgue and identify the bodies if they so chose. Though this would seem reasonable, it conflicts with current practice.

A public information officer at the FAC explained to families who were assembled there what the OCME policy was regarding visible presumptive identification. Then the public information officer (PIO) unfortunately asked the families for a "show of hands" of those who wanted to view the remains of their loved ones in case that could be arranged.

Viewing and identifying remains is a significant issue for victim survivors. Even though 303ervice303cation of the body by family members is not always considered scientifically reliable, for various reasons, victim survivors often want to make that decision for themselves. At Virginia Tech, families were frustrated with the lack of information from OCME and why it was taking so long to identify and release the victims' remains. Medical examiners must be sensitive to the waiting family members' need to be kept informed when there are delays and when they can expect a status update

The remains of persons killed in a crime become part of the evidence of the crime scene, and are legally under the jurisdiction of the OCME until released. The OCME can set the conditions it thinks are appropriate for the situation. The standard of care does not include presumptive identification using visual means. The public information officer who asked for a show of hands should not have done so.

When the protocol and policies of the OCME were explained to the families, some of the tension seemed to abate. The confusion and misunderstanding surrounding these issues involved misinformation, late information, no information, and the high emotional stress of the event. Had a public information officer with a background in the operations of the OCME been available or a representative from the OCME been present to answer these concerns, the controversy regarding this issue could have been reduced or eliminated.

IDENTIFICATION PROGRESS: The progress of the first day continued on the second day of morgue operations. The second-shooter theory had been discounted after it was determined forensically that Cho used two different weapons. By the end of the second day, another 20 autopsies had been completed, which meant that all 33 victims had received a post-mortem exam. At this point, there were 22 total identifications and 22 remains released to next

of kin. Morgue operations were conducted from 7:00 a.m. to 8:00 p.m.

Thursday, April 19 – The third day of morgue operations began at 7:00 a.m. It was determined that the OCME would work around the clock if necessary to complete the identification process this day. By this time, all of the ante-mortem records had arrived at the regional office.

The media had gathered in the area of the morgue and was covering the activities of representatives of the families—usually funeral homes—as they arrived to pick up the remains. Roanoke County law enforcement provided security.

All of the remaining decedents were identified and released by 6:00 p.m. The last case was a special challenge as there were no fingerprints on file and the victim did not have a dentist of record. The latent prints in the home were not readable. The identification was completed through a process of exclusion and definition of unique physical properties using the Victim Identification Protocol process. The Virginia OCME had completed 33 post-mortem exams and correctly made 33 positive legal identifications within 3 working days.

Figure 23 summarizes the statistics for 3-day morgue operations. The figure shows that not all of the remains were picked up by the end of morgue operations because Cho's family did not pick up his remains for several days after the operations were shut down.

**ISSUES**

T303erv major issues surfaced during panel interviews and the collection of after-action reports in regards to the actions of the Virginia OCME; these were primarily issues presented by some families of the deceased:

- Some felt the autopsy process took too long.
- Some felt families should have been allowed to go to the morgue and visibly identify their family members.

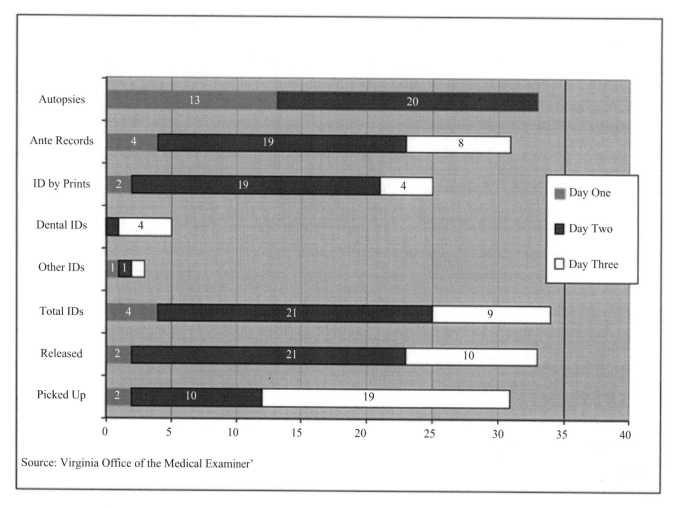

Source: Virginia Office of the Medical Examiner'

Source: Virginia Office of the Medical Examiner'

*Figure 23. Progress and Activity of the OCME Over the 3-Day Period April 17–19, 2007*

- Many felt the process of notifying the families and providing assistance to the families was disjointed, unorganized, and in several cases insensitive.

Speed – There is no nationally accepted time standard for the performance of an autopsy. The NAME standards mentioned earlier do not set time standards.

The average duration of the post-mortem exams was just under 2 hours. Had the OCME office been fully staffed, it may have been able to perform the identifications and examinations somewhat more rapidly. The OCME did have a disaster plan that it implemented upon notification of the events. The plan called for staff from the regional and central offices to deploy to the regional office where the disaster

occurred to meet the surge in caseload, which was done.

The OCME did not call for federal assistance, which is available from the Department of Health and Human Service's National Disaster Medical System (NDMS) program. That program can deploy a disaster mortuary operational response team (DMORT) composed of forensic specialists who can assist medical examiners in the event of mass fatality incidents. The DMORT system has three portable morgue units. DMORT resources (in this case, just personnel) could have been requested and probably [85]been in place within

---

[85] A member of TriData's support staff to the panel is a member of a DMORT and provided first-hand information on its operation.

24 hours of mobilization. For example, a DMORT was used in the Station Nightclub fire in Rhode Island in February 2003 to assist the Rhode Island medical examiner in the identification of the victims of that fire.

Once ante-mortem information had been gathered, DMORT personnel could have worked a second shift and might have reduced the elapsed time of morgue operations by 24 hours. Given the information regarding the performance of the family assistance center, which also was the responsibility of OCME, this early collection may or may not have occurred. The time delay for identifications came from delays in gathering ante-mortem information and then providing that information to the OCME, a task outside the control of the OCME.

Identification and Viewing – The second issue was the insistence by the OCME to perform forensic identifications of the victims as opposed to presumptive identifications. Forensic identifications use methods such as fingerprinting, dental records, DNA matches, or other scientific means for identification. Presumptive identification includes photographs, driver's licenses, and visual recognition by family or friends.

Some of the families wanted to go to the regional office of the OCME to view the remains and identify the victims. The OCME did not permit this for several reasons. For one, the regional office does not have an area large enough to display all the bodies for families to view each one to determine whether it is their family member

As noted earlier, the idea of families viewing their loved one and making a legally binding identification is not the current practice of the OCME because it is not considered scientifically reliable. Nevertheless, it was emotionally wrenching for families not to have a choice in this matter. Presumptive identification is acceptable in some communities under certain conditions. OCME noted that several female victims had no personal effects such as a driver's license or student identity card when they were transported to the hospital or morgue. At the same time, some families told the medical examiner's office about specific moles, scars, or other distinguishing marks that were far more reliable than a purse and could not be confused with another victim.

A textbook for students of forensic pathology discusses the identification of human remains. Regarding the topic of reliable visual identification:

> The operative word in this method of identification is reliable [italics added]. Personal recognition of visage or habitus, under certain circumstances, is less reliable than fingerprints, dental data, or radiology. It (this method) relies on memory and a rapid mental comparison of physical features under stressful conditions and often a damaged body....
>
> Another hazard in visual identification is denial. The situation may be so stressful or the remains altered by age, injury, disease or changes in lifestyle that identification is denied even if later confirmed by finger-prints or dental examination.[86]

In Clinics in Laboratory Medicine, Victor Weedn writes:

> Visual recognition is among the least reliable forms of identification. Even brothers, sisters and mates have misidentified victims. ...Family members may find it emotionally difficult and uncomfortable to carefully gaze at the dead body, particularly a loved one. Identification requires a rapid mental comparison under stressful conditions. The environment in which the identification is made and

---

[86] Spitz and Fisher, Medicolegal Investigation of Death, 3rd edition, Edited by Werner U. Spitz. 1993, pages 77–78.

the appearance of the person at death are unnatural and strange....[87]

Family Treatment – The third issue was the treatment of the families of the decedents regarding official notification and support while waiting for positive identification. Their treatment was haphazard, inconsistent, and compounded the pain and trauma of the event.

Victims of crime are afforded a number of rights, among them the right to be treated with dignity and respect. The right of respect speaks to victims being given honest and direct information free of any attempt to protect them from perceived emotional injury or their inability to process information. Crime victims rights are protected by federal and state laws. Basic rights for victim survivors generally include the right to be notified and heard, and to be informed.

In 1996, following several airline accidents, the families of the victims felt the airline companies and government officials did not address their needs, desires, or expectations. In that year, Congress passed the Aviation Disaster Family Assistance Act. This law holds airline companies and government officials, such as medical examiners and coroners, accountable to the National Transportation Safety Board for compassionate, considerate, and timely information regarding the disposition of their loved ones or next of kin.

The U.S. Department of Justice, through its Office of Justice Programs, has an Office for Victims of Crime (OVC) that can provide support for victims of federal crimes such as terrorism.

To this end, many medical examiners' offices have developed plans for the establishment of family assistance centers. A FAC serves several purposes. First, it is the location where families can receive timely, accurate, and compassionate information from officials. Second, medical examiner's office staff can collect vital ante-

mortem information from families there to assist in the positive identification of the deceased. Third, it can be the location where private, compassionate notification of the positive identification of the deceased can be conducted with next of kin.

A FAC was established in Oklahoma City in April 1995 following the Murrah Building bombing. Families were notified in private, before the media was notified. This model for the 306ervicesionate, accurate information exchange was [88]published by the federal OVC.

Although a FAC was established at The Inn at Virginia Tech, reports received by the panel indicate that what was provided was not adequate. Many complaints were lodged by families regarding what they perceived as an insensitive attitude and manner of communication from the medical examiner's office. Some families also objected to the rigid application of the scientific identification process. Among the complaints and questions relevant to the ME functions were the following:

- Inadequate communication efforts (lack of information).

- Lack of sensitivity to the emotions of survivors.

- Lack of a central point of contact for information for responders, victims, and family members.

- Lack of a security plan that resulted in an inability to distinguish personnel, responding service providers, and other agents with authority to enter the FAC and surrounding areas.

- Confusion regarding the Victim Identification Profile form.

- Confusion regarding the identification process as to length and method used and its necessity.

- Failure to provide adequate isolation for parents in receiving information.

---

[87] Victor Weedn, "Postmortem Identification of Remains," *Clinics in Laboratory Medicine*, Volume 18, March 1998, page 117.

[88] OVC, "Providing Relief After a Mass Fatality, Role of the Medical Examiners Office and the Family Assistance Center," Blakney, 2002

- Location of the media relative to the FAC; media management in general was lacking.

- Issues surrounding the source and responsibility for death notifications.

- Lack of personnel trained, skilled, and prepared to assist victims upon receipt of death notification.

- Concern that no one was addressing the needs of all family members, and awareness that some family members were having great difficulty in coping.

- No timely or consistent family briefings.

- Confusion about who is responsible for the death notifications and family assistance.

Some of these complaints are associated with the medical examiner's office, but others are not. In fact, no one individual agency or department of government is charged with the responsibility of organizing and maintaining a fully operational family assistance center. This is an oversight in federal and state policies. Existing planning guidance, such as the National Response Plan, parcels out pieces of the FAC function to various lead agencies, but places no one agency in charge. The OCME is clearly identified as being responsible for fatality management, including death notifications; also, the state plan calls for OCME to set up a family victim identification center within the FAC. Who is supposed to run the FAC is not addressed.

The university attempted to provide these services. In the Virginia Tech Emergency Operations Plan, the Office of Student Programs is responsible to:

> Develop and maintain, in conjunction with the Schiffert Health Center, Cook Counseling Center, the University Registrar, and Personnel Services, procedures for providing mass care and sheltering for students, psychological and medical support services, parental

notification and other procedures [89] as necessary,

A university the size of Virginia Tech must be prepared for more than emergencies of limited size and scope. Universities need plans for major operations. If the situation dictates the need for additional help from outside the university, then all concerned must be prepared to proceed in that direction.

The university turned to the state for help on Wednesday, April 17. It should have done so earlier. The Commonwealth Emergency Operations Plan in its "Emergency Support Function (ESF)" #8" addresses public health and fatality issues. The Health Department is the lead agency for this ESF. The OCME mass fatality plan is found in Volume #4, "Hazardous Materials and Terrorism Consequence Management Plan," part 14-D-2.

The OCME plan considers 12 or more fatalities in 1 day in one regional office to be the trigger point for implementation of the emergency plan. The plan calls for the establishment of both a family assistance center and a family victim identification center. At this location, the OCME and law enforcement agencies would conduct interviews to gather ante-mortem information and notify next of kin. The OCME, however, does not have sufficient personnel to perform this task, and its plan indicates as much (page 16). To their credit, the OCME has recruited a team of volunteers through the Virginia Funeral Directors Association to assist in the operation of a FAC. Funeral directors by training and disposition have experience in interactions with bereaved families. This group is an ideal choice to provide assistance to the OCME. Unfortunately, this team was not available for the Virginia Tech incident because the state requires background checks and ID cards for these teams and funding was not provided for them.

What evolved by Wednesday, April 18, was an uncoordinated system of providing family support. It was too late and inadequate.

---

[89] "VA Tech Emergency Response Plan," Appendix 10 to Functional Annex A, page 45.

## KEY FINDINGS

### Positive Lessons

The part of the OCME disaster plan related to post-mortem operations functioned as designed. The internal notification process as well as staff redeployments allowed the surge in caseload generated by the disaster to be handled appro308ervice308308 as well as existing cases and other new cases that were referred to the OCME from other events statewide.

Thirty-three positive identifications were made in 3 days of intense morgue operations.

The contention that the OCME was slow in completing the legally mandated tasks of investigation is not valid.

Crime scene operations with law enforcement were effective and expedient.

Cooperation with the Department of Forensic Services for fingerprint and dental comparison was good.

The OCME performed their technical duties well under the pressures of a high-profile event.

### Areas for Improvement

The public information side of the OCME was poor and not enough was done to bring outside help in quickly to cover this critical part of their duties. The OCME did not dedicate a person to handle the inquiries and issues regarding the expectations of the families and other state officials. This failure resulted in the spread of misinformation, confusion for victim survivors, and frustrations for all concerned.

The inexperience of state officials charged with managing a mass fatality event was evident. This could be corrected if state officials include the OCME in disaster drills and exercises.

The process of notifying family members of the victims and the support needed for this population were ineffective and often insensitive. The university and the OCME should have asked for outside assistance when faced with an event of this size and scope.

Training for identification personnel was inadequate regarding acceptable scientific identification methods. This includes FAC personnel; Virginia funerals directors; behavioral health, law enforcement, public health, and public information officials; the Virginia Dental Association; and hospital staffs.

Adequate training for PIOs on the methods and operations of the OCME was lacking. This training had been given to two Health Department public information officers prior to the shootings. However, since neither was available, information management in the hands of an inexperienced public information officer proved disastrous. This in turn, allowed speculation and misinformation, which caused additional stress to victims' families.

No one was in charge of the family assistance center operation. Confusion over that responsibility between state government and the university added to the problem. Under the currentstate planning model, the Commonwealth's Department of Social Services has part of the responsibility for family assistance centers. The university stepped in to establish the center and use the liaisons, but they were not knowledgeable about how to manage such a delicate operation. Moreover, the university itself was traumatized.

## RECOMMENDATIONS

The following recommendations reflect the research conducted by the panel, after-action reports from Commonwealth agencies, and other studies regarding fatality management issues.

X-1 The chief medical examiner should not be one of the staff performing the post-mortem exams in mass casualty events; the chief medical examiner should be managing the overall response.

X-2 The Office of the Chief Medical Examiner (OCME) should work along with law enforcement, Virginia Department of Criminal Justice Services( DCJS), chaplains, Department of Homeland Security, and other authorized entities in developing protocols and training to create a more responsive family assistance center (FAC).

X-3 The OCME and Virginia State Police in concert with FAC personnel should ensure that family members of the deceased are afforded prompt and sensitive notification of the death of a family member when possible and provide briefings regarding any delays.

X-4 Training should be developed for FAC, law enforcement, OCME, medical and mental health professionals, and others regarding the impact of crime and appropriate intervention for victim survivors.

X-5 OCME and FAC personnel should ensure that a media expert is available to manage media requests effectively and that victims are not inundated with intrusions that may increase their stress.

X-6 The Virginia Department of Criminal Justice Services should mandate training for law enforcement officers on death notifications.

X-7 The OCME should participate in disaster or national security drills and exercises to plan and train for effects of a mass fatality situation on ME operations.

X-8 The Virginia Department of Health should continuously recruit board-certified forensic pathologists and other specialty positions to fill vacancies within the OCME. Being understaffed is a liability for any agency and reduces its surge capability.

X-9 The Virginia Department of Health should have several public information officers trained and well versed in OCME operations and in victims services. When needed, they should be made available to the OCME for the duration of the event.

X-10 Funding to train and credential volunteer staff, such as the group from the Virginia Funeral Director's Association, should be made available in order to utilize their talents. Had this team been available, the family assistance center could have been more effectively organized.

X-11 The Commonwealth should amend its Emergency Operations Plan to include an emergency support function for mass fatality operations and family assistance. The new ESF should address roles and responsibilities of the state agencies. The topics of family assistance and notification are not adequately addressed in the National Response Plan (NRP) for the federal government and the state plan that mirrors the NRP also mirrors this weakness. Virginia has an opportunity to be a national leader by reforming their EOP to this effect.

## A FINAL WORD

The weaknesses and issues regarding the performance of the OCME and the family assistance process that came to light in the aftermath of the Virginia Tech homicides did not reveal new issues for this agency. In July 2003, the Commonwealth published "Recommendations for the Secure Commonwealth Panel." Appendix 1-3 of this report addressed mass fatality issues. Although the intent of the report was to assess the state of preparedness in Virginia for terrorist attacks, many of the issues that arose following the Virginia Tech homicides were identified in this report. Had the recommendations in this report been implemented, many of the problems cited above might have been averted.

Therefore, the panel also recommends that the recommendations found in Appendices 1-3 of the Secure Commonwealth Panel from 2005 be implemented.

## ADDITIONS AND CORRECTIONS

(No changes from original report.)

# Chapter XI.

## IMMEDIATE AFTERMATH AND THE LONG ROAD TO HEALING

In the hours, days, and weeks following Cho's calculated assault on students and faculty at Virginia Tech, hundreds of individuals and dozens of agencies and organizations from Virginia Tech, local jurisdictions, state government, businesses, and private citizens mobilized to provide assistance. Once again the nation witnessed the sudden, unexpected horror of a large number of lives being intentionally destroyed in a fleeting moment. Only those caught up in the immediate moments after the attacks can fully describe the confusion, attempts to protect and save lives, and the heartbreaking struggle to recover the dead. Reeling from shock and outraged by the shootings, students and faculty who survived Norris Hall and law enforcement officers and emergency medical providers who arrived on the scene will carry images with them that will be difficult to deal with in the months and years ahead.

Disaster response organizations including community-based organizations, local, state and federal agencies, and volunteers eager to help in any capacity flooded the campus. The media descended on the grounds of Virginia Tech with a large number of reporters and equipment, pursuing anyone and everyone who was willing to talk in a quest for stories that they could broadcast across the nation to feed the public's interest in the shocking events.

The toll of April 16, 2007, assaults the senses: 32 innocent victims of homicide, 26 physically injured, and many others who carry deep emotional wounds. For each, there also are family members and friends who were affected. Each of the 32 homicides represents an individual case unto itself. The families of the deceased as well as each physically and emotionally wounded victim have required

support specific to their individual needs. Finding resolution, comfort, peace, healing, and recovery is difficult to achieve and may take a lifetime for some.

The people whose lives were directly affected include:

- Family members of the murdered victims, who are often called co-victims due to the tremendous impact of the crimes on their lives.

- Physically and emotionally wounded victims from Norris Hall and their family members who, while grateful that they or their loved ones were spared death, face injuries that may have a profound effect upon them for a lifetime.

- Witnesses and those within a physical proximity to the event and their family members.

- Law enforcement personnel who faced life-threatening conditions and were the first to respond to Norris Hall and among the first to respond to West Ambler Johnston dormitory. They encountered a scene few officers ever see. Their families are not sparred from the complicated impact of the events.

- Emergency medical responders who treated and transported the injured. Their family members also share in the complexity of reactions experienced by emergency medical responders.

- Everyone from Virginia Tech who was part of the immediate response to the two shooting incidents and the aftermath that followed.

- Mental health professionals.

- Funeral home personnel and hospital personnel, who, while accustomed to traumatic events, are not necessarily spared the after-effects.
- Volunteers and employees from surrounding jurisdictions and state agencies, and others who worked diligently to provide support in the first hours and days.
- The campus population of students, faculty, and staff and their families.

This chapter describes the major actions that were taken in the aftermath of April 16. Many other spontaneous, informal activities took place as well, especially by students. For example, members of the Hokie band went to the hospitals and played for some injured students outside their windows. The madrigal chorus from Radford University sang at a memorial service for several students who had been killed. The private sector made donations and offered assistance. It is difficult to capture the true magnitude of the heartfelt responses and the special kindnesses exhibited by thousands of people.

At the time of publication of this report, recovery was only 4 months along in a process that will continue much longer. The following sections discuss the actions that key responders and entities took in the immediate aftermath of the shootings and during the weeks that followed.

## FIRST HOURS

After Cho committed suicide and the scene was finally cleared by the police to allow EMS units to move in, the grim reports began to emerge. The numbers of dead and injured rose as each new report was issued. Parents, spouses, faculty, students, and staff scrambled for information that would confirm that their loved ones, friends, or colleagues were safe. They attempted to contact the university, hospitals, local police departments, and media outlets, in an attempt to obtain the latest information.

Chaos and confusion reigned throughout the campus in the immediate aftermath. Individuals

and systems were caught unaware and reacted to the urgency of the moment and the enormity of the event. There was an outpouring of effort to help and to provide for the safety of everyone. Responders scrambled to offer solace to the despairing and to meet emergency needs for medical care and comfort to the injured. These initial spontaneous responses helped to stabilize some of the impact of the devastation as it unfolded.

Grief-stricken university leaders, faculty, staff, and law enforcement worked together to monitor the rapidly changing situation and set up a location where families could assemble. Some family members arrived not knowing whether their child, spouse, or sibling had been taken to a hospital for treatment for their wounds, or to a morgue. University officials designated The Inn at Virginia Tech as the main gathering place for families.

## ACTIONS BY VIRGINIA TECH

The immediate tasks were to provide support to the families of Virginia Tech students and particularly to the family members of the slain and injured. Countless responders including law enforcement officers, concerned volunteers, government entities, community-based organizations, victim assistance providers, faculty, staff, and students worked diligently to lend assistance in this uncharted territory, the impact of a mass murder of this scale. Many aspects of the post-incident activities went well, especially considering the circumstances; others were not well handled.

The incident revealed certain inadequacies in government emergency response plan guidelines for family assistance at mass fatality incidents. Also, certain state assistance resources were not obligated quickly enough and arrived late. Finally, the lack of an adequate university emergency response plan to cover the operation of an onsite, post-emergency operations center (and most particularly a joint information center) and a family assistance center hampered response efforts.

A variety of formal and informal methods were used to assist surviving victims and families of deceased victims.

University-Based Liaisons – The Division of Student Affairs organized a group of family liaisons, individuals who were assigned to two or more families for the purpose of providing direct support to victim survivors. The liaison staff was comprised of individuals from the Division of Student Affairs, the graduate school, and the Provost's Office. They were tasked to track down and provide information to families of those killed and to victim survivors, to assist them with the details of recovering personal belongings and contacting funeral homes, and to act as an information link between families and the university. Liaisons worked out the details on such matters as transportation, benefits from federal and state victim's compensation funds (as that information became available), coordination with the Red Cross, travel arrangements for out-of-country relatives, and much more. They also helped arrange participation in commencement activities where deceased students received posthumous degrees.

Interviews with victims' families revealed that many of the liaisons were viewed as sensitive, knowledgeable, caring, and helpful. Originally set up as a temporary resource for the early days and weeks following the shootings, the liaisons soon discovered that the overwhelming needs and expectations for their assistance would be ongoing. Many liaisons continued to help even as the weeks stretched on, while others were not in a position to continue on at such an intense level for an extended period of time. Still others were not prepared to serve in the capacity of a liaison and lacked training and skills needed to provide assistance to crime victims.

There were a few reports of poor communication, insensitivity, failure to follow-up, and misinformation, which added to the confusion and frustration experienced by a number of families. Largely, these problems occurred because Liaisons were volunteers untrained in responding to victims in the aftermath of a major disaster. Nevertheless, they were willing and available to fill an acute need while system based victim assistance providers awaited the required invitation before they were authorized to respond to Virginia Tech campus. The liaisons themselves had little if any experience in dealing with the aftermath of violent crime scenes and were grappling with their own emotional responses to the deaths and injuries of the students and faculty. Liaisons did not have adequate information on the network of services designed for victims of crime until at least 2 days later when most of the state's victim assistance team arrived.

In general, most families reported that their liaisons were wonderful and conscientious, and they were grateful for the tremendous amount of time and effort put forth by them on their behalf.

State Victims Services and Compensation Personnel – Assistance to survivor families and families of the injured could have been far more effective if executed from the beginning as a dual function between university-assigned liaisons and professional victim assistance providers working together to meet the ongoing needs of each family

Victim assistance programs throughout the nation are supported by federal, state, and local governments. Many victim assistance programs are community based and specific to domestic violence and sexual assault crimes, while other programs are system-based and operate out of police departments, prosecutor's offices, the courts, and the department of corrections. These programs provide crisis intervention, counseling, emotional support, help with court processes, links to various resources, and financial assistance to victims of crime. They represent a network of trained, skilled professionals accustomed to designing programs and strategies to meet the specific needs of crime victims. Moreover, all states have a victim compensation program charged with reimbursing crime victims for certain out-of-pocket expenses resulting from criminal victimization.

Patricia Snead, Emergency Planning Manager at the Virginia Department of Social Services (DSS), alerted Mandie Patterson, Chief of the

Commonwealth's Victim Services Section (VSS) at the Department of Criminal Justice Services (DCJS), at 12:21 p.m. on April 16, and asked that office to stand by for possible mobilization to support the needs at Virginia Tech. At that point, it was unclear whether DCJS staff from Richmond or local advocates would be needed to staff a family assistance center and whether Virginia Tech would request assistance for these services per the state's emergency management procedures. According to those procedures, before VSS staff can move forward, they must be authorized to do so from DSS. There was no further instruction that day from DSS.

The following day, April 17, the DCJS chief of VSS sent a broadcast e-mail to the 106 victim witness programs in Virginia to determine the availability of advocates with experience in working with victims of homicide. At 4:17 p.m. that day, DSS sent a message to DCJS, VSS and the victim advocates from local sister agencies indicating that they were authorized to respond to the needs of victims on the campus. The team of victim service providers arrived on April 18, 2 days after the massacre. Thus, even though the Commonwealth's emergency plan authorizes immediate action, the process moved slowly—a real problem given the substantial need for early intervention, crisis response, information and help in establishing the family assistance center. According to Snead, time was lost while officials from the state and the university worked through the question of who was supposed to be in charge of managing the emergency and its aftermath: the state university or the state government. Reportedly, the university was guarded and initially reluctant to accept help or relinquish authority to the Commonwealth for managing resources and response.

Mary Ware, Director of the Department of Criminal Injuries Compensation Fund (CICF), arrived on Tuesday around midnight. Early on Wednesday morning, she began providing the services of her office and talked to two on-scene staff from the Montgomery County Victim Witness Program. Kerry Owens, director of that

program, told the panel, "You have never seen such pain, sorrow, and despair in one place, and you have never seen so many people come together for a common cause." The CICF provides funds to help compensate victim survivors with medical expenses, funeral and burial costs, and a number of other out-of-pocket expenses associated with criminal victimization. At Virginia Tech, CICF enabled the rapid provision of funds to cover funeral expenses, temporarily setting aside certain procedures until they could be processed at a later date. CICF staff and the team of victim service providers orchestrated by DCJS arrived on Wednesday morning and proceeded to help in various capacities.

The delay in the mobilization and arrival of the victim service providers resulted in some families working directly with the medical examiner regarding that office's request for personal items with fingerprints or DNA samples to help identify the bodies. Though the university liaisons were helping, a number of families did not have the benefit of a professional victim service provider to support them in coping with the ME's requests. Many families had scattered and begun making arrangements with funeral homes, which had a direct line to the ME's office. Other nongovernmental service providers—many without identification or a security badge—appeared on the scene without having been summoned to help. As a consequence, some families received conflicting information about what the Red Cross would pay for, what the state would cover, and what they would have to manage on their own.

The victim assistance team comprised of the state's two relevant agencies—DCJS and CICF—had difficulty locating and identifying victim survivors. Victim Services and Crime Compensation staff became aware that the United Way was fund-raising on campus and sought out those individuals to ensure that there were no conflicts or duplications of effort. The victim assistance team provided assistance for family members by informing them of their rights as crime victims and offering assistance in a number of areas to include help with making funeral arrangements, childcare in some instances, arranging for transportation, emotional support and referral information. Unfortunately, when many of the family members returned home to other states or other parts of Virginia, they were not connected directly to available services in their local jurisdictions. Because of the need to respect privacy and confidentiality, victim assistance providers in the victims' hometowns had to refrain from intruding and instead had to await invitation or authorization by others to become linked to the families. There was a gap in the continuum of care as, in many cases, survivors returned home with little or no information regarding ongoing victim services in their jurisdictions. To the extent the liaisons had sufficient information about victim's assistance services to tell the families, they did. However, unless the liaison or other responsible on-scene providers provided families and victims with specific information regarding their local victim services office, they did not know what services were available or how to access them.

The Family Assistance Center – The Inn at Virginia Tech became the de facto information center and gathering place where everyone congregated to await news on the identification of the wounded and deceased. It also was designated as a family assistance center—a logical choice for families who needed lodging, information, and support. Accommodations at the inn (rooms, food, and staff service) were well received, and hotel staff offered special care to the families who stayed there. However, the sheer magnitude of the immediate impact coupled with the failure to establish an organized, centralized point of information at the outset resulted in mass confusion and a communications nightmare that remained unabated throughout the week following the shootings.

The official Virginia Tech FAC was set up in one of the ballrooms at Skelton Conference Center at the Inn. Over the first 36 hours, 15 victim advocates from several victim assistance programs arrived and formed a victim assistance team comprised of seven staff from the Office of CICF and other service providers and counselors. Additionally, staff from the Office of the Chief Medical Examiner (OCME) was assigned to supervise the family identification section (FIS) at the FAC. The FIS, according to the OCME Fatality Plan "will receive inquiries on identification, prepare Victim Identification Profiles, and collect Any materials, records, or items needed for confirmation of identification.

A FAC also is supposed to serve as a safe haven, a compassion center, and a private environment created to allow victims and surviving family members' protection from any additional distress brought about as a result of intrusive media. In addition to serving as an information exchange mechanism, the FAC affords victims and family member's refreshments, access to telephones for long-distance calls, and support from mental health counselors and victims' service providers.

Arriving media, unfortunately, were situated in a parking lot directly across from the inn. Families had to traverse a labyrinth of cameras and microphones to reach the front desk at the inn. The media were a constant presence because they were stationed in the same area rather than at a site farther away on Virginia Tech's large campus. The impact of the media on victim survivors is enormous. In high-profile murder cases the murderer instantaneously is linked to the victims and together become household names. Some members of the press were appalled at the tactics that some of their colleagues used to gather information on campus at the family assistance center.

There was little organization and almost no verifiable information for many hours after the shooting ended. The operative phrase was "go to the inn" but once there, families struggled to know who was responsible for providing what services and where to go for the latest news about identification of the dead victims. Some unidentified people periodically asked families if they needed counseling. Those offers were pre-mature in the midst of a crisis and information was the most important thing that families wanted at the time.

Family members were terrified, anxious, and frantic to learn what was happening. Who had survived? Which hospital was caring for them? Where were the bodies of those who had perished taken and how can one get there? There was no identified focal point for information distribution for family members or arriving support staff. For decades, disaster plans have underscored the importance of having a designated public information officer (PIO) who serves as the reliable source of news during emergencies. The PIO serving at the FAC was inexperienced and over-whelmed by the event. He was unable to adequately field inquires from victim survivors. Help from the state arrived later, but here again, repairing the damage caused by misinformation or no information at all became all but impossible.

Guests at the inn, officials from state government, and others reported a chaotic scene with no one apparently in charge. From time to time, small groups of families were pulled aside by law enforcement officials or someone working in public information to hear the latest information, leaving other families to wonder why they could not hear what was happening and what the information might mean for their own relative whose condition was in question. A number of victim families eventually gave up hope of learning the status of their spouse, son, or daughter and returned home.

Without a formal public information center, adequately staffed, the ability to maintain a steady stream of updates, control rumors, and communicate messages to all the families at the same time was seriously hampered. Here is where advance planning for major disasters provides jurisdictions with a template and a fighting chance to appropriately manage the release of information.

The university did establish a 24-hour call center where volunteers from the university and staff from the Virginia Department of Emergency Management responded to an enormous volume of calls coming into the school.

Two of the most deeply disturbing situations were the dearth of information on the status and identification of Cho's victims and the instances where protocol for death notifications was breached. The authority and duty for this grim task falls usually to law enforcement, hospital emergency room personnel, and medial examiner offices. Victim advocates, clergy, or funeral directors ideally accompany law enforcement during a death notification. Reports are that law enforcement, where involved, conducted sensitive and caring death notifications to family members.

Virginia State Police officers, in some instances with local law enforcement, personally carried the news no one wants to hear to victims' homes around Virginia late into the night of the 16th. Officers also coordinated with law enforcement in other states who then notified the families in those jurisdictions. Not all families, however, were informed in that manner. One family learned their child was dead from a student. In another case, a local clergy member took it upon himself to inform a family member that their loved one was dead while they were on an elevator at the Inn. The spouse of a murdered faculty member saw members of the press descend on her home before his death had been confirmed.

The victims were known to faculty and friends across campus. As a result, information circulated quickly through an informal network, which allowed a few family members, who lived in the immediate area and who arrived quickly at the inn, to connect with those who were helping to locate the missing. Families who lived out of the area had to rely on the telephone to obtain information. Lines were busy and connections were clogged. They were referred from one number to another as they tried to track down information that would confirm or deny their worst fears.

Until Friday, April 20, families reported that they had to think of what questions to ask and then try to locate the right person or office to answer the question. The intensity of their pain and confusion would have been diminished somewhat if they had received regular briefings with updates on the critical information sought by all who were assembled at the inn. It would have helped if there had been a point person through whom questions were channeled. The liaisons and the victim assistance team did the best they could, but for the most part they were in the dark as well.

To make room for all the individuals who needed to stay at the inn, many resource personnel like Virginia State Police and others were housed in dormitories at nearby college campuses like Radford University.

Counseling and Health Center Services – The university's Cook Counseling Center quickly led efforts to provide additional counseling resources and provide expanded psychological assistance to students and others on campus. They extended their hours of operation and focused special attention on individuals who lived at the West Ambler Johnston dormitory, surviving students, who were in Norris Hall at the time of the incident, roommates of deceased students, and classmates and faculty in the other classes where the victims were enrolled. The victims had participated in various campus organizations, so Cook Counseling reached out to them as well. Dozens of presentations on trauma, post-incident stress, and wellness were made to hundreds of faculty, staff, and student groups. The center helped make referrals to other mental health and medical support services. The center sent 50 mental health professionals to the graduation ceremonies several weeks later, recognizing that the commencement would be an exceptionally difficult time for many people. Resource information on resilience and rebounding from trauma was developed and distributed, including posting on the Internet.

Schiffert Health Center at the university sent medical personnel to the hospitals where injured victims were being treated to check on their well being and reassure them of follow-up treatment at Schiffert if needed. The medical personnel included some psychological screening questions into their conversations with the injured students so that they could monitor the student's psychological state as well.

Other University Assistance – The Services for Students with Disabilities Office began investigating classroom accommodations that might be needed for injured students and planned for possible needs among students with 317ervice317317y-cal disabilities. The Provost's Office announced Flexible options for completing the semester and for grading. The college deans, the faculty, and Student Affairs were helpful in advising students and helping them complete the semester. Academic suspensions and judicial cases were deferred.

Cranwell International Center provided complimentary international telephone cards to students who needed to contact their families abroad and assure them they were safe. Center staff called each Korean undergraduate and many Korean graduate students and, with the Asian American Student Union and Multicultural Programs and Services, assured each one of the university's concern for their safety. They especially addressed potential retaliation and requests from the press.

Residence Life asked resident advisors to speak personally with each resident on campus and make sure they were aware of counseling 317ervicees as they grappled with lost friends or room-mates. Housing and Dining Services provided complimentary on-campus meals for victims' families and friends at graduation. Several of the victims were graduate students at Virginia Tech. The graduate school helped open the multipurpose room in the Graduate Life Center as a place for graduate students to gather and receive counseling services. They also aided graduate assistants in continuing their teaching and research responsibilities.

Hokies United is a student-driven volunteer effort that responds to local, national, and international tragedies. In addition to a candlelight vigil, this group organized several well-attended activities designed to bring the campus community together.

Human Resources requested assistance from the university's employee assistance provider, which sent crisis counselors immediately. The counselors worked with faculty and staff on issues of self-care, recovery, how to communicate the tragedy to their children, and other subjects. After 4 weeks, more than 125 information sessions had been held and 800 individuals had been individually counseled.

## MEETINGS, VISITS, AND OTHER COMMUNICATIONS WITH FAMILIES AND WITH THE INJURED

President Steger, Governor Kaine, and Attorney General McDonnell visited injured students in area hospitals to reassure them of the university's and the Commonwealth's concern for their recuperation. President Steger also met with many families over the following weeks. Governor Kaine held a private meeting with families who were dealing with the death of their child, husband, or wife and another meeting with injured students and their families.

On April 19 Governor Kaine appointed the Virginia Tech Review Panel to examine the facts surrounding April 16. After appointment, panel chairman Gerald Massengill sent a letter to all families of the deceased to express condolences and offer to meet with anyone who wished a private audience with up to two members of the panel. (As noted in Chapter I, FOIA rules require that such meetings be public if more than two members participate.) The letter also offered them the opportunity to speak at one of the four public meetings that were to be scheduled in different parts of the state. Several families took advantage of a special web site that was created as a tool for collecting information and comments. Others communicated their thoughts through letters. The chairman sent a similar letter to injured students.

Over the next several weeks, a number of families communicated their desire to meet. Others preferred their privacy, which of course was respected. Panel members and staff held at least 30 meetings (in individual and group sessions) with families of the murdered victims and with injured students and their parents, and fielded more than 150 calls. The governor designated Carroll Ann Ellis as the panel's special family advocate. She spent many days initiating and returning calls to provide information and to help families regarding their individual issues and concerns. Many with whom the panel met or talked with by phone noted appreciation for the assistance and support they had received and for the work of the panel.

Several families raised concerns about poor coordination—what they saw as failings of the university, of responders, of communicators, of volunteers, of the panel and staff, and more. Some demanded financial restitution; most focused on relating what society had lost with those 32 lives, who by all measures were outstanding individuals whose achievements and character were making a difference in the world. The families asked the panel and the Commonwealth to find out what went wrong and change what needs to be changed so others might be spared this horror. That has been the overriding concern of the governor and of the panel.

Family members of homicide victims of mass fatalities tend to view their experiences and the impact of the crime from the following perspectives:

* The overwhelming event and the system response to the scale of the event. Very often, the victims become categorized as a group rather than as individuals (e.g., 9/11 and Oklahoma City victims). The particular needs of each victim can be overlooked as the public perceives them as a unit rather than as separate families. Victims are attuned to whether they received the information and care attention that they needed. Victim survivors want to know what happened, how it happened, and why their loved was killed. They look for resources that can adequately respond to their needs and answer their questions, though some answers may never be found.

* Death notifications have long-term impact on victims. Survivors typically remember the time, place, and manner in which they first learned of the death of their loved ones.

- Where is the justice? Victim survivors look to the criminal justice system to hold the murderer accountable for the crime. Cho ended his life and denied the criminal justice system and its participants the justice that comes from a conviction and eventual sentencing.

A homicide differs from other types of death because it—

- Is intentional and violent.

- Is sudden and unexpected.

- Connects the innocent victim to the murderer in a relationship that is disturbing to family members of the dead victim.

- Creates an aura of stigma that surviving family members often experience.

- Is a criminal offense and as such is associated with the criminal justice system.

- It has the problematic overlap of symptoms created by the victim survivor's inability to move through the grief process because of a preoccupation with the trauma experience cause by a homicidal death. This completed grief reaction is identified as traumatic grief.

- Is pursued by the media and is of interest to the public.

Meeting the overwhelming needs of the families of homicide victims and fulfilling those expectations to a level each one finds acceptable is extremely challenging when there is a mass murder. So many people need the same information and services simultaneously. Systems are severely tested because disasters cause the breakdown of systems and create chaos. Without a well-defined plan, navigating through the aftermath is an uphill struggle at best. Even when plans are in place, the quality and degree of response to victims of disaster are often inconsistent. A small change in the initial conditions of a sensitive system can drastically affect the outcome.

All deaths generate feelings of anger, rage and resentment. In the case of a murder, and especially when the shooter commits suicide, survivors are denied their day in court and the opportunity for the justice system to hold that person accountable. This adds insult to the terrible Injury they already are experiencing. In these cases, accurate information in real time is imperative if survivors are to develop a sense of trust in the very systems they now must count on to explain what happened, and why it happened. When for a variety of reasons that does not occur, relatives of homicide victims can experience increased trauma.

Each family has its own particular way of processing the death of a loved one, because each life taken was unique. Several grievances, however, were shared widely among the victims' families as well as questions they wanted the panel's investigation to address. Among the major concerns and questions were the following:

- What are the facts and details of the first responder and university response to the first shooting, including the decision process, timing, and wording of the first alert?

- What were the assumptions regarding the relationship between the first two victims, and why were they made?

- Did those assumptions affect the nature and timeliness of the subsequent first alert?

- What are the facts and details of the first responder and university response when the shooting at Norris Hall began?

- With so many red flags flying about Cho over a protracted period of time, how was it that he was still living in the dorm and allowed to continue as a student in good standing? Why were the dots not connected?

- Was Cho's family notified of any or all of his interactions with campus police, the legal system, and the mental hospital?

- Why was there no central point of contact or specific instructions for families of victims at The Inn at Virginia Tech?

- Why were identifications delayed when wallet identifications, photos, and other methods available would hasten the release of remains?

- Who was responsible for ensuring that the media was properly managed, and who was supposed to be the authoritative source of information?

- What is going to be done with the Hokie Fund and what about other crime compensation funds?

- What commonsense practices regarding security and well being will be in place before students return to campus?

- What changes to policy and procedures about warnings have been made at Virginia Tech?

These and many other issues all have been examined by the panel and the results presented throughout this report.

With regard to the individuals who Cho injured— physically and emotionally—their wounds may take a long time to heal if they ever can heal completely. Many of the men and women who were in the classrooms that Cho attacked and who survived, bravely helped each other to escape, called for help, and barricaded doors. Others were too severely wounded to move. These men and women in Norris Hall not only witnessed the deaths of their colleagues and professors, but on a physical and emotional level also experienced their dying. The terror of those who survived Cho's attacks in the classrooms was increased by the silence of death as the living harbored somewhere between life and death. Exposure to such an overwhelmingly stressful event quite often leads to post traumatic stress disorder (also known as critical incident stress) represented by an array of symptoms that range from mild to severe and which are not always immediately apparent.

The law enforcement officers and emergency medical providers who were the first to witness the carnage, rescue the living, and treat and transport the physically wounded were exposed to significant trauma. Their healing also is of concern.

## CEREMONIES AND MEMORIAL EVENTS

People seek ways to share their grief when tragic events occur. The university community came together in many ways, from small prayer groups to formal ceremonies and candle-light vigils. Cassell Coliseum was the site of convocation on Tuesday, April 17. President George Bush, Governor Tim Kaine, University President Charles Steger, noted author and Professor Nikki Giovanni, and leaders from four major religions spoke to a worldwide television audience and 35,000 people in attendance divided between the coliseum and Lane Stadium. Perhaps the most poignant event, however, was the student-organized candlelight vigil later that evening. One by one, thousands of candles were lit in quiet testimony of the shared mourning that veiled every corner of the campus. Stones were placed in a semicircle before the reviewing stand to honor the victims of the previous day's shooting. Mourners wrote condolences and expressed their grief on message boards that filled the area, while flowers, stuffed animals, and other remembrances were left in honor of the professors and students who died in a dorm room and in classrooms.

## VOLUNTEERS AND ONLOOKERS

Disasters draw an enormous response. At Virginia Tech, hundreds of volunteers came to offer their services; others arrived in unofficial capacities to promote a particular cause, and many drove to Virginia Tech to share the grief of their friends and colleagues. As occurs during many disasters, some special interest groups with less than altruistic intentions arrived in numbers and simply took advantage of the situation to promote their particular cause. One group wore T-shirts to give the impression they were bona fide counselors when their main goal was to proselytize. Others wanted to make a statement for or against a particular political position.

Legitimate resources can be a great asset if they can be identified and directed appropriately. An emergency plan should define where volunteers should report and spells out procedures for 321ervitration, identification, and credentialing. That way, available services can be matched to immediate needs for greater effectiveness.

## COMMUNICATIONS WITH THE MEDICAL EXAMINER'S OFFICE

With regard to identifying the victims, everything was done by the book and with careful attention to exactness as described in Chapter X. Therein, however, lay the crux of a wrenching problem for the families. From a clinical perspective, the ME's office can be credited with unimpeachable results. From a communications and sensitivity perspective, they performed poorly.

A death notification needs to be handled so that families receive accurate information about their loved one in a sensitive manner and in private with due respect. The OCME should have taken into consideration the wishes of the family and their care and safety once the news was delivered. Counseling services need to be available to families during the process of recovering the remains. The media needs to be managed with reference to families and their right to privacy, dignity, and respect. Finally, victims' families need to be given explanations for any delays in official notifications and then be provided crisis support in the wake of receiving that news.

For example, families needed to know what method was being used to identify their loved one, and when and how the personal effects would be retuned. Some families were told that identification would take 5 days and were given no explanation why. Some families did not understand why autopsies had to be performed. Some wondered about getting copies of the ME's reports and how they could obtain those. The ME's office attached this information to each death certificate, but they concur this may not have been sufficient.

## DEPARTMENT OF PUBLIC SAFETY

Many families interviewed by the panel praised Virginia Secretary of Public Safety John Marshall and the efforts of the Virginia State Police during the days following the murders. Marshall's leadership coalesced resources at the scene. The state police, with some help from campus police, mobilized to assist the medical examiner. They collected records and items from homes to help confirm the identities of the deceased and they carried official notification of death to the families. State troopers also provided security at The Inn at Virginia Tech to prevent public access to the FAC.

Finally, in the aftermath of April 16, the panel has discerned no coordinated, system-wide review of major security issues among Virginia's public universities. With the exception of the Virginia Community College System, which immediately formed an Emergency Preparedness Task Force for its 23 institutions, the responses of the state-supported colleges and universities appear to be uncoordinated.

While Governor Kaine covered a large conference on campus security August 13, to the panel's knowledge, there have been no meetings of presidents and senior administrators to discuss such issues as guns on campus, privacy laws, admissions processes, and critical incident management plans. The independent colleges and universities met collectively with members of the panel, and the community colleges have met them twice. The presidents of the senior colleges and universities declined a request to meet with members of the panel June 26, saying it was "not timely" to do so.

## KEY FINDINGS

Mass fatality events, especially where a crime is involved, present enormous challenges with regard to public information, victim assistance, and medical examiner's office operations. Time is critical in putting an effective response into motion.

Discussions with the family members of the deceased victims and the survivors and their family members revealed how critical it is to address the needs of those most closely related to victims with rapid and effective victim services and an organized family assistance center with carefully controlled information management Family members of homicide victims struggle with two distinct processes: the grief associated with the loss of a loved one and the wounding of the spirit created by the trauma. Together they impose the tremendous burden of a complicated grieving process.

Post traumatic stress is likely to have affected many dozens of individuals beginning with the men and women who were in the direct line of fire or elsewhere in Norris Hall and survived, and the first responders to the scene who dealt with the horrific scene.

While every injured victim and every family members of a deceased victim is unique, much of what they reported about the confusion and disorganization following the incident was similar in nature.

Numerous families reported frustration with poor communications and organization in the university's outreach following the tragedy, including errors and omissions made at commencement proceedings.

A coordinated system-wide response to public safety is lacking. With the exception of the Virginia community College System, which immediately formed an Emergency Preparedness Task Force for its 23 institutions, the response of the state-supported colleges and universities has been uncoordinated. To the panel's knowledge, there have been no meetings of presidents and senior administrators to discuss such issues as guns on campus, privacy laws, admissions processes, and critical incident management plans. The independent colleges and universities met collectively with members of the panel, and the community colleges have met with panel members two times. The presidents of the senior colleges and universities declined a request to meet with members of the panel June 26, saying it was "not timely" to do so.

## RECOMMENDATIONS

The director of Criminal Injuries Compensation Fund and the chief of the Victim Services Section (Department of Criminal Justice) conducted internal after-action reviews and prepared recommendations for the future based on the lessons that were learned. The recommendations with which the panel concurred are incorporated into the following recommendations.

XI-1 Emergency management plans should include a section on victim services that addresses the significant impact of homicide and other disaster-caused deaths on survivors and the role of victim service providers in the overall plan. Victim service professionals should be included in the planning, training, and execution of crisis response plans. Better guidelines need to be developed for federal and state response and support to local governments during mass fatality events.

XI-2 Universities and colleges should ensure that they have adequate plans to stand up a joint information center with a public information officer and adequate staff during major incidents on campus. The outside resources that are available (including those from the state) and the means for obtaining their assistance quickly should be listed in the plan. Management of the media and of self-directed volunteers should be included.

XI-3 When a family assistance center is created after a criminal mass casualty event, victim advocates should be called immediately to assist the victims and their families. Ideally, a trained victim service provider should be assigned to serve as a liaison to each victim or victim's family as soon as 322ervice322al. The victim service should help victims navigate the agencies at the FAC.

XI-4 Regularly scheduled briefings should be provided to victims' families as to the status of the investigation, the identification process, and the procedures for retrieving the deceased. Local or state victim advocates should be present with the families or on behalf of out-of-state families who are not present so that those families are provided the same up-to-date information.

XI-5 Because of the extensive physical and emotional impact of this incident, both short and long-term counseling should be made available to first responders, students, staff, faculty members, university leaders, and the staff of The Inn at Virginia Tech. Federal funding is available from the Office for Victims of Crime for this purpose.

XI-6 Training in crisis management is needed at universities and colleges. Such training should involve university and area-wide disaster response agencies training together under a unified command structure.

XI-7 Law enforcement agencies should ensure that they have a victim services section or identified individual trained and skilled to respond directly and immediately to the needs of victims of crime from within the department. Victims of crime are best served when they receive immediate support for their needs. Law enforcement and victim 323ervicees form a strong support system for provision of direct and early support.

XI-8 It is important that the state's Victims Services Section work to ensure that the injured victims are linked with local victim assistance professionals for ongoing help related to their possible needs.

XI-9 Since all crime is local, the response to emergencies caused by crime should start with a local plan that is linked to the wider community. Universities and colleges should work with their local government partners to improve plans for mutual aid in all areas of crisis response, including that of victim services.

XI-10 Universities and colleges should create a victim assistance capability either in-house or through linkages to county-based professional victim assistance providers for victims of all crime categories. A victim assistance office or designated campus victim advocate will ensure that victims of crime are made aware of their rights as victims and have access to services.

XI-11 In order to advance public safety and meet public needs, Virginia's colleges and universities need to work together as a coordinated system of state-supported institutions.

**ADDITIONS AND CORRECTIONS**

University-appointed Liaisons: p. 136, Correction – Each liaison assigned by Virginia Tech had one or more families to assist, not two or more.

# Appendix B.

## INDIVIDUALS INTERVIEWED BY RESEARCH PANEL

(Revised, with corrections to some names and titles.)

The Virginia Tech Review Panel conducted more than 200 interviews. The interviewees included family members of victims; injured victims; students; and individuals from universities, law enforcement, hospitals, mental health organizations, courts, and schools. During the course of the review, the interviews were conducted in person, through public meetings, by phone, and through group meetings. A number of people were interviewed multiple times.

The panel wishes to express its appreciation to everyone who graciously provided their time and comments to this undertaking.

In 2009 several changes were made to this list to correct titles and spellings of some names., and to reflect preferences for how some are listed.

| Virginia Tech | |
|---|---|
| Carl Bean | English Department Faculty |
| Cathy Griffin Betzel | Cook Counseling Center |
| Erv Blythe | Vice President for Information Technology |
| Tom Brown | Dean of Students |
| Sherry K. Lynch Conrad | Cook Counseling Center |
| Fred D'Aguilar | English Department Faculty |
| Ed Falco | English Department Faculty |
| Christopher Flynn, PhD. | Director, Cook Counseling Center |
| David R. Ford | Vice Provost for Academic Affairs |
| Nikki Giovanni | English Department Faculty |
| Kay Heidbreder | University Counsel |
| Bob Hicok | English Department Faculty |
| Zenobia Lawrence Hikes | Vice President for Student Affairs |
| Lawrence G. Hincker | Associate Vice President for University Relations |
| Maggie Holmes | Office Manager, West Ambler Johnston Hall |
| Jim Hyatt | Vice President and Chief Operating Officer |
| Frances Keene | Director, Judicial Affairs |
| Gail Kirby | Associate Vice President for Student Affairs |
| Judy Lilly | Associate Vice President |
| Heidi McCoy | Director of Administrative Operations, News and External Relations |
| Jim McCoy | Capital Design and Construction |
| Lenwood McCoy | Liaison of University President to Panel |
| Jennifer Mooney | Coordinator Undergraduate Counseling |
| Jerome Niles | Dean, College of Liberal Arts and Human Sciences |
| Lisa Norris | English Department Faculty |
| Lynn Nystrom | Director, News and External Relations, College of Engineering (faculty in Norris Hall) |
| Ishwar Puri | Chairman, Engineering Mechanics Dept. (faculty in Norris Hall) |
| Kerry J. Redican | President, Faculty Senate |
| Lucinda Roy | Past Chair, English Department |
| Carolyn Rude | Chair, English Department |
| Joe Schetz | Aerospace and Ocean Engineering Faculty |
| Maisha Marie Smith | Cook Counseling Center |
| Ed Spencer | Associate Vice President for Student Affairs |

| Charles Steger | President |
|---|---|
| *Other Universities and Colleges* | |
| Richard Alvarez | Chief Financial Officer, Hollins University |
| Grant Azdell | College Chaplain, Lynchburg College |
| Mary Ann Bergeron | Virginia Community Services Board |
| Walter Bortz | President, Hampden-Sydney College |
| William Brady, MD | University of Virginia, Department of Emergency Medicine |
| William Thomas Burnett, MD | Medical Director of the Virginia State Police Div 6 SWAT Team |
| Valerie J. Cushman | Athletic Director, Randolph College |
| Susan Davis | University of Virginia, Special Advisor/Liaison to the General Counsel, Office of the Vice President for Student Affairs |
| Chris Domes | Chief Admissions Officer, Marymount University |
| Roy Ferguson | Executive Assistant to the President, Bridgewater College |
| Pamela Fox | President, Mary Baldwin College |
| Ken Garren | President, Lynchburg College |
| Nancy Gray | President, Hollins University |
| Robert B. Lambeth | President, Council of Independent Colleges in Virginia |
| Robert Lindgren | President, Randolph-Macon College |
| Greg McMillan | Executive Assistant to President, Emory and Henry College |
| Katherine M. Loring | Vice President for Administration, Virginia Wesleyan College |
| Courtney Penn | Special Assistant to the President, Roanoke College |
| Herb Peterson | Vice President for Business and Finance, University of Richmond |
| Richard Pfau | President, Averett University |
| Jeff Phillips | Director of Administrative Services, Ferrum College |
| Michael Puglisi | President, Virginia Intermont College |
| Robert Reiser, MD | Department of Emergency Medicine, University of Virginia |
| James C. Renick | Senior Vice President, American Council on Education |
| Robert Satcher | President, Saint Paul's College |
| LeeAnn Shank | General Counsel, Washington and Lee University |
| Wesley Shinn | Dean, Appalachian School of Law |
| Douglas Southard | Provost, Jefferson College of Health Sciences |
| Phil Stone | President, Bridgewater College |
| Loren Swartzendruber | President, Eastern Mennonite University |
| Melvin C. Terrell | Vice President of Student Affairs, Northeastern Illinois University |
| Madelyn Wessel | Special Advisor/Liasion to the General Counsel |

| | and Chair, Psychological Assessment Board, University of Virginia |
|---|---|
| William Woods, MD | Department of Emergency Medicine, University of Virginia |
| Andrea Zuschin | Dean of Student Affairs, Ferrum College |
| *National Higher Education Associations* | |
| Robert M. Berdahl | President, Association of American Universities |
| George R. Boggs | President and CEO, American Association of Community Colleges |
| Susan Chilcott | Vice President for Communications, American Association of State Colleges and Universities |
| Charles L. Currie | President, Association of Jesuit Colleges and Universities |
| Benjamin F. Quillian | Senior Vice President, American Council on Education |
| James C. Renick | Senior Vice President, American Council on Education |
| David Ward | President, American Council on Education |
| *Law Enforcement* | |
| Donald J. Ackerman | Assistant Special Agent-in-Charge, FBI Criminal Division (NY) |
| Joey Albert | Captain, Virginia Tech Police Department |
| Richard Ault | Supervisory Special Agent for the FBI, (ret.), Academy Group Inc. |
| Kenneth Baker | Supervisory Special Agent for the FBI, U.S. Secret Service (ret.), Academy Group Inc., Manassas, VA |
| Ed Bracht | Director of Security, Hofstra University |
| David Cardona | Special Agent-in-Charge, FBI Criminal Division (NY) |
| Rick Cederquist | Counter-Terrorism Coordinator, Union County (NJ) Sheriff's Office |
| Don Challis | Chief, College of William and Mary Police Department |
| Kim Crannis | Chief, Blacksburg Police Department |
| Lenny Depaul | U.S. Marshal's Service (NY/NJ), Fugitive Task Force |
| Robert C. Dillard | Chief, University of Richmond Police Department and President, Virginia Association of Chiefs of Police |
| Jonathan Duecker | Assistant Commissioner, New York Police Department |
| Chuck Eaton | Special Agent, Salem, VA, Virginia State Police |
| Samuel Feemster | Supervisory Special Agent for the FBI, Behavioral Science Unit |
| Martin D. Ficke | SES Resources International/ Special Agent-in-Charge (ret.) Immigration and Customs Enforcement (NY) |
| W. Steve Flaherty | Superintendent, Virginia State Police |

| | |
|---|---|
| Wendell Flinchum | Chief, Virginia Tech Police Department |
| Kevin Foust | Supervisory Special Agent for the FBI, Roanoke, VA |
| Vincent Giardani | New York Police Department Counter-Terrorism Division |
| Michael Gibson | U. Va Chief of Police |
| Christopher Giovino | SES Resources/Dempsey Myers Co. |
| Ray Harp | SWAT Team Commander and Homicide Detective, Arlington County (VA) Police Department (ret.) |
| Charles Kammerdener | New York Police Department, Special Operations Division |
| Robert Kemmler | Lt. Col., Virginia State Police; Deputy Director, Bureau of Administration and Support Service |
| Kenneth Lanning | Supervisory Special Agent for the FBI (ret.) |
| Jeff Lee | Active Shooter Training Program, International Tactical Officers Organization |
| Stephen Mardigian | Supervisory Special Agent for the FBI (ret.), Academy Group Inc. |
| George Marshall | New York State Police |
| Raymond Martinez | New York Police Department Counter-Terrorism Division |
| Bart McEntire | Resident Agent-in-Charge, Bureau of Alcohol, Tobacco, Firearms and Explosives, Roanoke, VA |
| William McMahon | Special Agent-in-Charge, Bureau of Alcohol, Tobacco, Firearms and Explosives, Roanoke, VA |
| Ken Middleton | High-Intensity Drug Traffic Agency (NY/NJ) |
| Terrence Modglin | Executive Director, College Crime Watch |
| Andrew Mulrain | Nassau County, New York Police Department. |
| Eliud P. Pagan | Office of Homeland Security, State of New York |
| Chauncey Parker | Director, High-Intensity Drug Traffic Agency (NY/NJ) |
| Robert Patnaude | Captain, New York State Police |
| Alfred Perales | Sergeant, University of Illinois Police Department, Chicago, IL |
| Kevin Ponder | Special Agent, FBI Criminal Division (NY) |
| David Resch | Chief, Behavioral Analysis Unit, FBI, Quantico, VA |
| Anthony Rocco | Nassau County, New York Police Department. |
| Jill Roark | Terrorism and Special Jurisdiction, Victim Assistance Coordinator, Federal Bureau of Investigation |
| Bradley D. Schnur Esq. | President, SES Resources International Inc. |
| Dennis Schnur | Chairman, Police Foundation of Nassau County Inc. |
| Andre Simons | Supervisory Special Agent for the FBI, Behavioral Analysis Unit, Quantico, VA |
| Sean Smith | Sergeant, Emergency Response Team Virginia |

|  | Tech Police Department |
|---|---|
| Philip C. Spinelli | Union County, New Jersey Office of Counter-Terrorism |
| Matt Sullivan | Detective/Lt. Suffolk County, New York Police and Hostage Negotiation Team |
| Bob Sweeney | Lieutenant, Suffolk County, New York Police Emergency Services Bureau |
| Thomas Turner | Director of Security, Roanoke College |
| Shaun F. VanSlyke | Supervisory Special Agent for the FBI, Behavioral Analysis Unit, Quantico, VA |
| Anthony Wilson | Sergeant, Emergency Response Team, Blacksburg Police Department |
| Jason Winkle | President, Active Shooter Training Program, International Tactical Officers Organization |
| Joan Yale | Nassau County, New York Police Department |
| *Families of Victims* | |
| Ms. Lynnette. Alameddine | Mother of Ross Alameddine |
| Stephanie Hofer | Wife of Christopher James Bishop |
| Mr. and Mrs. Dennis Bluhm | Parents of Brian Roy Bluhm |
| Mr. and Ms. Cloyd | Parents of Austin Michelle Cloyd |
| Mrs. Patricia Craig | Aunt to Ryan Christopher Clark |
| Ms. Betty Cuevas | Mother of Daniel Alejandro Perez |
| Mrs. Linda Granata | Wife of Kevin P. Granata |
| Mr. Gregory Gwaltney | Father of Matthew Gregory Gwaltney |
| Marian Hammaren and Chris Foote | Mother and Stepfather of Caitlin Millar Hammaren |
| Mr. John Hammaren | Father of Caitlin Millar Hammaren |
| Mr. Michael Herbstritt | Father of Jeremy Michael Herbstritt |
| Mr. and Mrs. Eric Hilscher | Parents of Emily Jane Hilscher |
| Mrs. Tracey Lane | Mother of Jarret Lee Lane |
| Mr. Jerzy Nowak | Husband of Jocelyne Couture-Nowak |
| Mr. William O'Neil | Father of Daniel Patrick O'Neil |
| Mrs. Celeste Peterson | Mother of Erin Nicole Peterson |
| Mr. and Mrs. Larry Pryde | Parents of Julia Kathleen Pryde |
| Mr. and Mrs. Peter Read | Parents of Mary Karen Read |
| Mr. and Mrs. Joseph Samaha | Parents of Reema Joseph Samaha |
| Mrs. Holly Adams-Sherman | Mother of Leslie Geraldine Sherman |
| Mr. Girish Suratkal | Brother of Minal Hiralal Panchal |
| Mr. and Mrs. Paul Turner | Parents of Maxine Shelly Turner |
| Ms. Liselle Vega-Coates Ortiz | Wife of Juan Ramon Ortiz |
| Mr. and Mrs. White | Parents of Nicole Regina White |
| *Cho Family* | |
| Mr. and Mrs. Cho | Parents of Seung Hui Cho |
| Sun Cho | Sister of Seung Hui Cho |
| Wade Smith | Attorney at Law, Tharrington Smith, Raleigh, NC; Advisor, Friend to Cho Family |
| *Injured Victims and Their Families* | |
| Alec Calhoun | Student, Virginia Tech |
| Colin Goddard | Student, Virginia Tech |

| Suzanne Grimes | Mother of Kevin Sterne |
|---|---|
| Emily Haas | Student, Virginia Tech |
| Mrs. Lori Haas | Mother of Emily Haas |
| Jeremy Kirkendall | Virginia National Guard |
| Mrs. Miller | Mother of Heidi Miller |
| Erin Sheehan | Student, Virginia Tech |
| *Rescue Squads* | |
| Allan Belcher | Carilion Patient Transportation Services |
| Sidney Bingley | Blacksburg Volunteer Rescue Squad |
| William W. Booker IV | Virginia Tech Rescue Squad |
| Charles Coffelt | Carilion Patient Transportation Services |
| Paul Davenport | Carilion Patient Transportation Services |
| Jeremy Davis | Virginia Tech Rescue Squad |
| Jason Dominiczak | Virginia Tech Rescue Squad |
| Kevin Hamm | Christiansburg Rescue Squad |
| Matthew Johnson | Captain, Virginia Tech Rescue Squad |
| Tom Lovejoy | Blacksburg Volunteer Rescue Squad |
| Alisa Nussman | Virginia Tech Rescue Squad |
| John O'Shea | Blacksburg Volunteer Rescue Squad |
| Neil Turner | Montgomery County EMS Coordinator |
| Colin Whitmore | Virginia Tech Rescue Squad |
| *Hospitals* | |
| Carole Agee | Legal Counsel, Carilion Hospital |
| Deborah Akers | Lewis-Gale Medical Center |
| Pat Campbell | Director of Nursing, New River Valley Medical Center |
| Candice Carroll | Chief Nursing Officer, Lewis–Gale Medical Center |
| Loressa Cole | Montgomery Regional Hospital |
| Susan Davis | Special Advisor/, Liaison to the General Counsel, Office of the Vice President for Student Affairs |
| Michael Donato, MD | Carilion Roanoke Memorial Hospital Emergency Room |
| Robert Dowling, MD | Lewis–Gale Medical Center |
| Patrick Earnest | Carilion New River Valley Medical Center |
| Ted Georges, MD | Carilion New River Valley Medical Center |
| Carol Gilbert, MD | EMS Regional Medical Director |
| Mike Hill | Director, Emergency Department, Montgomery Regional Hospital |
| Scott Hill | Chief Executive Officer, Montgomery Regional Hospital |
| Anne Hutton | Manager, CONNECT, Carilion Hospital |
| Judith M. Kirkendall | Administrator, Criminal History Records, Richmond, VA |
| David Linkous | Director, Staff Development and Emergency Management, Montgomery Regional Hospital |
| Rick McGraw | Carilion Roanoke Memorial Hospital Emergency Room |

| William Modzeleski | Assistant Deputy Secretary, U.S. Department of Education |
| John O'Shea | Lieutenant and Cardiac Technician, Blacksburg Volunteer Rescue Squad |
| Fred Rawlins, DO | Carilion New River Valley Medical Center |
| Mike Turner | Clinical Support Representative, Carilion St. Albans |
| Holly Wheeling, MD | Montgomery Regional Hospital |
| *Federal, State, and Local Agencies* | |
| Marcella Fierro, MD | Chief Medical Examiner, VA |
| Robert Foresman | Director of Emergency Management, Rockbridge County, VA |
| Mandie Patterson | Chief Victim Service Section, Department of Criminal Justice Services, VA |
| Patricia Sneed | Emergency Planning Manager, Virginia Department of Social Services |
| Jessica Stallard | Assistant Director, Victim Services, Montgomery County, Virginia |
| Karen Thomas | Virginia Department of Criminal Justice Services |
| Mary Ware | Director, Criminal Injuries Compensation Fund |
| *Mental Health Professionals* | |
| Harvey Barker, MD | Director of Crisis and Intervention, New River Community Service Board |
| Richard Bonnie | Director, Institute of Law, Psychiatry and Public Policy, University of Virginia |
| Gail Burruss | Director, Adult Clinical Services and Crisis Intervention, Blue Ridge Behavioral Healthcare |
| Pam Kestner Chappalear | Executive Director, Council of Community Services |
| Lin Chenault | Executive Director, New River Community Service Board |
| Katuko T. Coelho | Center for Multicultural Human Services |
| Roy Crouse | Independent Evaluator for Commitment |
| Joan M. Ridick Depue | Clinical Psychologist, Pastoral Counseling, Culpeper, VA |
| Russell Federman | Director, Counseling and Psychological Services, University of Virginia |
| Kathy Godbey | New River Community Service Board, pre-screener for commitment |
| James Griffith, MD | Psychiatrist, Center for Multicultural Human Services |
| Kathy Highfield | Blue Ridge Behavioral Healthcare |
| Dennis Hunt | Executive Director, Center for Multicultural Human Services |
| J. Ida | Clinical Psychologist and Executive Director, National Asian American and Pacific Islander Mental Health Association |
| Jerald Kay, MD | Chair, College Mental Health Committee for the |

| | |
|---|---|
| | American Psychiatric Association, Chair of the Department. Of Psychiatry, Wright State School of Medicine |
| Wun Jung Kim, MD | Psychiatrist and Professor, University of Pittsburgh |
| Jeanne Kincaid | ADA/OCR, Attorney with Drummond Woodson |
| Francis Lu, MD | Chair, APA Council on Minority Mental Health and Health Disparities, Professor of Clinical Psychiatry, UCSF |
| James Madero | Clinical Psychologist, Former NIMH Staff/School Violence Specialist, California School of Professional Psychologists at Alliant International University |
| Kent McDaniel, MD | Consultant Psychiatrist to the Office of the Inspector General, VA |
| Jasdeep Migliani, MD | Staff Psychiatrist, St Albans Medical Center, Carilion Health System |
| Frank Ochberg, MD | Former Director of Michigan Department of Mental Health |
| Carrie Owens | Director of Victim Services, Montgomery County, VA |
| Annelle Primm, MD | Director, Division of National and Minority Affairs, American Psychiatric Association |
| Andres Pumariega, MD | Chair of the Diversity Committee for the American Psychiatric Association, Chair Department of Psychiatry, Reading Hospital, PA |
| James S. Reinhard | Commissioner, Virginia Department of Mental Health, Mental Retardation and Substance Abuse Services |
| Gregory B. Saathoff, MD | Executive Director, Critical Incident Analysis Group, University of Virginia |
| Les Saltzberg | Executive Director, New River Community Service Board |
| Jim Sikkema | Executive Director, Blue Ridge Behavioral Healthcare |
| Bruce Smoller, MD | President-elect, Medical Association of Maryland; HPC |
| James W. Stewart III | Inspector General, Virginia Department of Mental Health, Mental Retardation and Substance Abuse Services |
| Terry Teel | Attorney for Commitment |
| Clavitis Washington-Brown | Blue Ridge Behavioral Healthcare |
| Richard West | Psychologist, Research on Preventing Campus Mental Health-Related Incidents |
| *Courts/Hearing Officials* | |
| Paul Barnett | Special Justice |
| Donald J. Farber | Attorney at Law, San Rafael, CA |
| Lorin Costanzo | Special Justice, Virginia |

| John Molumphy | Special Justice, Virginia |
|---|---|
| Joseph Graham Painter | Attorney, Former Special Justice |
| *High School Staff* | |
| Dede Bailer | Director, Psychology and Preventative Services, Fairfax County Public Schools |
| Rita Easley | School Guidance Counselor, Westfield High School |
| Frances Ivey | Former Assistant Principal, Westfield High School |
| *Students at Virginia Tech* | |
| Joseph Aust | Cho Roommate |
| Chandler Douglas | Resident Advisor |
| John Eide | Cho Roommate |
| Andy Koch | Cho Suitemate |
| Austin Morton | Cho Resident Advisor |
| Melissa Trotman | Resident Advisor |
| *Business* | |
| Kathleen Schmid Koltko-Rivera | President, Professional Services Group, Winter Park, FL |
| Mark E. Koltko-Rivera | Executive Vice President, Professional Services Group, Winter Park, FL |
| *Other* | |
| Steve Capus | President, NBC News |
| Steven Erickson | Father of Stalking Victim |
| Mr. Gibson | Father of Stalking Victim |
| David McCormick | Vice President, NBC News |
| Luke Van Heul | Former Member, Delta Force |

# PLEASE DO NOT READ THE FOLOWING CRITIQUES OF THE GOVERNOR'S REVIEW PANEL REPORT ADDENDUM UNTIL YOU HAVE WRITTEN YOUR ANALYSIS

Below is the list of timeline events given for your consideration in writing your analysis, along with a brief comment on the significance of each. These are followed by an example analysis of the Addendum. It is not necessary for you to have written your analysis in exactly the same way, but as you compare the writings, ask yourself if you feel you have covered the most important points and reflect on the significance of any differences between your own analysis and the example.

1. **October 10, 2005**: Professor Giovanni forwards a request and copy of Cho's violent writings to Virginia Tech's student affairs vice president, who sends it to the school's top discipline official. *This should have been included in the timeline because it gives specific details dealing with the school's awareness of Cho's potential violent behavior.* (add to page 23 of timeline)

2. **October 19, 2005**: The Student Affairs Dean asks English department chair Lucinda Roy to warn Cho that he could face disciplinary action. She offers to tutor him if he leaves Giovanni's class. *This should have been included because it is an early warning of the seriousness of Cho's aberrant behavior.* (add to page 23 of timeline)

3. **November 2, 2005**: Cho's roommates and dorm residents say they think Cho sets fires in dorm lounge and report it to the police. *More evidence of Cho's troubled, violent personality.* (add to page 23 of timeline)

4. **November 27, 2005**: A female student (allegedly harassed by Cho) wants to testify at a disciplinary hearing for Cho, but no hearing is ever held. *More evidence of Cho's deviant behavior and at least one student's willingness to testify to that fact; it needs to be added to the timeline entry for that date.* (add to page 23 of timeline)

5. **December 6, 2005**: Resident assistant reports that Cho has knives in his room and mentions that the harassment victim is scared. Resident assistant expresses concern that no one has talked to Cho. *The evidence continues to grow that Cho was unstable and a threat to others.* (add to page 24 of timeline)

6. **April 16, 2007**: At 0730, a housekeeper in Burruss Hall told the Associate Vice President for Student Affairs and member of the Policy Group, Dr. Ed Spencer, that a Residential Advisor in West Ambler Johnston Hall was murdered. She had received a phone call from a friend who is a housekeeper in that residence hall. *This fact needs to be added because it is evidence of how early members of the university's Policy Group were being notified of the initial double homicide.* (add to page 27 of the timeline)

7. **April 16, 2007**: 0816-0924: Students Henry Lee and Rachel Hill are cleared to leave West Ambler Johnston Hall for their 0905 class. Both were shot and killed in that class in Norris Hall. *The timeline simply says students were allowed to leave, but makes no mention of the fact that these two were killed. The school's failure to lockdown West Ambler Johnston Hall and the deaths of Lee and Hill are critical to judging the school's decision not to lockdown—a lockdown that would have saved those two lives.* (add to page 28 of the timeline)

8. **April 16, 2007**: 0825: The police cancel bank deposit pickups. *The timeline should include this fact as an indication of the level of concern the police had for security on campus.* (add to page 28 of the timeline)

9. **April 16, 2007**: 0840: A Virginia Tech Policy Group member notifies the governor's office of the two murders in West Ambler Johnston Hall. *The time of this notification needs to be added to the timeline to give the reader a sense of the Policy Group's order of priorities of notification.* (add to page 28 of the timeline)

10. **April 16, 2007**: 0845, a Virginia Tech official reminds a Richmond colleague, "Just try to make sure it doesn't get out." *This time and fact needs to be added to the timeline as an indicator of the extent to which the school was concerned about bad publicity.* (add to page 28 of the timeline)

11. **April 16, 2007**: 0850: The Virginia Tech Policy Group begins composing a notice to the university about the two murders at West Ambler Johnston one hour and thirty-five minutes earlier at 0715. Larry Hinkler, Associate Vice President for University Relations, is unable to send the message before classes changed at 0905 due to technical difficulties with the wireless LAN connection. The Policy Group decided to wait for more information and hold the notification until the next class change at 0955. *This fact needs to be added to the timeline as an indicator of the time that lapsed between the double homicide and the initial stages of campus notification.* (add to page 28 of timeline)

12. **April 16, 2007**: At 0924 a Virginia Tech Police Department captain arrives at the Policy Group meeting to act as liaison and provide updates. He reported one gunman is at large possibly on foot (on campus). *The arrival of the police captain at the Policy Group meeting over two hours after the murders of Emily Hilscher and Ryan Christopher Clark should be added to the timeline as an indication of the failure of authorities to move promptly and swiftly when it was clear from the outset that a murderer was on the loose and probably on campus.* (add to page 29 of the timeline)

# CRITIQUE OF THE FINAL REPORT THE ADDENDUM

The long-awaited revision to Governor Kaine's Review Panel Report on the mass murders at Virginia Tech makes only minor progress toward analyzing the nation's worst school shooting, does not totally correct a badly flawed timeline, and never addresses the questions of accountability and responsibility. The revision is inadequate and only confirms the impression the report writers' goal was not to analyze, not to make clear and concise judgments, and not to make hard-hitting conclusions and recommendations needed to help prevent future school shootings. The report writers' goal appears to be to cover-up and to obfuscate.

The number of revisions, clarifications, and additions to the timeline are, by my count, around twenty. That number alone is an indictment of the initial report. Crime Analysis 101 stresses the importance of the timeline in order to unravel and solve any crime. Yet, the timeline and almost all text corrections are thanks to the hard work of the victims' families. And, the state of Virginia rewards TriData for flawed work by giving them another $75,000 to correct the report—based on the work of others.

The Addendum never really addresses the question of responsibility and accountability, TriData makes just enough revisions to give them the fig leaf of being able to say, "We listened to the families; we made revisions." Okay, let's lift up the fig leaf and take a look at one of the revisions. The timeline entry on page 28 for 8:16-9:24 now reads:

> "Police continue canvassing WAJ (West Ambler Johnston Hall) for possible witnesses. VTPD, BPD, and the VSP continue processing Hilscher's room (4040) crime scene and gathering evidence. Investigators secure identification of the victims. Police allow students in WAJ to leave; some go to 9:00 a.m. classes in Norris Hall."

TriData did not put in the Addendum the fact that two of the students allowed to leave, WAJ, Rachael Elizabeth Hill and Henry J. Lee, were killed at Norris Hall. It would appear that the report writers apparently wanted to gloss over Virginia Tech's failure in handling the crisis of April 16, 2007. The failure of the school to issue a warning and lock-down cost these two students their lives—there can be no doubt of that fact. A lock-down would have meant Hill and Lee would not have been able to leave a police-secured environment—they would be alive today. Furthermore, there is nearly a 100% chance a campus-wide lock-down would have saved all the lives at Norris Hall.

Now, let's take a look at one of the criticisms about the text of the report. In response to a question about the relevancy of the testimony by Dr. Jerald Kay on the frequency of shootings on campus—specifically whether his words were an attempt to downplay the seriousness of the Virginia Tech shootings in light of other dangers to students such as drunk driving; here is TriData's response:

"The Review Panel invited Dr. Kay's presentation for two reasons: First to consider the risk from guns as part of the larger picture of campus emergency planning. The Review Panel wanted colleges and universities to consider, as part of emergency planning, the whole range of threats and their likelihood, not just guns. Second, this testimony was of interest as part of the discussion of whether guns should be allowed to be carried on campuses. The frequency and nature of shootings on campus was very relevant to the deliberations of the Review Panel in making recommendations regarding these issues. It also was relevant in understanding the risk of a further shooting faced by the Policy Group after the double homicide."

Here is the quote about Dr. Kay in the report:

"The panel heard a presentation from Dr. Jerald Kay, the chair of the committee on college mental health of the American Psychiatric Association about the large percentage of college students who binge drink each year (about 44 percent), and the surprisingly large percentage of students who claim they thought about suicide (10 percent). College years are full of academic and social stress. The probability of dying from a shooting on campus is smaller than the probability of dying from auto accidents, falls, or alcohol and drug overdoses."

1.  Nowhere does the report state that Dr. Kay says anything about guns as part of emergency planning.
2.  Where does the report tie Dr. Kay to the discussion of guns on campus?
3.  If the frequency and nature of shootings on campus was relevant to the Review Panel deliberations, why is Dr. Kay not quoted on the subject?
4.  What insight did Dr. Kay provide on understanding the risk of a further shooting faced by the Policy Group after the double homicide?

Is TriData trying to tell us binge drinking played a role in the killings at Virginia Tech? As for the sentence: "The probability of dying from a shooting on a campus is smaller than the probability of dying from auto accidents, falls, or alcohol and drug overdose." What possible reason could there be for this sentence in the report than to downplay the significance of gun violence on campuses?

TriData's response is that they wanted colleges and universities to examine the whole range of threats. Fine, but that was not the Panel's mandate, nor was it the duty to emphasize those threats at the expense of analyzing the Virginia Tech shootings. There is nothing in the Panel's mission statement telling them to go into a broader range of campus threats. Here is the Review Panel's Mission Statement:

"The Panel's mission is to provide an independent, thorough, and objective incident review of this tragic event, including a review of educational laws, policies, and institutions, the public safety and health care procedures and responses and the mental health delivery system. With respect to these areasof review, the Panel should focus on what went right, what went wrong, what practices should be considered best practices, and what practices are in need of improvement. This review should include examination of information contained in academic, health and court records and by information obtained through interviews with knowledgeable individuals. Once that factual narrative is in place and questions have been answered, the Panel should offer recommendations for improvement in light of those facts and circumstances."

The Addendum is poor research and writing at the taxpayers' expense. The Addendum is a conundrum—an unanswerable puzzle within a puzzle. The Review Panel Report and the Addendum are riddled with inaccuracies.

The *Daily Press* (Hampton/Newport News, Virginia) captured the failure of the TriData-written report beautifully when it wrote on December 10, 2009, "What could and should have been a last, official effort to get to the truth about the Virginia Tech shootings was used, instead, to tidy up the archives."

"The choice was made by Governor Tim Kaine. When evidence came to light that the official inquiry failed to uncover and consider some significant information, he had options. He could ignore it, but victims' families were pushing hard and he has tried to be responsive to them. He could reconvene the panel to reconsider its assessment of what happened that awful morning in April, 2007, when a deranged student killed 33 people and wounded others. Or he could turn over to a contractor the job of updating the report's facts without changing the conclusions or recommendations or judgments."

"He sent it to the rewrite man. What a shame."

"... The panel failed to get the timeline of that morning right. That's critical..."

"... Only relentless digging by reporters and families revealed that a version of the timeline accepted by the panel wasn't accurate. ... (the changes) shed a different light on their (the school administration's) failure to warn the campus, which allowed students and faculty to gather in Norris Hall, where Cho gunned down so many of them, then himself."

"... with failures of this magnitude there's another piece of clean-up: accountability. No one has been publicly reprimanded, no consequences assigned."

The *Daily Press* is absolutely right. As long as no consequences are assigned, as long as there are no public reprimands, the job remains unfinished. As a consequence, our schools are not as safe as they need to be. It is nothing short of a tragedy that an opportunity has been lost to make a difference, to find some sort of meaning in a horrific tragedy. As long as people are not held responsible for their actions or inactions, nothing meaningful will be done to protect our campuses.

# ANNEX III

# A Critique of the Original Governor's Review Panel Report on the Virginia Tech Shooting

The following pages contain a critique of the first version of the Governor's Review Panel Report. The critique was done at the request of several of the Virginia Tech victims' families.

# CRITIQUE OF THE INITIAL REVIEW PANEL REPORT

## GENERAL COMMENTS

The Governor's Review Panel Report is badly damaged because of the serious flaws in the analysis and writing of the report. While corrections can be made, the report will probably go down in history as a poorly researched, poorly analyzed, and poorly written document. For example, the Review Panel Report does not address problems central to the causes behind the shooting and shies away from making the tough recommendations needed to get at the heart of the problem and prevent future shootings on school grounds. The reader is left with the impression that the incentive to produce a candid and objective report was low.

Parts of the report can be salvaged, but it must be understood that many of the report's flaws stem from decisions made before a word of it was written. In the first place, the idea of a state-sponsored panel investigating a state institution is a conflict of interest. That conflict of interest probably explains why the report does not hold anyone accountable for anything. Furthermore, from the outset, the credibility of the Review Panel and their report was undermined because of the failure of the Review Panel to have subpoena power and the inability of the panel to have people interviewed under oath. The inaccurate timeline and Cho's missing medical records (which have now turned up) do serious damage to the document's credibility. ***If the original report is based on an inaccurate timeline, then the analytical narrative flowing from that timeline is, by definition, flawed and requires a major rewrite.***

The systemic flaws in the panel itself play out in the final report. There appear to be eight major failings:

<u>First</u>, the report did not address issues such as identifying mistakes in judgment and the individuals who should be held accountable for their actions or inactions. Indeed, the report is an exercise in avoiding accountability and legal liability.

<u>Second</u>, the panel itself, which investigated the tragedy and wrote the report, is a prime example of conflict of interest. A state panel examining the behavior of state employees and a state organization cannot be completely objective. To even suggest that the panel was completely objective is sheer folly—particularly when the state was so well represented and not one member of the victims' families was a panel member. Instead, there is the state-selected family representative and spokesperson on the panel—again, a conflict of interest that is not conducive to impartiality.

<u>Third</u>, several key players did not fully cooperate with the review panel. This lack of cooperation is both disheartening and puzzling. Specifically, the Virginia State Police, the ATF, and the gun dealers: "declined to provide the panel with copies of the applications" Seung-Hui Cho completed when he bought the weapons that would eventually kill over thirty innocent people. The report notes that "the Virginia State Police…did describe the contents of Chou's gun purchase applications to members of the panel and its staff." The state police's willingness to "describe" is a limp attempt to explain their failure to fully cooperate and provide the panel with documents related to the shootings is a major flaw in the report—it is inexcusable.

<u>Fourth</u>, the report repeatedly falls back on passive voice sentences that obscure who did what and when; who knew what and when; and who acted and didn't act. The authors of the report carefully chose their words in order not to identify any individual by name.

<u>Fifth</u>, the panel was impeded in its work by the FOIA rules that did not allow more than two members to meet together or speak by phone without it being considered a public meeting. This is bureaucracy at its worst. The report needs to be more specific in detailing the problems this bureaucratic obstacle presented.

<u>Sixth</u>, the report sugar-coats glaring errors and problems: for example, on page 10, the report talks about its findings and recommendations being of two different kinds: "What was done well," and "what could have been done better." The report should talk about people in positions of authority *failing* to do their jobs—"*could have been done better*" is backing away from holding individuals and institutions accountable for their actions.

<u>Seventh</u>, the report appears to make excuses for the decision of the university's Policy Group not to put out a campus-wide alert following the discovery of the first two bodies. But the previous August, the university had put out an alert that a convict named William Morva had escaped from a nearby prison and killed a law enforcement officer and a guard. The alert indicated the murderer was on the loose and could be on campus. The university set its own standard in August of 2006 by issuing that alert, and then violated that standard in April 2007. The report skirts this critical point.

<u>Eighth</u>, the panel should not have been chaired by a former head of the state police. This is another example of a conflict of interest. The result appears to have been a downplaying of the mistakes made by the police on the day of the shooting—and probably mistakes they made in not placing Cho's name on the list of those people prohibited from buying guns.

In connection with systemic flaw eight, the report says that the police *may* have made an error in reaching the premature conclusion that their initial lead (following the discovery of the first two shooting victims) was a good one and that the person of interest was probably not on campus. *May* have made an error? They did *make a very serious error* by jumping to a premature conclusion and giving the wrong impression to school officials. This error should not be glossed over.

In sum, the report fails to do its job in critical areas; it is bland, and raises no real red flags. The report is the equivalent of reading a book with no thesis. The recommendations indicate this or that "should" be done. The "shoulds" relate to such things as analyzing, training, complying with this or that act, police being members of panels, and so on and so forth. Yes, these "shoulds" need to be done. But, nowhere does the report say that individuals must be held accountable for their actions or inactions; that organizations and individuals must be held accountable when they break their own standards and it results in over thirty lives being lost.

The report is impressive in size and unimpressive in content. It falls short of what it needed to do: make clear that everyone in a position of responsibility must be held to the highest standards of safety, and that failure to meet those standards will result in stiff penalties. Instead, the reader is left wandering from page to page in an effort to tie ends together and make his or her own conclusions.

## STRUCTURAL PROBLEMS

There are structural flaws in the report centering on the **Key Findings and Recommendations**. Most people who look at a report this size will only read those two parts. Professional writers are taught to put one or both of these sections at the beginning of the chapters or the report itself because it is a well-known principle among professional writers that the Key Findings and Recommendations are the meat. By placing them at the end, and by watering them down, the writers are weakening the significance of the Key Findings and Recommendations. In other words, the report is written more as an on-going investigative report, rather than an analysis of a major crime. TriData Corporation employs professional writers who know this. Who would benefit from non-specific conclusions? The state of Virginia. Who hired TriData? The state of Virginia.

If you go through and just read the Findings and Recommendations you more often than not get broad, watered-down generalizations and lack of specificity. The net result is the Findings and Recommendations do not accurately reflect the content of the report.

## SPECIFICS

Here are sections that typify errors found throughout the report. Let's take a look at some specific examples: A major concern is the apparent selection of words in the report to downplay failings and mistakes. For example, the topic sentence on page 18 in the paragraph in the middle of the page needs to be replaced:

| Original Sentence | Reasons for Replacing | Replacement Sentence |
|---|---|---|
| "Shootings at universities are rare events, an average of sixteen a year across 4,000 institutions." | Reason: To correct the report's downplaying of the seriousness of the threat and to be factually correct. Site: *The Journal of College and University Law*, a peer-reviewed journal published by the Notre Dame Law School, Professor Helen de Haven, "The Elephant in the Ivory Tower: Rampages in Higher Education and the Case for Institutional Liability," —the citation for the article is 35 JC&UL 503, 2009. | "Shootings at universities are becoming more and more frequent and now average sixteen a year across 4,000 institutions. Even before the rampage at Virginia Tech, a growing body of legal opinion held that the nation's colleges and universities have a legal and moral responsibility to protect students, faculty and staff." |

Another example is found on page 52—here, **The Key Findings** need to be rewritten to accurately reflect the magnitude of the school's failings. These failings are documented on pages 46 through 52:

| Original Sentence | Reasons for Replacing | Replacement Sentence |
|---|---|---|
| "The lack of information sharing among academic, administrative, and public safety entities at Virginia Tech and the students who had raised concerns about Cho, contributed to the failure to see the big picture." | Reason: vague language, inaccurate reflection of the magnitude of the failings and over use of platitudes such as "big picture." | The numerous failings of Virginia Tech to respond to warning signs that Cho was a serious threat to himself and others should not, and cannot, be glossed over. Members of the school administration and campus police failed to heed the warnings and take the initiative to head-off what became the nation's worst school shooting. Overly strict, and at times incorrect, interpretations of federal and state privacy laws combined with bureaucratic ineptitude to make the shooting rampage possible |

There are also discrepancies in logic and reasoning that need to be reconciled. For example on page 43 the reader will no doubt be confused over what constitutes a threat. Left hand column, first full paragraph, third sentence through the end of the paragraph reads: "She (Dr. Giovanni) contacted the head of the English Department, Dr. Roy, about Cho and warned that if he were not removed from her class, she would resign. He was not just a difficult student, she related, he was not working at all. Dr. Giovanni was offered security, but declined saying she did not want him back in class period. She saw him once on campus after that and he just stared at the ground."

**Problem**: If a professor is threatening to resign because she feels threatened, then Frances Keene, Judicial Affairs director, needs to give a better explanation of why Cho's threatening behavior was not actionable under the abusive conduct-threats of the UPSL.

All of page 43 is confusing and is intellectual mumbo-jumbo—it may have been intentionally written that way to hide the shortcomings and failures of the school to act.

## PASSIVE-VOICE SENTENCES

The report's excessive use of passive voice sentences appears to be intentional and meant to obscure. Passive voice sentences are the preferred sentences of members of the legal profession because they allow for greater courtroom interpretation and argumentation. In an historical document such as this, passive voice sentences should not be used, unless the writer has no other choice.

Let's take a look at a couple of examples. Look at page 43 and how the passive voice is intended to hide who knew what: "However, it is known that the university did not contact the family to ascertain the veracity of home town follow-up for counseling and medication management." Known by whom? Was the individual or department responsible for this failure ever questioned?

Lucinda Roy, in her book "No Right to Remain Silent," gives an excellent example of passive voice sentences obscuring information. When referring to Vice Provost of Student Affairs David Ford's statement to the panel on May 21, 2007, she writes, "As Ford revealed in his prepared statement, the president and the Policy Group were advised by the police that a suspect was being tracked—slain student Emily Hilscher's boyfriend.

*"Information continued* **to be received** *through frequent telephone conversations with Virginia Tech police on the scene. The Policy Group* **was informed** *that the residence hall was being secured by Virginia Tech police, and students within the hall* **were notified** *and asked to remain in their rooms for their safety. We* **were further informed** *that the room containing the gunshot victims* **was immediately secured** *for evidence collection, and Virginia Tech police began questioning hall residents and identifying potential witnesses. In the preliminary stages of the investigation, it appeared to be an isolated incident, possibly domestic in nature." (Pages 81and 82 of the Review Panel Report.)*

In commenting on the above, she writes, "It's difficult to know why this last assumption was made, though there is little doubt that the term "domestic violence" has connotations which can lead people to assume that the violence has somehow been contained within the domestic sphere and is therefore less likely to be visited upon those outside it."

She then adds, "When the passive voice is used in sentence construction it is hard to pin down who the subject is. In the first sentence of the above quote, for example, we would normally say "So-and-so continued to receive information," but instead we have "Information continued to be received," which makes it hard to know who was actually receiving it. Although this description begins as what appears to be a first-person, eyewitness narrative, it seems to dissolve into an account of an event viewed at a considerable distance. The phrase "The Policy Group was informed," for example, raises the question of who did the informing. It seems by the end of the paragraph as though everyone is receiving all the information at the same time, but given how chaotic the situation must have been, this seems somewhat unlikely. Usually teachers of writing try to dissuade students from using the passive voice construction because it tends to result in accounts that lack specificity and removes a subject from his or her own action, as it does in this case." The TriData Corporation specializes in report writing—they knew exactly what they were doing. TriData may have been following instructions, or did not want to be too specific and alienate the state of Virginia, a state that might hire them again.

## EXCUSES

While you are on pages 81-82 of the report checking Roy's quote, look at the section on page 82 entitled "Decision Not To Cancel Classes or Lock Down:"

"… Most police chiefs consulted in this review believe that a lockdown was not feasible."

This statement is clearly intended to make excuses for a bad decision not to act. My question is how many police chiefs were asked, how many said the school should be locked down? In my talks with campus security representatives from colleges and universities, 100 percent said the school should have been locked down. The sentence also runs counter to the school's own past practices—the Morva case is the most noteworthy. In that case, the school didn't believe the killer was on the campus, yet it locked down.

On the next page (83) the excuses continue: "In the *Morva* incident, when the school was closed, it took over an hour and half for traffic to clear despite trying to stage the evacuation." An hour and a half is a small price to pay to save thirty lives.

## THE PARAGRAPHS ON LAW ENFORCEMENT RECORDS ARE ESPECIALLY DISTURBING

Please turn to pages 63-64 and look at: "Law enforcement agencies must disclose certain information to anyone who requests it. They must disclose basic information about felony crimes: the date, location, general description of the crime, and name of the investigating officer. Law enforcement agencies also have to release the name and address of anyone arrested and charged with any type of crime. All records about non-criminal incidents are available upon request. When they disclose non-criminal incident records, law enforcement agencies must withhold personally-identifying information such as names, addresses, and social security numbers."

. . .

"Most of the detailed information about criminal activity is contained in law enforcement investigative files. Under Virginia's Freedom of Information Act, law enforcement agencies are *allowed* to keep these records confidential. The law also gives agencies the discretion to release the records. However, law enforcement agencies across the state typically have a policy against disclosing such records."

Many actions may be legal, such as withholding vital information in the nation's worst school shooting, but to do so is morally and ethically repugnant. *The panel should have made that point.* Furthermore, the police, in order to remove any suspicion that they did not do their job in connection with Cho's purchase of weapons, should have willingly released all documents.

## CHAPTER VI: GUN PURCHASES AND CAMPUS POLICIES

This chapter (pages 71-76) is important and is a disappointment. Perhaps nowhere else in the report is it as evident as it is on these pages that the panel members did not want to address critically sensitive issues.

Page 71—"In investigating the role firearms played in the events of April 16, 2007, the panel encountered strong feelings and heated debate from the public. The panel's investigation focused on two areas: Cho's purchase of firearms and ammunition, and campus policies toward firearms. The panel recognized the deep divisions in American society regarding the ready availability of rapid fire weapons and high capacity magazines, but this issue was beyond the scope of this review." *This borders on stating the obvious; how does it help? This paragraph should be dropped.*

The chapter is filled with inconsistencies and contradictions:

Page 71—"Cho was not legally authorized to purchase his firearms, but was easily able to do so. Gun purchasers in Virginia must qualify to buy a firearm under both federal and state law. Federal law disqualified Cho from purchasing or possessing a firearm. The federal Gun Control Act, originally passed in 1968, prohibits gun purchases by anyone who has "been adjudicated as a mental defective or who has been committed to a mental institution." Federal regulations interpreting the act define "adjudicated as a mental defective" as "(a) determination by a court, board, commission, or other lawful authority that a person, as a result of...mental illness...is a danger to himself or to others." Cho was found to be a danger to himself by a special justice of the Montgomery County General District Court on December 14, 2005. *Therefore, under federal law, Cho could not purchase a firearm.*

"The legal status of Cho's gun purchase under Virginia law is less clear. Like federal law, Virginia law also prohibits persons who have been adjudicated incompetent or committed to mental institutions from purchasing firearms. However, Virginia law defines the terms differently. It defines incompetency by referring to the section of Virginia Code for declaring a person incapable of caring for himself or herself. It does not specify that a person who had been found to be a danger to self or others is 'incompetent'. Because he had not been declared unable to care for himself, it does not appear that Cho was disqualified under this provision of Virginia law." *The report should have done a better job of reconciling Cho's legal status to buy a gun. First the report says "under federal law, Cho could not have purchased firearms." Then it implies that there are exceptions under Virginia law. When you read the following, perhaps the reason for the obfuscation is clearer.*

…

Page 72–"This uncertainty in Virginia law carries over into the system for conducting a firearms background check. In general, nationally, before purchasing a gun from a dealer a person must go through a background check. A government agency runs the name of the potential buyer through the databases of people who are disqualified from purchasing guns. If the potential purchaser is in the databases, the transaction is stopped. If not, the dealer is instructed to proceed with the sale. The agency performing the check varies by state. Some states rely on the federal government to conduct the checks. In yet other states, such as Virginia, the state conducts the check of both federal and state databases. **In Virginia the task is given to the state police.**" *It would appear that there is a motive for the obfuscation; in Virginia the state police ensure that the name is on the list of those prohibited from buying guns. Did the police not do their job? The report never even attempts to address that point.*

…

Page 72–**"In Virginia, the Central Criminal Records Exchange (CCRE), a division of the state police is tasked with gathering criminal records and other court information that is used for the background checks.** Information on mental health commitments orders "for involuntary admission to a facility" is supposed to be sent to the CCRE by the court clerk *(was this done?)* who must send all copies of the orders along with a copy of form SP 237 that provides basic information about the person who is the subject of the court order. *(was this done?)* As currently drafted, the law only requires a clerk to certify a form and does not specify who should complete the form. Because of the lack of clarity in some jurisdictions *(which jurisdictions—the one where Cho bought his firearms?)* do not send the information unless they receive a completed form. Recommendations to improve this aspect of the law were given in Chapter IV."

Page 73–"The state police did not permit the panel to view copies of the forms in their investigation but indicated that Cho answered "no" to this question (have you ever been adjudicated mentally defective, which includes having been adjudicated incompetent to manage your own affairs) or have you ever been committed to a mental institution? It is impossible to know whether Cho understood the proper response was "yes" and whether his answers were mistakes or deliberate falsifications. In any event, the fact remains that Cho, a person disqualified from purchasing firearms, was readily able to obtain them." *Again, the reader will be confused, Cho was disqualified to purchase firearms, but he was readily able to obtain them.*

Page 74–Now the reader is told, "Federal law prohibited Cho from purchasing ammunition."

Page 74–"Virginia Tech has one of the tougher policy constraints of possessing guns on campus among schools in Virginia." *(Yes, but how does that policy compare with schools in other states?)*

Page 75–The last paragraph before the Key Findings appears to be an intentional inclusion to downplay the threat of guns on campus. **Drop the paragraph**:

"The panel heard a presentation from Dr. Jerald Kay, the chair of the committee on college mental health of the American Psychiatric Association about the large percentage of college students who binge drink each year (about 44 percent) *(Was Cho a binge drinker? How does this fit into the equation?),* and the surprisingly large number of students who claim they thought about suicide (10 percent) *(Okay, tie this into Cho's mental condition).* College years are full of academic stress and social stress. *(The panel brought in the chair of the committee on college mental health of the American Psychiatric Association to state the obvious?)* The probability of dying from a school shooting on campus is smaller than the probability of dying from auto accidents, falls, or alcohol and drug overdoes." *(This sentence has a particularly unsavory flavor—it appears to be an intentional effort to downplay the threat of increasing gun violence on our campuses.) After reading this paragraph, you are left wondering, this cannot be all Dr. Kay said, but if this is all he said of note, what a waste of time and money.*

Page 75–The Key Findings are weak and clearly represent the timidity of the panel when confronting a politically sensitive issue—gun ownership and guns rights. Indeed, the Key Findings are so weak as to be meaningless.

Page 75–The topic sentence, first paragraph of Key Findings is another example where strong editing is needed.

| Original Sentence | Reasons for Replacing | Replacement Sentence |
|---|---|---|
| Cho was able to purchase guns and ammunition from two registered gun dealers with no problem, despite his mental history. | The Recommendations should include a recommendation that the governor issue an executive order requiring the state police and gun dealers to turn their documentation over to the panel for review. | Under federal law, Cho could not purchase a firearm or ammunition, yet despite his mental history he was able to do so from two registered gun dealers with no problem. The refusal of the state police, the ATF, and the gun dealers to give the panel access to copies of the forms Cho filled out to purchase the weapons was a major impediment to the panel's work. This refusal, while legal, is morally and ethically questionable. |

Page 75–The second paragraph of the Key Findings simply states the obvious, again an indication of the panel's timidity and lack of dedication to tackling difficult issues.

| Original Sentences | Reasons for Replacing | Replacement Sentence |
|---|---|---|
| Cho was able to kill 31 people including himself at Norris Hall in about 10 minutes with the semiautomatic handguns at his disposal. Having the ammunition in large capacity magazines facilitated his killing spree. | It simply restates the obvious and adds nothing to the findings. | Cho's ability to kill 33 people, including himself, is a clear indication of a systemic problem that permeates Virginia's legal and law enforcement system when it comes to keeping guns out of the hands of the mentally ill. |

Page 75–The third and final paragraph of the Key Findings needs to be completely rewritten:

| Original Sentences | Reasons for Replacing | Replacement Sentence |
|---|---|---|
| There is confusion on the part of universities as to what their rights are for setting policy regarding guns on campus. | It does not address Virginia Tech specifically, and is in fact far too general in every respect. | Virginia Tech has one of the tougher policy constraints among Virginia schools concerning possessing guns on campus, yet this did not prevent the killings on April 16, 2007. Moreover, there is confusion on the part of universities in Virginia as to what their rights are for setting policy regarding guns on campus. The panel finds this confusion to be a major weakness in improving campus safety. Moreover, the panel finds that no matter what the policies are, if organizations responsible for keeping guns out of the hands of those who are a danger to themselves or others, do not do their job, campus security is seriously undermined. This is evident by the failure to have Cho's name on the list prohibiting him from purchasing weapons. |

Now, let's look at the Recommendations on page 76. By definition, the reader will assume that recommendation number one is the most important and deals specifically with the Virginia Tech tragedy. Instead, the recommendation is a broad generalization of what *should* be done at the federal level on background checks. *Was the panel's primary charter to make recommendations at the federal level?*

**VI-1 All States should report information necessary to conduct federal background checks on gun purchases.** There should be federal incentive to ensure compliance. This should apply to states whose requirements are different from federal law. States should become fully compliant with federal law that disqualifies persons from purchasing or possessing firearms who have been found by a court or other lawful authority to be a danger to themselves or others as a result of mental illness. Reporting of such information should include not just those who are disqualified because they have been found to be dangerous, but all other categories of disqualification as well. In a society divided on many gun control issues laws that specify who is prohibited from owning a firearm stand as examples of broad agreement and should be enforced. *(Note, I do not disagree with the point that is being made, but the recommendations should have gone from the specific—Virginia Tech and the state of Virginia, to the broader—the federal level.)*

Recommendation number two should have been the first recommendation. Indeed, recommendations two through six do address Virginia-specific issues related to the shooting. Some of the recommendations contained in numbers VI-2 though VI-6 may have been implemented, but that notwithstanding, I would change the reading of recommendation two to the following:

**VI-2 The Virginia General Assembly should immediately adopt legislation requiring background checks for all firearms sales including those at gun shows.** To ensure that these background checks are thorough and done promptly, Virginia should adopt stiff penalties for guns sold without a background check and later used in a crime. In an age of sophisticated information technology, it should not be too difficult for anyone, including private sellers to contact the Virginia Firearms Transaction Program for a background check that usually only takes a few minutes. The program already processes transactions made by registered dealers at gun shows. The practice should be expanded to all sales.

Recommendation VI-2 currently reads:

*VI-2 Virginia should require background checks for all firearms sales, including those at gun shows. In an age of widespread information technology, it should not be too difficult for anyone, including private sellers, to contact the Virginia Firearms Transaction Program for a background check that usually only takes minutes before transferring a firearm. The program already processes transactions made by registered dealers at gun shows. The practice should be expanded to all sales. Virginia should also provide an enhanced penalty for guns sold without a background check and later used in a crime.*

I would change recommendation VI-3 to read:

VI-3 **Anyone found to be a danger to themselves or others by a court-ordered review must** *(I have changed should to must)* **be entered in the Central Criminal Records Exchange database regardless of whether they voluntarily agreed to treatment.** Some people examined for a mental illness and found to be a potential threat to themselves or others are given the choice of agreeing to mental treatment voluntarily to avoid being ordered by the courts to be treated involuntarily. If they agree to voluntarily seek treatment, nothing is placed in the Central Criminal Records and they are free to purchase guns. This policy should be changed, and even if a person voluntarily seeks treatment, he or she should be added to the list of those who may not buy guns. *(If you remember, one of the problems surrounding Cho and the Cook Counseling Center rested on the fact that he had to voluntarily seek help. The panel missed the opportunity to draw the parallel with Cho and to make the point that the mentally ill may not be in a position to do anything "voluntarily.")* Some highly respected people knowledgeable about the interaction of mentally ill people with the mental health system are strongly opposed to requiring voluntary treatment to be entered on the record and be sent to a state database. The objection of these mental health professionals pales when you consider the fact the two school shootings in Virginia were carried out by individuals who had sought mental health treatment and still bought guns. It is not logical to allow someone found to be dangerous to be able to purchase a firearm.

Recommendation VI-3 currently reads:

*VI-3 Anyone found to be a danger to themselves or others by a court-ordered review should be entered in the Central Criminal Records Exchange database regardless of whether they voluntarily agreed to treatment. Some people examined for mental illness and found to be a potential threat to themselves or others are given the choice of agreeing to mental treatment voluntarily to avoid being ordered by the courts to be treated involuntarily. That does not appear on their records, and they are free to purchase guns. Some highly respected people knowledgeable about the interaction of mentally ill people with the mental health system are strongly opposed to requiring voluntary treatment to be entered on the record and be sent to a state database. Their concern is that it might reduce the incentive to seek treatment voluntarily, which has many advantages to individuals (e.g., less time in hospital, less stigma, less cost) and to the legal and medical personnel involved (e.g., less time, less paper work, less cost). However, there still are powerful incentives to take the voluntary path, such as a shorter stay in a hospital and not having a record of mandatory treatment. It does not seem logical to the panel to allow someone found to be dangerous to be able to purchase a firearm.*

I would strengthen recommendation VI-4 so that it reads:

**VI-4–The existing attorney general's opinion regarding the authority of universities and colleges to ban guns on campus needs to be clarified immediately.** The Virginia attorney general and the state legislature need to move quickly to codify the right of all colleges and universities to ban weapons on school grounds. Currently the state's institutions have interpreted the law in different ways—that needs to change. The Commonwealth's attorney general has provided some guidance to universities, but additional clarity is needed from the attorney general and the state legislature regarding guns on university and college grounds.

Recommendation VI-4 currently reads:

*VI-4 The existing attorney general's opinion regarding the authority of universities and colleges to ban guns on campus should be clarified immediately. The universities in Virginia have received or developed various interpretations of the law. The Commonwealth's attorney general has provided some guidance to universities, but additional clarity is needed from the attorney general or from state legislation regarding guns at universities and colleges.*

I would keep recommendation VI-5 as is (it is on the mark):

**VI-5–The Virginia General Assembly should adopt legislation in the 2008 session clearly establishing the right of every institution of higher education in the Commonwealth to regulate the possession of firearms on campus if it so desires.** The panel recommends that guns be banned on campus grounds and in buildings unless mandated by law.

I would change recommendation VI-6 to say the following:

**VI-6–Universities and colleges should make clear in their literature, as well as in their orientation programs, what their policy is regarding weapons on campus—and what the penalties are for disregarding those policies.** Again, the panel recommends that guns be banned on campus grounds and in buildings unless mandated by law. Prospective students and their parents, as well as university staff, should know what the policies related to concealed weapons are, and the severe penalties for breaking those policies.

Recommendation VI-6 currently reads:

*Universities and colleges should make clear in their literature what their policy is regarding weapons on campus. (Prospective students and their parents, as well as university staff, should know the policy related to concealed weapons so they can decide whether they prefer an armed or arms-free learning environment.)*

# CHAPTER VII

## DOUBLE MURDER AT WEST AMBLER JOHNSTON

Time and time again, the report soft-pedals the mistakes made by the police. Look at page 79: "… the police may have made an error in reaching a premature conclusion that their initial lead was a good one, or at least in conveying that impression to the Virginia Tech administration." *The word "may" needs to be dropped—it **was** a mistake.*

And again on page 80: "The police did not tell the Policy Group that there was a chance the gunman was loose on campus or advise the university of any immediate action that should be taken such as canceling classes or closing the university. Also, the police did not give any direction as to an emergency message to be sent to the students…. Not until 9:25 a.m. did the police have a representative sitting with the Policy Group, a police captain." This is a clear example of stifling bureaucracy preventing prompt response to an emergency. The police had the authority, but no means to send a message.

Page 81–"Even with the police conveying the impression to campus authorities that the probable perpetrator of the dormitory killings had left campus and with the recent past history of the "panic" caused by the alert nine months earlier, the university Policy Group still made a questionable *(should read: made a wrong)* decision. They sent out a carefully worded alert an hour and half after they heard that there was a double homicide, which was now more than two hours after the event." *Once again the school displayed bureaucratic timidity and 30 people lost their lives. That point needs to be made.*

Page 82–In the section entitled "Decision Not To Cancel Classes or Lock Down:"

"…Most police chiefs consulted in this review believe that a lockdown was not feasible." This statement is clearly intended to make excuses for a bad decision not to act. First, it runs counter to the decision the school made nine months earlier; and second, the reader is not told how many police chiefs were asked, how many said the school should have been locked down, and were any of the police chiefs from other states with no ties to the police in and around Blacksburg."

## CHAPTER VIII

## MASS MURDER AT NORRIS HALL Pages 89-99

Once again the report puts a positive foot forward when talking about the police. See page 98–Key Findings:

"Overall, the police from Virginia Tech and Blacksburg did an outstanding job in responding quickly and using appropriate active-shooter procedures to advance to the shooters location and to clear Norris Hall." *The danger of this type of positive lead is that many people do not read a report this size, they skim it. How do you skim? Usually the reader reads the topic sentences of each section carefully and then skim over the rest. So, for the quick reader, what is the impression? "Overall the police from Virginia Tech and Blacksburg did an outstanding job…" This topic sentence technique is well known to professional writers and I am sure TriData is well aware of it.*

The recommendations for this section are so broad as to be meaningless. Many will only read the Key Findings and the Recommendations. If you have not read the chapter, you would not understand the importance of the failings when it came to Norris Hall. The Recommendations need to be specific and give examples. Look at page 99.

**VIII-1–Campus police everywhere should train with local police or instructions by phone to people in a shooting or facing other emergencies.**

**VIII-2–Dispatchers should be cautious when giving advice or instructions by phone to people in shootings or facing other threats without knowing the situation.** This is a broad recommendation that stems from reviewing other U.S. shooting incidents as well, such as the Columbine High School shootings. For instance, telling someone to stay still when they should flee or flee when they should stay still can result in unnecessary deaths. When in doubt dispatchers should just be reassuring. They should be careful when asking people to talk into the phone when they may be overheard by a gunman. Also, local law enforcement dispatchers should be familiar with the major campus buildings of colleges and universities in their area.

**VIII-3–Police should escort survivors out of buildings, where circumstances and manpower permit.**

**VIII-4–Schools should check the hardware on exterior doors to ensure that they are not subject to being chained shut.**

**VIII-5–Take bomb threats seriously. Students and staff should report them immediately, even if most do turn out to be false alarms.**